"At last—an alternative to cynicism! Jane Caputi has created a Rosetta stone that decodes popular culture's hidden agendas of biocide and misogyny, uncovering the missing pieces of the twenty-first-century puzzle. Her insights reveal the magic, power, and joy available to those who dare to imagine a world of mutual respect and natural harmony."

—Kay Leigh Hagan, author of
Fugitive Information: Essays from a Feminist Hothead

"Jane Caputi's work burns with earned vision. . . . always intelligent and brave, she reports unflinchingly what she sees. . . . this book is like its subject: deep, radiant, and necessary."

—Barbara Mor, author of The Great Cosmic Mother

"Jane Caputi has unearthed and diagnosed the male-centered popularisms of rapine, plunder, genocide, mayhem, and denial, and done so with a panache not ordinarily associated with such ordeals. In fact, it is her lightness of touch and scintillating range that readies the reader for a whole new appreciation of the strange and fertile chaos lurking in our future."

—Dr. Michael Tobias, author of
Deep Ecology, Voice of the Planet, and Life Force

"I appreciate the challenge to look at the nuclear issue in a working way—by changing our attitudes, our language, our thought processes. . . .This is a good way to look at generating transformation in our society—to create a new path, a new way."

—Bobbie Hall, artist and daughter of one of the men
who helped create the first atomic bomb

"Jane Caputi captured my mind with her pristine, avid attention to correct research and translations. The lyric poetry and the easy ebb and flow of her writing captured my heart and touched the 'knowings' in me. . . . Even the difficult, dark truths in this book are presented to the reader with beauty and laser humor. . . . Everyone should read *Gossips, Gorgons & Crones*."

—Oh Shinnah, singer, teacher, and ceremonialist

Ricki Klages © 1993

GOSSIPS, GORGONS & CRONES

The Fates of the Earth

by Jane Caputi

foreword by
Paula Gunn Allen

BEAR & COMPANY
PUBLISHING
SANTA FE, NEW MEXICO

LIBRARY OF CONGRESS CATALOGING-IN-PUBLICATION DATA

Caputi, Jane.
  Gossips, gorgons & crones : the fates of the earth / by Jane Caputi ;
foreword by Paula Gunn Allen.
      p.   cm.
  Includes bibliographical references (p.   ) and index.
  ISBN 1-879181-05-3
  1. Feminist theory. 2. Patriarchy. 3. Nuclear energy. 4. Ecofeminism.
I. Title. II. Title: Gossips, gorgons, and crones.
HQ1190.C37 1993   93-18885
305.42'01—dc20   CIP

Bear & Company, Inc.
Santa Fe, NM 87504-2860

Cover illustration: "Crow Mother over the Rio Grande" by Meinrad
Craighead © 1988, from *The Litany of the Great River* by Meinrad
Craighead (Paulist Press, 1991).

Cover & interior design: Marilyn Hager

Author photo: Annette Peláez

Editing: Gail Vivino

Typography: Marilyn Hager

The illustrations for the title frontispiece and part 2, 3, and 4 opening pages
are by Ricki Klages © 1993. The illustrations for the half title and part 1
opening pages are by L. Crespin © 1993.

Printed in the United States of America by R.R. Donnelley

1 3 5 7 9 8 6 4 2

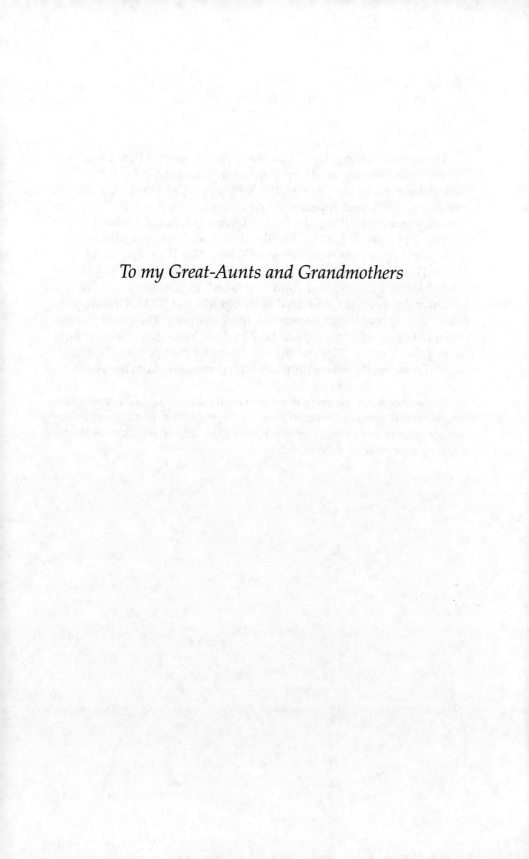

To my Great-Aunts and Grandmothers

PERMISSIONS

The poems "Dying Back," "Mother Nature Sends a Pink Slip," and "When Earth Becomes an It" by Marilou Awiaka are reprinted from her book *Selu: Seeking the Corn-Mother's Wisdom* (Golden, CO: Fulcrum Publishing, 1993), and appear with permission from the poet. The poem "the earth is a living thing" by Lucille Clifton is reprinted from the *Book of Light*, copyright © 1992 by Lucille Clifton, and appears with permission from Copper Canyon Press, P.O. Box 271, Port Townsend, WA 98368. The excerpt from the poem "Monster" (copyright © 1970 by Robin Morgan) is reprinted from "Monster" in *Upstairs in the Garden: Selected and New Poems 1968–1988* by Robin Morgan (W.W. Norton, publisher) and appears with permission from the poet. The poem "Gettin Down to Get over" (copyright © 1989 by June Jordan) is reprinted from *Naming Our Destiny: New and Selected Poems* by June Jordan (Thunder's Mouth Press, publisher) and appears with permission from the poet.

The author has made every effort to trace the ownership of all copyrighted material and to secure permission from copyright holders. In the event of any question arising as to the use of any material, we will be pleased to make the necessary corrections in future printings.

CONTENTS

ACKNOWLEDGMENTS

I have been aided in this work by many friends and students who have helped in various ways, alerting me to relevant items of nuclear culture or research sources, discussing ideas with me, critiquing my writing, offering dream interpretations, and so on. I thank Augusta Walden, Gerry Shapiro, Hugh Gusterson, A.J. Johnston, Vince Murphy, Sharon Welch, Cynthia Alcala, Amy Estelle, Sue Nance, Maura Daly, Evan Heimlich, Marmika, Kathy Nielsen, Allison Freese, Karman Kregloe, Martha Yates, Leslie Myrick, and Steve Hesske.

Sandy Boucher offered advice when I was writing my first proposal for the book. Ruthann Robson, Annette Peláez, Yolanda Retter, and Amy Estelle read all or parts of the manuscript in an early draft and offered extremely helpful comments. Alice Trabaudo, Susan Hammock, and Dorothy Johnson read a much later version, and I greatly appreciate their suggestions and interest. Gordene MacKenzie, Ann Scales, Helene Vann, and Fran Chelland read the manuscript at various stages and provided invaluable advice and insight.

Anna Livia and Deena González helped me with translations. Gordene MacKenzie and Susan Hammock via Tiska Blankenship, respectively, led me to the inspirational artwork of Ricki Klages and Les Crespin. I thank my friends Michael Bailey, Ann Scales, Joan Balter, Helene Vann, Dorothy Johnson, Gordene MacKenzie, Fran Chelland, Nicholas Tarnawsky, and Betty Holyan for their ever-present inspiration, conversation, advice, comfort, and fun. I also thank my parents, Elizabeth and Robert, and my siblings, Margaret, Kathleen, Anne, Mary, Jacqueline, Robert, and Daniel, for all of their support and love.

I thank my publisher, Barbara Hand Clow, for her interest and support in this work from its initial stages. I also thank everyone I have worked with at Bear & Company—Gail Vivino, Gerry Clow, Jerry Chasen, Jody Winters, Angela Werneke, and Hanna Fields—all of whom have been most gracious and helpful. I especially thank

Barbara Doern Drew for her fine editing skills, her discernment, and her wit, and Marilyn Hager for the beautiful design of this book.

Of great aid to me in writing this book was institutional support from the University of California at Berkeley, where I was a Beatrice Bain Affiliated Scholar through its women's studies program for the academic year 1989–1990. I also thank the University of New Mexico for granting me a course release from my teaching in the spring semester 1992.

I also would like to express my admiration and gratitude to those thinkers whose writings have most instructed and inspired me: Paula Gunn Allen, Gloria Anzaldúa, Marilou Awiakta, Mary Daly, Andrea Dworkin, bell hooks, June Jordan, Robert Jay Lifton, Catharine MacKinnon, Barbara Mor, Diana Russell, Leslie Silko, Monica Sjöö, Alice Walker, and Barbara Walker.

FOREWORD

In the great feminine mysteries of Eleusis, the event of the birth resulting from the union between Persephone and Dionysus was announced as: 'Brimo given birth to Brimos!' Brimo is one form of the Goddess; her name means 'the power to arouse terror . . . to rage'; she was closely associated with Pluto and Dionysus. . . . The experience of terror and chaos was understood by the initiates to be inextricably linked to the birth of a new consciousness.

—*Nathan Schwartz-Salant*[1]

The Gossips say that in 1939, the year I was born, some uranium was dug up from Laguna Pueblo land. They say that the uranium went into the making of the Bomb, those exploded in New Mexico and over Hiroshima and Nagasaki. A few days before I began to write this foreword, my father, Elias Lee Francis, former lieutenant governor of New Mexico and a man who delights in personal reminiscences, mentioned that he saw the bomb blast, though whether it was "Fat Boy" or the other one, I don't know. He was receiving livestock out around Zuni, and even at that distance he saw the cloud. "What did it look like?" I asked. "Like smoke," he said. "It looked like smoke."

I guess he didn't know exactly what he'd seen for some time; maybe he realized what it was when Americans learned that the United States had dropped the bombs on Japan. It must have frightened them—my father, my mother, and her family—for Bobby, my mother's then eighteen-year-old brother, was somewhere over there. In the Pacific, anyway. Under wartime security, the people of New Mexico—of Cubero and Laguna—didn't know much about what was going on. Surely they didn't know that the earth the strangers (who had to be Anglos—Eastern Anglos, at that) dug up and took away would be milled somewhere and transformed into radiant death.

In the 1950s, we school children were subjected to frequent bomb alerts—some of the many acts of terrorism, euphemistically called "civil defense," visited upon our cowed heads. In the wake of one of these, my best friend, Teresa Baca, and I talked about the Bomb. She told me that her mother, Concepcion, had told her that the people of Cubero saw a ring around the Moon a few days before the first bomb test and that they knew that something awful (awe-full) was about to occur. (We probably get more information relying on our senses and our particular traditions than from textbooks or media!)

I think Concepcion saw the smoke the same day my dad did. They were both very far away from Stallion Gate, where it was detonated—one was up around Zuni, one in Cubero. But in New Mexico in the 1940s you could see forever. The people in Nagasaki and Hiroshima saw forever—became forever—when the sky exploded above their unsuspecting heads a couple of months after my dad and my friend's mom saw the omen of global transformation.

Following the Gossips' hints, my mother and I visited the area where we thought the original uranium had been dug up forty years before. We walked over the rough land, trying to locate the site of the first uranium dig. It lay somewhere near the old road that had led from Laguna to its daughter village, Paguate, but even its traces had been obliterated when the new paved road was built to expedite hauling huge supplies of "yellowcake," raw uranium ore, from the mine. We both knew that the petrified body of the old giantess that my great-grandmother, Meta Atseye Gunn, used to tell me about marked one side of that vanished road, and her equally petrified head, flung far from the torso, marked the other. We knew that the road had opened off old Highway 66 just about directly across from the door to Laguna Trading Post, almost at the door of the old Gunn house behind the store, where we went to eat on Feast Day at Laguna.

Mother and I figured that the giantess's remains lay close to the site we were seeking. But even knowing that, we failed to find it. It was ever so much easier to find the huge tract of land overturned by Anaconda Company's vigorous mining near Paguate village. The huge rectangular heaps of flat-topped earth eerily resemble the sandstone mesas that dot the surrounding terrain, but they are not sandstone. Piled close upon one another, they are clearly human-made, and in their arrangement they also resemble Eastern cities, towering artificial structures huddled together in fear and pain.

Growing up with legends not only from Laguna but from around the world—my mother was a literary sort with eclectic, albeit refined tastes—it was easy enough to see some weird correlations between the Bomb, the mine, and the stories, correlations that reveal the transformational nature of the powers nuclear fission unleashed. As I mentioned, the raw ore from which uranium is milled is called yellowcake, and a supernatural female, featured in much of the ritual tradition, is named Yellow Woman (which signifies Yellow Corn Woman). I don't think it is an accident that yellowcake is found in great abundance in the lands of Yellow Woman, where yellow corn grows in abundant sweetness. It is interesting that the Mayan word for *corn* is the same as for *dawn*, though exactly what that correspondence signifies at Laguna is unclear. It is also strangely coincidental that some naturalists see yellow corn as an antidote to poisoning by strontium 90, a hazardous isotope present in radioactive fallout; many narratives in the oral tradition assert that no natural poison exists that is not closely accompanied by its antidote. And, too, the color of woman there is not pink but yellow.

There is an old story about Yellow Woman (or a number of supernatural women of that name) in which she is abducted by Whirlwind Man (in other versions she is abducted by Evil Kachina or Sun Man). According to the story, Yellow Woman went to the river to get water for her sisters and herself. There she was accosted by Whirlwind Man, who compelled her to go with him. She left her water jar by the river, a clue to her plight. Whirlwind Man carried her off to the other world, where he remanded her to his mother's custody. There she performed the tasks that every intended wife must perform for her future in-laws. Meanwhile, her concerned sisters, Red Corn, White Corn, and Blue Corn, set about trying to find Yellow Woman and eventually succeeded. Appropriate to Keres custom, Whirlwind Man sent Yellow Woman home laden with lavish gifts from his mother for herself and her sisters.

There is another story that has bearing on the whole question of nuclear fission and its effects. This one is far more central to Laguna thought than even the Yellow Woman ritual narratives, for it is at the heart of Laguna cosmogony. Naotsete, Sun Woman, was one of the original goddesses who with her sister, Icsity, and Spider Woman created the heavens, the Earth, the gods, the animals, the plants, the arts, the laws, and all institutions, abilities, and phenomena needful for planetary life. Eventually, she and her sister quarreled over who was the elder, and Naotsete decided to go away. She, like her sister, had a "medicine" bag that contained a number of yet-to-be born qualities or phenomena, and they discussed who would keep the various items. Naotsete took writing, or so some of the stories say, along with metal, mining, and metallurgy because her sister didn't want them. Accompanied by one of her sons (the other stayed with Icsity), she went away "to the east," but it was known that someday she would return. Some say that she came back when the Spanish and later the Anglos found their way into Pueblo country, but tribal Gossips say that when the Bomb was exploded, that was her return.

No versions that I have heard or read suggest that the end of the world follows closely upon her return; indeed, given the facts of the past five hundred years, I'd say that the Bomb is as likely to result in the liberation of the people as in their (continued) demise. Gossips hint that her return signals the end of Western colonial domination and the destruction of the patriarchy. But maybe it heralds some event we can't conceptualize—something only Grandmother Spider, Thought Woman, can dream. But I think it is clear that the fission of the atom signals loud and bright that something sacred is going on in the universe. And it is equally clear that respect for that Great Mysteriousness—the kind of respect that Whirlwind Man and his mother showed for Yellow Woman and her people—is demanded in such a sacred time.

This is not to suggest that nuclear fission is an unmitigated blessing, but rather to reiterate a point that all ritualists know: the approach of the sacred is fraught with great danger; the liminal state, which one enters at the moment of transformation, is as likely to yield disaster as its obverse. True ritualists go through long periods of cleansing and isolation before they are so bold as to approach the sacred, clearly aware of the danger such an approach occasions. Modern people, of course, do not recognize the peril. Raised on Walt Disney's notions of supernatural events coupled with the intellectual-

ly toxic "empirical" (the word comes from the same source as "impe-
rial") thought, they play with the sacred as though it were a toy, then,
shocked at its devastating response, look angrily around for someone
to blame for their folly.

In November of 1991, my Laguna mother died of cancer. Or, at
least, that's what they put on her death certificate. She had oat cell
cancer of the lung, a kind of cancer that is unlikely to kill its host
quickly, particularly when the person is elderly. But she accepted the
treatments that Western doctors offered—chemotherapy and radiation—and the cancer metastasized to her brain. More chemo, more
radiation. She died—whether of the disease or of the cure, we'll
never know. It is presently fashionable to attribute her illness to her
lifelong smoking and not at all fashionable to point out that cancer of
any sort was almost unheard of until after World War II, when it
became all too ordinary.

In a special report on February 28, 1993, CNN told the story of a
doctor who, seeing a single case of lung cancer in 1936, called in several students. He wanted them to observe this "rare disease that
[they] might never see again." It was ten years before he saw another
case, the report went on, and, of course, the incidence has risen pre-
cipitously since. CNN blamed the rise in lung cancer and other
"smoking-related diseases" on the huge amounts of cigarettes the
GIs toted in their C ration packs! Not a word was said about the
increase of cancer in relationship to the Bomb, nuclear testing, or the
horrifying proliferation of radioactive waste all over the country. For
that matter, not a word was said about the proliferation of electrical
apparatus—power plants, power lines, electrification of every home
in the modern world—that also accompanied the rise in cancer and
other respiratory and immune-system-dysfunction–related illnesses.

You see, blaming the victim is an old patriarchal game; it fits
quite neatly into disinformation systems and possesses the even
neater potential of terrorization, social control, and mind warp. Held
in its sway, we become not only each other's policemen and enemies,
but our own. I am intrigued by the oddity of proposed taxes on cigarettes, alcohol, and luxury foods being called "sin taxes." Having
read *Gossips, Gorgons & Crones*, I am certain the cause of life, freedom,
and survival would be better served if "sin taxes" were levied on

assault weapons, weapons of mass destruction, and pornography!

In 1936, Ethel, my mother, didn't enjoy electricity in her stone-walled Cubero home; by the mid-seventies through mid-eighties, when she was diagnosed with lupus, perocarditis, asthma, and diverticulitis, she had enjoyed every benefit of modern technology. In 1936 there was little, if any, nuclear toxicity in western Valencia (now Cibola) County. By 1976, when my younger brother commissioned an analysis of our Cubero water, the level of lethal radiation-associated toxins was extremely dangerous. Gee, Ma, you shouldn't have smoked so much!

Gossips suspect that it is more than coincidental that, according to the New Mexico Tumor Registry in 1976, Native Americans in New Mexico did not contract lung cancer. Nor is it a fluke that the New Mexico Cancer Control Project, for which I worked for a time, refused to deal with radiation, toxic waste, asbestos mining—all demonstrably implicated in carcinogenesis—though they were avidly engaged in an antismoking campaign as a major aspect of what they were pleased to call their "cancer prevention program."

The years between 1932 and 1962 were years of terrible drought in our part of the world. The yellowcake blew back and forth over us; sometimes the dust was so thick we could barely see across the room, despite stuffing doors and window frames with cloth and newspapers in vain attempts to keep it out. As we watched the huge dust clouds form and sweep overhead, we used to quip, "There goes some more Enchantment!" Little did we realize the truth of our joke, though indeed we should have: one of the prime characteristics of the sacred is its wit.

I met Jane Caputi a year or so after I realized that a large percentage of Native American writers were addressing the issue of nuclear life—the Bomb, its aftermath, its possibilities. Simultaneously, I noticed some commonalities the Yellow Woman/yellowcake shared. They are from the same land; they are the same color; they are each radiant beings, vast intelligences whose barest acquaintance we've made. Then, there is the curious assignment of the color yellow to signify the female. I thought about these connections and the terrifying beauty and power of the Bomb—its ritual force whereby it transforms all number of living things into something other than what they were before its touch. "She's come back!" I thought, and began working on a novel that would explore this theme.

A year or so later, I realized that a larger than average number of Native American writers were also preoccupied with the confluence of the nuclear and the sacred, and I determined to teach a course about it. The following year, Jane sat in on another class where I pursued some of the ideas raised in the earlier course. Recently she told me that my approach to the Bomb as a sacred matter led her to do some rethinking of her already wide-ranging understanding of "nuclear" issues and their relationship to the feminine and to the sacred, and that some of the consequent visions and revisions inform *Gossips, Gorgons & Crones.*

Drawing from a variety of sources, Caputi uncovers a pattern of thought that, after reading her book, I style "nuke-think." Nuke-think is simultaneously pornographic and terrorist, becoming, as great social phenomena will, another weapon in the struggle for control of the planet's resources, be they human or otherwise. Far more devastating than the bomb itself, nuke-think invades our minds and consciousness, permeating every idea, belief, attitude, and value we possess with utter conviction in the absolute supremacy of He-Who-Owns-the-Bomb. Our only hope of regaining control of our consciousness is discerning the underlying pattern and unraveling it. According to an old story, there is a Crone who every day weaves and weaves an intricate blanket, and every night her dog unravels it. Should the Old Woman ever complete the blanket, the universe would come to an abrupt end.

Certainly, unraveling nuke-think is one thing popular culture attempts, however awkwardly, with its jokes, puns, witticisms, and absurdities. Caputi mentions a few: "A little nukey is good for everyone," emblazoned on a T-shirt; "nuke it," meaning cooking dinner in a microwave; and menus featuring dishes like "Atomic Blast," "Meltdown," and "Atomic Tacos." In 1984, Bay Area musician Lauralee Brown wrote a song called "Atom Dance," about how much of Nothing we face. She dedicated it to Albert Einstein when she first performed it:

What're you worried about
Your kids, your love, your money?
Are you wondering if they'll amount to something?
When the things around the middle spiral out
    from the center
What will it mean?
Nothing, Nothing at all
Everything is NOTHING AT ALL.

The refrain is almost lost in the shrieking wail of electric guitars and equally wailing vocals. The unraveling includes barefaced jokes, like one circulating during the Iran hostage affair in the late 1970s: "What's one hundred kilometers long, eighty-five kilometers wide, and glows in the dark?" Answer: Tehran.

Terror is no laughing matter, one might object. But, as those who are profoundly engaged in the ways of the sacred realize, complete acknowledgment of the awesome depth of the Great Mysteriousness that surrounds and permeates every aspect of our being requires the sacred art of ungainly humor. It offers a respectful demonstration of our acute recognition of the terror human encounters with the sacred evoke. The deeper and more pervasive our fear in the face of that which we cannot control, the more hyperbolic becomes the attempt at release, the more essential the clarity of perception humor offers, and the more urgent unraveling the profane pattern of nuke-think becomes.

This is the significance of *Gossips, Gorgons & Crones*. In it, the pattern made by the Bomb and society's carefully orchestrated response to it are revealed, and the entirely proper conclusion to Caputi's analysis is offered: this is the time of the end—the end of patriarchy, the end of the profane. It is the time of the Grandmothers' return, and it is a great time indeed.

Having guided us through the tangled landscape of nuke-think, Caputi brings us to the heart of her exploration. In the Cherokee writer Marilou Awiakta's account of her childhood encounter with the Black Goddess, we find ourselves face-to-face with the truth, ancient and arcane, contemporary and awe-full. When she was a child, Awiakta's father told her that scientists called the reactor "The lady" and, in moments of high emotion, referred to her as "our beloved reactor." He described "The lady" further: "They tell me she has a seven-foot shield of concrete around a graphite core, where the atom is split." Discovering from her father that graphite is black, the child "imagined a great black queen, standing behind her shield, holding the splitting atom in the shelter of her arms."

At last our descent yields to the seeker who knows the proper question to ask when faced with the fact of the sacred. Caputi's discussion is as enlightening as the nuclear event itself. She acknowledges the power of language as mysterious, fraught. And so it is: millions of people—Buddhists, Christians, Jungians, and, most recently, New Agers—have intensely prayed for enlightenment; they have longed to enter the light; they have invoked the engulfing powers of the Sun.

The advent of patriarchy signaled its determination to dominate the vast power of the Sun. From Goddess, she became god (Egypt, India, Persia, Europe, Mayaland) or she was subject to the mediation of emperor (Japan, Peru) and shaman/priest (Cherokee, Keres, Natchez, Lakota). During the millennia of her usurpation, men attempted to subject her to their will. Finally she blasted forth, furious at their presumption, ripping apart earth and sky with her pain and rage.

Unfortunately, those who have prayed for enlightenment over the millennia haven't bargained for the devastating fact of light. They have wanted the bright, the powerful, the utterly overwhelming, the male (the Indo-Germanic root of Aryan is *ar*, meaning "bright," as in bright or brilliant light). Why now complain? The supplicants have been answered with the blinding, deafening whirlwind that is the face and voice of the Great Mystery when it is aroused.

We have for all too long loathed the shade—shadows, night, the dark of the Moon. We have found the shadows so repugnant, the darkness so repulsive, that we have given the Goddess only three parts—maiden, mother, and crone—thoroughly repressing the fourth, that of mystery. But in the final sections of her book, Caputi invokes it: Gossip, Gorgon/Medusa, Crone, and, finally, Chaos.

Chaos, the Grandmother of all that is, now comes among us, just as we discover that she is the source of all order and that she is infinitely generative, infinitely fecund. It is as the old ones have told: the name of the Female Principle is "Thought," and she is more fundamental and varied than time and space.

Perhaps through *Gossips, Gorgons & Crones*, readers will come to understand something Carl Jung wrote in ways that had not previously been so clear: "One does not become enlightened by imagining figures of light, but by making the darkness conscious." To his remark I'd add, ". . . realizing that it is the darkness, the female, that sources and nurtures life." Faced with the terror of our situation vis-à-vis the sacred, perhaps we can learn what we so urgently need to know: the powers that inform our universe must be treated with respect. The transformational process is sacred and is to be approached cautiously, humbly, and in awareness of its actual nature. At the very least, perhaps we will realize that it is futile to imagine ourselves as threatening the Earth's survival when the truth is quite otherwise. Should we attempt to nuke the planet, we can be sure she alone will survive.

> I die, but the earth remains forever.
> Beautiful earth, you alone remain.
> Wonderful earth, you remain forever.
> —*Kiowa Death Song*

Paula Gunn Allen is the author of Grandmothers of the Light: A Medicine Woman's Sourcebook *and* The Sacred Hoop.

PREFACE

For a number of years, I have investigated violence against women as a form of sexually political terrorism. Simultaneously, I have explored the interconnections between technology and sexual violence, focusing increasingly upon nuclear technology. In my earlier book, *The Age of Sex Crime*,[1] I first brought these concerns together by discussing the correlations between the serial mutilation murder of women by men and technological, particularly nuclear, violences.

This was, admittedly, bleak work—a trek, as in an ancient story, to the edge of the world, the ends of the Earth. However, my encounters with the extremes of male domination did not remain untempered. Around the same time that I was completing *The Age of Sex Crime*, I worked with Mary Daly on *Websters' First New Intergalactic Wickedary of the English Language*.[2] Drawing from all of the new words created in Daly's earlier works, including *Pure Lust*, in which she first conceived the idea of a *Wickedary*,[3] we invoked extremes of female Powers, beings such as Gossips, Gorgons, Crones, Hags, Spinsters, Prudes, Nags, and Fates. The *Wickedary*, in Daly's words, is a "Wicked/Wiccen dictionary; dictionary for Wicked/Wiccen Women," containing all manner of new words.[4]

Gossips, Gorgons & Crones: The Fates of the Earth springs from both of these prior works and is, in many ways, a double-edged venture. It is extremely painful and horror-stricken, but it is also exhilarating and Hag-ridden. I continue to relentlessly interrogate the confluence of male supremacist ideology and practices such as incest with technological beliefs and violences. Yet I simultaneously invoke female Powers to confront and confound these atrocities and their perpetrators.

Essentially, my perspective in this book is based in the feminist critique that a complex of patriarchal traditions is producing conditions of analogous private and public horror (from the nuclear family to nuclear war) and tempting the "end of the world." These traditions include a sex and gender system that continually invents male and female as two opposed and unequal entities and legitimates "masculine" domination of the "feminine" in whatever forms these take (for example, males and females, whites and people of color, technology and nature); the refusal to acknowledge the intelligence and soul of life-forms other than the human form; the idolization of the machine; the romanticization of patriarchal taboo violation ("to go where no man has gone before"); the worship of a humanized and solely male divinity; and the denial of Chaos.

Simultaneously, *Gossips, Gorgons & Crones* is an invocation of a worldview that promises an amelioration of these conditions—a worldview that although young, is also very old, for it is rooted in tribal, non-Western, and premodern European traditions. This worldview imagines and passionately invokes the nonviolent end of the world, the demise of patriarchal cosmogony, and an ongoing encounter with the Powers of Chaos. The new world Chaos I envision is founded upon principles that include tolerance, egalitarianism, autonomy, communal harmony, equal distribution of goods, a focus upon responsibility rather than rights,[5] a transformation of the normative sadomasochistic power ethos that infuses all aspects of everyday life, a transcendence of oppositional sex and gender, and an embrace of "familiar values"—those that recognize the interconnectedness and sacredness of all life-forms.

Many people scoff at such imaginings, claiming them to be rooted in some illusory past that probably didn't exist. Even if it did, they arrogantly but wearily chide, "you just can't go back." Such a point of view is, of course, tethered to a linear model of time in which existence marches like a little toy soldier along an unswerving, progressive path. Yet time is not straight. It is curved or, more precisely, coiled. From the spiraling eyes of ancient Eye goddesses to the spiraling arms of star beings (galaxies), we know that the shape of time is that of a helix. Things do come around again, but always with a slightly different twist of fate. In the parlance of many diverse groups, the Goddess is returning (with, as we shall see, a vengeance) to a patriarchal world long out of balance. But that metaphor doesn't mean we are simply returning to some utopian, matriarchal, nontechnological past. Quite the contrary. The cosmic serpent, time, is sending out a new coil, which, while retaining strands of past gynocentricities, will transmute them and introduce elements never before experienced, ones we can't even yet imagine.

GOSSIPS,
GORGONS
& CRONES

INTRODUCTION

Female Powers at the Ends of the Earth

> The prophecies foretelling the arrival of the Europeans to the Americas also say that over this long time, all things European will eventually disappear. The prophecies do not say that European people themselves will disappear, only their customs. The old people say that this has already begun to happen, and that it is a spiritual process that no armies will be able to stop. So the old people laugh when they hear talk about the "desecration" of the Earth. Because humankind, they know, is nothing in comparison to the Earth. Blast it open, dig it up, or cook it with nuclear explosions: the Earth remains. Humans desecrate only themselves. The Earth is inviolate.
> —*Leslie Marmon Silko*[1]

One of my purposes in writing this book is to investigate the metaphysical implications of a confluence of events as we approach the curve in the bend of time otherwise known as the end of the twentieth century. These events include the invention of nuclear technologies, the worldwide environmental crisis, the worldwide feminist movement, the approaching Christian millennium, and the felt resurgence of sacred female Powers.

As many investigators attest, after forty-five years of nuclear development much of the former Soviet Union, particularly in the aftermath of the Chernobyl disaster, is a toxic wasteland. One scientific expert, Jay M. Gould, has even suggested that the widespread illness caused by the radiation released by the disabled Chernobyl power plant was a deciding factor in the disintegration of the Soviet Union. As he sees it, that illness contributed heavily to the "despair and outrage that helped unravel the social fabric of Soviet society after the accident [and] . . . may help to explain the mystery of why the Soviet Union collapsed so quickly after 1986, with a suddenness that completely upset the geopolitical balance."[2]

With the demise of the USSR, our nation's "evil twin" (can the U.S. be far behind?), and the institution of the new nuclear world order, including welcome reductions in arsenals and weapons tests, some might suppose that nuclear concerns are now less urgent. Yet people all over the world, particularly indigenous people, continue to find their lands and waters contaminated by radioactive waste and targeted for dump sites.[3] More and more countries are acquiring the knowledge and means to build nuclear weapons. Former Soviet nuclear scientists are now free to take their knowledge wherever they choose. Nuclear power plants in Eastern Europe and the former Soviet Union stand in great danger of neglect and hence assured disaster. There is deepening evidence of an illegal underground market in radioactive materials.

Gross lack of foresight and extreme mismanagement have marked the operations of nuclear production facilities in this country as well as in the rest of the world. Plutonium, a manmade product, is generated in nuclear reactors and provides reactor fuel as well as fissionable material for much of the world's forty thousand or so nuclear warheads. From the human standpoint, plutonium remains toxic for so long that it is virtually eternal. It and other radioactive wastes have been dumped carelessly into soil, oceans, rivers, and ground water (and hence, into the bodies of creatures, including humans, with lethal effects on their immune systems) and stored in leaky, corroding tanks, where they interact with water and chemicals to form highly explosive gases. And even these deeply foolish containment measures are only temporary. So far, no one has figured out how to dispose safely of radioactive waste permanently, and perhaps no one ever will.

Meanwhile, the patience of the Earth's ozone layer—which scientists analogize to a human body's immune system—grows thin. Corporate and colonial interests continue to foment the destruction of the planet's "lungs"—the old-growth forests, both tropical and temperate. Free animal life, which, as writer Alice Walker intuits, is "the spiritual equivalent of oxygen," continues to be extincted with cartoonlike lethal abandon (though some would say it is the animals who are abandoning us).[4] Precious planetary bodily fluids—rivers, lakes, and oceans—are thoughtlessly used by corporations as sewers for toxic waste. The geocidal threat, brought to a head in the mushroom cloud, is far from over.

Certainly the leaders of the superpowers and the scientific, military, and corporate elite must be held responsible for these atrocities. Yet at the same time we must not succumb to their carefully nurtured belief in their own "super" power. Frederick Soddy, a chemist working with Ernest Rutherford on the properties of radioactivity, speculated in 1904 on the possible applications of atomic power:

> If it could be tapped and controlled what an agent it would be in shaping the world's destiny! The man who put his hand on the lever by which a parsimonious nature regulates so jealously the output of this store of energy would possess a weapon by which he could destroy the earth if he chose.[5]

This was one of the first utterances of what has come to be a nuclear-age cliché, ironically promulgated by nuclear advocates and resisters alike: the notion that "mankind" shapes destiny and holds the very fate of the Earth in its hands. Implicit in this notion is the idea that the Earth revolves around men—that men are the prime movers, responsible for nearly all that transpires on Earth, including the impending "destruction" or "salvation" of a passive planet. If we consent to this cockaludicrous[6] conceit—if we believe that the Earth is a lump of unconscious matter owned by elite men—we are far more susceptible to the belief that we are equally powerless, passive, and possessed.

As the millennium approaches, it is impossible to deny that we are coming to a crossroads. Apocalyptic, "endtime" thinking is in the air, even where we least expect it. For example, a 1989 ad for *Time Frame*, a Time-Life book series, promotes the series with the phrase "The History of Civilization from Start to Finish." Two pictures illustrate this concept: on the left is a cave painting; on the right, a mushroom cloud. The first book in the series opens up civilization's saga with *The Age of God Kings 3000–1500 B.C.*; the series closes with *The Shadow of the Dictators, 1925–1950.* The message couldn't be clearer:

civilization = patriarchy. Yet, simultaneously, it is difficult to miss a rather subversive companion message: that civilization/patriarchy is "finished." Superficially, the ad suggests that nuclear war will accomplish that end. More subterraneanly, however, the redolent cloud acts as a metaphor for the bomb that has exploded in consciousness in the last fifty years.

In 1984, one of my students made an MTV-like video for a class assignment, setting a parade of images to a Patti LaBelle song. The lyrics told of a woman who had been imprisoned by patriarchal convention but had broken free. The first part of the video showed very traditional feminine images; the second, liberated feminist ones. To separate these segments, the student spliced in an image of an exploding atomic bomb. I asked why he chose to use the image of a mushroom cloud, and he said he wanted to convey a change of unprecedented magnitude, fundamental and permanently transformative.

Semiotically, this student was marvelously astute. For all of its devastations, the invention of atomic weaponry has induced a revolution in consciousness. Writing in the *New York Times* on August 8, 1945, Anne O'Hare McCormick declared that the atomic bomb had caused "an explosion in men's minds as shattering as the obliteration of Hiroshima." As postwar U.S. culture indicates, the first preservative response of mainstream culture to this shock was, as social historian Elaine Tyler May illuminates, a desperate attempt at sociocultural "containment."[7] This attempt involved the institutional idealization of a kind of Disneyland of the soul, epitomized by the suburban, white, middle-class, "Father Knows Best" type of nuclear-family life as depicted on television. But the proverbial handwriting was now on the wall, or rather the sky: the explosion of the Bomb had clearly spelled out the mass murderous and the fundamentally suicidal absurdity at the core of patriarchal culture. Chaos had dropped in along with the Bomb and the center could no longer hold, as William Butler Yeats so well foretold in "The Second Coming."

As the Nuclear Age progresses, things continue to fall apart— things such as Enlightenment myths of individualism, rationality, science, progress, and mind/body dualism.[8] Simultaneously, as the manifold liberation movements of the postwar years demonstrate, there are profound challenges continuously being posed to all manner of supremacist orders and doctrines, including those of sexual supremacy, racial supremacy, species supremacy, and so on.

There is hope in these transformations. Still, the possibility remains strong that "civilization" ultimately will destroy all of us along with itself in a global nuclear holocaust or environmental disaster. But that future is not fixed. It is up to us to willfully imagine other possibilities, to prophesy other possibilities, to reconceptualize reality through conscious mythmaking, and to read other meanings into these signs of the (end)times by attempting to fathom the passages of the Earth from a perspective in which neither men nor humans in general are the center of the universe.

In truth, it behooves us to undertake the ancient Dreamtime journey to the ends of the Earth. *End*, of course, connotes demise, death, or termination—yet that is by no means the whole story. My use of the word *end*, while intended to evoke the end of the patriarchal world, also draws upon some of that word's complementary and very crucial meanings, for *end* also means "goal, ultimate intention, purpose," or, in philosophical terms, the "final cause" of any movement.[9] History might be finished, but the intentional Earth endures and pursues her own purposes, her own final cause, her own Fates.

Intending to endure as well, runaway women and men[10] are developing the senses and Powers to discover and align ourselves with the ends of the Earth. By doing so, we might not so much "save the planet," for humans don't really have the ability to destroy her. Rather, we seek to understand and place ourselves in balanced relation with the ends of the Earth so that we might save ourselves. Pumped-up, masculinist hubris permeates the invention, use, discourse, and iconography of nuclear technology, culminating in the threat/boast that such technology can be used to "end the world." Yet perhaps an unfaced truth of our age is that the world the nuclear fathers ultimately will shatter is their very own. In "The Fifties," Hopi poet Wendy Rose recalls her childhood during the Cold War years of the 1950s, when she and other schoolchildren practiced "how to die / in a foetal position" under their desks at school. Thirty or so years later, she concludes,

Once again
we scan our western expanse of sky
not for bombers and Russians
but for a thing more final
than antique atom bombs.
Like earthquakes
crawling up the Richter scale
the ghosts of our future
are unpredictable
and out of control.

This is a weather report:
who knows what will end
in the fury of the storm?[11]

Waiting for the End of the World

It's the end of the world as we know it and I feel fine.
—R.E.M.[12]

Manmade nuclear power, with its unprecedented capacity for destruction, is the inevitable fulfillment of perhaps the most familiar of all patriarchal notions: that of *power* itself. Lavina White, a Haida elder, offers a biting assessment of that notion:

> *Let's quit talking like men.* We talk a lot about power and empowerment, let's talk about responsibility, that's man's talk . . . power. There are many words that are being used; the buzz sentence right now is "management of environment." That shakes a person like me . . . we should be managing mankind, not environment. . . . we can't play God. Which reminds me, I've heard some arguments whether God is female or male. In our way, there is no genders. . . . try our way. . . .
> They've trashed the lands, they've trashed the oceans, they've trashed the rivers, and now the air . . . it must come to an end . . . if we don't put a stop to it . . . Mother Nature will . . . and I want to leave you with that.[13]

In 1974, Françoise d'Eaubonne was one of the first in the European feminist tradition to elucidate a clear connection between patriarchal "power" and environmental destruction:

> Patriarchal man is therefore above all responsible for the demographic madness, just as he is responsible for the destruction of the environment and for the accelerated pollution which accompanies this madness, bequeathing an uninhabitable planet to posterity.
>
> Thus a transfer of power [to "awakened women"] is urgently needed, then, as soon as possible, a destruction of power.[14]

D'Eaubonne further declares that what she envisions for the future is not a reversal of the current system of sexual domination: "Not 'matriarchy,' to be sure, nor 'power-to-the-women,' but destruction of power by women." White and d'Eaubonne are telling it exactly right. *Power*, as presently conceptualized, is man's talk and more. It is (to use the Oglala Sioux word) the *wasichu*[15] (conqueror and consumer) way of knowledge; it is patriarchy's ruling and most fundamental conceit.

The word *power* derives from an Old French word, *poer*, which means "to be able." There is nothing inherently oppressive about this definition. Nevertheless, *power's* primary modern definitions according to *Webster's*[16] smack of inequality and violence: "a position of ascendancy; ability to compel obedience; control, dominion." Examples of power in the dictionary refer to "dictators" and "control over nature." Immediately following these are more, equally cruel meanings: "a military force or its equipment; ability to wage war."

Despite these negative connotations, I am reluctant to abandon completely the notion of power, since some of the biggest lies hammered into our consciousness are that only elite men are potent and that only high-powered "snools" ("normal inhabitants of the sadosociety, characterized by sadism and masochism combined")[17] or the leaders of the so-called superpowers are able to affect the world. It is imperative that those of us who oppose the snoolish world order acknowledge that we are able to effect revolutionary change, although our ways, to be sure, are not the ways of patriarchal power.

The dictionary does list some far more egalitarian meanings of the word *power*: "capability of acting or of producing an effect; a mental or physical ability: faculty, talent." Of even greater interest is one of the definitions of its plural form, for *powers* can be "a supernatural being or occult force." More information on this surprising meaning can be found in Mary Daly's *Pure Lust*. In a great leap of spirit, Daly allies feminist philosophy with elemental beings, that is, those "intelligences ensouling the stars, animating the processes of earth, air, fire, water." Two groups of such elementals are the angels known in ancient tradition as the Principalities and Powers:

> The third order is that of the Principalities, and their task is to hie themselves to the places where the clouds rise from the ends of the earth . . . and to cause the rain to descend from thence upon the earth. All the changes in the air, rain and hail and snow and dust-storms and showers of blood are all produced by them, and to them also belong the storm-clouds and the lightning.
> The fourth order is that of the Powers, and their task is the government of all light-giving bodies, such as the sun and the moon and the stars.[18]

In these surprising meanings of *Powers*, I find a way to dissever *power* from its inherently oppressive connotations. Throughout this work, I use *Powers* not only to signify my aversion to patriarchal notions of ascendancy, obedience, dominion, and control, but also to acknowledge the link between female-identified potency and elemental or supernatural beings. The Gossips, Gorgons, and Crones I invoke are such Powers.

While I frequently refer to resistant women as Gossips, Gorgons, and Crones, indicating our participation in these Powers, it is important to stress that these quite inhuman, supernatural beings are by no means mere magnifications or reflections of human females. They are *not* women. Rather, they are completely and utterly inhuman—supernatural beings, occult forces with a marked talent for ending the patriarchal world. Simultaneously, Gossips, Gorgons, and Crones can be understood as symbols expressing intuitions and other perceptions about the nature of the universe. They are monsters, portents, and metaphors, describing imagistically the nearly indescribable workings of human and nonhuman souls. As symbols, they "open up levels of reality otherwise closed to us and they unlock dimensions and elements of our souls which correspond to these hidden dimensions and elements of reality."[19]

As female Powers, Gossips, Gorgons, and Crones are, of course, utterly unfeminine. That is, they are not gendered according to phallocentric standards; their femaleness does not compel the enactment of a certain set of subordinate behaviors, capacities, or moods. Phallocentric belief has it that traditional masculinity (loosely, every "positive" trait known to *man*) and traditional femininity (loosely, every "negative" trait known to *man*) are the natural expressions of biological maleness and femaleness. Yet, these gender roles are patriarchal constructs, enforced and defended because their maintenance is fundamental to sexual inequality. As argued most persuasively by such theorists as Gayle Rubin and Gordene MacKenzie, to end patriarchy we must end the culturally constructed and enforced bipolar sex and gender system.[20] In transcending that system, we deny hierarchical dualism its due—enmity, inequality, and stupidity—and realize wholly other modes of being. For example, the Lesbian, as conceptualized by Monique Wittig, is a being incomprehensible to and uncontainable by the patriarchal category of sex.[21]

The characteristic atrocity of the hierarchical sex and gender system is *gynocide*: the systemic, institutionalized, and multifarious patriarchal war against women, as well as any form of life associated with femaleness. Gynocide is everywhere—from the latest exploits of the characteristic American psychos, serial killers, through the rapist campaigns of overt wartime. In January of 1993, a team of investigators from the European Community estimated that twenty thousand women had been raped as Bosnian Serb soldiers terrorized Muslim towns and villages in Bosnia and Herzegovina. Their report read in part,

> The indications are that at least some of the rapes are being committed in particularly sadistic ways, so as to inflict maximum humiliation on the victims. The delegation also received information strongly suggesting that many women, and more particularly children, may have died during or after the rape. . . . The delegation frequently heard—including from some individual witnesses—that a repeated feature of Serbian attacks on Muslim towns and villages was the use of rape, or the threat of rape, as a

weapon of war to force the population to leave their homes. . . .
Overall, the delegation accepted the view that rape is part of a
pattern of abuse, usually perpetrated with the conscious intention of demoralizing and terrorizing communities, driving them
from their home regions and demonstrating the power of the
invading forces. Viewed in this way, rape cannot be seen as inci-
dental to the main purpose of the aggression but as serving a
strategic purpose in itself.

Every
rape is
Genocide

The headline over this story reads, "Rape Becomes 'a Weapon of
War.'"[22] Here, rape is rightfully being acknowledged as a conscious
stratagem of genocide, or what the Serbs call "ethnic cleansing." Yet,
as feminist theorists have long argued, rape, however committed and
in whatever context, is *always* an act of war and one serving the
strategic purpose of terrorizing women and maintaining male
supremacy.[23] In short, any and all rapes are weapons of war; any and
all rapes are acts of gynocide.

Mary Daly and Andrea Dworkin each have spoken of *gynocide*,
defined by Dworkin as "the systematic crippling, raping, and/or
killing of women by men . . . the relentless violence perpetrated by
the gender class men on the gender class women."[24] Throughout
male supremacist societies, all women (even the most tokenized,
privileged, and/or numb among us), by virtue of our femaleness, are
variously beaten, brainwashed, disrespected, objectified, incested,
harassed, mutilated, battered, raped, tongue-tied, defamed, enslaved,
or systematically murdered by men.

On November 5, 1991, the *New York Times* reported on the conclu-
sions of various economists and demographers who warn that, glob-
ally, "100 million women are missing," sixty million of them in Asia.
These include females of all ages: females who, after fetal testing, are
aborted; females who are killed at birth; females who are routinely
starved when the bulk of available food is given to males; females
who receive no health care or receive damaging health care; and
females who are killed by fathers, brothers, sons, spouses, lovers,
friends, and strangers for reasons including profit, passion, power,
and pleasure, as well as fear and hatred.

Yet these atrocities are barely noticed, for misogynistic violence is
so normal on the planet that it is frequently invisible. In every coun-

try of the world, violence against women remains protected by custom, indifference, glamorization, and denial.[25] Concomitantly, the culture, language, traditions, myths, social organizations, and members of gynocentric cultures, such as those of North American Indians, have been slashed and trashed.[26] Moreover, as I will demonstrate, the basic myths, motivations, and methods behind *geocide*—the wasting of the organic and elemental worlds and the attempted annihilation of the planet—are rooted in gynocidal and misogynist paradigms.

To resist, survive, and end this longstanding gynocidal/geocidal rampage, we desperately need to speak of female Powers. That *we* includes antipatriarchal males who declare disloyalty to male-supremacist manhood. Unlike Robert Bly and company, who ceaselessly pump Iron John—that is, endorse, propagate, and profit from traditional masculinity—such males do not seek themselves in sexist fairy tales and run off to form a "no girls allowed" born-again men's movement.[27] Rather, they welcome feminist fury, take it upon themselves to educate other men about sexism in all of its forms, begin to imagine nonsexist, elemental metaphors of male, cross-sexed, and intersexual Powers, and second feminist commotion.[28]

Conscious Mythmaking

I have spoken of Gossips, Gorgons, and Crones as highly potent symbols. Folklorist Barre Toelken tells a story about a personal experience with the efficacy of Navajo symbolism:

> When I lived with Yellowman's family in Montezuma Canyon, I once came down with what appears to have been pneumonia and was diagnosed by a Navajo practitioner as one in need of the Red Ant ceremony. A medicine man (in Navajo, literally a "singer") was sent for who knew the ceremony, and I was later advised I was being treated for red ants in my system which I had no doubt picked up by urinating on an anthill. Some time after the ritual, which was quite successful I must point out, I had occasion to discuss the treatment with the singer: Had I really had ants in my system, did he think? His answer was a hesitant "no, not ants, but Ants" (my capitaliza-

tion, to indicate the gist of his remark). Finally, he said, "We have to have a way of thinking strongly about disease."

We also very much need to have ways of "thinking strongly" about both female efficacy and the global ills that we need to diagnose and cure.[29]

A time-honored way of dominating females is to drench us with ways of thinking weakly about ourselves. Thus, patriarchal texts, from religious parables through prime-time television, construct us as victims, fembots,[30] fulfilled martyrs, and other such dreary types. Simultaneously, avenues to reach female Powers are blocked and camouflaged. Resistors are labeled gossipy biddies, silly geese, castrating and evil bitches, and sexless and useless old bags and hags.

While many feminists renounce these caricatures, we simultaneously recognize that immured within these distortions are, in the archaic sense of the word, *pregnant* (that is, *cogent, convincing, forcible, and pressing*) presences. These freed presences, when released and reclaimed, become prime ways of thinking strongly about contemporary female passions and Powers. Moreover, these presences can act as especially forceful, *pregnant* symbols, enabling us to give birth to faculties hitherto hidden or constrained. My constellation of the Gossip, Gorgon, and Crone is literally that: an assemblage of three shimmering metaphors. These metaphors are capable of initiating us into the realm of the Powers. They inspire us to feats of intuition, comprehension, and articulation, enabling us to see and speak the truth about nuclear/sexual dominations. At the same time, they are capable of summoning necessary transmutational faculties.

Discussing the mythological system of ancient Egypt, Egyptologist R.T. Rundle Clark stresses that its symbols provided a way to describe the "origin and development of consciousness," to comprehend "the nature of the human soul and nature and God." He further avers that these purposes were "realized by the Egyptians themselves, although not in modern terms. When they mythologized they knew what they were doing."[31] So, too, when we consciously mythologize, we perform deliberate steps of comprehension. We choreograph, intuitively *and* deliberately, a system of symbols and stories that dance our insights about chaos, cosmos, and the nature of being. These symbols invoke world-changing Powers—from without and from within.

Such metaphors are invariably paradoxical. They transport us to a time and space beyond rationality, hierarchical dualisms, and false oppositions such as life and death, chaos and cosmos, past and future, essence and change, and spirit and flesh. To convey this, Gossips, Gorgons, and Crones appear most frequently in figurations of three. These Powers are emanations of the Fates, the most ancient trinity of female supernaturals ("older than all the gods"[32]) found in oral traditions worldwide. The Fates are the three Weird Sisters who weave destiny, spin and cut the thread of life, and dwell on the "edge of the depths of woods, water, and the unconscious—places where things can turn into their opposites."[33] The Fates, though they appear in a threesome, are distinct from many emanations of the Triple Goddess in that they are not a combination of the young, the middle-aged, and the old—the Virgin, the Mother, and the Crone. Rather, like the Gossips, Gorgons, and Crones, *they all are old*.

The word *fate* comes from the Latin *fatum*, meaning a "prophetic declaration, oracle . . . destiny, fate," which, in turn, is from *fari*, "to speak" (*Webster's*). As mythographers such as Barbara Walker and Robert Briffault have amply demonstrated, in prepatriarchal times the faculty of prophecy, and indeed the faculty of all magical utterances, was specifically the lot of women, particularly old women.[34] Yet prophecy these days, whether of the technological futurist or the evangelical variety, is everywhere paraded as the eminent domain of men. For example, fools[35] such as Hal Lindsey and Pat Robertson endlessly reiterate the evangelical endtime message—the promise of a "rapture" (a bodily assumption into heaven of all true believers) and the subsequent divine destruction of the Earth by (nuclear) fire. This message is spread in bestselling books, on the airwaves of the Christian Broadcasting Network, in films, in comic books, in church sermons, and so on.[36]

For the past century, another brand of patriarchal prophet, the techno-utopian futurist, has envisioned impending "White Cities"— that is, gleaming, perpetually lit, shiny clean, energy-abundant centers of civilization. This is a fantasy in which we can discern not only racist longings, but also a denial of the tidal movements of abundance and scarcity, a loathing for the dirt and the dark, and a refusal to come to terms with the realities of waste.[37]

Yet patriarchy's grip on prophecy is a very tenuous one indeed. *Be-Speaking*, that is, "Auguring, foretelling, Speaking of what will be . . . bringing about a psychic and/or material change by means of words; speaking into be-ing,"[38] truly is the province of the Fates and those who participate in these most nonpatriarchal of Powers. *Gossips, Gorgons & Crones*, then, is a reclamation of those prophetic Powers so dangerously and foolishly appropriated by snools. I write with the full understanding that much of the efficacy of prophecy is obtained through the Be-Speakers' determined use of the Powers of myth and language to change consciousness, to set world-changing metaphors into motion, and to suggest images that can be collectively realized. My basic message is this: It *is* the end of the world as we know it. Patriarchy is finished. As Alice Walker might add, "Pass it on."[39]

To Grandmother's House We Go

The Grandmother is the oldest voice I know—the soul of Mother Earth, who is her first face. —*Marilou Awiakta*[40]

While I was writing this book, I had several dreams in which I stood face-to-face with a very old woman. Sometimes she was someone known to me, and sometimes she was a stranger. In each dream, I stood so close I could appreciate every line etched upon her face, could feel her breath, and could look into her eyes.

Cherokee/Appalachian poet and essayist Marilou Awiakta reiterates in nearly everything she writes, "The Grandmothers are coming back." Female Powers *are* returning to our sphere. It is imperative that we welcome, honor, and face these Powers now journeying toward us. Thus, I imagine the progress of this book to be somewhat akin to that archetypal visit to the Grandmothers' house—a journey over rivers, through deep woods, and across seas of time to greet the returning Fates of the Earth.

Before setting out on that extensive journey, I first conduct a brief survey of the terrain of patriarchal nuclear myth and metaphor, looking at the ways that phallocentric associations with the Bomb have been insinuated into our consciousness through everyday imagery, particularly in the areas of sexuality and divinity. This investigation provides a necessary springboard for the latter part of *Gossips, Gorgons & Crones,* where I concentrate upon reconceptualizing nuclear myth through a perspective that admits and respects female Powers.

In the second part, inspired by the Gossips, I embark with you on our journey, scathingly assessing the sexually abusive practices and beliefs of the nuclear fatherland. The Gossips whisper to us of the magical Powers of language, motivating us to shed the ordained role of the living dead and to become, instead, psychic activists.

In the third part, we arrive at the abode of the Gorgon and there find ourselves facing the unfaceable. We reconsider patriarchal definitions of knowledge and taboo, finding surprising and even shocking connections between female Powers and nuclear technologies.

In the fourth part, guided by the Crone, we visit the house of the Grandmothers. There we envision our participation in a cosmic change of life, a climacteric occurring in the very life cycle of planet Earth. We contemplate the workings of Chaos in the evolution of human history. And, there, as the Old Wives say, we endeavor to meet our Fates.

PART ONE

Waiting for the End of the World

Toxic Terminology: We Are What We Speak

They all—all of them whitefolks ruling the country—they all talk that talk, that "standard (white) English." It is the language of the powerful. Language is political. . . . We will not survive by joining the game according to the rules set up by our enemies; we will not survive by imitating the doublespeak/bullshit/non-think standard English of the powers that be.
—*June Jordan*[1]

The women say the language you speak poisons your glottis tongue palate lips. They say, the language you speak is made up of words that are killing you.
—*Monique Wittig*[2]

In contemplating the end of the patriarchal world, I would like to begin by examining its origins. An insight that recurs in countless ancient myths and stories is that *in the beginning is the word*. Language—including naming, dreaming, and imaging—does not merely reflect or describe reality, it constructs it. Simultaneously, it forms the consciousness and social selves of individual speakers. Language is a

language is patriarchal

primary locus of socialization. Embedded in "standard" white English, correct grammar, common vocabulary, elite jargon, prevailing slang, and conventional imagery (in advertising, film, television, and so on) are the perspectives, agendas, and imposed realities of those who are in power.)

Feminist linguist Julia Penelope writes, "Language is an intangible, almost invisible weapon. Its messages are implanted in our minds when we are babies and left there to maintain our allegiance to men and their institutions."[3] A network of images and metaphors similarly maintain our enmeshment in and loyalty to *nuclearism*.[4] By *nuclearism*, I mean a worldview combining disrespect for the atom with the exploitation, eroticization, and worship of nuclear technology as a means to extend elite men's dominion over the elements and the Earth.

A 1991 issue of *Nuclear News* (a trade magazine for the nuclear industry) contains an advertisement for a company called Nuclear Wear, promising "Hot Styles to Come and Glow In!" Nuclear Wear pushes nuclear war by hawking T-shirts bearing such slogans as "Totally Rad," "Up and Atom," "Alpha, Beta, Gamma," "Nuclear Workers Make Better Lovers—They're Hot," and "Nuke Kids on the Block." This is but one fairly specialized instance of popular nuclearist images and language.

During the 1950s, when the U.S. government was testing bombs above ground in Nevada, the "Atomic Cocktail" was a big seller in bars along the Las Vegas strip. One can still order "Los Alamos Atomic Tacos" at an Albuquerque restaurant. In a link between sex appeal and nuclear imagery, the swimsuit name "bikini" is derived from the 1947 test bombing (and virtually eternal contamination) of the South Pacific Island named Bikini. A connection between eroticism and intense radioactivity resonates as well in these lyrics from a 1985 rock song: "Well, I'm not uptight, not unattractive. Turn me on tonight, 'cause I'm radioactive."[5] One of the most popular "Bomb songs" of the 1950s, and there were many, was the oft-recorded "Jesus Hits Like an Atom Bomb."[6] This association between nuclear power and the divine has continued: some contemporary Christian fundamentalists identify nuclear war with the biblically prophesied destruction of the world by fire and the second coming of Jesus Christ.[7]

However inconsequential or absurd some of these images and references seem, all such verbal and visual metaphors play a key role in the overall "nuclearization" of contemporary life. They comprise a symbolic nuclear vocabulary and must be understood in their political role of daily constituting and reconstituting nuclearist reality.

Political theorist Glenn Hook argues that the nuclearization of language has played a crucial role in "making nuclear weapons easier to live with . . . structur[ing] reality in such a way as to make the political pact with weapons of mass destruction appear normal and acceptable." Hook further notes that to understand how nuclearization works, it is crucial to comprehend language "as a form of power, exercised consciously or unconsciously, in the structuring of nuclear reality."[8]

This proposition is explored in great depth by another theorist of nuclear culture, Carol Cohn, who spent several years as a participant observer at an unnamed university's center on defense technology and arms control. At the center, she was immersed in the virtually all-male (save the secretaries) world of defense intellectuals—civilians who "formulate what they call 'rational' systems for dealing with the problems created by nuclear weapons: how to manage the arms race; how to deter the use of nuclear weapons; how to fight a nuclear war if deterrence fails."

This venture required Cohn to learn to speak a specialized language, what she calls a "technostrategic" jargon—an ultrarational, abstract, and dispassionate discourse based not on bodily experience and sensory reality but on computer-generated models of war. In this jargon, the ultimate reference point is not human beings but rather nuclear weapons themselves. Not surprisingly, technostrategic discourse is comprised of the blandest of terms and the most extreme euphemisms. For example, a "clean bomb" is a nuclear device often a thousand times more powerful than those that devastated Hiroshima and Nagasaki, but one that does not produce as much radioactive fallout as "dirty" devices. Cohn comments,

"Clean bombs" may provide the perfect metaphor for the language of defense analysts and arms controllers. This language has enormous destructive power, but without emotional fallout, without the emotional mass murder, mangled bodies, and unspeakable human suffering. Defense analysts talk about "countervalue attacks" rather than about incinerating cities. Human death, in nuclear parlance, is most often referred to as "collateral damage."

Such language declares war to be a permanent state of existence. It tells a story of incipient mass murder, but at the same time it masks that theme and pronounces a ban on alternative futures. Not surprisingly, the word *peace* does not exist in the vocabulary of technostrategic speak.

As Cohn became a fluent speaker of this discourse, she found herself quite naturally beginning to see the world through the perspective of the nuclear strategists: "As I learned their language, as I became more and more engaged with their information and their arguments, I found that my own thinking was changing. Soon, I could no longer cling to the comfort of studying an external and objectified 'them.' I had to confront a new question. How can I think this way? How can any of us? . . . over and over I found that I could not stay connected, could not keep human lives as my reference point. I found I could go for days speaking about nuclear weapons without once thinking about the people who would be incinerated by them."[9]

Cohn could think this way, as could any of us who had been through this process, because the language itself ordains certain thoughts and precludes others. In essence, we would think this way because we would have undergone fissioning and mutation through learning the language. Learning technostrategic speak is not merely a matter of adding words to our vocabulary. Rather, in Cohn's words, it is a "transformative process." It creates a personality that we might think of as a "warhead." This personality identifies with nuclear weapons, assumes the subjectivity of a missile, and "gossips" with bombs.

This poses a clear problem. If those of us who lament and hope to uninvent the nuclearization of life don't become fluent in the father tongue, our voices are dismissed as infantile, uninformed, and irrelevant babble. Yet if we do begin to speak this language, we stand a good chance of becoming "nuclear fashioned," reborn from the heads of these nuclear fathers. Cohn concludes that the task of feminists and others who "seek a more just and peaceful world, then, is both deconstructive and reconstructive." That is, we cannot imitate the "doublespeak/bullshit/nonthink standard" of patriarchal power. Rather, we must critique and divest ourselves of the language and symbol system that produces nuclearist reality. However, at the same time we must invent new languages, images, and metaphors to re-conceptualize the world.

The greater part of *Gossips, Gorgons & Crones* is devoted to that re-conceptualization. However, to lay a foundation for that reconstructive work, I first undertake the deconstructive work through an analysis of everyday nuclear metaphor in part 1. My focus will be primarily upon popular words and images. Cohn and several other observers have amply critiqued many varieties of technostrategic language or "nukespeak," the words and metaphors regularly employed by experts—militarists, journalists, scientists, politicians, and so on. My attention is instead focused on the common language and images of jokes, slang, toys, comic books, advertising, songs, and movies.

CHAPTER ONE

Nuclear Fashion

The effects could well be called unprecedented, magnificent, beautiful, stupendous, and terrifying. . . . The whole country was lighted by a searing light with an intensity many times that of the midday sun. It was golden, purple, violet, gray, and blue. It lighted every peak, crevasse, and ridge of the nearby mountain range with a clarity and beauty that cannot be described but must be seen to be imagined. It was that beauty the great poets dream about but describe most poorly and inadequately.

> —*Brigadier General Thomas Farrell's response*
> *to the explosion of the first atomic bomb,*
> *Trinity site, New Mexico, July 1945*[1]

BURSTING FURY: Atomic Inspired Pin and Earring.—New fields to conquer with Atomic jewelry. The pearled bomb bursts into a fury of dazzling colors. . . . As daring to wear as it was to drop the first bomb.
> —*Advertisement,* Fascination, *July 1946*

In October 1983, Goldwater's, a major Southwestern retailer, decorated its Albuquerque store windows with several mannequins in blue-denim outfits. Spray-painted on the wall behind them was the headline "Nuclear Fashion. Energize Your Look." The word *fashion* means "the way in which something is formed." It is semantically

An early example of "nuclear fashion."

related to such words as *habit* and *costume* and hence to the words *habituate* and *accustom*. I use the phrase *nuclear fashion* to mean those everyday words and images that form and reflect consciousness in the nuclear age. Some of these are ironic or campy. Others are uniform, working to accustom us to nuclearist notions, to habituate us to the horrors of living in the nuclear-armed and geocidally inclined warhead world.

This denial of the dangerous effects of radiation has a long history. In his 1950 government-sponsored book, *How to Survive an Atomic Bomb*, Richard Gerstell, a radiologist and consultant to the Pentagon's office of civil defense planning, dismisses as rumor the notion that contact with "fallout stuff" could cause cancer. Similarly, he ridicules reports of other dire effects such as loss of hair, blindness, sterility, and global environmental damage as utterly spurious. "Much of the danger of radioactivity is mental," he avers.[2] Gerstell, with blessings from the Pentagon, is engaging in big-time deception, perhaps even of himself. Still, his words carry some inadvertent truth, for they draw our attention to the psychological danger of radiation—that is, to some of the psychic consequences of living in the nuclear age.

In a series of books and articles, psychologist Robert Jay Lifton focuses analytic attention on the nuclearist psyche and on the psychological mechanisms that structure and sustain that consciousness:

> We are just now beginning to realize that nuclear weapons radically alter our existence. It is true that none of our actions, problems, or symptoms is caused by nuclear weapons alone. But it is also true that nothing we do or feel—in working, playing, and loving, and in our private family and public lives—is free of their influence. The threat they pose has become the context for our lives, a shadow that persistently intrudes upon our mental ecology.[3]

Some of the social effects Lifton ascribes to this all-pervasive, if shadowy, nuclear influence include a new ephemeralism; a prevailing sense of radical futurelessness due to an expectation of annihilation in our lifetimes; widespread fundamentalism; a sense of radical absurdity; psychic numbing, including the blocking of sensation, the repression of disturbing thoughts and images, and a dulling denial, even to the point of creating a "double life"; and a tendency to identify with the Bomb and even, as we shall see, to worship it.

Lifton focuses almost completely upon the ways that the invention of nuclear technology has degraded consciousness or threatened contemporary life. Still, it is important to also listen to and work with the insights of cultural theorists such as Paula Gunn Allen and Derrick de Kerckhove, who insist that the Bomb, paradoxically enough, has also acted culturally as a transformer, radically reordering perceptions and identities and raising our ecological and spiritual consciousness.[4] For example, the invention of the Bomb has elicited a consciousness of planetary interconnectedness. At the same time, the sense of radical nuclear absurdity that Lifton observes can serve to shock us out of denial and illuminate the total and fundamental folly of masculinist power, domination, and control. It can provide a framework in which those common claims of infallible Western progress and knowledge are rendered transparently ridiculous. That same radical absurdity can also contribute to a desire to seek radical change. Indeed, the core message of nuclear myth and symbol is profound alteration or transmutation—the qualitative transformation of elements or essences, the passage from death into rebirth.[5]

Throughout *Gossips, Gorgons & Crones*, particularly its latter sections, I consider and explore the beneficial transmutations of consciousness coincident with the advent of the Bomb, including the disruption of the reigning power/knowledge paradigm, the awareness of the need for limits and taboos on technological "progress," and the awareness of the return of female Powers. In part 1, however, my primary purpose is to deconstruct nuclearist myth and metaphor, disrupting and hopefully aiding in demolishing that narrative. With the nuclearist narrative rendered impotent and obsolete, Gossips can generate radically different and transformational nuclear symbols and stories, completely reconceptualizing the reigning narratives.

Every Mushroom Cloud Has a Silver Lining

One of the more remarked-upon items at a toy convention in New York City in 1987 was a mushroom cloud night-light. Who knows what the manufacturers had in mind? Humor, irony, fashion, marketability? Perhaps they were merely reflecting the normalcy of nuclear imagery in our everyday culture. As cultural theorist Derrick de Kerckhove aptly puts it, "Forty years after Hiroshima, we wake up to the feeling that the bomb has become a major icon within our mental structures."[6]

The mushroom cloud is the most common signifier of the Bomb. Yet, despite its omnipresence, any attempt to assign definite symbolic significance to the mushroom cloud is haunted by ambiguity, paradox, and contradiction. As nuclear historian Spencer Weart perceptively writes, the mushroom cloud is an extremely redolent "folk symbol."[7] The shape of the cloud associated with atomic bombs was originally described in a variety of ways: as a column, a funnel, and even a brain. Yet it was the *mushroom* association that caught the popular imagination. Weart recognizes that mushrooms have long held traditional associations with "witches and fairies, or in short with magical powers," with hallucinations, with shamanistic rituals, and even with psychedelic experience. Most significantly, the mushroom, while symbolically linked with rot and death, is simultaneously an emblem of life, of food or umbrellalike protection. Weart concludes, "The mushroom, whether an atomic bomb cloud or simply a knob growing on a rotting log, could represent life opposing death—perhaps even life arising from within death, that is, transmutation."

Another nuclear historian, Paul Boyer, notes that since 1945 the mushroom cloud has remained "the universally recognized symbol of atomic-age menace."[8] The nuclear disarmament movement has effectively employed that image in numberless pins, posters, and bumper stickers to convey dread of nuclear war. Yet, at the same time, in military environs (such as the National Atomic Museum in Albuquerque and the Bradbury Science Museum in Los Alamos) the mushroom cloud is flaunted as "an undisputed sign of military might."[9] Finally, as any alert consumer knows, the mushroom cloud is flagrantly and frequently employed as a marketing device.

The bomb blast or simply the word *atomic* is used as a kind of shorthand in any number of ways to suggest awesome heat and/or power, evidenced in the brand names "Atomic Horseradish" and "Atomic Skis." A mushroom cloud appears on the cover of the October 1985 issue of *Guns & Ammo* magazine. The gun of the month is a ".454 casull 'atomic class' magnum!" set against the background of a billowing mushroom cloud. Apparently, gun enthusiasts want to envision themselves as packing the power of the atom bomb.

An extraordinary advertisement hawking real estate appeared in 1971 in the *Los Angeles Times*. It, too, shows a towering mushroom cloud. Underneath, the copy reads, "Even if they drop a bomb on it . . . you still own the hole! And when the dust settles, it will probably go up in price."

Twenty years later, Oakley sunglasses, in a state of even greater abandonment of truth, promise their wearers lenses crafted with "plutonite" (sounds like plutonium), which they boast offers "thermonuclear protection." In a 1993 commercial shown on MTV, a super cool, rich, young white dude is awakened by the flash of an H-bomb. Hey, no sweat. He pushes a few buttons that instantly pull down some high-tech shades all around his deluxe house. He then goes to a cabinet, takes out his Oakley "thermonuclear protection" lenses, pops them into a frame, and dons a monkish, black hooded cape. The sound of medieval chanting rises on the soundtrack as our hero strides out into the dawn of a nuclear fireball—the Bomb can't touch him! The Oakley slogan appears on T-shirts, caps, and bumper stickers and probably appeals to those eager to deny not only nuclear but also ozone-layer anxiety.

Nuked Food: You Are What You Eat

Differences between radioactive waste and food have been confused for some time. Atomic Fireball candy has been around for decades; its box shows the candy rising out of a mushroom cloud. A new candy, "Mega Warhead," came onto the market in 1992. Its package shows a cartoonlike face of a boy who just has eaten something really "hot." From the top of his head, a mushroom cloud blooms. In 1988, I visited the Phoenix Sheraton and found "Chernobyl Chicken Wings" on the menu. As a resident of Albuquerque, I already had encountered "Atomic Tacos" and other such "hot" fare, yet I was flabbergasted when faced with food named after an unqualified nuclear disaster (and one that contaminated food throughout much of Europe).

Yet, why should I have been surprised? Many other nuclear sites, including the original ground zero, Trinity site in New Mexico, and the Three Mile Island nuclear power facility, have become active centers for tourism. At the Three Mile Island gift shop, one can purchase coffee mugs in the shape of the cooling towers as well as a cookbook, *T.M.I.*, standing for "Tasty Meal Ideas."[10]

Rockwell International, the corporation that operated the Rocky Flats nuclear weapons complex outside of Denver, desperately contaminated the surrounding area for years and in 1992 pled guilty to ten charges of environmental violations. In its long and sorry history of deception, one episode stands out. In 1989, Rockwell officials tried to minimize the plant's hazards by passing off a spill of toxic chromic acid as "guacamole" from the employees' cafeteria. This radioactive "guacamole" was then (supposedly by accident) pumped into Rocky

Flats's sewage treatment plant and from there channeled into the drinking water of Broomfield, Colorado.[11]

"Nuked" food recently has attained a reality far beyond microwavable products, candies, euphemisms for toxic waste, or flamboyant menu items. In early 1992, the first food-irradiation plant, Vindicator, began operation in Florida. There, foods like strawberries are bombarded with gamma rays from radioactive sources such as cesium 137, a waste byproduct from the manufacture of nuclear weapons. Scientific opinion is now divided over the safety of this process, but as Dr. Samuel Epstein remarks, "To allow the entire U.S. population to consume radiation-exposed foods is unacceptable, especially when the cancer rate is already at near-epidemic proportions."[12] The symbol for irradiated food, the "radura," is a leafy flower enclosed in a half-broken circle. Dr. Ronald Engel of the Food Safety and Inspection Service of the United States Department of Agriculture explains, "It was meant to be kind of like a smiley face so people would recognize irradiated food and want it."[13] The underlying message, I suppose, is that if you do get cancer, die smiling.

War Toys

An astonishing array of nuclear sentiments can be found in the world of toys. In 1946, General Mills offered the children of America an "Atomic Bomb Ring." For only fifteen cents and a Kix cereal box top, they could peer into that ring and see "genuine atoms SPLIT to smithereens." Current offerings continue to promote the recreational value of nuclear imagery and with far greater sophistication, frequently by visualizing world nuclear war. Board and video games such as "Missile Command" and "Ground Zero" let teenage boys (the primary consumers of such games) play at the same games that defense intellectuals get paid for—those that simulate nuclear war.

Children's and adults' comic books, films, and TV shows are rife with nuclear themes. Frequently, in these, as in many Cold War Hollywood films (such as *The Atomic Kid*, 1954), one of the most common ways for an ordinary modern mortal to become a superhero is to be exposed to something nuclear. Superheroes created in this fashion include Spiderman, Captain Atom, Firestorm, and the Incredible Hulk.[14]

One example of the packaging of this theme in a contemporary toy is the "Toxic Crusaders," manufactured by Troma, Inc. The toy's hero is "Toxie," formerly a "local mop boy" and "nerd-about-town" who fell into a vat of radioactive "toxic-transforming waste," effecting his rebirth into a "hideously deformed creature of superhuman size and strength!" Toxie teams up with "other human environmental accidents from the toxic waste dump," a platoon of "deformed do-gooders" to fight the forces of evil, in this case evil space aliens who want to take over the planet.

It seems that a certain "Dr. Killemoff," a pollution-breathing alien from the planet "Smogula" (who, significantly, looks very much like a cross between a vampire and a drag queen), has emigrated to Earth. This feminine male alien, working through his multinational corporation, "Apocalypse, Inc.," deliberately produces smog and toxic waste. His plan is to make the entire Earth unfit for human habitation. This alien corporate head is aided by four "bad guys," including the "Radiation Ranger," who delivers this quite chilling soliloquy:

> Don't think of us as strange. Think of us as your future. Humorless, radioactive, and cold. Some day, when Dr. Killemoff's corporate goal has been completed, all humans will wear our atomic armor and become humanoid radiation rangers. It is useless to resist us. We are great in number. We breathe the pollution you create and grow stronger every day. Nothing can destroy us.

There is a kind of ground zero humor in this soliloquy, as well as an eerie evocation of that central facet of nuclear consciousness described by Robert Jay Lifton as "radical futurelessness." If there is no future, these toys tell us, it's because we humans have done it to ourselves. We create the pollution that feeds and strengthens our "alien" enemies and frankly continue to do so through our ongoing contamination of the planet. Still, these toys ultimately celebrate the contamination.

In the one-dimensional world of the Toxic Crusaders, both "good" and "bad" guys (and they are all guys) come packing a

"SECRET TOXIC GLO-IN-THE-DARK WEAPON: So radioactive we've put it under wraps!" Everyone is nuclear armed and proud to be. Moreover, Toxie's disturbing trademark is the Earth skewered by a mop. It seems that the good guys are also symbolically raping the Earth. Toxie and crew not only use the same weapons as their "alien" opposites, but they are equally alienated from the Earth. While consumers are meant to be thrilled by the magical transmutation of the "nerd" into the superhero, they are not supposed to notice the accompanying utterly unmagical transformation of the Earth into a toxic dump. Toxie himself is colored a kind of radioactive guacamole green, but this only flaunts what we have lost. In Toxie's world, the Earth, in poet Marilou Awiakta's words, has taken "all green into her heart."[15] There are no trees, animals, flowers, or people, but only those beings, "good" and "bad," who flourish in total toxicity. Isn't Troma, Inc., then, very much like Apocalypse, Inc., thriving on, profiting from, and ultimately promoting environmental trauma?

At the same time, Troma, Inc. apparently intends this toy to raise some kind of ecological consciousness, for on the package back they invite children to become members of Kids Against Pollution. Yet I find it hard to believe that this toy's scenario, bereft of female presence and predicated upon the utterly unmourned destruction of animals, trees, and the elements, promotes ecological awareness among its targeted group, children "ages 4 and up." First of all, in science fiction scenarios, no matter how bizarre, the bottom line is that the future is now and the aliens are us. To encounter beings who thrive on waste and seem intent on turning the world into their sewer, we need look no further than many of our political, corporate, military, and scientific warheads.[16] To encounter humans hideously mutated by toxic and radioactive waste, U.S. citizens need only turn to our own Texas-Mexico border and face the alarming number of children victimized by environmental racism and being born there without brains.[17]

Certainly, there will be various interpretations given to these toys by those children who are attracted to them. For example, sophisticated consumers might enjoy the heavy irony. At the same time, some children (and some adults) might even identify with these bizarre creatures simply because they are mutants and aliens, signifying qualitatively different beings born with entirely new minds, ways of thought, ways of seeing and perceiving, models of the radical transmutation to which we aspire.[18] Nevertheless, just as Barbie dolls invite girls into a future world of objectification, anorexia, cosmetic surgery, and silicone implants, the Toxic Crusaders can be understood as preparing children for proliferating toxicity, horrific mutations, endless warfare, and, most pragmatically, future occupations as toxic-waste cleanup workers—slang terms for whom include *glowboys, jumpers, fresh meat, minutemen,* and *radiation sponges.*[19] Certainly, the rhetoric of transmutation informs the Toxic Crusaders. Still, at their core, the Toxic Crusaders remain war toys, structured by power play and the all too familiar erasure and scapegoating of the alien and the feminine.

Nuke Talk

If many popular artifacts and images make nuclear technology and weaponry seem playful and personalized, then slang words, particularly the technical terms incorporated into everyday language, create a similar effect. Robert Lifton scorns what he sees as a prevailing domestication of weapons: "In calling them 'nukes,' for instance, we render them small and 'cute,' something on the order of a household pet."[20] Curiously, according to Spencer Weart, the word *nuke* was originally deployed at the Strategic Air Command (SAC) during the 1950s as a deliberately dry and asexual alternative to the provocative imagery associated with bombs and bombers during and after World War II (such as the atomic bomb dropped on Bikini, which had a picture of Rita Hayworth painted on it and was nicknamed "Gilda").[21] While the word *nuke* originated in the military establishment, ironically it was the antinuclear movement itself that first did a great deal to promote its use with the widespread slogan "No Nukes."

Though first popularized as a noun, *nuke* also frequently appears in general speech as a verb—and one with the wide range of meanings usually associated with obscene expressions. One of its first entries into popular jargon was in the phrase "nuke the whales" (1979). Originally part of the lyrics to a song by a student punk band, the expression soon began to appear as campus graffiti, then on T-shirts, then on bumper stickers. "Nuke Iran" and "Nuke Jane Fonda" soon followed.

Curiously, the verb *nuke* is commonly used to refer to microwave cooking, as in "Let's nuke some pizza." While we could read this as yet another domestication of nuclear effects, the slang term *nuke* in this context also indubitably registers some anxieties about the alleged safety of microwave ovens. This unease also informs a song, "Nuke It," sung in the early 1990s by first graders in the Albuquerque school district. It concerns a man who has stopped worrying and learned to love his microwave. He praises its ability to "[make] leftovers glow" and concludes,

> Now, I'm a microwave king.
> And I love this machine.
> It's my own little Three Mile Island.[22]

The ironic reference to Three-Mile Island might initially be lost on the first-graders, but its resonance may linger and eventually provide some food for thought.

The technical word *meltdown* connotes the extremely hazardous melting of the core of a nuclear reactor, an event that would contaminate the area surrounding a nuclear power plant and kill and sicken untold numbers of people. Curiously enough, the same word, often positively inflected, has entered into everyday slang. For example, in 1988 an ad for Toyota enthusiastically proclaimed a "performance verging on meltdown," and *Family Circle* magazine that same year urged its readers to "lose weight, feel great" by embarking upon a "meltdown diet." Perhaps most astonishing was an ad for motor scooters that appeared in the *Albuquerque Journal* on July 25, 1987. A year-end sale on the bikes was signaled by the headline "*Meltdown '87.*" That phrase, incredibly, was surrounded by the words "*FINAL DAYS! FINAL DAYS!*" and an exhortation to "*TAKE THE RIDE OF YOUR LIFE.*" The methodology of this ad was somewhat analogous to that of a fundamentalist preacher invoking doomsday in order to spur adhesion to the faith; here, however, the desired reaction to the evocation of doomsday was an urge to impulsively spend and buy.

A cheeseburger named "Meltdown" was sold in Harrisburg, Pennsylvania, after the 1977 Three Mile Island near disaster. The his-

meg-ă-deth), n. (1) a unit of
measure equal to the death of a
million people by nuclear explosion.
2) Megadeth, n. the world's state-of-the
art speed metal band.

Megadeth poster, 1987.

tory of nuclear development has shown that government and corporate officials regularly deny contamination from both everyday
nuclear production and storage procedures as well as from overt
accidents. Yet, as this slang term reveals, residents of the Three Mile
Island area were acknowledging, albeit in an oblique way, that their
food was contaminated by radiation.

A Los Angeles–based Japanese-American jazz band is named
"Hiroshima." Whereas that name unmistakably recalls the historical
use of nuclear weapons, the name of the popular heavy-metal band
"Megadeth" seems to welcome their mass use. A 1987 poster for
Megadeth portrays a giant skeleton rearing up on the horizon, one
outstretched hand reaching to crush a tiny, faceless mass of humans

below. A mushroom cloud sporting a fetuslike face appears just over the skeleton's shoulder. At bottom right is a dictionary definition of the band's name: "(*meg-a-deth*), n. (1) a unit of measure equal to the death of a million people by nuclear explosion (2) . . . the world's state of the art speed metal band." Viewers are invited to identify, rather sadistically, with the agent of nuclear mass murder. Yet, ironically, such identification is ultimately masochistic for we, in truth, are represented by the vanquished humans.

Although it is beyond my scope here to provide anything other than a cursory mention, it is important to note that nuclear themes pervade contemporary music in every genre, from heavy metal through funk, rap, hip-hop, punk, folk, and pop. For example, superstar Prince anticipates heavy partying at the nuclear end of the world in his funky "1999."[23] Still, in many ways the most expressly techno-apocalyptic genres are punk and heavy metal, as indicated by such characteristic band names as "Megadeth," "Sex Pistols," "Anthrax," "Nuclear Assault," "Slayer," "Suicidal Tendencies," and "Annihil-ator." In punk and heavy metal's costuming, iconography, and song lyrics, themes such as destruction, waste, environmental contamination, and genocide are not only cynically celebrated but also frequently criticized. As sociologist Deena Weinstein points out, mixed in with the misogyny, racism, and homophobia that all too frequently mar the messages of heavy metal are pointed critiques of the governmental and corporate corruption, the horrors of environmental con-tamination, the traumatization of children, and the alienation of adults.[24] Basically, through its characteristic imagery and themes, punk and metal music asks us to acknowledge that we *already* are living through the apocalypse.

Searing, apocalyptic representations of wasted bodies and landscapes appear in the "Garbage Pail Kids," a series of bubble gum cards aimed at preteens and originated by graphic artist Art Spiegelman (who is most well known for his bestselling accounts of his parents' experiences of the Holocaust in *Maus* and *Maus II*).[25] The Garbage Pail Kids loudly mock the Cabbage Patch happy nuke-family vision. The cards make plays on given names to create characters such as "Adam Bomb," "Michael Mutant," "Impaled Gail," and "Toxic Wes." These characters are depicted as children in various

Michael Mutant and Toxic Wes of the Garbage Pail Kids, Art Spiegelman's surreal-istically thrown away children. Topps © 1993.

states of surreal neglect, death, and/or mutilation. For example, Toxic Wes is a disembodied huge, round face through whose open mouth pour all sorts of sewage, corpses, and garbage. The abuses heaped upon Spiegelman's surrealistically thrown-away children offer a pointed, though undeniably ambivalent critique of the social order—whose neglect and abuse of children is a microcosm of the larger neglect of the future, manifested in the pollution of earth, air, and water and in the systematic preparations for nuclear war. The Garbage Pail Kids thus both reflect and indict the cosmically wasteful and lethally self-centered "Make Room for Daddy" culture.

In her poem "Dying Back," Marilou Awiakta elucidates the connections between our garbage-pail society's methodical wasting of nature and the wasting away of human consciousness, soul, and intelligence:

On the mountain
the standing people are dying back—
hemlock, spruce and pine

turn brown in the head.
The hardwood shrivels in new leaf.
Unnatural death
from acid greed
that takes the form of rain
and fog and cloud.

In the valley
the walking people are blank-eyed.
Elders mouth vacant thought.
Youth grow spindly, wan
from sap too drugged to rise.
Pushers drain it off—
sap is gold to them.
The walking people are dying back
as all species do
that kill their own seed.[26]

Air pollution is but one of many threats now being leveled against the trees, or the "standing people." Since 1982, thanks to the Reagan administration, only the very oldest sequoias, those more than two thousand years old, are protected at Sequoia National Forest. Less ancient sequoias and their surrounding trees have provided fair game for commercial logging. Environmentalist Lee Green reports on the jargon of the Forest Service: "In official documents, forestlands are not logged but 'managed.' Clearcutting is known as 'regeneration cutting.' Trees are 'standing inventory.'" Green describes the results of such "management": a few two-thousand-year-old trees standing alone in a razed area, "no longer surrounded by pines and firs, incense cedar and dogwood, beat clover, manzanita, and bracken fern." Most significant is Green's revelation that "'nuked' is the term these [deforesting] forest rangers use privately to describe their own actions, as in, 'We nuked the place.'"[27]

As viewers were told endlessly by every other vacant elder at the 1992 Republican national convention, the Cold War is over thanks to the leadership of those consummately hollow men Reagan and Bush. To such committed wastemakers, the nominal enemies (be they the

Soviets or the Iraqis) were and are mere decoys. The blue and green world is the real "evil empire" to these toxic crusaders. For, in truth, "nuclear war" now is being waged—against the waters, the atmosphere, the animals, and the forests. It is these "peoples" who, even as we do not speak, are being "nuked."

CHAPTER TWO

Nuclear Pornography

A little nukey is good for everyone.
—*Slogan on a pro-nuclear T-shirt, c. 1980*

Air Force Magazine's advertisements for new weapons . . . rival
Playboy as a catalog of men's sexual anxieties and fantasies.
—*Carol Cohn*[1]

It is very ironic that the SAC thought it was desexualizing nuclear weapons by calling them "nukes," for, as any examination of
popular usage reveals, *nuke* is frequently meant as a synonym for
fuck. A sexually sadistic attack or obliteration is always implicit in the
phrase "fuck you." An example of how it is equally implicit in the
use of the word *nuke* was the action of a counter-demonstrator at the
Women's Encampment for a Future of Peace and Justice in Romulus,
New York. This man took one of the encampment T-shirts and sten-
ciled onto it, "NUKE THE BITCHES."[2]

This sex-violent use of the technical term *nuke* speaks eloquently
to feminist insights about sex and violence under male supremacy. In
that system, male and female are defined as inevitably attracted to
each other and, at the same time, inherently unequal. Domination is
identified with masculinity, submissiveness with femininity. (Hence,

43

any unsubmissive women are labeled "bitches.") The male partner in the heterosexist relationship is supposed to be taller, stronger, richer, and older—in short, more powerful. The female partner is supposed to be shorter, weaker, poorer, and younger—in short, powerless. As feminist legal theorist Catharine MacKinnon has argued, under this system of male supremacy, inequality itself becomes sexy. Dominance and submission themselves become heavily invested with eroticism. Inevitably, then, sex and violence become "mutually definitive," and "acts of dominance and submission, up to and including acts of violence, are experienced as sexually arousing, as sex itself."[3]

Acts of technological dominance participate in this sex-violence continuum. In this world ordered by patriarchal power, "fucking" and "nuking" are deeply interconnected expressions of domination. The "NUKE THE BITCHES" T-shirt, moreover, is by no means unique. It is characteristic of much of the verbal and visual imagery of what I call nuclear pornography. These images link nuclear technology, weapons, and warfare to patriarchal constructions of desire and eroticism.

The 1987 film *Full Metal Jacket* first exposes and then embraces the misogyny that constructs the male warrior, tracing the transformation of boys into men as they proceed from marine boot camp to Vietnam. In boot camp, the initiates are abused, demoralized, and incessantly verbally harassed by an abusive father figure (the drill instructor). In his mouth, every woman is "Mary Jane Rotten Crotch," and the worst epithet for a recruit is "lady" or its equivalent. The film climaxes when some of these same marines are targeted by sniper fire in Vietnam. When one soldier, a cowardly braggart, critically wounds the sniper, she is revealed to be a teenaged girl. With this slaying, the annihilation of the feminine begun in boot camp comes full circle. At this virile and victorious moment, the shooter gloats, "Am I a heartbreaker; am I a life taker!"

In the nuclear age, the quintessential or ritual act—upon which other culturally charged actions are then modeled—is the splitting of the atom, the attempted rape or breaking of what Marilou Awiakta calls the "mother heart" of the universe.[4] For about two centuries, *split* in low slang has meant to "copulate . . . as in . . . 'I'd like to split that one.'"[5] The sexual violence in that term—adhering as well to *fuck, screw, hammer, nail, bang,* and *pound*—everywhere informs the language of nuclear technology.

It is important, first, to define *pornography* and to distinguish it from *erotica*. By *erotica*, I mean nonsexist sexual words and pictures, ones premised upon equality, respect, and consent between sexual partners. By *pornography*, following Catharine MacKinnon and Andrea Dworkin, I mean "the graphic sexually explicit subordination of women through pictures and/or words." Pornography is sexually explicit material that sexualizes male power, female subordination, taboo-breaking, objectification, and violation. It consists of words and pictures that are veritably *documents* of sexual abuse.[6] The history of scientific imagery and metaphor provides a rich study of such pornographic worldviews and practices.

Traditionally, the Earth, nature, and matter have been understood as female, usually in the nurturing sense. The word *nature* is from the Latin word *nasci*, "to be born." The word *matter* is from the Latin word *mater*, meaning "mother." All of the English words for Earth beginning with the prefix *geo* (such as *geology)* come from the Greek word *ge*, which invokes both the Earth and the Earth Goddess. As these etymologies indicate, in Western culture, women and the Earth have long been mutually associated. Environmental historian Caroline Merchant traces the implicit sexual violence of the seventeenth-century scientific revolution as revealed through its characteristic metaphors of "mastering," "disrobing," and "penetrating" nature as a female form. Merchant also describes the objectification of the Earth as, during this time, the planetary body became seen as a mechanism or a corpse, though still a feminized one.[7] Such metaphor rapidly became habitual and provided the basis for much of twentieth-century nuclearist imagery. Spencer Weart notes:

> Twentieth-century scientists and journalists who wanted to stimulate public interest in physics found their most striking phrases in this old metaphor of aggressive pursuit. Atomic scientists investigated "the most intimate properties of matter," indeed "penetrated" hidden mysteries, "tore away the veils" to reveal inner secrets, and "laid bare" the structure of atoms. Language about breaking apart the indivisible atom could be openly belligerent. Already in 1905 a friend told Rutherford that anoth-

er physicist was "so anxious to bust atoms artificially that . . . he would have tried it with a cold-chisel before long." A quarter-century later Millikan wrote of the "satisfaction in smashing a resistant atom."[8]

Weart is being somewhat coy here, for the stimulation he refers to resides not so much in the metaphor of aggression, but in images of *sexual* aggression—rape, mutilation, and matricide.

A question arises: Wouldn't it be better just to rid the Earth of its female associations—to simply call the planet "it" and thereby disrupt this rapist, essentially incestuous ("motherfucking") paradigm? Some postmodern thinkers prefer the pronoun *it* to refer to the Earth because they refuse allegiance to oppositional patriarchal categories of sex and disavow any collusion with an ideology of "essentialism" (a belief in fixed, essential sexual natures).[9] Yet I don't think using *it* will provide any solutions. Certainly, runaway women, those abandoning patriarchal worldviews, resist essentialist notions of a fixed female nature, since these notions have been used by patriarchs for millennia to define and construct femaleness as a state of unchanging and inescapable domestic and bodily slavery. But to counter this trap, we need not disavow the concept of essential femaleness. Rather, we must radically refuse sexist constructions of female and male natures and simultaneously expand our understanding of *essences*. Essences exist, but, contra the prevailing notions, they are not fixed but are themselves mutable. Essences, including female and male essences, are always moving, always transmuting.[10]

Many feminists also are rightfully wary of nurturing, maternal metaphors in a sexist culture in which motherhood is still not only mandatory but also so pseudo-sacralized and so simultaneously scapegoated. Nevertheless, the solution is not to deny the planet's femaleness but to abandon such sexist notions of femininity. Gossips redefine the terms of the argument so that to be female in no way means being passive, endlessly nurturing, willing to constantly clean up the messes of wasteful and disrespectful dependents, and perpetually open to invasion and possession. Rather, to be female is to be "pregnant" with Powers—not only Powers of life, but also Powers of death.

I also suggest that modern, technology-dependent Western people listen carefully to the many indigenous peoples who have always spoken of the Earth as female, not only symbolically female but also in the realm of physical reality. Cherokee/Appalachian poet Marilou Awiakta, in her poem "When Earth Becomes an It," affirms that the Earth is female and a mother and cautions that we had best speak of her in that way:

> When the people call Earth "Mother,"
> they take with love
> and with love give back
> so that all may live.
>
> When the people call Earth "it,"
> they use her
> consume her strength
> Then the people die.
>
> Already the sun is hot
> out of season.
> Our mother's breast
> is going dry.
> She is taking all green
> into her heart
> and will not turn back
> until we call her
> by her name.[11]

Calling the planet "it," whatever our intentions, potentially colludes with pornotechnology's objectification and attempted rape of the planet and nature. It, moreover, can numb us to the awareness that the planet is a sentient, ensouled body with means and ends all her own.

On Orgasmic Meltdowns and Sex Bombs

> Tell me that you don't have to fuck yourself on
> the reactor core of an intense meltdown
>   to show your importance
> Tell me that you have no desire

to be the first one to fuck
                    into the fission of a fusion
                        of a fucking holocaust.
        —*Jayne Cortez*[12]

Metaphors linking sexuality to elemental forces such as heat and fire are extremely common (as in "C'mon, Baby, light my fire"). Spinning off from these metaphors are recurrent comparisons of both male and female sexuality to nuclear fire, including nuclear power plants:

"He's like Three Mile Island inside, just ready to blow." . . . "I think he's going to be a heterosexual Montgomery Clift." That's what movie biggies are saying about Tom Cruise.[13]

Many observers find in the ascendancy of Michael Jackson the ultimate personification of the androgynous rock star. His high-flying tenor makes him sound like the lead in some funked-up boys' choir, even as the sexual dynamism irradiating from the arch of his dancing body challenges Government standards for a nuclear meltdown.[14]

Why Is A Beautiful Woman Like A Nuclear Power Plant? In order to remain beautiful she must take good care of herself. . . . She schedules her rest regularly. . . . When she is not feeling well she sees her doctor. . . . She never lets herself get out of shape. . . . She is as trim now as she was ten years ago. . . . In other words, *she is a perfect example of preventative maintenance.*
            —*Advertisement in* Nuclear News Buyer's
                Guide *(Crouse Group of Companies, 1976)*[15]

In each of these descriptions, sexuality is somehow linked to a nuclear reactor—male sexuality with the reactor's propensity to blow, female sexuality with its ability to be contained or controlled. Such metaphors participate in a dominant sexual paradigm that feminist historian Martha Vicinus has characterized as both "overwhelmingly male and heterosexual"—the "energy-control (or hydraulic) model."[16] In this "energy-control" paradigm, sexuality is seen as an "independent force or energy disciplined by personal and social constraints." Such sexuality is understood as both a powerful force seeking explosive release as well as a force that can be controlled and made socially useful. It is only in a culture conditioned by such a paradigm that a nuclear meltdown can be understood as erotic—as the irresistible, blissful spilling over of repressed energy (making nuclear meltdown especially attractive to a fascist, over-controlled, and sexually repressed culture).

An even more familiar association insists on the connection between nuclear *weaponry* and sexuality, specifically between the bomb blast and sexual orgasm. In 1945, special War Department historian and journalist William L. Laurence won much acclaim for his eyewitness accounts of the first atomic bomb blasts. These accounts resounded with delight in the "come shot"—the primary pornographic spectacle of male ejaculation. In one Pulitzer Prize–winning description, his account of the bomb burst over Nagasaki, Laurence wrote, "The mushroom top was even more alive than the pillar, seething and boiling in a white fury of creamy foam, sizzling upward and then descending earthward, a thousand geysers rolled into one."[17]

Throughout the 1950s, scores of popular songs promoted our culture's orgasmic surrender to nuclear technology. For example, in 1957 Little Caesar and the Red Callender Sextette sang of their "Atomic Love": "Ooh, something exploded down inside/and rushed tears up in my eyes./Oh yes, I have that funny feeling./I guess it's my atomic love for you." Thirty years later, in "Disco Inferno" the Trammps wailed, "Satisfaction came in a chain reaction."[18] In 1982, Artist Mimi Smith served up her ironic version of nuclear safety: a drawing of a mushroom cloud with a diaphragm vainly trying to contain it. "Better Safe Than Sorry," read the caption.[19] Not to be outdone, the phenomenally bestselling writer Stephen King had one of his female characters describe her orgasm—which was actually King's fantasy of female orgasm—in this way: "She became aware that this wasn't going to be just a come; it was going to be a tactical nuke."[20]

Such sexual boasting probably covers a multitude of denials. For does anyone believe that the invention of nuclear weaponry, capable of wiping out our species, actually promotes erotic joy? Sardonic commentary on this can be found in abundance in the campy 1982 sex film *Cafe Flesh*. The story is set in a post–nuclear-holocaust future, where the vast majority of people have completely lost their capacity for bodily pleasure and must enslave the few still functional "sex positives" to perform for them in Cafe Flesh:

In a world destroyed, a mutant universe, survivors break down to those who can and those who can't. Ninety-nine percent are Sex Negatives, call them erotic casualties. They want to make love, but the mere touch of another makes them violently ill. The rest, the lucky one percent, are Sex Positive, those whose libidos escaped unscathed. After the Nuclear Kiss, the Positives remain to love, to perform, and the others, we Negatives, can only watch, can only come to Cafe Flesh.[21]

As we watch people having sex in the film, we can't help but identify ourselves, the viewers of the filmic sex show, with the abusive Sex Negatives, who, due to postnuclear trauma, can only watch others perform and who frankly enslave them to do it. *Cafe Flesh* thus mockingly explores not only the effects of nuclear numbing on the human libido, but also the ultimately numbing effect of objectification on the capacity for actual and consensual fleshy interaction.

This film also provided an early commentary on the havoc that another harbinger of apocalypse, AIDS, has wreaked upon sexual expression. Following the 1992 Winter Olympics, an extremely bizarre prime-time music and dance costume number sent out a similar message. Scores of young people, isolated in plastic bubbles, danced around and sang, "Now that we've found love, what are we gonna do with it?" As cultural theorist Ann Larabee observes, AIDS is an ironic successor to nuclear weaponry, ensuring that it is now sex that "is perceived as MAD, that is, mutually assured destruction."[22]

Despite such glaring paradoxes, a recurrent mainstream metaphor continues to insist upon identifying sexual pleasure with nuclear explosion. One image, though, is a bit more truthful about the nature of this particular pleasure. It is an illustration by well-known rock artist Raymond Pettibone that is used for the cover of a mid-1980s avant-garde compilation rock album. It shows a naked man strangling and raping a naked woman. Outside, a mushroom cloud blooms, signifying both his orgasm and her annihilation.[23] These and all other such images invite us to reconsider the sex appeal of nuclear weapons—as well as the apocalyptic lethality of normative patriarchal sexuality.

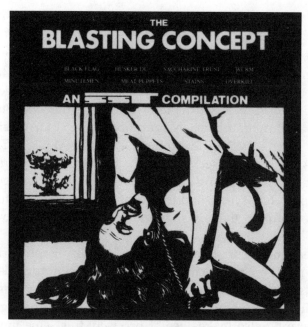

Raymond Pettibone's artwork for The Blasting Concept—
*one of many cultural images linking sexual murder to
nuclear weaponry.*

Safer than Sex?

I wish you were the town of Hiroshima and I *la bombe atomique
pour tomber dessus* [and I the atomic bomb so that I could fall on
you].
> —*The master of ceremonies to a female
> performer in an Athens nightclub, 1945*[24]

Nuclear Energy—Safer than Sex
> —*Slogan of a women's pronuclear group, S.A.F.E.
> (Society for the Advancement of Fusion Energy),
> 1977*[25]

A political cartoon by Lou Myers shows two military men duel-
ing with extended penises that are designed as missiles, one marked
U.S., the other *USSR*.[26] Similarly, a political cartoon in the *Los Angeles
Times* shows a number of upright nuclear missiles with the caption
"Speaking of the need for condoms."[27] What these humorists mock,

however, is taken seriously and blithely exploited by others. For example, Ronald Reagan, in the most repeated lines of his famous March 23, 1983, "Star Wars" speech, promised that his plan would be able to render nuclear missiles "impotent and obsolete." More deliberately jocular, Mr. Reagan employed the same sexualized association in his world-televised remarks following the 1984 Superbowl. Chatting with winning coach Tom Flores of the L.A. Raiders, the president joked, "I've already gotten a call from Moscow. They think Marcus Allen is a new secret weapon. They insist we dismantle it." Warming to his metaphors, the "Great Communicator" continued, telling Flores that if he would turn over his football team to the government, "we'd put them in silos and we wouldn't have to build the MX missile."[28]

In Reagan's commentary, idealized virility is powerfully and gleefully fused both to weaponry and to a mass-murderous lethality. His words are recognizable as part of an omnipresent stream that we might call the pornography of everyday life. Not surprisingly, explicit pornography also makes use of precisely this same metaphor of weaponry. A 1987 adult video catalog highlighted one feature, *The Incredible Mr. MX*, a porno film about a man with a monstrously long penis, with the words, "Take a long look at the real weapon of the '80s!! . . . See his 16 1/2-inch missile."

This same association appeared much earlier in Stanley Kubrick's extraordinary 1964 comedy, *Dr. Strangelove: Or How I Learned to Stop Worrying and Love the Bomb*. In this film, the madman militarist who triggers a world nuclear holocaust is named after the legendary sex killer Jack the Ripper. *Dr. Strangelove's* General Jack D. Ripper, obsessed with what he sees as a worldwide communist plot to pollute his "purity of essence" through fluoridation of the water, decides to wipe out the Soviet Union on his own initiative. He instructs airborne SAC bombers to launch a nuclear attack, a move ultimately resulting in the detonation of the Soviet's "doomsday machine." The film ends with the end of the world, but before doomsday, General Ripper elaborates on his ideas to his captive, Colonel Mandrake:

Mandrake: Tell me, Jack, when did you first become . . . well, develop this theory.
Ripper: Well, I first became aware of it, Mandrake, during the

physical act of love . . . yes—a profound sense of fatigue, a feeling of emptiness followed. Luckily, I was able to interpret those feelings correctly—loss of essence. I can assure you, it has not recurred. Women . . . women sense my power, and they seek the life essence. I do not avoid women, Mandrake, but I do deny them my essence.

Kubrick's naming of the crazed general, however much a potshot it seems, actually was aimed with deadly accuracy. General Ripper's criminal namesake killed and mutilated five prostitutes in London in 1888. He did not rape his victims, so his actions were not immediately recognized as sex crimes. Soon, however, with the conceptual aid of Sigmund Freud and German neurologist Richard von Krafft-Ebing, Jack the Ripper's knife (as well as every other weapon) became understood to be a symbolic penis. Public opinion apprehended that although the killer did not rape his victims, "the murderous act and subsequent mutilation of the corpse were substitutes for the sexual act."[29] Like his prototype and namesake, *Dr. Strangelove's* General Jack D. Ripper finds his ultimate satisfaction in violent assault, using a sexualized weapon in place of his penis. In the general's case, however, the mutilation sex murder takes the form of an all-out nuclear attack, and the victim is planet Earth.

I have extensively discussed the connections between sexual and nuclear violences in earlier writings,[30] arguing that

1. Violence against women and violence against the Earth, legitimated and promoted by both patriarchal religion and science, are interconnected assaults rooted in the eroticization of domination. The gynocidal culture's image of woman as object and victim is paralleled by contemporary representations that continually show the Earth as a toy, machine, or violated object, as well as by the religious and scientific ideology that legitimates the possession, contamination, and destruction of Mother Earth.

2. In a symbolic system in which the penis is consistently linked with weaponry and nuclear blasts with ejaculations, nuclear holocaust is frequently celebrated, however subtly, as the ultimate orgasm, the ultimate matricide, and the ultimate "snuff" scene.[31]

3. The ubiquitous metaphors linking virility with weapons of cosmic destruction are, then, no mere figures of speech, but symbols and images actively structuring reality. Discussing the significance of metaphor, cultural theorist David Edge has commented, "To use a metaphor is to overlap two images . . . our sense of both is subtly altered, by a sort of elision."[32] Ideal masculinity is already commonly associated with weaponry. As that weaponry has progressed to the destructiveness of nuclear arms, that culturally constructed virility has become ever more spectacularly virulent. For example, this virility is presently manifesting in unprecedented forms and rates of multicide, including serial sex murder and mass murder. In response to the pronuclear slogan "Nuclear Energy—Safer than Sex" (which, significantly, preceded the AIDS crisis), it could be argued that it is not so much that nuclear energy is safer than sex but that sexual danger is intimately linked with nuclear danger.

In my discussion of nuclear pornography, I have so far concentrated primarily on the metaphors that link the standard male-dominant heterosexuality with nuclear weaponry. In that system, men are weapons and women are targets. Still, even nuclear pornography recognizes that in the Bomb there are also female energies. As in ordinary pornography, the female characters in nuclear pornography are sexist stereotypes—projections of self-serving fantasies that perceive women as objects, evil seducers, bitches, bombshells, and scapegoats.

The Atom and Eve

Atom bomb baby, loaded with power,
Radioactive as a TV tower,
Nuclear fission in her soul,
Loves with electronic control.
            —The Five Stars, "Atom Bomb Baby," 1957[33]

What spreads faster than radiation?—Jane Fonda
            —Bumper sticker, late 1970s

Discussing the nicknaming of the Bikini test bomb as Gilda, film critic Michael Wood wrote:

The bomb dropped on Bikini was called Gilda and had a picture of Rita Hayworth painted on it. The phallic agent of destruction underwent a sex change, and the delight and terror of our new power were channeled into an old and familiar story: our fear and love of women. We got rid of guilt too: If women are always to blame, starting with Eve perhaps, or Mother Nature, then men can't be to blame.[34]

It is indeed interesting that the much-touted male-conceived, male-fathered, and male-"birthed" atomic bomb would so soon be associated in nuclearist representations with *female* sexualities, particularly scapegoated and pornographically inflected versions of those sexualities.

During the 1950s, Las Vegas casinos held beauty contests for a "Miss A-Bomb." In 1953, the same year it was being hit with especially "dirty" fallout from the Nevada test site, the town of St. George, Utah, paraded a small, crowned girl called "Our Little A-Bomb," who sat atop a facsimile of a mushroom cloud. In such figurations, atomic Powers are trotted around as the captives, the playthings, and even the children of "man." [35]

The cover of the November 1982 *Penthouse* was dominated by a voluptuous woman wearing a crown and dressed in black. Untypically, she assumed a mocking pose and gave "the finger" to the observer. She was a "bitch," marked by her attitude of challenge or menace. On her right the headline read, "Souvenir Issue: PET OF THE YEAR." On her left was a headline for an inside story on disarmament reading, "ISN'T LEARNING TO LOVE THE BOMB WHAT LIFE IS ALL ABOUT?"

In my previous writings, I have argued that media messages, both broadcast and in print, are constructed via a process of *flow*.[36] In order to get the full meaning of any media text, one has to see it in its context, taking into account the influence of whatever precedes, follows, and surrounds it. Essentially, a magazine cover comprises a complex package of interconnecting items that one must read together in order to comprehend their total message. Although only the message on the right purportedly referred to the woman, arguably *both* messages did. She was "the Bomb" that *Penthouse* dwellers had to learn to "love," but really to hate: the epitome of the pornographic dream of the aggressive, nonsubservient woman who needs only a "good fuck" to be put back in her place.

In 1950s jargon, experts promised that the atom could be "tamed" to serve "man." As social historian Elaine Tyler May argues, these pronouncements paralleled the domestic ideology that the "female bombshell could be 'harnessed for peace' within the home."[37] So too, it seems, could the 1982 *Penthouse* bomb/pet, for inside the cover she was naked, sitting on Bob (the publisher of *Penthouse*) Guccione's lap. A page later, she was on her back, legs spread, groveling, posed and possessed.

Michael Wood recognized another theme in the symbolization of the Gilda bomb: the scapegoating and displacement of guilt achieved by making women and not men responsible for the destructiveness of the Bomb. He further placed such scapegoating into its archetypal tradition, epitomized in the Western world by the myth of Adam and Eve. This myth was invoked in one of the earliest atom bomb songs, "The Atom and Evil," sung by the Golden Gate Quartet in 1949. In

Woman as (Sex) Bomb.

this song, the power itself is male—the archetypically innocent Adam/Atom, who is being tempted by the equally archetypical Eve/Evil: "Now Atom was a sweet young innocent thing/ Until the night that Miss Evil took him under her wing." The song cautions, "If we don't break up that romance soon/We'll all fall down and go boom, boom./We're sitting on the edge of doom, doom, doom."[38]

The 1950s was also the decade of Marilyn Monroe, the consummate "sex bomb." Monroe's endlessly duplicated image has appeared in several complex nuclear contexts. Nicholas Roeg's 1986 film, *Insignificance*, is a surrealistic meditation on the meaning of god, fame, and nuclear weapons as explored through four characters representing Monroe, Albert Einstein, Senator Joseph McCarthy, and Joe Dimaggio. They interact one night in the 1950s. Monroe has come to Einstein's hotel room to seduce him, but due to various interruptions and the scientist's reluctance, she never succeeds. Clocks and time figure prominently, and Einstein dreads the hour of 8:15 a.m., the moment when Hiroshima was struck.

Indeed, at 8:15 a nuclear blast seems to strike just near their hotel room. We experience the devastation as, along with Einstein, we watch the burning figure of Monroe, who flames and swirls in agony in her famous white dress (the one blowing up around her legs in *The Seven Year Itch*). Such imagery recalls the biblical book of Revelation in which the "whore of Babylon" is burned so that "the smoke from her goes up for ever and ever." Not surprisingly, this imagery simultaneously evokes a pornographic "snuff" scene, in which the object of desire is not fucked but climactically tortured and murdered.

If Monroe can represent the bombed city of Hiroshima, she also, paradoxically, can represent the Bomb itself. In a 1980s "Hiroshima Appeals" peace poster by Japanese artist Takeshi Otaka, four blown-up and increasingly distorted images of Monroe's laughing face form a mushroom cloud.[39] It is difficult for me to understand how this image can be read as a peace poster. One message conveyed by this poster is that the Bomb, like the Hollywood star, is quintessentially American. Yet why is Monroe depicted and not, for example, the warrior John Wayne? The underlying message seems to be that the Bomb is female and a sex symbol, akin to Monroe, the consummate sex goddess of the twentieth century. Moreover, this Bomb, like woman in a patriarchal world, is both loved and hated, feared and desired, worshiped and scapegoated. Under the normative sado-masochism that structures patriarchal, power-based relationships, sexuality signifies, simultaneously, pleasure and danger. In this poster there is an underlying suggestion that nuclear explosion just might be the "fuck of the century."[40]

In a culture founded upon sexual inequality and the concomitant eroticization of dominance and submission, sadism is not truly a deviation but is itself the norm. Ritual and nonconsensual sado-masochism is institutionalized throughout the culture and infuses such power-driven and sexually charged systems as the military, the priesthood, and the nuclear family. The connection between patriarchy's normative sadistic sexuality and the cosmic domination taking shape in the desire to end the world can be traced to the origins of the technological era in the pornographic writings of the Marquis

Marilyn Monroe, the sex goddess as Bomb.

de Sade. In *The 120 Days of Sodom*, written in 1785, a group of socially elite men gather scores of young boys and girls whom they then torture and rape at will. Still, they lament that something is missing. One "libertine" affirms their joint perception that the greatest pleasure comes from committing the most terrible crime and violating the most profound taboo. Another, a bishop, agrees, but whines, "My imagination has always outdistanced my faculties; I lack the means to do what I would do, I have conceived of a thousand times more and better than I have done, and I have ever had complaints against Nature who, while giving me the desire to outrage her, has always deprived me of the means."

Yet another, a banker, concurs, claiming that there are but two or three crimes worth committing: "All the rest is inferior; you cease any longer to feel. Ah, how many times, by God, have I not longed to be able to assail the sun, snatch it out of the universe, make a general darkness, or use that star to burn the world! Oh that would be a crime."[41] Here de Sade, through his definitive grasp of the extremes of sadistic masculinity, anticipates the invention of weapons capable of burning the Earth. The ultimate mass murder he imagines grows out of his sexual desire and is the global equivalent of individual sexual murder.

Curiously enough, not only a similar sadistic desire but also a similar inability to feel underlie both sexual murder and the imagination of nuclear annihilation. Let us then understand that the origins of the nuclearist threat lie not only in economics, politics, and the assumed inevitable progress of science and technology but also in the porno-normal cultural notions of desire.

De Sade's scenario was unique not so much for its burning of the Earth—for that long had been imagined as the proverbial act of god in countless mythologies, including those of Christianity. Rather, it is distinguished by the way de Sade puts that act into an erotic context. If man can burn the Earth and get ultimately turned on, the implication is that god can too.

In nearly all serial sex-killer fiction, the line between the sadistic killer and the law-abiding pursuer is continually blurred, suggesting a hidden bond between the two as well as the inherent normalcy of sexual murder. *Red Dragon* by Thomas Harris first introduces

Hannibal Lecter, the master killer of *The Silence of the Lambs*, Harris's later smash hit. The imprisoned, cannibalistic serial killer Lecter writes to Will Graham, the FBI expert on serial killing, telling him that he knows Graham also finds pleasure in killing: "Think about it, but don't worry about it. Why shouldn't it feel good? It must feel good to God—He does it all the time, and are we not made in His image?"[42]

Currently, as the millennium approaches, many people, some with great joy and anticipation, expect god to commit the ultimate act of erotic mass murder by destroying the Earth with fire as prophesied in the gospel of Saint Peter.[43] Perhaps this provides a partial explanation for why more and more people (nearly all white men) are finding ways to emulate that divine role model. Since World War II, there has been an extraordinary rise in both serial and mass murder. Mass murder, which is the killing of three or more people at one time, was committed on the average of twice per month in the United States in 1991, an unprecedented rate.[44] As more and more men seek to "play god," it is clear that the origins of both gynocide and geocide lie not only in sadistic sexuality but also in sadistic religion. That is, their origins lie in the now reigning pornographic constructions not only of desire but also of divinity.

CHAPTER THREE

Nuclear Theology

[God] by His most powerfull Hand . . . holdeth backe the Sythe
of Tyme from destroying or imparying the Universe. . . . The
same Hand shall at last destroy the Whole by Fire.
— *George Hakewill, 1630*[1]

Atomic power, atomic power, was given by the mighty hand of
God.
— *The Buchanan Brothers, "Atomic Power"*[2]

In countless cultural references, nuclear technology is imbued
with a sacred aura. Frequently, it is cast as either a deity or a direct
manifestation of the deity's will on Earth. A 1988 ad in *Guitar* magazine exploits that cultural tendency to genuflect to the Bomb. The ad
is for "The Overlord," an electronic tube. The illustration shows the
tube held between two male fingers; the top third of the oblong tube
is opaque, the bottom third transparent. Inside that visible zone is a
mushroom cloud in full bloom. The copy announces, "The Power of
the Lord. Explained." Indeed, the invention of atomic weaponry does
explain a great deal about the patriarchal god, who has come a long
way (Baby), all the way from appearing in burning bushes to mani-

festing as a techno-deity who now, his followers say, can instantaneously torch the world.

Religious historian Ira Chernus argues that nuclear weapons carry descriptive symbolic meanings that are extremely similar to traditional religious descriptions of the attributes of divinities. For example, they are said to have "awesome and limitless power, omniscience, eternity, and omnipresence," as well as mystery and irrationality. Exploring the various symbolic ramifications of the Bomb, Chernus concludes that we must understand its meaning through religious symbolism and, moreover, face the fact that our "technological culture has made a death-machine its deity."[3]

Chernus's work contains many insights; nevertheless, his study is flawed by a lack of any gender analysis. Just as the images of nuclear pornography reveal a connection between patriarchal sexuality and nuclear weaponry, so the images of nuclear theology reveal an underlying bond between patriarchal religious tradition and the invention and embrace of weapons that, some nuclearists proudly claim, are capable of destroying the Earth. The connections between nuclear weaponry and patriarchal religion are, however, only one part of my story, and in chapter 9, I undertake an extended discussion of the relationship of sacred female Powers to nuclear technology.

Religious associations are rampant in the early development of the atomic bomb. J. Robert Oppenheimer, scientific leader of the team at Los Alamos, code-named the first atomic explosion "Trinity," conjuring in most people's minds the Christian godhead. Upon witnessing the first fireball, he broke into a recitation from the *Bhagavad-Gita*: "I am become Death, the shatterer of worlds." General Thomas Farrell, deputy to General Leslie Groves, military chief for the project, had an equally revealing response: "We puny things were blasphemous to dare tamper with the forces heretofore reserved to the Almighty."

After ordering the first military use of the bomb, Harry Truman informed the American public that this act represented the "harnessing of the basic power of the universe." He further intoned, "We thank God that it has come to us instead of to our enemies, and we pray that He may guide us to use it in His ways and for His purposes." Perhaps most flagrant of all were the litanies of journalist

William L. Laurence, describing his vision at the Trinity site: "It was as though the earth had opened and the skies had split. One felt as though he had been privileged to witness the Birth of the World—to be present at the moment of Creation when the Lord said: 'Let there be Light.'"[4]

Soon country, pop, and gospel musicians were incorporating many of these themes into their tunes, coming up with such winning numbers as "Jesus Hits Like an Atom Bomb." In their 1951 song, "Atomic Telephone," the Spirits of Memphis Quartet ascribed the sacred power once found in menstrual blood to male divinity: "I just talked to Jesus on the atomic telephone./ No man knows the power, only God alone./ It can cure the sick or destroy the evil./ With one sweep of power known by God alone."[5] An identification of nuclear technology with religious, awesome, terrible, life-giving, and death-dealing forces continues to inform popular culture. This can be seen in such Hollywood mega-hits as *Star Wars* (1977), *Star Trek II: The Wrath of Khan* (1982), and *Raiders of the Lost Ark* (1981), all of which link nuclear power with ambiguous, mystical forces that, however, can be harnessed by elite men.

Ted Post's 1970 film *Beneath the Planet of the Apes* mocks the religious ardor permeating popular notions of nuclear weaponry. In this thought-provoking film, postholocaust mutants literally bow down before the Bomb-god that by film's end destroys them. A Bomb-god also appears in Alan Moore's 1986 cult comic book series, *The Watchmen*, which features a nuclear superhero, "Dr. Manhattan," a scientist who disintegrated in a nuclear accident only to reform as a "wholly original entity [with a] . . . complete mastery of all matter." Dr. Manhattan, who clearly functions as a symbol of nuclear technology itself, is simultaneously understood as a divinity. In *The Watchmen*, a university professor discusses the global impact of this new superhero:

> "God exists and he's American." If that statement starts to chill you after a couple of moments' consideration, then don't be alarmed. A feeling of intense and crushing religious terror at the concept indicates only that you are still sane. . . . I do not believe we have made a man to end wars. I believe we have made a man to end worlds.[6]

Readers easily accept the logic equating Dr. Manhattan, the man who can end worlds, with "god" because common (non)sense first equates masculinity purely with destruction and then ordains god to be purely masculine, hence characteristically death-dealing. As Chernus notes, "While all other gods are seen as sources of death, they are also sources of life. Only in our own day has a God appeared that is capable of providing death but not life."[7] The invention of the Bomb as the ultimate death machine is the end result of patriarchy's massive denial of female Powers, those uncontrollable forces who hold the capacities not only for death but also for rebirth. It is, moreover, rooted in the fundaments of a *christotechnological*[8] world order, one in which patriarchal technology and spirituality have united in a geocidal project, attempting to accomplish an "elemental cleansing."

Another strain of popular stories kneels to the same lethal-weapon god, hailing the detonation of nuclear weaponry as an expression of divine righteous wrath. From this perspective, nuclear holocaust accomplishes the expurgation of the wicked and provides. a planetary cleansing. For example, the Bomb plays an explicitly salvific role in two bestsellers: Stephen King's 1978 novel, *The Stand*, and Clive Barker's 1990 novel, *The Great and Secret Show*.[10]

The recurrent nuclear motif of transmutation, death followed by transformation and rebirth, informs both Robert MacCammon's *Swan Song* and *Golden Days* by Carolyn See (both 1987). In these novels, nuclear war and its aftermath become occasions for planetary spiritual renewal, leading to rebirth and, in the more romantic *Swan Song*, a new Eden on Earth.[11] In the more realistic *Golden Days*, one character makes the seemingly obvious statement that these are indeed "terrible times" only to be contradicted by the central female character:

> But I was filled with a terrible rage and light, and I stood up and put out my arm to quiet her. "No!" I said. "Some people say these are bad times, but I say they are good times. We have bravery! We have love! We have the future. We have the Beginning! . . . This fire! This blessed fire! Some say it was a bad thing, but I say it was a good thing."[12]

See, by laying claim to optimism, is trying to achieve balance and counter the profound despair resulting from living in a nuclear-armed world. Still, I would caution that the metaphor that bonds nuclear war to spiritual resurrection—like that linking nuclear explosion to orgasm—functions for many only to make nuclear holocaust an eminently desirable event. Can we instead imagine a spiritual transmutation engendered by, and at the same time resulting in, a radical avoidance of nuclear war?

Kurt Saxon, the so-called father of the survivalist movement, also sees many beneficial side effects of planetary nuclear holocaust. This overtly racist leader happily tells us that he has "learned to love the Bomb and welcome the chaos which will come from it because I know that's all necessary to cull the degenerate urban masses so that we can finally get to the nuclear renaissance."[13] Saxon also has much in common with the *necro-apocalyptic*[14] Christian fundamentalists. These fundamentalists await nuclear holocaust as a signal of the second coming of Christ and a fulfillment of biblical prophecy re-garding the consumption of the Earth by fire.

One can find many flaming examples of this particularly sorry strain of Christianity in Paul Boyer's comprehensive study *When Time Shall Be No More: Prophecy Belief in Modern American Culture.*[15] In one citation, Robert Gromacki, an Idaho Baptist minister, exhorts his flock to welcome "the destruction of the world by fire . . . and pray for its nearness." In another example, far more fulsome foolishness is propounded by David Wilkerson, an Assemblies of God minister:

> Are we so blind, so earthbound, that we want God to keep us alive physically, only to live in a contaminated, hostile environment? Why can't we see that a holocaust can only dissolve this earthly body; but that very dissolving brings us into a celestial one. It will be instant glory. How can we who are already dead to the world be adversely affected by a holocaust? As for me, I died to the world—its pleasures, its pains, its destruction—so that a meltdown simply brings me into the fullness of an inheritance I already possess in measure.

Wilkerson's "death" to the world—his cessation of feeling or dissociation from pain and pleasure, which is so similar to that experienced by de Sade's jaded libertine—sounds like a full-blown case of psychic numbing. Sealing himself into this veritably senseless state, he claims he has nothing to worry about from nuclear holocaust: it can't touch him. Ironically, Wilkerson fails to see how his own and others' indulgence in such a heart- and brain-dead condition contributes mightily to the very "hostility" and "contamination" he warns against. His attitude facilitates human preparations for nuclear and environmental holocaust—not only by allowing people to blot out realizations of atrocity, but also because, in such a state of psychic numbing, only a sadistic touch can be felt.

A Christian poster from the late 1970s features a towering and unmistakably phallic mushroom cloud. In the center is posed the ultimate nuclear question: "Is there a future?" At the bottom right is our answer: a crucifix on a hill with the words "Yes. I'm coming.—Jesus Christ." Here male ejaculation, nuclear apocalypse, and religious ecstasy all indelibly fuse.

A similar story line governs the picture on the January 7, 1990, cover of *Image* magazine from the *San Francisco Examiner*. It illustrates an inside story about the preponderance of end-of-the-world narratives as our culture approaches the second Christian millennium. The illustration is a variant on the famous Sistine chapel scene in which god awakens Adam. This time, god (that familiar old white man with a beard), surrounded by angels, reaches out a long finger to touch a vulnerable Earth. What we are seeing is an obscene fantasy of nuclear pornography and theology. Education aimed at forewarning children about sexual abuse teaches them to distinguish between a "good" touch that is safe and a "bad" touch that is molesting. In this picture of "God the Father" reaching out with his long finger to destroy an infantilized Earth, the consummate "bad touch" of a nuclear father god is immediately recognizable.

The nuclear longings of contemporary Christianity continue this religion's long history of unwavering commitment to earthly apocalypse. American historian Perry Miller traces Christian eschatological thought during the time of the scientific revolution and Puritan America, showing that after the shifts of the scientific revolution, theologians struggled mightily to demonstrate the continued "feasibility of destruction." They argued that an "explosion" rather than an

is there a future?

Yes.
I'm coming.

*One of many cultural images linking
Christian prophesy with nuclear warfare.*

"arbitrary influence" was now required to destroy the Earth and proposed such forces as comets to do the job. Miller writes:

> There is no more curious phenomenon in the history of our civilization than the fact that the triumph of modern physics over the imagination of mankind was achieved by a sustained effort to prove that such a triumph was not only compatible with the cherished hope [for the end of the world] but that actually it was a confirmation, a veritable guarantee, of an approaching, colossally violent catastrophe.[16]

Twentieth-century physicists have come the closest to making good on that guarantee. By inventing the Bomb, they demonstrated to their satisfaction the scientific "feasibility of destruction." By thus providing a practical means that they believed could incinerate the Earth, the atomic scientists honored, and perhaps in part acted from, patriarchal religion's ardent desire for apocalyptic fires.

In *Pure Lust: Elemental Feminist Philosophy*, Mary Daly provides a great deal of insight into the patriarchal desire for nuclear warfare. She identifies a distinctive Christian crusade against the "elemental spirits of the universe," that is, against the "spirits, angels, and demons . . . manifesting the essential unity and intelligence of spirit/ matter . . . [the] Intelligence ensouling the stars, animating the processes of earth, air, fire, water." She cites Saint Paul's demands that we not only "die to" such spirits, but set our "mind on things that are above, not on things that are on the earth." In a similar necro-apocalyptic vein, Saint Peter states: "But the day of the Lord will come like a thief, and then the heavens will pass away with a loud noise, and the elements will be dissolved and the earth and the works that are upon it will be burned up." Daly quotes this biblical Ripper and then comments that "as self-fulfilling prophecy and manifesto of necrophilic faith, this 'inspired' text is one among many that have paved the way for modern technological war against the elements, which takes such forms as nuclearism and chemical contamination."[17]

In trying to fathom why Western science invented the technology of atomic destruction, we also might recall Alice Walker's insight that it is "not inventiveness that characterizes the Wasichu, but rather unnaturalness." She asks us to realize "that even tiny insects in the South American jungle know how to make plastic, for instance; they have simply chosen not to cover the Earth with it."[18] Atomic technology continues to be pursued not because Western patriarchy is the most "advanced" culture on Earth but because nuclearist power so completely recapitulates the dominant paradigms of phallic sexuality, power, and divinity.

The intermeshing of sexual and sacred patriarchal power paradigms, as well as their relation to nuclearism, is vividly expressed in Russell Hoban's 1980 novel, *Riddley Walker*. In his postholocaust world, humanity has lost a good measure of its intelligence, evidenced by the illiteracy and vulgar spelling of the ensuing civilization. On a quest for the nuclear power that destroyed the old world, the hero, Riddley Walker, journeys to Canterbury ("Cambry"), the site of the most powerful nuclear blast. Musing on his search for the "Big Power," which he alternately refers to as the "Spirit of God," Riddley undergoes an epiphany:

> Funny feeling come on me then I fealt like that Power *wer* a Big Old Father. . . . I wantit it to come in to me hard and strong long and strong. Let me be your boy, I thot.
> Stanning on them old broakin stoans I fealt like it *wer* coming in to me and taking me strong. Fealt like it wer the han of Power clampt on the back of my neck fealt the Big Old Father spread me and take me. . .
> And stil I fealt a nother way. . . . I knowit Cambry Senter ben flattent the werst of all the dead town senters it ben Zero Groun it ben where the wite shadderd stood up over every thing. Yet unnder neath that Zero Groun I lissent up a swarming it wer a humming like a millying of bees it wer like 10s of millyings. I begun to feal all juicy with it. Juicy for a woman. Longing for it hard and hevvy stanning ready. Not jus my cock but all of me it wer like all of me were cock and the worl a cunt and open to me.[19]

Two desires result from Riddley's mystical-sexual experience of nuclear power as a Big Old Father. First, he feels himself to be puny and willingly succumbs to being fucked by that incestuous father; second, he wants to take the almighty phallic power and use it himself to incestuously (mother)fuck, that is, destroy, the Earth. (He does find that he is not man enough for that.) This passage neatly expresses the pact men have made with their god: If they bow (boy) to the Big Old Father (god), the payoff is their ultimate assumption of that divine paternal privilege to rape, dominate, and destroy others.

Bowing to the god War has long promised men similar benefits. One Vietnam veteran described his experience:

> I had a sense of power. A sense of destruction. . . . In the Nam you realized you had the power to take a life. You had the power to rape a woman and nobody could say nothing to you.

That godlike feeling you had was in the field. It was like I was God. I could take a life. I could screw a woman.[20]

Here again, phallic notions of power, sexuality, and divinity collapse into one unholy trinity:[21] god the rapist, god the ripper, god the self-promoted shatterer of words, wombs, and worlds.

Conclusion

In part 1, I have described the popular language and symbol system that constructs and maintains nuclearist reality. Most of the "stories" I have told in this section are, to be sure, terrible ones that fully enrage the Gorgon in us. But it is imperative to remember that they and the world they invoke are not fixed. They are utterly subject to the Crone—that is, to Chaos, and to sudden, unpredictable change. Moreover, as the Gossip reminds us, there are wholly other stories.

In her extraordinary novel *Ceremony*, Leslie Marmon Silko describes "a world made of stories, the long ago, time immemorial stories, as old Grandma called them. It was a world alive, always changing and moving; and if you knew where to look, you could see it, sometimes almost imperceptible, like the motion of the stars across the sky."[22] If we did know where to look, we would journey to that place at the ends of the Earth where the Gossips dwell. It is a place by a river—a river of memory, not of forgetfulness—a flowing, profoundly black river filled with twinkling stars/stories. There, at the very source of the oral tradition, we can begin to learn how to untell nuclearist stories—tales of power, domination, and control. Simultaneously, we can learn to retell and thereby, in poet Barbara Mor's words, "respell the world,"[23] summoning other words, and remembering and inventing other stories that are strong enough to invoke a wholly other world out of the ashes of the nuclear fatherland.

PART TWO

The Gossip:
What the Little Bird
Told Me

Ricki Klages ©1993

Word Magic: A Praisesong for the Gossip

I hold to the traditional Indian views on language, that words have power, that words become entities. When I write I keep in mind that it is a form of power and salvation that is for the planet. If it is good and enters the world, perhaps it will counteract the destruction that seems to be getting so close to us. I think of language and poems, even fiction, as prayers and small ceremonies.
                              —*Linda Hogan*[1]

I cure with Language.
                    —*María Sabina*[2]

In an autobiographical essay, "From the Poets in the Kitchen," novelist Paule Marshall gives us a portrait of the artist as a young woman: "I grew up among poets. Now they didn't look like poets . . . .They were just a group of ordinary housewives and mothers, my mother included, who dressed in a way (shapeless housedresses, dowdy felt hats, and long, dark, solemn coats) that made it impossible for me to imagine they had ever been young." These women, most of whom were immigrants from Barbados, did not make their livings as writers; they were cleaning ladies for white housewives. At the end of the day, they would sometimes gather in the basement kitchen of Marshall's house, where they would drink tea or cocoa and talk "endlessly, passionately, and poetically, and with impressive range. No subject was beyond them." As Marshall now understands it, that rich flow of talk was "therapy," enabling the women "to overcome the humiliations of the work-day."

However, this women's talk was far more than that: it was creative expression, a refuge into familiarity in a strange and frequently hostile land. The talking was also a weapon, a "way for them to feel they exercised some control over their lives and the events that shaped them. 'Soully-gal, talk yuh talk!' they were always exhorting each other. 'In this man world you got to take yuh mouth and make a gun!'" In recognition of their poetry, philosophy, and linguistic grace, Marshall extols these

> giants whom I always acknowledge before all others: the group of women around the table long ago. They taught me my first lessons in the narrative art. They trained my ear. They set a standard of excellence. This is why the best of my work must be attributed to them; it stands as testimony to the rich legacy of language and culture they so freely passed on to me in the wordshop of the kitchen.[3]

Marshall's homage is somewhat unusual, for women's daily talk is all too often trivialized and denigrated, not least of all by designating it "gossip." Yet there is another side to this story. Jungian mythographer Nor Hall relates that poet Meridel LeSueur once told her that words have two uses: "The first is for analysis and the second is 'to heat you and move you on.'" That is, words generate energy. When Hall asked how she could realize this second aspect, LeSueur told her to "go and listen to the rhythm of country gossip. Gossip is worth listening to: it means 'god speaking through a woman.'"[4] Although *gossip* is currently understood to be, at best, idle or small talk and, at worst, malicious backbiting, these are relatively recent connotations. The word *gossip* is formed from the words *god* and *sib*. *Sib* means "kin, someone who is related to you." Centuries ago, a Gossip was understood to be an intimate companion, one to whom another was linked by a spiritual bond, a midwife, a powerful communicator, a purveyor of wisdom.[5] However, in the twentieth century, gossiping has become synonymous with a nasty and trivial form of talk and, simultaneously, it has become indelibly associated with women.[6] Nevertheless, the powerful and wise Gossip is still here, waiting to be encountered in the most unexpected places.

An advertisement for *Sophia* perfume appeared in the October 1985 issue of *Good Housekeeping* magazine. It features three old white women who, save for their race, bear an uncanny resemblance to Paule Marshall's kitchen poets. These utterly drab women, about whom it is almost "impossible . . . to imagine they had ever been young," stand behind a heavy iron fence, wearing "dowdy felt hats and long, dark, solemn coats" and peering intently ahead. They are photographed in black and white. Etched across their image is the phrase "Let them talk."

The reader of *Good Housekeeping* is not supposed to identify with these women. On the contrary, they represent everything she should aspire *not* to be. An insert, featuring a small, square color photograph of Sophia Loren's face and a (larger) bottle of the perfume, is superimposed over the bottom midsection of the three gossiping biddies. It contains this advice from "Sophia":

> They say you're not as
>   innocent as you seem.
>
> They say you have a past.
>
> They say you cry too easily
>   and laugh too much.
>
> They're right, you do.
>
> So do I.
>
> Now wear my perfume.
> And let them talk.

These words from "Sophia," a name that in Greek means "holy female wisdom," are deeply unsettling. On its surface, the ad is indubitably both ageist and sexist. Old women are made to represent sex-

The Gossips speak to us even from the pages of Good Housekeeping *magazine.* Coty, N.Y., © 1985.

ual repression and it is implied that they are attempting to ban freedom, emotionalism, and experience. Their "talk" is represented as injurious, the kind of "vicious sniping of old crones" that a coroner's jury once concluded was responsible for a young woman's suicide.[7] Moreover, the allegedly free and sensuous woman, Sophia (Loren), is incongruously boxed in, represented by only a tiny, closely cropped photograph. All of these images and judgments display the common contradictions and doublethink we regularly encounter in the commercial media. However, if we look beyond the overt meaning of the ad and reach more deeply into its background or subtextual space, other meanings begin to assert themselves.

Sophia is the Gnostic name for the supreme female being. Akin to the Hindu goddess Shakti, she is cosmic energy, life itself, the spirit of female wisdom, the world soul, represented as both the Tree of Life and the dove of Aphrodite.[8] Sophia, then, has a mythic background and so, significantly, do the three old women. Looking at this ad through a mythic lens, the old women, or Gossips, kept beyond our reach by that imposing fence, start to bear a resemblance to the Fates, the Norns, or the Weird Sisters—the ancient trinity of female supernaturals who spin and weave human destiny and rule past, present, and future in nearly all Western mythologies.[9]

Despite the surface foolishness of this ad, canny readers can recognize the archetypal and wondrous beings masked by its superficial and sexist front. Such readers may find themselves going beyond the superficial implications of the ad and zeroing in on the phrase "Let them talk." Those canny readers may start to say of the Gossips or Fates pictured in their characteristic covey of three, "Yes indeed, let them talk!"

Old women commonly are figured as birds: old hens (biddies), dangerous snipes, and forbidding crows—rather like the Gossips in this ad. Gossips graciously accept these comparisons, for they, in truth, are profoundly akin to birds. They are the winged creators such as the Great Primeval Spirit in Egyptian myth, the Goose or Great Cackler whose voice sang out the first word "while the world was still flooded in silence."[10] The Gossips are shades of that magical great Witch, Mother Goose, the originator of all the world's stories.

Gossips also are akin to the birds that the poet Chrystos invokes in her antinuclear lamentation: "No bird ever called me crazy No rock scorns me as a whore. . . . With their songs, they know the sacred I am in a circle with that soft, enduring word In it is the wisdom of all peoples."[11] Amazingly, the birdy/wordy Gossips, speakers of the first and enduring words of wisdom, are framed by the Sophia perfume ad as scorning Wisdom or Sophia herself as a "whore." This splitting of the elemental self, or fragmentation of female cogency, is a characteristic method of control in the Age of Fission. Yet such forced opposition is based in deception. In truth, the Gossips *are* Sophia, the very soul of female wisdom. They are the Powers of speech, the keepers of our oral tradition.

Referring to the oral tradition of the Pueblo people, Leslie

Marmon Silko writes, "We make no distinctions between the stories—whether they are history, whether they are fact, whether they
are gossip."[12] It is only in the patriarchal tradition that talk is set into
a hierarchy and that woman-identified gossip is feared, belittled, and
censored. This occurs because Gossips speak about the unspeakable:
specifying and exposing perpetrators, telling truths, satirizing and
ridiculing, talking back, prophesying, and foretelling. In short,
Gossips possess the faculty of *word-magic*,[13] which is the ability to
influence reality through talking or storytelling. Through word-
magic, Gossips can avert (or cause) disasters and conjure Powers
through the utterance of words.

The three old women in the Sophia perfume ad might stir memories not only of the Fates, but also of another ancient magical trinity of speaking sisters. The Keres peoples are a language group
of Southwestern Pueblo Indians. In their cosmogyny,[14] the creator
is Ts'its'tsi'nako, also known as Thought Woman or Spider Grandmother. Whatever Thought Woman thinks about, dreams about, or
names comes into being. According to Leslie Silko's poetic telling of
this original story, Thought Woman first thinks of her two sisters,
Nau'ts'ity'i and I'tctsi'ity'i, who together with her create the
Universe, the world we know, and the worlds that exist below.[15]

Sacred Gossipry, or word-magic, is akin to the primal, creative,
thinking, and naming faculties of Thought Woman. As Paula Gunn
Allen explains, "The thought for which Grandmother Spider is
known is the kind that results in physical manifestation of phenomena: mountains, lakes, creatures, or philosophical-sociological systems."[16] Unbalanced, phallocentric thought, on the other hand,
results in the physical manifestation of phenomena such as social
inequality, pollution, nuclear weapons, genocide, and gynocide.

In 1963, the notorious nuclear strategist Herman Kahn, alarmed
that Americans believed nuclear war was so horrible that they were
refusing to conceptualize its practicality, urged us all to "think about
the unthinkable."[17] Of course, we can understand more fully if we
reverse this memorable phrase. Nuclear war is eminently *thinkable*;
its technology, we are told over and over again, is the crowning
achievement of Western thought.

As Gossips, then, we must prepare ourselves to *unthink the think-*

able; that is, we must *unthink* nuclear war, environmental devastation, the destruction of the forests, and so on. As Gossips, we must gather, talk back, and refuse and refute these thoughts. At the same time, we must foray into the realm traditionally forbidden our kind—the realm of the symbol makers and mythmakers. When we do so, we become *psychic activists*, employing thinking, naming, imaging, and speaking as elemental female Powers, exercised consciously and/or intuitively in the deconstruction of masculinist thought systems and the realities they effect. Reality is, as Mary Daly writes in *Pure Lust*, "nothing less than an Ontological Battleground. The risks are ultimate."[18] As Gossips, we respond to that call, like Paule Marshall's kitchen poets, by making our mouths into "guns."

Gossips are supernatural entities, but they are realized in common women who are deeply connected to the rhythms and activities of everyday life. Paula Gunn Allen writes:

> There are always the women, who make pots and weave baskets, who fashion clothes and cheer their children on at powwow, who make fry bread and piki bread, and corn soup and chili stew, who dance and sing and remember and hold within their hearts the dream of their ancient peoples—that one day the woman who thinks will speak to us again, and everywhere there will be peace.[19]

This is a dream I share. The Gossips are here. They are irrepressible, traveling to speak to us even from the pages of *Good Housekeeping* magazine. Open the gate to let them in. Recognize that they *are* Sophia. And, above all: *Let them talk. Let them talk. Let them talk.*

CHAPTER FOUR

Speaking About the Unspeakable

Now we are the "betrayers of the lie." In our speaking and writing, we betray what has harmed us and held us down. We tell on those who hurt us. We give away the truths of oppression. . . . This is just a beginning, this truth-telling, this courageous facing of inner reality and outer facts.
　　　　　—Linda Hogan[1]

Hell hath no fury like a man exposed.
　　　　　—Catharine MacKinnon[2]

Over the past seventeen years, I have collected a wide variety of fashion advertisements. All of them are visually distinct and pitch different products, but all, nonetheless, deliver the same message: female silence. One nightgown ad from 1975 shows a group of real women arranged like mannequins or, in the hateful slang, *dummies*, in a department store window. In *Webster's*, a *dummy* is defined as "one that is incapable of speech, one that is habitually silent." The copy reads, "If you happen to wake up one morning in the window of your favorite store, don't worry, you'll look terrific."

A 1977 ad for designer eyeglasses carries an illustration of seven feminized dummy heads pointing inward and forming a circle, looking eerily like the numbers on a clock. The head at 6 o'clock is clearly human; most of the others are just as clearly plastic. Yet one head, positioned at 9 o'clock, is unclassifiable, signifying some blend of woman and simulacrum.

Another advertisement, from the Canned Food Information Council in 1985, is more aggressively predictive. Representing canned food in the ad is an uncanny, voluptuous, high-heeled, horizontal female robot. The copy reads, "In the year 3000, food will come in amazing containers . . . convenient. Time-saving. Versatile. Healthy . . . cans." Conveniently, for those who aim to contain female Powers, the subliminal message being simulcast in this ad is that "in the year 3000" women will be reduced to containers—disposable, time-saving, versatile, healthy fembots.

An ad for perfume, dating from the mid-1980s, displays a woman's severed head on the floor. Her face is expressionless; her mouth is closed. There is not, as would be expected, shreds of skin and shards of bone and gristle hanging from her neck. Rather, her neck devolves fantastically into a spiral of paper, creating an effect something like a curling ribbon on a gift package. Despite the prettiness of the picture, what we are seeing is female *decapitation*. A more subtle decapitation structures a 1989 ad for shoes, bizarrely titled "A State of Mind." Well-shod female legs point up into the air. Focusing on this spectacle, we might not even notice that the woman's body above the thighs has been severed. Whose snuff state of mind do such images reflect? And to what god are these gifts/sacrifices being offered?

In another set of ads, female heads are replaced, partially or completely, by consumer products. In one ad from the late 1970s, a woman's head is replaced by a *Redbook* magazine; her body is posed before a stove, happily cooking. Another ad, this one from 1980, again features a disembodied female head, half of which has been replaced by a bar of soap. Brainwashed women viewers shouldn't mind at all. Frankly, such pictures seem to suggest that women have no minds. Viewing these ads recalls to me those ridiculous but terrifying words of the Stepford wife who, after suffering an injury in an auto accident, kept repeating, "Don't worry, it's just my head."

The beautification of female decapitation.

The Stepford Wives, which is both a novel and a film, is a prescient parable about a final solution for the "woman problem" devised by a group of professional suburban men.[3] These husbands, bonding together in a "men's association," kill their wives and replace them with look-alike robots. Their new and improved "wives" keep a cleaner house, boast more voluptuous figures, and speak only from a vocabulary list programmed into them by the "men's association." The men literally have put their words into the women's mouths.

While snools[4] of every stripe whine incessantly about their castration anxieties and complexes, such blather covers up a much more pressing danger facing women: decapitation, along with the related horror of robotization. French philosopher Hélène Cixous illustrates this danger with an old Chinese story about women, men, and the making of the warrior. It seems that a king wanted his preeminent military strategist, Sun Tse, to make soldiers of his 180 wives, teaching them to march to the beat of his drum:

But instead of learning . . . the ladies started laughing and chattering and paying no attention to the lesson, and Sun Tse, the master, repeated the lesson several times over. But the more he spoke, the more the women fell about laughing, upon which Sun Tse put his code to the test. It is said in this code that should women fall about laughing instead of becoming soldiers, their actions might be deemed mutinous, and the code has ordained that cases of mutiny call for the death penalty. So . . . [Sun Tse] with his sabre beheaded the two women commanders. They were replaced and the exercise started again, and, as if they had never done anything except practice the art of war, the women turned right, left, and about in silence and with never a single mistake.

As Cixous remarks, the moral of this story is clear: Women, "if they don't actually lose their heads by the sword . . . only keep them on condition that they lose them—lose them, that is, to complete silence, turned into automatons."[5] Adding insult to injury, it is when women refuse to roll over and play fembot—when we most vehemently resist decapitation by refusing to be silenced—that we are deemed by cockocrats to be the most "castrating."

Gossips call it many things: breaking silence, speaking out, ranting, raving, railing, consciousness raising, scolding, specifying, soothsaying, talking, and testifying. And we are called many names for doing it: nags, bitches, shrews, ballbusters, dykes, man-bashers, madwomen, and, most of all, liars. And what is it that we are doing? We are gossiping—that is, we are telling the truth, dishing the dirt, speaking about those things that have been deemed unspeakable, such as male sexual abuse.

I Just Want to Testify

I felt that I had to tell the truth.
I could not keep silent.
—*Anita Hill, testimony before the Senate*
Judiciary Committee, October 11, 1991

Anita Hill told the truth. She testified before the entire nation about Clarence Thomas's verbal sexual harassment of her. Her words were disbelieved, of course, by a majority of the all-white and nearly all-male Senate—perhaps because these men perceived a woman testifying, let alone an African-American woman testifying, as constituting an unnatural act, if not a castration. The word *testify* is derived from the Latin root *testis*, meaning "witness." Significantly, the English word *testis* (the male reproductive gland) shares that same origin, as *Webster's* notes, "perhaps from it being evidence of maleness." When Clarence Thomas thundered that he was being subjected to a "high-tech lynching" with all its implications of castration, this was a reversal. For, in truth, it was his maleness, literally his testes, that made his testimony persuasive, even though it consisted almost completely of denial. Meanwhile, Anita Hill's lucid, detailed, and low-key revelations were mocked and dismissed by the injudicious men of the Senate.

As many African-American commentators have pointed out, racist and sexist assumptions governed the hearings. They influenced Clarence Thomas's self-presentation and believability as a victim, Anita Hill's lack of credibility as a black woman, the concomitant wanton disrespect accorded Hill by many of the interrogating senators, and the fixation of white America on black sexual bodies.[6]

This racist and sexist mockery also pervades a Pepsi commercial that was run during Superbowl 1992 and is apparently modeled after the Clarence Thomas hearings. It features Ray Charles and three anonymous African-American women, suggesting a configuration of lead and background singers. A panel of men sit on a raised platform, clearly designed to recall the visual iconography of the Thomas hearing before the Senate Judiciary Committee. They first interrogate the three nearly identical women, who are demurely dressed in gray frocks with Peter Pan collars, representing Hill. The fragmentation of Hill into three women subtly strips her of both her individuality and her integrity. She is, moreover, symbolically decapitated. These three women can respond only "uh-huh" to inane queries regarding a "secret ingredient" in Diet Pepsi. In the context of Hill's allegations, this mindless "uh-huh" can be read as signifying consent to Thomas's advances.

The questioners in the commercial next interrogate Ray Charles, representing Clarence Thomas, who also responds "uh-huh" and then overturns the table to reveal a piano. As he exposes his instrument and begins to play, the women throw off their modest clothing to reveal sexy dresses, confirming the rapist culture's belief in the "inner whores" lurking behind the proper fronts of all women, most particularly women of color. The women then act "whorishly" by suggestively draping themselves around Charles/Thomas, sitting on his lap and petting his shoulders. This commercial recasts the hearings, overtly valorizing Thomas by making him the "star," yet subliminally suggesting that he is only a yes-man for the establishment (for he, too, can only say "uh-huh"). Hill is treated with no respect at all in this commercial—overtly or covertly. She is reduced to an anonymous background singer. The commercial further suggests that a depersonalized, vamped-up, and fissioned Hill desired and consented to the great man's attentions.

Despite the many attempts to discredit Anita Hill and her testimony, the word was out, and the power of Hill's gossiping has unfolded in numerous ways. The Senate is no longer all white; in fact, 1992 heralded the election of an African-American woman, Carol Moseley Braun, from Illinois. Moreover, the nation has become immersed in a massive consciousness-raising and breaking-silence session on male sexual abuse. The Equal Employment Opportunity Commission (Clarence Thomas's old stomping grounds) reported that sexual harassment charges filed in the first half of 1992 were 50 percent higher than those filed the previous year. All over the country, there are reports of women speaking out and fighting back—in high schools, medical schools, churches, and the military.[7]

A vast network of sanctioned sexual abuses is being exposed in the United States military. In 1990, the Pentagon itself concluded that more than a third of military women experience some form of harassment, including touching, pressure for sexual favors, and rape. Its report described a pervasive derogation of women, hidden by a veil of denial, trivialization, and enforced silence.[8] While policies against sexual abuse exist, they are routinely ignored. Women who do report rape or other offenses are most commonly ordered to forget about them. Then they themselves are written up for sexual misconduct, leered at, mocked by Veterans Administration counselors, and asked, "What's the big deal?" Outrages against U.S. servicewomen are quite common enough. Yet most U.S. military sexual abuses are aimed at Third World women on and near U.S. military bases.[9]

The long-standing silence about the internal abuse in the military was broken in the furor surrounding an episode of mass sexual abuse in September 1991. This episode occurred at a three-day convention of navy and marine pilots in Las Vegas sponsored by the Tailhook organization. Eighty-three women and seven men, including officers and civilians, were accosted by up to two hundred naval and marine officers, fresh from the Persian Gulf War. During the event, the pilots (described by *New York Times* columnist Anna Quindlen as "guys with nuclear hands") formed gauntlets in the hallways of the Hilton. When unsuspecting women, both conference attendees and hotel guests, happened by, the military men shoved them down the line, grabbing at their breasts and buttocks, and stripping off their clothes. Investigators said the men used hand and verbal signals to identify which women to assault.[10]

Lieutenant Paula Coughlin complained that night and then continued to complain. The ensuing official investigation resulted in the resignation of Naval Secretary H. Lawrence Garrett 3d (who was sipping beer very near the hallway, but alleged that he saw no misconduct), yet it named only two suspects from amongst the five thousand conventioneers. This original report blamed those pathetic results on a "wall of silence" created by the aviators and their commanders and aided by the insularity of the military brethren. The inspector general's report concluded that "inappropriate sexual behavior" at the Tailhook convention had been "accepted, tolerated, and condoned over the years" by senior pilots, "making it now the norm."

Ironically, this very report itself has been castigated for its participation in the normalcy and toleration of abuse. By September 1992, the Pentagon had concluded that senior officials in the navy had conspired to undermine their own investigation and cover up the offenses. Two admirals were forced to retire and another was reassigned.[11] Finally, by April 1993, yet another report issued from the Pentagon. It recommended that 140 officers face punishment for sexual assault, lewd behavior, and conduct unbecoming an officer. Derek J. Vander

Schaaf, the Pentagon's acting inspector general, said that the conduct
was so outrageous—and had occurred at Tailhook conventions for so
many years—that it "raised serious questions about the senior leadership of the Navy."[12]

I introduced the subject of the Tailhook Convention in one of my
classes. Afterward, a student brought me a T-shirt sold at the convention that belonged to a friend's husband. On the front was a fighter
plane bearing the slogan "We Train Hookers." On the back was a
large, naked, aggressively muscled, hairless white man. His face was
obscured by a gas mask with a long hose extending from his nose
area. At the level of the man's crotch was a bomber. It is not difficult
to see how men imbued with this top-gun–style masculinity would
find sexual harassment normal. My student told me that I had to get
the T-shirt back to her as soon as possible: her friend needed it back
because her husband liked her to wear it when they had sex!

Not surprisingly, the Tailhook incident has also been rewritten
and represented in an abuser-friendly manner in popular imagery.

Tailhook T-shirt: sexual abuse as an ideal of masculinity.

Just as the Diet Pepsi ad serves up a vicious portrayal of a revamped and consenting Anita Hill, the April 1992 *Harper's Bazaar* proffers a completely *cock-eyed*[13] view of the Tailhook assault. The magazine contains a photo spread entitled "Maritime Dash," which highlights women's clothing with a military flair. The pictures were shot aboard the U.S.S. Elliot, not at the Las Vegas Hilton, but the connection to the Tailhook event is unmistakable. Nearly all of the photos feature a single woman flanked by rows of uniformed men. The first image shows a woman striding through a gauntlet of eight saluting sailors. The naughty copy reads, "Today's nautical report: the navy is coming." A subsequent photo shows the female model lifted adoringly in the arms of six uniformed men, one of whom, if you look closely, is fondling her breast. The last photograph portrays the model looking arch and utterly in control while six sailors flank her, rubbing broom handles in frustrated obeisance. This photo essay recalls the sexist Tailhook assault, but with a significant twist: the woman is smiling and the gauntlet is friendly. The photos seem to say, "She wants it. She loves it. *She* is in control."

One of the core conceits of pornography is that it portrays rapes, verbal denigrations, and various forms of torture as activities not only avidly encouraged but controlled by women, activities that *she* in fact desires and directs. This inverted, pornographic perception was vividly displayed by men's-movement guru Warren Farrell in his comments on a May 1992 ABC broadcast, "Peter Jennings Reporting: Men, Sex and Rape." During the broadcast, a video clip from a stag party was shown to Jennings's guests. In it, a near-naked woman, dressed only in a flimsy teddy, lay across the laps of five men who poured beer over her vulva. The video's all-male crowd cheered, gave encouraging hand and verbal signals, and leered. The woman in the video, paid to take this abuse, smiled as she was being metaphorically pissed on.

Jennings's female guests, Cassandra Thomas, Susan Faludi, Catharine MacKinnon, and Naomi Wolf, agreed that this ritual was pornographic in that it presented the woman as an object, passed around for appropriation, degradation, and consumption. Farrell (who, James Twitchell reports, has written an unpublished book advocating incest)[14] insisted they were dead wrong. It was the woman, he declared, who was "in control." Sure. If you believe that, you are probably also convinced that Anita Hill was in love with Clarence Thomas.

The Tailhook convention also opened with female "party favors," that is, live women being passed around by men. These women were paid strippers, who generally ended up nude and participated in both real and simulated sexual acts with the conventioneers. The organizers also showed pornographic films continually over the three-day period of revelry.[15] Perhaps, inevitably, the spirit of abuse toward women implicit in these snoolish party practices spilled out of bounds, and many conventioneers began treating any woman who happened by as a target. If there were a trial of these Tailhook harassers, Warren Farrell might testify that the pilots had felt threatened and diminished by the all-powerful women strippers and were only acting in justified frustration over their lack of control. Due to the deep internalization of the pornographic mindset in our culture, the jury might well believe him.

Speaking in April 1993 to the Senate Armed Services Committee, Secretary of Defense Les Aspin suggested that, in the words of journalist Mark Thompson, "Tailhook's fallout is not all negative." Aspin told the committee, "There's going to be some changes in the American policy about women in combat. There's going to be a new world by the end of this decade about women being sexually harassed."[16] Patriarchy's great "wall of silence" is crumbling. There are going to be big changes, and there *is* going to be a new world— though perhaps not quite the one Aspin is imagining. This world will be brought into being in part by the explosive speech of women and its ensuing, transmutational "fallout."

Harper's Bazaar has it wrong. The navy isn't coming. Rather, Gossips are becoming. And, as Hélène Cixous prophesied in 1975, "We'll keep on becoming."[17] Our "waves of speech," as feminist theorist Amy Curtis-Webber proclaims, burst the "wall of silence with our stories . . . washing us onto a new country of the body, of the mind."[18]

Talking Dirty/Talking Dirt

Her power [women generally, but particularly old women] was that of pronouncing curses. . . . It was a dreaded power.
—*Robert Briffault*[19]

I curse you, I say. . . . Until you do right by me, I say, everything you even dream about will fail. I give it to him straight, just like it come to me. And it seem to come to me from the trees. . . . A dust devil flew up on the porch between us, fill my mouth with dirt. The dirt say, Anything you do to me, already done to you.
—*Celie to Mr.* ———, The Color Purple[20]

Snools regularly use pornography as a tool of sexual harassment, not only when they are coming on to women but also when they want to humiliate women and force them to leave their jobs. Common tactics include hanging pictures of naked women on office walls, leaving things like dildos on women's desks, and using objectifying and demeaning language.

Pornography was a central, though circumvented, issue at the Clarence Thomas hearings. Although scores of Thomas's acquaintances, particularly those from his law school years, told the press about his pronounced penchant for pornography and his habit of regaling his listeners with scenes from his favorite sex movies, the Judiciary Committee did not delve into any possible connection between his pornography habit and his alleged sexual harassment. Yet, if we take Anita Hill at her word, Thomas's sexual harassment, like countless other incidents of sexual abuse, was clearly linked with pornography, for Thomas' harassment consisted of verbal molestations culled mostly from pornographic films.

Questioned by Senator Biden about the flavor of Thomas's utterances, Anita Hill responded, "They were very ugly. They were very dirty. They were disgusting." That was in October 1991. Remarkably, the February 1992 *Harper's* magazine had an article by Sally Tisdale entitled "Talk Dirty to Me: A Woman's Taste for Pornography." It seems impossible that Tisdale and the editors of *Harper's* could be numb to the significance of such a title in the wake of Hill's testimony regarding Thomas's talking dirty to her against her will. Tisdale, with no apparent ironic intent, defines pornography as "whatever we will not talk about."[21] Clarence Thomas, of course, talked about pornography all the time. Tisdale neglects to notice this; nor does she refer to the disbelief Anita Hill had to endure in her resolve to reveal "the dirt" on her former boss. Rather, Tisdale tells us about her long-term pleasurable involvement with pornography, her desire to claim pornographic images for herself, and her penchant for "talking dirty."

Like Tisdale, I fully support women's efforts to resist puritanical prohibitions on active female sexuality and to explore and produce sexual imagery.[22] Yet, unlike her, I believe that when we do so, we must simultaneously be aware of the ways that some forms of sexual imagery, even if one personally finds them exciting and liberating, simultaneously document the subordination, abuse, harassment, and violation of women and girls and, moreover, are used to further other abuses.[23] This awareness and sense of responsibility is wholly absent in Tisdale's account and thus profoundly diminishes her argument.

Anita Hill testified that Clarence Thomas "spoke about acts that he had seen in pornographic films involving such matters as women having sex with animals and films showing . . . rape scenes." In other words, pornography frequently presents forced sex.[24] Tisdale acknowledges (in about two lines) that pornography does indeed present such material, but she immediately dismisses its consequences by claiming that such material is about *violence*, not about sex, and therefore irrelevant to her discussion. By so doing, she ignores the bloody implications of the fusion of sex and violence in a culture founded upon male dominance, where the phrase "I want to fuck you" can mean either "I want to have sex with you" or "I want to destroy you completely."

This curious coincidence occurs because under male dominance, *power*—control, possession, and the ability to compel obedience—has become inextricably merged with sex.[25] As such, forms of domination such as slavery and colonialism acquire an undeniably sexual component for the dominators. Concomitantly, "sex" itself is constructed as and identified with heterosexist domination—in pornography as in marriage—and intercourse itself is practiced as a ritual of male supremacy.[26]

*An image of female fragmentation
and psychic imbalance.*

Another of the core injuries wrought by the pornographic mind is the fragmentation or fissioning of female cores. As Tisdale herself uncritically describes pornography, "When I stand among the shelves . . . I am standing in a maze of female images, shelf after shelf of them, hundreds of naked women smiling or with their eyes closed and mouths open or gasping. I am just one more image in a broken mirror, with its multiple reflections of women, none of them whole."[27] We see such fragmentation as well in the pornography of everyday life. In any number of the advertisements I have collected, women are depicted as "parts": legs, breasts, hands, faces, eyes, buttocks. So normative is this type of presentation that we, as viewers, rarely comprehend that we are looking at a breakdown—a veritable dismemberment of the female body.

Fragmentation takes other forms as well. An ad for a 1979 movie called *Angel*, about a girl who is a "high school honor student by day, a Hollywood hooker by night," shows her split precisely down the middle: she is the stereotypic innocent on one side, the inviting whore on the other. Similarly, a 1992 ad for M + J Savitt jewelers presents a disembodied female head sliced down the middle. Half of the head faces the viewer directly; the other half is in partial profile, resulting in an image of eerie psychic imbalance.

Conveying the same message, though using a slightly different strategy, is a 1986 ad for hair gel. In it, a collage of photographs, all different, present small sections of a woman's face. Nowhere do we see the face in its integrity; we see only twenty-odd shattered fragments. Another ad shows a whole woman at the center of the page. But, as if the Bomb has gone off, there are identical, though larger, images emanating from this central figure, rather like the concentric circles around ground zero in conventional nuclear depictions. Such images intend the internal fissioning, dissociation, and self-mutilation of women.

Curiously, Tisdale finds that pornography somehow heals an inner sexual brokenness: "I have always just been trying to make peace with my abyssal self, my underworld. Pornography helps; that's simple." It is difficult for me to fathom how pornography genuinely helps, since it both creates and remains utterly dependent upon the maintenance of an inner sexual schism. Pornography owes its existence to and utterly depends upon its alleged opposite: prurience or patriarchal morality. That is, it depends upon religiously legitimated disgust and hatred for the body and sexuality, particularly female sexuality, which is identified with dirt, filth, "whoredom," evil, and monstrosity. It is only when, consciously or not, we buy into this patriarchal religious ideology that sex and sexual depiction become taboo but, at the same time, deeply desired. Only under such a religious ideology can pornography be conceptualized and taboo-breaking be sexualized.

From this false dichotomy of morality and pornography proceed a number of related false oppositions: the madonna (or virgin) and the whore, the lover and the batterer, the boy next door and the serial killer, the priest and the pedophile, and so on. I understand and applaud the female desire to be "bad"—that is, to be transgressive in a culture that constructs active female sexuality as either "sinful" or "criminal." Yet the pornographer's path that Tisdale recommends actually serves to contain and defuse female transgression. Yes, it will help women to get in touch with our "inner whores," in much

the same way that former subhead of state Dan Quayle's "family values" are designed to help women get in touch with our "inner
madonnas." Yet why should we speak to either of these contrived
and self-defeating selves? Neither, to be sure, knows how to gossip.

Trying to heal the divided, repressed and robotized female sexual
self with pornography is like fighting nuclear monsters with radioactive bullets—a favorite tactic of 1950s sci-fi films. Talking dirty according to patriarchal pornographic codes is by no means speaking
the unspeakable: it really is just another way for phallocentric fools
to put their words into women's mouths. It diverts us, moreover,
from our essential work, which is *talking dirt*. Gossips talk dirt in
many ways. One way is by gossiping out "dirty, " that is, earthy, lust-
ful, undomesticated, bawdy, erotica—with allegiance to *no* patriarchal values, puritanical or pornographic. At the same time, *talking
dirt* implies another aspect of Gossipry—exposing depredations and
cursing perpetrators.

In the autumn of 1992, popular singer Sinead O'Connor ripped
up a picture of Pope John Paul II on the television show "Saturday
Night Live." While doing so, she exhorted the audience to "fight the
real evil." O'Connor was widely condemned in the press, and some
days after the original event, she was booed off the stage at a musical
tribute to Bob Dylan.

The week after O'Connor's defiant gesture, the film actor Joe
Pesci hosted "Saturday Night Live." Pesci opened the show by wishing everyone a happy Columbus Day and then holding up the same
picture of the pope, but now it was scotch-taped together. He then
verbally trashed O'Connor and said that if he had been hosting that
show, he would have punished her by "smacking" her and forcibly
grabbing her by the head. These threats were accompanied by sug-
gestive hand gestures. The audience laughed and applauded.
Obviously, physical abuse is seen as an appropriate punishment
when a woman steps out of her subordinate and speechless place
and betrays the lies of the fathers. Fearless female truth-telling is
extremely threatening to the status quo, particularly when that
woman is denouncing sacred male authority.

O'Connor, intrepid Gossip that she is, stated subsequently that

she was protesting the complicity of the Catholic Church in child sexual abuse, including her own sexual abuse. O'Connor is not alone.
That complicity continues to be exposed with increasing frequency.
For example, in July 1990, the archbishop of Newfoundland, Al-
phonsus Penney, was forced to resign in the face of charges that the
Roman Catholic Church's hierarchy had ignored, for more than ten
years, complaints about priests and laymen sexually abusing altar
boys, orphaned youths, and other children. Penney refused to deal
with the charges, reserved his pastoral concern for the offending
priests, and unleashed his venom against victims and their mothers.
For example, in 1986, a mother charged that a priest had molested
her infant son. Penney accused the mother of "spreading gossip."[28]
In the feminist sense of the word, she indubitably was.

This enraged mother was giving us "the dirt" on that offending
priest. One of the meanings *Webster's* gives for *dirt* is "common scan-
dalous gossip about discreditable personal behavior . . . suppressed
information whose disclosure would be highly damaging." That
mother's gossip, conjoined with a chorus of others, was highly damaging and extremely effective. The archbishop resigned, confessing
his shame. Church attendance has been radically reduced, and some
say the scandal—mirrored by scores of similar and continuously unfolding incidents in the United States[29]—has broken the
church's influence and authority in the Newfoundland region. Let it
stay broken—there and everywhere!

Gossips deliberately give the dirt, spilling even the best-kept
secrets, specifying the perpetrators, and broadly pointing to the related dangers inherent in the abusive acts of nuclear fathers—be they
priests, judges, scientists, strategists, militarists, or family men.
Significantly, two antinuclear activists, Patricia Ellsberg and Elissa
Melamed, note the parallel between antinuclear resistance and the
willingness to repudiate and expose the authoritarian father. Each
prefaces her own "nuclear story" by reconsidering the propaganda of
her childhood. Ellsberg reveals, "I grew up with a sense of gratitude
to the nuclear bomb. When I was an adolescent, my father told me
that nuclear weapons would make the world safe. . . . His words carried great weight with me, not only due to his authoritative personal-

ity, but also because in the thirties he had befriended many of the men who were to become the great generals of World War II."

Melamed also begins her story with acid recollection: "Daddy was the greatest, he knew everything, he was always right." She concludes, "Along with the dread of nuclear holocaust, I was dealing with more subtle fears. . . . I would have to take Daddy on . . . the struggle to retain my integrity of vision never ends. Each time, there is a moment of 'how dare I?' as I expose Daddy for all the world to see."[30] Decisive truth-telling begins at home, and this word work is at the heart of our most undomesticated art: Gossipry.

CHAPTER FIVE

The Nuclear Family Goes Critical

One nuclear bomb can ruin your whole day.
—*Bumper sticker, c. 1983*

One nuclear family can ruin your whole . . . life.
—*Bumper sticker, c. 1990*

In 1959, *Life* magazine staged a publicity event in which a couple of newlyweds were sealed in a well-stocked bomb shelter to spend a two-week honeymoon. Social historian Elaine Tyler May cites this as one of those picture-perfect popular moments, providing "a powerful image of the nuclear family in the nuclear age: isolated, sexually charged, cushioned by abundance, and protected against impending doom by the wonders of modern technology." In a way, the hidden model for the 1950s nuclear family was itself a bomb shelter, for that "self-contained home held out the promise of security in an insecure world."[1] Of course, prison offers maximum security too.

The isolated, sexually charged, and paternally dominated nuclear-family home was, in truth, precisely the inverse of its "safe" image. Just as those seeking refuge from an atomic bomb attack in a fallout shelter might instead find themselves roasted alive, those seeking security in the nuclear family might instead find themselves under attack in the form of battery, rape, and incest. Affirming the dire effect of the Bomb on personal life, and in subliminal recognition of the often apocalyptic experience of American family life, the phrase *nuclear family* established itself firmly in the vernacular by 1947. The nuclear family, as defined by one of its fans, is one "focused on the procreation of children . . . [and structured by] a legal, lifelong, sexually exclusive, heterosexual, monogamous marriage, based on affection and companionship, in which there is a sharp division of labor (separate spheres) with the female as full-time housewife and the male as primary provider and ultimate authority."[2]

In June 1992, Dan Quayle created a great stir by chastising TV character Murphy Brown for having a child out of wedlock—in other words, for removing the child from the influence of the nuclear family and father. As they scuffled unsuccessfully for reelection, Bush and Quayle offered paeans at every opportunity to the mythic American family. For example, on July 4, 1992, Bush chose to visit Faith, North Carolina, an all-white town where the Ku Klux Klan recently had marched. The assembled crowd cheered him loudly as he lauded small-town America and its enduring faith in "family values."

Such a setup comes very close to exposing the corrupt reality behind this vaguely reassuring and nostalgic phrase. The original and chief institution of male supremacy is the family, and the family's principal value is as a boot camp for the status quo. American "family values" are historically rooted in the white-racist, small-town, middle-class nuclear unit. These patriarchal "family values" include hierarchical power based on sex and age; heterosexism (forced heterosexuality based in an eroticized inequality between men and women); the inculcation of racist beliefs and attitudes; the reproductive and sexual slavery of women, with variations rooted in class; religious intolerance and persecution; economic and emotional dependency; isolation; reality control; unqualified loyalty; manipulation through guilt and shame; the efficacy of violence; uniformity; materialism; and, let us not forget, the pursuit of the consumer good. One economist at the Massachusetts Institute of Technology, Paul R. Krugman, reports that the richest 1 percent of American families reaped 70 percent of the growth in average family income from 1977 to 1988. Now that's family value.[3]

The word *family* comes from the Latin and describes an ancient social unit consisting "of animate and inanimate property, of wife, children, slaves, land and goods, all held together by subjection to the despotic authority of the eldest male."[4] While this reality has been tempered through the centuries, the fact remains that the American family remains a prison for countless women and children who are subjected to physical, sexual, and emotional abuse. The apocalyptic violence made "flesh" in nuclear weaponry is but an out-size reflection of the violence that simmers at the core of any nuclear family.[5] Despite all the shimmering images of nuclear bliss depicted throughout pop culture, the institution of the nuclear family remains the single most unsafe place for women and children—the most like-ly setting for sexual abuse, battery, and murder.

Three to four million women are beaten every year by their male partners, and domestic violence is the single largest cause of injury to women in the United States. In addition, more than 50 percent of all husbands who batter their wives also abuse their children. While, due to feminist activism, marital rape now is recognized as a crime in most states, juror and court prejudice often deny its reality, no matter how compelling the evidence. For example, in South Carolina in April 1992, a jury acquitted a man shown on videotape raping his wife while she was tied up and her mouth and eyes were taped shut. The defense claimed it was a consensual S&M "sex game." The vin-dicated husband explained to the press, "No, I didn't rape my wife. How can you rape your own wife?"

A 1992 government-financed survey estimates that at least 12.1 million adult females in the United States have been the victims of rape at least once in their lives; that's one in every eight women. Researchers spoke to just over four thousand women about rapes that had occurred in the last year as well as sexual assaults during their lifetimes. Of those women who had been raped, 36% were assaulted by a family member, 16 percent by a relative not in the immediate family, 11 percent by a father or stepfather, and 9 percent by a husband or former husband. Finally, about one-third of all women killed in this country are slain by their boyfriends or husbands.[6] Not all families present such violent profiles. Many people do love their relatives and have found genuine affirmation, trust, support, and emotional comfort within their families. Yet these reflect not the basic nature of the patriarchal/nuclear family, but a triumph of spirit against a historically oppressive institution.

Despite Bush's and Quayle's nostalgic exhortations, the fact remains that the image of the family they invoke is a figment of the imagination—an "ahistorical amalgam of structures, values, and behaviors that never coexisted in the same time and place," according to historian Stephanie Coontz, author of *The Way We Never Were: American Families and the Nostalgia Trip.*[7] Right now, only about one in every four American families resembles the idealized image. Family researcher Judith Stacey finds that many people are participating in looser networks—"postmodern families" formed by "complex patterns of divorce, remarriage, and stepkinship."[8]

Many right-wing critics blame any number of ills—child abuse, welfare dependency, crime, violence, drugs, and so on—on the alleged breakup of the nuclear family. However, this is a diversionary tactic that keeps our attention from other incriminating factors such as racism, the threat of nuclear war, sexism, unequal educational opportunities, the violence inherent in socially constructed masculinity, and the lack of sex education and simple, effective birth control. Moreover, in the glut of acclaim for family values, there is little critical attention given to the problems that riddle traditional families. Such problems include corporate crime of the type that some claim has been handed down through three generations of George Bush's family,[9] as well as the entrenched prescription drug and alcohol problems of white, middle-class, nuclear-familied America.

"Family values" have a reactionary and exclusionary character (as is indicated by Bush's July 4th visit to a Klan-friendly town to preach them to the converted). They encompass racist social policies from the slavery era to the present that have violated kinship bonds among African Americans. As legal scholar Patricia J. Williams writes, "The insignificance of family connection was consistently achieved through the suppression of any image of blacks as capable either of being part of the family of white men or of having family of their own."[10] Family values are also inherently heterosexist. While some municipalities and two states as of 1993 have in limited ways recognized lesbian and gay relationships, these relationships are regularly denied family status and privilege.[11] Female-headed families are also severely discriminated against. They are socially punished with poverty, bureaucratic soul murder, and all-around vulnerability (including targeting by the former Mr. Vicepresidenthead).

Still, the answer to these injustices does not lie in aspiring to the inherently unequal, patriarchal nuclear-family model. Rather, those of us who radically question the value of the traditional family need to invent, encourage, and support gender-equal, safe living networks and associations. We must create a nuclear-free home zone, something along the lines of what bell hooks describes as "homeplace"—a site of support, resistance, and liberation struggle.[12] Concomitantly, we need to articulate and live out such homeplace values as the abolition of ownership, consensual sexual and religious diversity, egalitarianism, harmony, and communal responsibility.

In the patriarchal family, children and women learn the value of material possessions, for we are treated as property and are frequently without rights over our bodies, our spirituality, our space, or our time. In that same institution we learn the value of privacy, but only for abusers. Children and often women have none. It is in the family that we internalize unreal loyalties and are instilled with a profound taboo against speaking out about any horrors we endure. It is in the family that our unconscious is paved according to patriarchal patterning, with dire consequences for adult life.

For example, as nuclear children we internalize values that support militarism, such as hierarchy, obedience, absolute authority, loyalty, misogyny, and uniformity. Both girls and boys learn to devalue the feminine and the mother and to exalt the masculine and the father, even when it hurts. A case in point is the charges of severe physical and emotional abuse that have been made by former child patients against the revered psychiatrist Bruno Bettelheim. No one disputes the fact that Bettelheim used corporal punishment and humiliation, but some therapists claim that Bettelheim was merely functioning as a "kind of surrogate father—often stern, certainly feared, but at the same time loving and devoted."[13]

This is precisely the "Godfather" style of male parenting with which we are imprinted in the nuclear family. Trained from birth to conflate worship and fear, hate and desire, we are opened to the abusive embrace and contradictory seductions of subsequent power-based protector/annihilators, including teachers, therapists, husbands, bosses, governmental leaders, commanding officers, torturers, and even the Bomb.

However, we *can* change our unconscious. Even as we speak, these embedded patterns are being radically subverted by the survivors of this original nuclear devastation. As the family goes critical, its (war)head—the nuclear father—is being subjected to searing criticism by those who have suffered at his whim. More and more, overtly and subtly, in word and in image, his name is being called.

The Nuclear Father

The effect of fatherhood on males, specifically, is to make them "Men," that is, highly defensive of all impulses to passivity, faggotry, and of desires to be female. . . . The effect of fatherhood on females is to make them male—dependent, passive, domestic, animalistic, nice, insecure, approval and security seekers, cowardly, humble, "respectful" of authorities and men, closed, not fully responsive, half dead, trivial, dull, conventional, flattened out, and thoroughly contemptible. . . . It is the increase of fatherhood, resulting from the increased and more widespread affluence that fatherhood needs in order to thrive, that has caused the general increase of mindlessness and the decline of women in the United States since the 1920s. . . . The effect of fathers, in sum, has been to corrode the world with maleness. The male has a negative Midas Touch—everything he touches turns to shit.
                    —*Valerie Solanas*[14]

What is the half-life of my father's influence?
                    —*Ann Scales*[15]

An uncanny image appears on the cover of a 1985 children's comic book, *The Outsiders*. A band of tiny costumed heroes, ready for battle, approaches an enormous mushroom cloud, upon which is inscribed a face that is broadly reminiscent of a 1950s sitcom dad. A pipe juts from his mouth, and his expression is a lordly know-it-all smirk. His sadistic eyes say it all.

*A comic book representation of the nuclear
father.*

A similar image appears in Llyn Foulkes's 1990 art installation
"Pop," set in the living room of an American home. A pop-eyed
father, with a Superman uniform peeking out beneath his shirt and
a holstered gun on his hip, sits staring crazily at a television. On
his wall hangs a calendar with a picture of a mushroom cloud. It
indicates that the date is August 6—the date of the Hiroshima bombing. This image and the one on the comic book are but two of many
linking nuclear weaponry with domineering, abusive, and insane
fatherhood.

Writing in 1937, Gertrude Stein gossiped out the relationship of
the coming horrors of world war to abusive fatherhood: "There is no
doubt about it fathers are depressing. Everybody nowadays is a father, there is father Mussolini and father Hitler and father Roosevelt
and father Stalin . . . and there are ever so many more ready to be
one."[16] Indeed, the world was soon to behold the coming of the ultimate patriarch, the nuclear father.

In his astute study *Fathering the Unthinkable*, physicist and historian Brian Easlea points to a predominance of metaphors of male birth and fatherhood in the language of the Manhattan Project, the U.S. government's mission to develop the atom bomb. He perceives these metaphors as indicators of the masculinist bias steering the development of nuclear weapons. For example, at Los Alamos in 1945, as scientists struggled to produce an atomic bomb before the war ended, they took bets on whether they would produce a dud or a success—in their lingo, a "girl" or a "boy." Their project was a success, and the bomb dropped on Hiroshima was nicknamed "Little Boy." The National Baby Association reacted to this birth/explosion by naming J. Robert Oppenheimer "Father of the Year."[17] Oppenheimer remains the paradigmatic father figure in a select nuclear club that includes such men as Edward Teller, "father of the U.S. H-bomb"; Glenn Seaborg, one of the "five fathers of plutonium"; Andrei Sakharov, "father of the Soviet H-bomb"; and Admiral Hyman B. Rickover, "father of America's nuclear navy."

Oppenheimer, Teller, and other "fathers of the bomb" were widely heroized after World War II. Astutely, their colleague Leo Szilard observed, "It is remarkable that all these scientists . . . should be listened to, but mass murderers have always commanded the attention of the public, and atomic scientists are no exception to this rule."[18] This linkage of fatherhood and mass murder is eerily reflected in the contemporary nuclear family, where murderous mayhem is an increasingly common event.

Another kind of nuclear father was exemplified by forty-one-year-old Ernie Lasiter, a Roswell, New Mexico, man who in January 1992 strangled his wife and four of his children and then shot himself. A couple of days earlier, his seventeen-year-old daughter had been removed from the home by police, who were investigating her complaint of incestuous assault by Lasiter. In the aftermath of the atrocity, a number of friends confirmed, as is typical in such cases, that Lasiter was a "good guy" and fine family man. A secretary in the highway department where he worked added, "He was very conscientious and a hard worker. He was almost like a machine."[19]

The machine that a family (war)head like Ernie Lasiter most resembles is the unendingly lethal nuclear weapon. Not only does the apocalyptically raging nuclear father have an immediate mass kill from his "blast," but the effects of his lethality linger forever in the bodies and psyches of his survivors. Eerily, the mass murder/suicide pattern of the nuclear father mirrors the probable fate of any nation that initiates nuclear war.

Not surprisingly, nuclear-family men such as Lasiter seem omnipresent these days. Other recent family mass murderers include John List, Jeffrey MacDonald, Ramón Salcido, George Franklin, Gene Simmons, and even the god-identified, apocalyptically aimed, and allegedly sexually abusive father figure of the Branch Davidian Christian cult, David Koresh.[20] This nuclear father is also represented by fictional "pop" figures such as Leland Palmer in "Twin Peaks," Jerry Blake in *The Stepfather*, "De-Fens" in the despicably racist *Falling Down*, and Freddy Kruger in *A Nightmare on Elm Street*. Moreover, in all sorts of stories with explicit themes of nuclear weaponry and power—from comic books through popular films and elite literature—abusive fathers appear as prime metaphors for the Bomb. Examples include the novels *The Nuclear Age* by Tim O'Brien, *Falling Angels* by Barbara Gowdy, *The Mosquito Coast* by Paul Theroux, and *The Prince of Tides* by Pat Conroy; the films *Star Wars*, *Forbidden Planet*, and *Desert Bloom*; and even, humorously, the hit television show "The Simpsons."[21]

Of course, in his original mythic manifestations, primarily in television sitcoms, the fictional nuclear father is the benevolent patriarch who always "knows best." During the 1950s, the heyday of atomic culture, fatherhood became a much valorized role, and Father's Day became for the first time a holiday of national significance.[22]

In her 1963 book, *The Feminine Mystique*, Betty Friedan connected the cult of the family with a national psyche scarred by "the loneliness of the war and the unspeakableness of the bomb," for, faced with such "frightening uncertainty [and] the cold immensity of the changing world, women as well as men sought the comforting reality of home and children." These conditions, she argued, made women particularly vulnerable to "the feminine mystique," the belief that the highest value for women was fulfillment in a femininity characterized by "sexual passivity, male domination, and nurturing maternal love."[23] At the same time, women and men also were vulnerable to a "masculine mystique," the illusion that a man's rightful position was head of the family, where he was all-powerful, protective, a provider, benevolent, omniscient, and essentially godlike—attributes simultaneously ascribed to America's newest weapon.

The 1982 film *Atomic Cafe* is a witty compilation of clips from 1950s government and military pronuclear propaganda.[24] These clips demonstrate the efficacy of that inflated fatherly image for pronuclear propaganda. Throughout them, there is a clear and insistent emphasis on "family values." Over and over, they present heavily iconic white-family images: dads coming home from work, moms in the kitchen cooking, and Dick-and-Jane–type kids in the living room, watching TV. One of the most hilarious yet chilling scenes occurs at the very end of the film. In it, a nuclear attack on the United States is awaited. An emotionally cold man and woman (who could be either parents or teachers) huddle with a boy and girl in what appears to be a basement shelter. The father figure tells the others that when they hear an explosion, they must wait for a minute and then go out and see what the world looks like. An explosion then occurs. Afterward, the man sighs with relief and says, "that wasn't so bad." He tells the kids to clean up the broken glass and debris, then concludes, "Nothing to do but wait for orders from the authorities and relax."

Relaxation and authoritarianism may seem oxymoronic to Gossips, but their juxtaposition was the norm for those who promoted this kind of "bomb shelter" model family. This nuclearist genuflection to paternal authority, private and governmental, was equally apparent in mainstream popular culture in the 1950s. So dominant was the image of the white, middle-class, patriarchally ordered family in such television shows as "Ozzie and Harriet," "Leave it to Beaver," and "Father Knows Best" that one critic claimed, "Dad's authority around the house appeared to be the whole point of the spectacle."[25] Of course, that televised paternal authority also served to legitimate and ordain "Dad's" authority around the whole globe. Such rigid unreality was bound to fissure. By the early 1960s, the nuclear children of the white middle class were beginning to speak explicitly of the ways that growing up under the shadow of the Bomb had worked to radicalize them.[26]

Benevolent nuclear-(grand)father imagery, along with the attendant Cold War rhetoric, was cynically resurrected and expediently accepted by many during the Reagan years. Throughout the Reagan-Bush era, the federal government spent four billion dollars per year on the Strategic Defense Initiative, or Star Wars—Reagan's proposed space-based nuclear "defense" system. Though Reagan cast this system as a defensive project, anybody can figure out that space nuclear weapons, if ever perfected and placed in orbit, will serve just as ably for offensive purposes. In order to persuade Americans to place their trust in him and his plan, Reagan not only employed the double-speak of "defense," but he smoothly donned the mask of the father protector, promising that his plan would offer a "new hope for our children in the twenty-first century."

Reagan's "good father" image continued in a 1985 television commercial produced by High Frontier, a pro–Star Wars lobbying group. The ad opened with a childlike drawing of a simple house; stick figures represented a family, and there was a gloomy-faced sun. A syrupy little-girl voice chirped, "I asked my daddy what this Star Wars stuff is all about. He said that right now we can't protect ourselves from nuclear weapons, and that's why the president wants to build a Peace Shield." At this point, large red missiles appeared to threaten the house, but they harmlessly disintegrated when they were met by a blue arc in the sky. Like magic, the grumpy sun began to smile and the arc transformed into a shimmering rainbow.

This scenario was about as believable as Reagan's hair color. Yet credibility was not really the point. The essential message of this little package was that we, the much vaunted "American people," are children, in need of the loving protection of the all-powerful father/president. See, he can even make the Sun smile.

Reagan again assumed the mask of the benevolent nuclear father in his 1984 address to the peoples of Micronesia acknowledging the cessation of their "trust" relationship with the United States. In 1947, the United Nations had made the United States the administrator of Micronesia as a "strategic trust." This action authorized the United States to use the area, which encompasses more than two thousand islands, for military purposes. In exchange, the United States would "protect" the islands from invaders. Ironically, over the next eleven years, the real invader was the protector—the United States itself.

The U.S. government tested sixty-nine atomic and hydrogen bombs on the islands, rendering some of them permanently uninhabitable.

Diana Davenport, a native of Rongelap Atoll, remembers witnessing the blast of the hydrogen bomb "Bravo," dropped on neighboring Bikini Atoll in 1954:

> Seething, filthy clouds rose tens of thousands of feet in the air. Waves of heat and sound and motion broke across our atolls, blowing tin roofs off our huts. Electricity crackled through my father's body, and during the flash my mother saw all her bones, her arms and legs, and hips, glowing through her skin. Windows shattered, animals bled through their eyes. Bikini Atoll became debris. . . . Six hours after the "Bravo" blast, something rioted down on us, on our water and food. Like starflakes, or shavings of the moon. We danced in it, we played with it. It didn't go away. . . . We were caught in the fallout that scientists named "Bikini Snow."

Within twenty-four hours, everyone on Rongelap showed signs of radiation sickness. The legacy of this contamination continues in the form of all sorts of health calamities, including "Blindness. Thyroid tumors. Miscarriages. Jellyfish babies. Mental retardation. Sterility. Lung cancer. Kidney cancer. Liver cancer. Sarcoma. Lymphoma. Leukemia. . . . Retardation. Infants born who leaked through one's fingers like breathing bags of jelly. Others with long, twisted pincers like crabs."[27] More than 50 percent of the deaths on Rongelap each year are children under five.

Childbirth has become, in Davenport's word, a "metaphor" for the monstrosity of the future in a postnuclear world. With no sense of irony, Reagan employed a metaphor of healthy children growing up and leaving home in his formal 1984 good-bye to the Marshall Islands:

> Greetings. For many years a very special relationship has existed between the United States and the people of the trust territory. . . . Under the trusteeship, we've come to know and respect you as members of our American family. And now, as happens to all families, members grow up and leave home. I want you to know that we wish you all the best. . . . We look forward to continuing our close relationship to you in your new status. But you'll always be family to us.[28]

In this speech, Reagan was the ultimate unthinking and unthinkable father. His own role and the "American family" to which he referred represented, on a global scale, the "toxic parenting" and "dysfunctional family" of scores of bestselling recovery books— including a gossipy book by his own disaffected daughter, Patti Davis.[29] The "family" he described is one afflicted by a severely disordered and abusive father—one who more or less destroys the next generation, physically and/or psychically, and then denies his own horrendous behavior and tries to coerce everyone else into the denial as well. Not everyone, however, can be so bamboozled. As one sage Gossip, an elder from the Marshall Islands who was interviewed in the 1986 film documentary *Half Life*, commented, "I used to think the Americans were smart, but now I think they are crazy." She then laughed and added, "Well, yes, they're smart, smart at doing stupid things."[30]

During the 1980s, while the smiley-faced father occupying the White House mouthed feel-good truisms, a scar-faced, monstrous double rampaged through popular culture, tossing off deadly witticisms as he molested and murdered children. This phenomenally popular creation of the 1980s was Freddy Krueger of the six-part *A Nightmare on Elm Street* movie series. In the story, the loquacious and deadly funny Freddy Krueger was a janitor who preyed upon the children of Springwood, a picture-perfect, white, upper–middle-class suburb. Tried for his crimes, he was freed on a technicality, so some local parents got together, tracked him to his boiler room (marked with radiation and fallout-shelter symbols), and burned him to death. But Freddy lives on, accosting the children of these parents in their dreams. His visage is as vicious as Reagan's was pretty. On one hand, he wears a glove with five razor-sharp knives for fingers. Freddy's tongue is equally sharp. When he drowns one teenaged boy in a water bed, he quips, "How's this for a wet dream?"

In one survey, conducted in 1989, children aged from ten to thirteen were found to be more familiar with Freddy than with such historical figures as George Washington. Indeed, Freddy does comprise something of a new founding father. Wes Craven, director and writer of the original *A Nightmare on Elm Street*, describes his own creation: "Freddy is the most ruthless primal father. The adult who wants to slash down the next generation."[31] Robert Englund, the actor who played Freddy, amplifies, "He is the nightmare in suburbia. He is the nightmare in white America, and he's reminding you that you can't escape IT."[32] As such, Freddy might invite viewers to identify with him as a completely unrepressed individual—a revolutionary figure who disregards and destroys traditional mores and values, and one who exposes as fraud the image of the happy nuclear family and ideal suburban community.

A rather astonishing story, "A Nightmare on Sesame Street," stems from such a perspective and displays a sense of apocalyptic humor akin to Freddy Krueger's own. It was written in 1988 by a ten-year-old boy and turned in as a classroom assignment:

> It was a pleasant day, everybody was happy. "Play ball," shouted Big Bird one bright sunny day, but his friends disagreed. Which game should they play? Grover spoke first. He said, "Please let's play catch." But Henry suggested a quick soccer match. "Hey buddies," said Ernie, holding his bat, "how about baseball? I'd really like that." "I agree," Betty Lou said, flexing her mitt. But Oscar retorted, "Not enough grit." Cookie completely ignored the debate. "I get a kick out of football," said Bert. But Oscar continued, "Not enough dirt." "My racket is tennis. We'll take turns," Big Bird said averting a brawl. And that's what they did. And they each had a ball . . . until . . . There he was, Freddy Krueger. He said, "A is for Aim, B is for Blades. C is for Cut and D is for Dead." He popped Grover's ball, then he sliced him. He stabbed Ernie and threw him somewhere. He stabbed Bert when he said he wanted to play football. He sliced Cookie Monster's cookies. "What's going on here?" said Big Bird. "Run," said Henry. "He will kill you." "Nonsense, I'll ask him to be my friend." "Will you be my friend," Big Bird said. Not a chance. "Ffft ouch I'm dying." Krueger kills the rest of the people at Sesame Street. And his next stop is Mr. Rogers' Neighborhood.[33]

This piece certainly bespeaks a rage against the TV version of banally happy, middle-class nuclear-family life and childhood experience. Yet, if this story is a rebellion, it is a self-defeating one, for Freddy Krueger—the child molester and murderer—is not a stranger to that nuclear-family life, but a direct product of it. He is the alter ego, not the true opposite, of our culture's original Founding Fathers, who were slaveholders, aristocrats, Indian and buffalo killers, and "virgin land" rapers. At the same time, he is the hidden face of that cultural icon, the all-knowing and authoritative suburban dad/ bomb. Krueger is Ward Cleaver unrepressed, running amok, wielding his cleaver. He is the incestuous, alcoholic, abusive, murderous father, hidden behind the placid facade of Elm Street, U.S.A. Moreover, he is a consummate nuclear father, signifying imminent apocalypse.

Freddy, like all nuclear fathers (Reagan included) is a child abuser and killer. Actor Robert Englund is, again, quite eloquent on the meaning of this motif:

> Child Killer? What are children? Children are the future. Freddy's killing the future. Freddy hates beauty. He hates youth. He hates the future. . . . It's kinda political y'know. Freddy hates the future. He's killing the future. Parents are weary. They don't want to defend the future anymore. The kids see it, and Freddy's killing the kids.[34]

Killing the future. Abused children frequently express a disbelief in the possibility of any future for themselves. Antinuclear author Robert Jay Lifton points out that "radical futurelessness—the belief that the world has no future—is a condition particularly afflicting children and teenagers in the nuclear age. It is commonly accepted that monsters from 1950s horror and science fiction, such as Godzilla and giant ants, were metaphors for the Bomb.[35] Yet current film monsters continue to carry nuclear and apocalyptic meanings. As a murderer of the future, Freddy is a symbolic evocation not only of the reality of rampant child abuse, but also of the everyday potential for nuclear annihilation and environmental destruction.

But why, then, is Freddy Krueger so popular? First of all, identification with the perpetrator is a common response of abused children. One incest survivor, Judy Bierman, describes something of her own real horror:

> i didn't have a mommy
> i was a last frontier for someone else.
> he explored me

eager to plant a flag somewhere.
he caressed me, he loved me with
the smile of first possession
he held me open and mined
my inner reaches
he built a fence around the outskirts
to keep everybody else at bay
to mark his territory.
and i loved him.[36]

The love bestowed upon a flagrant abuser is akin to a phenomenon that Lifton describes as a "nuclear high"—a desperate
attempt to deny or escape nuclear destruction through identification with and love for the agent of that destruction. Thus, consummately lethal weapons are mythicized as beautiful, awesome,
omnipotent, and even divine—as the "only form of transcendence
worthy of the age."[37]

Lifton illustrates this "nuclear high" with one of the final images
from *Dr. Strangelove*. In this scene, Major Kong (Slim Pickens) "rides
bomb to its target while uttering a wild Texas yodel." Interestingly,
an episode in the TV series "Freddy's Nightmares" tells the story of a
teenage girl who dreams presciently of a nuclear holocaust. In her
visions, she sees a young father—a military man who works at the
local missile silo—playing Scrabble with his family. He spells out
words like *apocalypse*. And, yes, he is another nuclear father: he
slaughters his wife and children and then heads for work, hoping to
initiate mass murder on a global scale.

Throughout the episode, the commentator, Freddy, appears with
a mushroom cloud blooming from his head. Then he is seen out in
space, riding a missile down to the Earth. He takes off his hat and
waves it, yelling "Yee ha," clearly in homage to the well-known *Dr.
Strangelove* scene. Then he reconsiders, turns the missile around, and
says, "Nah, I'd rather get you little buckaroos one at a time." Freddy
is something like a personalized nuclear bomb. He is a new founding
father for an unremittingly apocalyptic culture, pointing to a future
of random, individual violences at unprecedented rates, fissionable
families, no safe sex ever, militarized starscapes, beaches spiked with

toxic waste, extincted species, razed forests, global warming, and nuclear war.

Not surprisingly, the suburban parents of the Elm Street children all are nightmares in their own ways. They are alcoholic, neglectful, narcissistic, abusive, and promiscuous. They disbelieve their children's horrific experiences, feed them sleeping pills, dismiss their terror, and in various bungling ways expedite Freddy's depredations. Of course, Freddy is nothing but the monstrous mirror image of these parents, particularly the fathers. "You're all my children now" is his cry in *Nightmare Part III*. In *Part IV*, Freddy infuses the fetus of one pregnant teen with his being, then croons to her, "Alice, come to Daddy." The incest theme could be no clearer. Freddy's characteristic grin is precisely what Bierman calls the "smile of first possession." Assuredly, the nuclear father is the incestuous father, the one who fucks his own children.

CHAPTER 6

Unthinkable Fathering

Like the arms race during the Cold War, the incestuous father is also out of control. He fails to honor his most basic responsibility as a parent—to protect the child. . . . His fathering is unthinkable.

—*Amy Estelle*[1]

> You are the rapist,
> Pa.
> You are the rapist whose knife I swing back burning,
> You are the rot that festers this Earth.
> Your poison slop filthy crap cancer trap
> Pollutes this planet
> Her psyche,
> Our lives.
> —*Marty O. Dyke*[2]

The cover of *Newsweek*, October 7, 1991, features a mushroom cloud. Inscribed over it are the words "THE FUTURE OF THE BOMB." Underneath this heading are three questions: "Will Bush's Plan Work? Can We Trust the Soviets? What is Saddam Hiding?" This is fairly ordinary weekly-news-magazine matter. Yet the whole meaning of this communiqué changes when the blurb at the top of the page is factored in. Above the *Newsweek* logo, referring to another inside story, is the headline "SURVIVING INCEST. Can Memories Be

Trusted?" Again, in order to get the full picture, we must take media flow into account—factoring in the ways that the various elements on the cover relate to one another.[3] The message of this particular *Newsweek* cover is that there are profound, if hidden, bonds between incest and the Bomb.

In his critique of the patriarchal bias of nuclear development, *Fathering the Unthinkable*, Brian Easlea notes that at the beginning of the modern scientific era, "the metaphor of 'mother nature' is explicitly attacked and rejected, sexual penetration into 'mother nature' having forbidden overtones of mother-son incest." To avoid this association, nature was remetaphorized as either an "alluring virgin" or "mere matter, lifeless, barren, unmysterious, above all unthreatening, but still female."[4] Curiously enough, following this abandonment of "Mother Nature" was the assumption by scientists of the metaphoric mantle of cosmic fatherhood, as inventors were hailed as "fathers" of various devices, from the telephone to the bomb.[5] Ironically, this mythic fatherhood identity carried an incest burden all its own.

An examination of cultural products with nuclear themes—films, novels, songs, and so on—as well as incest survivors' accounts reveal that the theme of incestuous fatherhood occurs with alarming regularity. In this chapter and the next, I explore various strands of this compelling connection between incest and nuclearism, including (1) the nuclear-father figure; (2) the predominantly masculine character of the abusive cohort;[6] (3) the desecration of the future; (4) the betrayal of trust; (5) insidious long-term effects after the initial harm; (6) victim identification with the abuser; (7) the shattering of safety; (8) the cult of secrecy, aided by psychological responses of denial, numbing, and splitting (in both survivor and perpetrator); (9) the violation of life-preservative taboos; and (10) survival.

Nuclear-Father Power

My impression of power was what my father was—abusive, destructive, and unloving.
                —*Inez*[7]

In August 1992, the press broke the story of fifty-six-year-old Woody

is Mia Farrow's adopted daughter. Allen had been Farrow's lover—
and hence a father figure to her children—since 1980. Moreover,
Farrow accused Allen of sexually abusing their four-year-old adopted daughter, Dylan. Allen responded to Farrow's charges by suing
for custody of the three children he shared with her, including Dylan.
In June of 1993, New York judge Elliott Wilk denied Allen's suit,
denounced him for carrying on an affair with Soon-Yi, and stated
that although a team of experts had concluded that Dylan was not
abused, he had found the evidence incon- clusive.

In a 1992 letter to a friend, Farrow described her feelings of
extreme betrayal and wrote that these events had brought her "per-
ilously close to a genuine meltdown of my very core."[8] The nuclear
imagery that Farrow employed is compelling, but not unique. She
joins legions of other women who turn to nuclear metaphors to
describe the indescribable.

In her essay "The Color of Holocaust," novelist Patricia A.
Murphy uses nuclear metaphors to describe both her incest experience and the interior self of her father/perpetrator:

> The nuclear winter resonates through our culture reaching
> into our global imagery as expressed through television. It
> extends into the secret heart of the family and finally into that
> private space inside our own skins.
>
> The color of this winter is ash, which seems to be the color
> of all holocausts public and private.
>
> My father and I were once children of the sky. That great
> blue bowl which hangs over the limitless prairie where we both
> experienced our childhoods a generation apart. He is the color
> of ash now like a stain on that sky. He smudges life itself. . . . My
> father has surrendered to the nuclear winter within.[9]

Murphy reminds us that there are congruencies between the external
and the internal: that there would not be an external bomb unless a
bomb also existed in the hearts of men and that the nuclear winter is
not only a physical state of blight but a psychic one as well. Her
father, she tells us, is an artificial season, a destroyed atmosphere, a
stifler of breath, life, and color—a sorry substitute for that older, original nurturing father she simultaneously invokes, Father Sky.

Barbara Gowdy's *Falling Angels* also sets up a metaphoric link between nuclear devastation and incest.[10] This novel tells the story of a 1960s nuclear family consisting of a tyrannical and crazed father, a nearly catatonic alcoholic mother, and three daughters. The secret at the heart of this family is that some years earlier, inexplicably, the mother dropped or threw her infant son to his death during a family trip to Niagara Falls. One Christmas, the father bestows minimal and despised presents on his daughters, telling them that in the summer they will take a trip to Disneyland. However, in the spring, heeding media messages of an imminent Soviet attack, the father begins frenzied work on a basement bomb shelter.

When summer arrives, his daughters find that instead of going to one newly constructed, controlled environment, Disneyland, they are to spend two weeks together in another such environment: their father's brand-new bomb shelter. Once inside, their father makes them conform to his "Regime," consisting of twenty-four-hour scheduled activities such as the "Pep Talk," "Inventory," and "Supper and Cleanup."

The experience in the bomb shelter is, of course, hell on Earth. The water supply is insufficient and everyone drinks whiskey incessantly; the oldest daughter gets her first period, to her unbearable shame; the father grows increasingly cranky, angry, and unpredictable; the air is foul; and the toilet backs up, leaving an unbearable stench. The metaphor is unmistakable: nuclear-family life, while advertised like Disneyland, to be "the happiest place on Earth," actually is a lot more like life in a bomb shelter: waiting in cramped quarters amidst insane behavior for the "Bomb" to drop. In Gowdy's novel, of course, some years later it does. The father eventually makes incestuous advances toward the oldest daughter, and the mother eventually kills herself by jumping off the roof of the house. The daughters, with varying degrees of damage, manage to survive.

The incest-nuclear connection also appears in the excellent though rather obscure 1986 film *Desert Bloom*, a movie that could easily be subtitled *Or How I Learned to Stop Worrying and Love My Stepfather*. The setting of the film is Las Vegas in the early 1950s as the city awaits an impending bomb test. There are Miss A-Bomb swimsuit contests, "atomic gas" stations, and a final, climactic mushroom cloud.

Against this backdrop, the film focuses upon a family composed of a mother, Lilly; her three daughters; and a stepfather, Jack, who is a World War II veteran, wounded in both body and spirit. Jack desperately seeks esteem and power through possession of "secret" information obtained via his shortwave radio. Significantly, the family keeps a number of secrets of its own. Jack is an alcoholic and a bully, lording it over his stepdaughters and his wife, who placatingly calls him "Daddy." Jack's relationship with Rose, the "blooming" pubescent oldest daughter, is charged with sexual tension: we see him verbally and physically abuse her. She alternately loathes and loves him. Moreover, Rose tells us that "Momma had a way of not seeing things." In these and other ways, the film strongly implies Jack's sexual abuse of Rose, although that subject is dealt with only in a covert way.

Though hinting broadly at incest, the film's narrative overtly refers only to a safer form of forbidden family sexuality: Jack's interest in his wife's sister. When eventually Jack makes a pass at her, the adults begin to brawl and Jack begins to beat Lilly. Witnessing this breach and the ensuing climactic explosion of her nuclear family, Rose picks up her stepfather's rifle and orders him to stop beating her mother. She then decides to run away, but makes it only as far as the test site, where she is rounded up by the authorities and returned to Jack, who has followed her trail. As they drive back to the house, he tells her that he just wants to "protect" her. "From whom?" Rose asks pointedly.

This is the most radical moment in the film. The final scene portrays the family gazing up at a mushroom cloud dawning on the horizon. The youngest child exclaims, "It's beautiful," and, in a voice-over, an older Rose tells us that things with Jack were much better from that point on. This ending is rather incoherent; nevertheless, the film's very lucid parallel between the incestuous/abusive father and nuclear weapons is extremely persuasive. Each purportedly protects the family, and yet each, in reality, invades it and threatens to destroy its members.

Robert Jay Lifton writes about the psychological and social consequences of nuclear weaponry. In his view, the radical futurelessness occasioned by nuclear invention has caused "a break in the human chain," specifically between familial generations:

> Consider the radical new situation between parent and child. Undermined now in that relationship is the fundamental parental responsibility: that of "family security," seeing the child safely into some form of functional adulthood. The parent must now doubt his or her capacity of just doing that. And the child must also sense, early on, the parental doubt and associate it with the overall inability of the adult world to guarantee the safety of children.[11]

Lifton's point is well meaning but nonetheless mired in denial about the fundamental insecurity of women and children in the patriarchal/nuclear family. Just as nuclear weapons, in his terms, give only an "illusion" of security, so do the nuclear family and father. Before parents can begin to think about saving children from the Bomb or from pollution and ozone depletion, and so on, they must make sure that children are safe from exploratory, imperialistic, and apocalyptic adults—including those closest to them and seemingly most deserving of trust: their parents.

"Trust Me"

> A world once divided into two armed camps now recognizes one sole and preeminent power, the United States of America. And they regard this with no dread. For the world trusts us with power, and the world is right. They trust us to be fair, and restrained. They trust us to be on the side of decency. They trust us to do what's right. . . . As long as I am President we will continue to lead in support of freedom everywhere, not out of arrogance and not out of altruism, but for the safety and security of our children.
> —George Bush, State of the Union Address, 1992[12]

> The incest survivor can be said to be incapable of experiencing trust. She has in fact learned that words don't mean what they say, that things are not always what they seem, and that what appears safe is generally not to be believed.
> —E. Sue Blume[13]

Trust is one of the key words linking incest and the Bomb on the *Newsweek* "Future of the Bomb" cover. Witness the similarity between the incest headline, "Can Memories Be Trusted?" and the Bomb headline, "Can We Trust the Soviets?" Frankly, both of these questions desperately displace the really important concerns about trust. Can we trust our fathers, grandfathers, uncles, brothers, priests, old family friends, neighbors, doctors, and teachers? is the question that is more to the point. Similarly, based upon past deceptions and egregious errors in judgment, it seems absurd to place much trust in the United States government, military, and associated nuclear facilities around issues of nuclear safety.

When I was about twelve, the older boys in my neighborhood, including my cousin, used to insist that we girls play a game with them called "Trust Me." A boy would put his hand on the top button of a girl's blouse, unbutton it, and ask, "Trust me?" The girl was supposed to say yes, even as he proceeded to uncover her breasts or shove his hand down her pants, all the while reiterating, "Trust me?" Even if she did just say no, the boy rarely listened. This was an early lesson in doublethink/doubletalk. The boys' words functioned to cloud the girls' minds with reversal, to distract us from what was actually happening, and to give an appearance of consent and mutuality. Our words were disappeared, while our bodies were invaded.

During the 1950s, United States military and government officials played "Trust Me" not only with the Pacific peoples of the United Nations "trust territory," but also with countless United States citizens. These citizens included lower-echelon military personnel who, as part of their duties, were exposed to radiation from bomb tests; the residents of northern Arizona, Nevada, and Utah who regularly were hit with fallout from above-ground testing; uranium miners—a great number of whom were Lakota, Kaibab Paiute, Navajo, and Pueblo Indians; and the residents of areas where nuclear production facilities were located.

The U.S. government exploded 126 bombs at the Nevada test site between 1951 and 1963—each releasing levels of radiation comparable to the amount released after the 1986 explosion of the Soviet nuclear reactor at Chernobyl. To document the seriousness of the continuing damage to people, animals, and environment, Carole

Gallagher both photographed and interviewed scores of the victims of this secret nuclear contamination and experimentation. Her 1993 book is titled *American Ground Zero: The Secret Nuclear War*. This was a covert war waged by the government against its own citizens.[14]

Throughout the era of this secret nuclear war (1951 to 1963), the Atomic Energy Commission and the United States government engaged in a "sustained and wide-ranging effort" to fool the public about the dangers associated with nuclear development and aboveground bomb testing.[15] In the aftermath of the attacks on Japan, the U.S. government actually denied the lethal and disabling effects of the radiation from the Hiroshima and Nagasaki bombs by dismissing reports of these as "Japanese propaganda." By 1950, the Federal Civil Defense Agency was claiming that nuclear war survival was simply a matter of "keeping one's head" and making sure to "duck and cover." In 1953, President Eisenhower advised the Atomic Energy Commission to keep the public "confused" about any hazards associated with radiation. Despite warnings from scientists such as Linus Pauling, the official line was that "low" levels of radiation were perfectly safe, that people could trust the government to protect them, and that bomb tests were in our best interest. By and large, U.S. citizens believed the government, embraced the Bomb through a million popular songs and artifacts, and accepted the notion of the "peaceful atom." Many of these people later developed cancer, sterility, and other serious and frequently lethal health problems in return for their trust.

Now, after decades of enforced secrecy, information is beginning to be released about the massive extent of this betrayal of trust and years of the most desperate deception by the nuclear industry, the Atomic Energy Commission, and their supporters throughout the government. For example, in 1990 a panel of radiation and health experts concluded that one in every twenty residents of ten counties surrounding the Hanford nuclear weapons plant in Richland, Washington, had absorbed "significant" levels of radiation in the three years from 1944 to 1947. During that time, the plant's officials had secretly authorized the largest releases of radiation from a nuclear-weapons facility that has yet been made public.

In April 1991, the Department of Energy disclosed that at least

444 billion gallons of waste had been dumped into soils surrounding Hanford, mostly in the 1940s, 1950s, and 1960s. Studies also revealed that radioactive gases regularly were vented and that, until 1971, when the practice was ended, millions of gallons of water from the Columbia River were pumped through the cores of eight of Hanford's nine nuclear reactors. These factors have combined to make "the Columbia the most radioactive river in the world." While all residents of the Richland area are at risk, some researchers suggest that those in the greatest danger are the members of the eight Native American tribes, including the Yakima and Klickitat, who long have depended upon the river for food and water.[16]

Tom Baile, a resident of the Hanford area, characterizes his experience as a virtual *rape* since the day he was born:

> As "downwinders," born and raised downwind of the Hanford Nuclear Reservation in Washington, we learned several years ago that the government decided—with cold deliberation—to use us as guinea pigs by releasing radioactivity into our food, water, milk and air without our consent.
>
> Now, we've learned that we can expect continuing cancer cases from our exposure in their "experiment." Is this what it feels like to be raped?
>
> The exposure began the same day our lives began.[17]

Baile observes that even after the government admitted that radioactivity had been released, residents were continually reassured there would be no "observable" health consequences. However, the reason that negative health consequences were not observable was not because there was an absence of harm, but because the consequences of radioactive contamination were perceived as normal. Baile comments, "Unknowingly, we had been seeing the effects for a long time. For us, the unusual was the usual!" He recalls nuclear cleanup crews, "men dressed in space suits," wandering around his town throughout his childhood—nice guys who gave him candy. He remembers the "neck massages" he and other children received from the school nurse (who was actually looking for thyroid problems), farm animal mutations, technicians coming in to sample milk and water, a high rate of human and animal miscarriage, and a high local cancer rate.

To Baile, all of this was perceived as "normal," including his own horrific health consequences: "I was born a year after my stillborn brother. I struggled to breathe through underdeveloped lungs, and suffered to overcome numerous birth defects. I underwent multiple surgeries, endured paralysis, endured thyroid medication, a stint in an iron lung, loss of hair, sores all over my body, fevers, dizziness, poor hearing, asthma, teeth rotting out and, at age 18, a diagnosis of sterility."

Baile's perception of the normalcy of abuse corresponds almost perfectly with testimony from people who literally were raped from birth. One incest survivor, Kyos Featherdancing, tells her story:

> From the time I was a baby until I was nine, I loved my father more than anything in the entire world. No one could say anything bad about him to me. His favorite thing was to suck my cunt when I was a baby. When I was three years old, I first remember him actually putting his prick into my vagina. That was something that we had between each other. He made me believe that every father did that with their daughter. So I believed that. And I became that. And I loved it too.
>
> My parents didn't let me go to other people's houses very much. I know now my father didn't want them knowing what he was doing. But when I was nine, I went to stay with a friend, and when it was time to go to bed, her father and mother tucked us in and gave us a kiss on the forehead and said, "Good night." I thought that was real strange. I kept wondering if anything else was going to happen. And finally I nudged my friend and said, "Hey, does your father come in and give you nookie?"
>
> And she was like, "What? What are you talking about?" She told her parents about it, and they said we couldn't be friends anymore after that. That was the first time I realized not everybody had a father like that.[18]

Like Baile, Featherdancing not only mistook the abnormal for the normal, but suffered long-term damage from the abuse. In her case, this included drug addiction, alcoholism, and self-hatred.

Robert Jay Lifton points to the shame, the "sense of impaired body substance," and the "unending lethal influence" of nuclear materials: "Radiation effects . . . are such that the experience has had no cutoff point. Survivors have the possibility of experiencing delayed but deadly radiation effects for the rest of their lives. That possibility extends to their children, to their children's children, indefinitely into the future."[19]

Like many survivors of Hiroshima, the survivors of incest often are also frightened to have children, for the effects of incest, like the effects of radiation, are insidious, long term, and transmitted through generations. They lie harbored in the victim until they later erupt into disease or disorder, just as toxic and radioactive waste lies "safely buried" until it leaches out into the environment and affects all life-forms. Some of the long-term effects of incest include fear, anxiety, anger, and hostility; eating disorders; allergies and asthma; shame; low self-esteem; guilt; depression; inability to trust or to establish relationships; phobias; multiple personality disorder; sexual dysfunction; a tendency toward revictimization through participating in such activities as prostitution, drug addiction, alcoholism, self-mutilation, and suicide.[20]

Many survivors, like Featherdancing, speak of a period of intense identification with and love for their abusers. Again, this is analogous to the experience of the nuclear community, where residents (like children upon a father) are economically dependent. For example, researcher Paul Loeb visited Richland, Washington, in the 1970s and found a town openly throwing bouquets to the Bomb. There were local businesses with names such as "Atomic Foods" and the "Atomic Body Shop," a high school football team named the "Bombers" (with a mushroom cloud insignia on their helmets), and city streets called, "Proton," "Argon," and "Nuclear Lane."[21] Simultaneous with these declarations of love, these residents were secretly being abused.

Official Secrecy

In the case of the bomb . . . the mystique of the secret held sway from the very beginning.
—Robert Jay Lifton[22]

The essence of incest is secrecy.
—Judith Herman[23]

Except possibly for the word *silence* and maybe the word *safety*, the

the word *secret* recurs more than any other in feminist discussions of incest. Psychiatric social worker Florence Rush calls the sexual abuse of children patriarchy's "best kept secret." Sociologist Diana Russell speaks of incest as "the secret trauma," marked by "a vicious cycle of betrayal, secrecy, unaccountability, repetition, and damaged lives."[24] Similarly, as any analyst of nuclear culture knows, an unprecedented and profoundly enforced official secrecy is the most prominent feature of the history of nuclear development.

Gossips believe strongly in breaching this official silence, for secrecy, which has ironically been made synonymous in the nuclear age with "security," is fundamental to the abuse of power—sexual and otherwise. Protected by the cult of secrecy, fathers molest their daughters, priests violate their flocks, bosses harass their "secretaries" (by definition, those who "keep secrets"), governments test nuclear weapons on human populations, including their own, and weapons laboratories and defense contractors plan, manufacture, and mismanage weapons without public knowledge, scrutiny, or criticism. Secrecy in the nuclear world, moreover, creates a select club of those "in the know," bestows a sense of privilege, and fosters ingroup loyalty. It encourages the arms race, allows safety problems to remain uninvestigated and unresolved at any number of nuclear weapons facilities in both the United States and the former Soviet Union, and has enabled disastrous accidents to be completely covered up.

So, too, is the truth about child sexual abuse covered up regularly. At the outset, children are told by abusers that their sexual activity is a secret that must never be told, frequently under threat of abandonment or death (for themselves or loved ones). If the children disregard that prohibition and tell the truth, they all too often are not believed. The invalidation of children's words, the characterization of their reports as fantasy, and massive community denial have long histories in psychoanalytic theory and everyday practice.[25]

Psychiatrist Ronald Summit, strongly decrying this continuing tradition of denial and adult skepticism, describes the case of a nine-year-old boy from Los Angeles who one day refused to go to his new school. He complained first of illness and then

blurted out an unbelievable story. He said he had been invited by an older boy to join a noontime club and taken to a classroom blindfolded for an initiation by a teacher that included being stripped, orally raped, and both threatened into silence and invited into continuing participation.

Luckily, the child's mother instigated an investigation that implicated one of the most trusted and indispensable teachers in the district, whom Summit calls "Mr. Friendly." A search of his classroom cabinets yielded sexual devices, cameras, and large quantities of both still and motion pictures depicting Friendly in oral and anal group sex with students. It turned out that Mr. Friendly had molested almost every fifth- grade boy in town over the past four years, a suspected total of more than a hundred children. In order to enforce secrecy among the children, he manipulated them using information he had gleaned from the school's confidential files. He would say such things as, "I know your mother has been in a mental hospital. If she found out what you're doing it would put her right back into the booby hatch."

This was a small town, and word tended to get around; yet despite glaring clues, the townspeople universally avoided considering the trusted teacher as a suspect. Summit notes that after Friendly's "arrest, the cover-up became deliberate and victim punitive." The secrecy was a concerted community effort involving police, fellow teachers, and mental health specialists who tried to exonerate the trusted teacher. He was, however, convicted and sentenced to prison. At this point, "the community sealed over without a trace of its scandal . . . the active efforts of the public were directed toward containment, avoidance, and erasure."[26]

This scenario of silence, secrecy, denial, avoidance, erasure, embrace of the trusted father figure/abuser, and victim blaming unerringly mirrors the typical responses of nuclear communities to complaints against the institutional abusers in their midst. Tom Baile reveals what happened when his family blew the whistle on the devastation caused by Hanford:

> Our patriotism has been impugned, our credibility questioned. We have been redlined by the banking community since 1985; the Farmers Home Administration foreclosure notice is sitting on my desk. We have been put off by politicians. . . . We have

been slandered as the "glow in the dark family" by friends and strangers alike. We have been told to shut up and received numerous death threats. I survived one attempt on my life. . . . Moscow was condemned for its three days of silence after the Chernobyl nuclear accident. What about Washington's 40 years of silence?

Marylia Kelley is a resident of Livermore, California—home of the Lawrence Livermore Laboratory. She is also a founder of Tri-Valley CARE (Citizens Against a Radioactive Environment). When she moved to Livermore in 1976, she knew there was some "super secret government facility" where almost everyone worked, but neither she nor anyone she spoke to seemed to have a clear idea about what went on there. There was some awareness that nuclear weapons work was occurring there, but most people dismissed it as comprising only a small proportion, maybe 10 percent, of the lab's actual endeavors. (In truth, weapons work accounted for about 90 percent of the lab's activities.)

As antinuclear activists increasingly converged upon Livermore in the 1980s, local residents like Kelley became interested in finding out the truth. Yet local activism faced a certain measure of resistance since so many community members were economically dependent on the nuclear facility. After several years of deliberate noncooperation, some of the churches agreed in 1989 to sponsor a series of talks entitled "Pathways to Peace," to be held in neighboring Pleasanton. Lectures on "Peace and the Law," "Media Images of Peace," and so on were given over a six-week period, but, Kelley reports, not once did anyone mention Lawrence Livermore Lab. As she puts it, "I felt like the community was keeping a dirty secret and it was breaking a taboo to speak the name Livermore in a public way."[27]

In other words, making genocidal bombs isn't taboo, but speaking out against them is. So, too, as many observers note, incest is not really taboo in our culture, but speaking out against it is. The "dirty secret" scenario Kelley describes parallels the protection by family members of a trusted and/or economically powerful child abuser and the concomitant silencing of victims. Kelley concludes that one of the most important features of CARE's activism is to overcome this obeisance to secrecy and to get people to "name things by their true names, to find their voice." Indeed, in order to thwart both child sex-

ual abuse and nuclearism, we must gossip or, in the phrase commonly used by survivors, "break silence." We must begin to spill those
long-held and closely guarded secrets and, concomitantly, believe the
unbelievable, be it that a fine churchgoing family man is sexually
abusing his daughter or that high rates of thyroid and brain cancer
(such as those in Los Alamos) are due to radioactive contamination.[28]

Earlier, I discussed the fragmentation of the female body as a
standard motif in fashion, advertising, and pornographic imagery.
Fragmentation depictions subliminally refer to and simultaneously
invite the psychic fissioning induced by a sexually victimizing culture. This process of fissioning has been described in countless testi-
monials from survivors. For example, Miss America of 1958, Marilyn
Van Derbur Atler, who exposed her father as subjecting her to sexual
abuse for thirteen years, recalls, "In order to survive, I split into a day
child, who giggled and smiled, and a night child, who lay awake in a
fetal position, only to be pried apart by my father. Until I was 24, the
day child had no conscious knowledge of the night child."[29]

Such splitting and repression of awareness is a common coping
mechanism of child victims, who are powerless either to protect
themselves or to manage the trauma that is being visited upon them.
Yet when they are able to remember and speak out, these disclosures
are essential not only for their own healing, but to disperse the smog
of secrecy that aids and abets the sexual abuse of children. Atler concludes her story with a warning to perpetrators: "Your child may not
speak your name today, but someday your child *will speak your
name*." Someday, too, more and more "downwinders" will speak the
names *Livermore, Los Alamos, Hanford, Savannah River*.

Keeping Secrets from Oneself

"What was your family life like, Savannah?" I asked, pre-
tending I was conducting an interview.
"Hiroshima," she whispered.
"And what has life been like since you left the warm, abid-
ing bosom of your nurturing, close-knit family?"
"Nagasaki," she said, a bitter smile on her face.
—*Pat Conroy*, The Prince of Tides[30]

Victims such as Atler seek refuge in numbing, denial, and massive repression, keeping their worst secret even from themselves because confronting incest in their own lives and families is truly "thinking about the unthinkable." Pat Conroy's bestselling novel *The Prince of Tides* elaborates a complex metaphor encompassing nuclear devastations, the secrets of family life, and child rape. The book's narrator, Tom Wingo, tells us that he and his twin sister, Savannah, "entered the scene in the middle of a world war at the fearful dawning of the atomic age." Their South Carolina island childhood was simultaneously haunted by a terror of their father's recurrent brutality, directed against themselves and their mother. While the world anticipated nuclear war, their "childhood was spent waiting for him to attack."

Tom further reveals that his is "a family of well-kept secrets and they all nearly end up killing us." His father, Henry Wingo, while trying to escape capture as a prisoner of war, strangles a German woman. Later, his utter repression of this memory makes him into "a father to be feared." Ultimately, Tom forgives his father and relegates him to the background. All attention is then focused upon the person against whom Tom nurtures his deepest resentments: his mother, Lila Wingo.

Lila is one of the few literary portraits of an abusive "nuclear mother," albeit one encouraged in that direction by her husband's misogyny and battery. She, too, commands a top-secret world, adamantly forbidding her three children to reveal their father's brutality, putting "the highest premium on 'family loyalty.'" In keeping with this policy, she conceals the fact that she has been stalked by a gigantic brute, a rapist and murderer whom the children nickname Callenwolde. Yet, inevitably, the repressed returns, this time with apocalyptic virulence. Callenwolde and two other men escape from prison and come to the family's home on Melrose Island while Henry is absent. They rape and try to kill Lila, Tom, and Savannah and are thwarted only because Luke, the oldest son, returns home and manages to disrupt the assaults and lead a lethal attack against the invaders.

As the family reels in the immediate aftermath, Lila orders everyone to render the event permanently unspeakable and unthinkable, meaning no one is ever to mention it to each other or anyone else and each must, simultaneously, wipe it from memory. They clean the house and bury the bodies. Though Tom can't stop himself from remembering, he brackets that knowledge and refuses to deal with its implications or speak of it. Savannah completely expunges this and other horrific memories from her consciousness. She goes on to become an extraordinarily gifted poet, yet she regularly descends into madness and attempts suicide.

Some years later, Lila divorces Henry, obtains the deed to Melrose Island as part of the property settlement, and then marries the most unethical but fabulously wealthy profiteer in town. Her new husband, who has been voraciously buying up all of Colleton country for years, happily sells off his holdings, including the Wingo family island, to the U.S. government so that it can build a nuclear weapons facility there. Utterly opposed to nuclear weapons and the destruction of his home territory, Luke becomes a one-man guerrilla army, battling the construction of the plant; in a few months, he is shot and killed.

Savannah Wingo's name is not arbitrary. One of the United States' primary nuclear weapons facilities is the Savannah River Plant, located in South Carolina. For years, it was the major source of tritium for U.S. nuclear weapons, but it was closed for the first time in 1988 due to its unsafe practices. As investigations in the late 1980s reveal, the Savannah River facility has a "long and shocking record of serious incidents of radioactive contamination and unsafe disposal of waste," hazards that the Department of Energy "has long attempted to keep . . . from public view."[31] The Savannah River, like the Columbia River, is one of the most toxic bodies of water in the world.

Savannah Wingo, like her namesake river, also has been profoundly polluted, made to serve as a repository for years of officially forgotten toxicity. Her twin, Tom, remembers the beatings and rape she has repressed and is able to maintain a facade of sanity. Nevertheless, his capacity for full emotional existence has been severely diminished. Before coming to terms with his past, Tom leads something of a half-life existence, unable to fully emotionally engage. He is classically, psychically numb. When Savannah asks him why the past hasn't harmed him, he replies, "I don't think about it. . . . I pretend it never happened." During his healing process, Tom pretends no longer. When he confronts his father about the incessant beatings he inflicted upon his children, Henry reveals the depth of his own numbness, responding that he is unable to recall ever battering his children.

Once again, abusive nuclear-family patterns serve as microcosmic mirrors for larger nuclearist abuse. Robert Jay Lifton and Eric Markusen detail that denial, numbing, dissociation or splitting, and even "doubling" ("the formation of a functional second self") are not only classic responses of victims but also characterize victimizer consciousness.[32] In special circles, these ways of numbing are celebrated and encouraged. For example, General Curtis LeMay, who oversaw the Hiroshima bombing and the creation of the Strategic Air Command (SAC), was popularly portrayed, with no onus attached, as "more machine than man." Spencer Weart notes that in his capacity as head of SAC, "LeMay took care to select only officers like himself, men who kept their feelings under strict control." Bombing, as one writer explained in the *Saturday Evening Post*, "had to be done 'mechanically, with swift, sure precision, undisturbed by emotion, either of fear . . . or pity."[33] LeMay himself recalled that when he flew bombers over Germany, "his imagination had caught a picture of a little girl down below, horribly burned and crying for her mother. 'You have to turn away from the picture,' he said, 'if you intend to keep on doing the work your Nation expects of you.'"[34]

While unapologetic incestuous abusers have not frequently described their mental states, I wager they might sound very much like LeMay: riveted on their own conquest or pleasure and steeling themselves to turn away from the "little girl down below," crying, injured, and annihilated. Just as the survivor splits into a "day child" and a "night child," so does the abuser create a second self, enabling him to perform atrocities and to keep the secret of his depredations even from himself. With such abusers, psychic numbing means never having to say you're sorry.

Another method of inculcating nuclear numbing is to render weapons work an always unfinished jigsaw puzzle. General Leslie Groves, who was the military chief of the Manhattan Project, initiated a policy of "compartmentalization of knowledge." This policy ensured that "each man should know everything he needed to know about doing his job and nothing else."[35]

The internalization of this mentality among nuclear workers guarantees that none of them needs to face what he or she is doing. Though I have lived in Albuquerque since 1982 and have spoken to scores of people who work at either Sandia or Los Alamos national laboratories, I have rarely met anyone who admits that she or he works on nuclear weapons. Nearly everyone claims to perform some specialized, unrelated task. Even those technicians who acknowledge that they are making weapons often mute their awareness with truly stunning doublethink. As one weapons designer at Lawrence Livermore Lab told an interviewer, "We're working on weapons of life, ones that will save people from weapons of death."[36] Similarly, many incesters deny that they are grievously injuring children. In their minds, they are pleasuring the children, helping them to attain adulthood, loving them, giving them only what they want, responding to their initiation of sex play, and so on.

The January 1991 issue of *Time* magazine opted to name George Bush "Men of the Year" and actually depicted a two-faced presidential image on its cover. Such doubling nominally referred to Bush's disparate record on international and domestic affairs. Yet this image simultaneously portrayed the "doubling" propensity of nuclear fathers and prepared the nation for Bush's role as commander in chief of the Persian Gulf War and mass murderous activities by the U.S. military.

A similar construction appeared in a 1991 advertisement for the Army National Guard. It depicted a young man whose face was split precisely down the middle. On the right, it was a relatively normal face. On the left, the face was heavily painted in camouflage style; the eye was widely opened and stared threateningly. This ad was stark testimony to the military's normative inculcation of a secret "killer self" within the soldier. It also portrayed the fissioned configurations of not only official femininity but also of official masculinity in the patriarchal state.

Masculine fragmentation in the service of war.

Familiar Values:
Or What Does the Owl Say?

So I learned from the old people that those spirits that come are my relatives. They learned that from the spirit. The spirit told them. "This Chanunpa [Sacred Pipe] is your relative. The Powers of the Four Winds are your relatives. Pray to them. Talk to them. They are your relatives. To the West, the Thunder Beings, they are your relatives. Send a voice out there. These are your relatives. Look to the North, the Buffalo Nation, the *White Buffalo-Calf Maiden*, the Chanunpa, these are your relatives. To the East, the Elk Nation, Black Elk, and the Elk Nation Woman that brings joy and happiness, these are your relatives. To the South, the Swan, the two-legged spirits that bring joy and happiness, the medicine people that bring health come from there. These are your relatives. Above you is the *Eagle Nation*. They watch, control, govern. They control the weather. They are the

true meteorologists. These are your relatives. Down to Earth, the stone-people are your relatives. So when you go back, tell your people that these are all your relatives."
        —*Wallace Black Elk*[37]

My art these days belongs to the dark of me, to that which has been hidden and has survived [incest] intact. So be it. I thank the stars for their insistence. I thank the moon for her grace. I thank the sky for offering me a safe passage home.
        —*Judy Bierman*[38]

The word *survivor* began to be used by incest victims sometime in the early 1980s. *Survivor* sheds some of the pain of the word *victim* and focuses on the time when the immediate danger is over and healing can begin. It also affirms a link between incest/child sexual abuse and what are, at least for the Western world, the two defining horrors of the twentieth century: the Nazi death camps and the use of atomic weaponry on Japan by the United States. While such an association may seem extreme, one medical expert, Dr. Judith Herman, who has been working on issues of incest and battery since 1976, affirms the profound connection. She describes the link "between public and private worlds" and the commonalities "between rape survivors and combat veterans, between battered women and political prisoners, between the survivors of vast concentration camps created by tyrants who rule nations and the survivors of small, hidden concentration camps created by tyrants who rule their homes."[39]

Just as neo-Nazis attempt to deny the reality of the Holocaust, so a confluence of forces consistently try to deny the reality and harm of incest. Most recently, there has been a growing movement to discredit memories that have been recovered by victims after years of forgetfulness.[40] Survivors of incest must then gossip widely, bearing witness to atrocity, renouncing numbing, and nurturing awareness. The word *survivor* as applied to incest also demands that we fathom the magnitude of the day-to-day inescapable devastations of this atrocity. We must understand its ongoing psychic and cultural consequences, its metaphorical enactment on the global scale, and its connection to other apocalyptic depredations.

One superb anthology, *She Who Was Lost Is Remembered: Healing from Incest Through Creativity*, contains a poem by Roseann Lloyd that makes the connection between incest and the Bomb more powerfully than anything else I have encountered. "Not Even a Shadow on the Sidewalk" opens as Lloyd recalls her reaction to an investigation of incest on the PBS news program "Frontline." In it, a woman returns to the room where she repeatedly was raped by her father. She points to a wall and describes how she would project herself into it during the assaults. Lloyd remembers that she was "jealous" when she heard this account:

> because I didn't go anywhere in particular
> when my dad climbed on my bed
> It's not that I can't remember where I went
> I didn't go anywhere
> I was just gone   like the people in Japan
> blown away by the atom-bomb
> Annihilated
> There wasn't even a shadow left
> on the sidewalk
> to say   someone's missing
>
> My symptoms developed   like the side-effects
> of nuclear war—numb hands   missing hands
> disconnected synapses
> wheezing chest
> damaged vision: staring at the white light
> weak limbs
> reamed out like the inside of a sewer pipe
> aphasia   memory loss   splitting
> headaches.[41]

Incest, Lloyd and others tell us as often as we will listen, is an apocalyptic, annihilating experience for the individual sufferer. Moreover, it signifies a greater apocalyptic event. For a society that fucks and fucks over its children is not only acting out an extreme form of male supremacy, but it is also fucking its own future, eating up the next generation, and indulging in the grossest excesses of consumerism, individual gratification, and final-frontierism. Ellen Bass, a poet and counselor who has worked with incest survivors for decades, elucidates some of these connections:

> It is very possible that in fifty years or less, life as we know it will not exist on Earth. Nuclear war could kill us all. Even without an explosion, the radiation emitted in the various phases of mining, milling, and constructing nuclear power plants and weapons is already so abundant that the continuation of our species is in grave danger. It is not odd that men whose desire for profit has superseded their own instinct for survival should so abuse their young. To stunt a child's trust in people, in love, in her world, to instill a fear that may take a lifetime to overcome, may never be overcome, to force one's body into the body of a child, of a baby, to desecrate children so is consistent for people who desecrate all life and the possibility of future life.[42]

A stunning display of this desecrating dynamic occurred early in June 1992, during a speech at an oil recycling plant in California by George Bush, the once self-proclaimed "environmental president." Some weeks earlier, the Bush administration had issued, in essence, a death sentence for many of the region's spotted owls by opening up a good portion of their Northwestern old-growth-forest home for logging. Bush referred to this during his speech, not by explicitly mentioning the owl, but by gesturing toward the sky and declaring that he cared as much as anyone else about those "little furry-feathery" things, but if those furry-feathery things got in the way of jobs and the mighty "family" (here a code word for corporate interests) they just had to go.

Mythically, the owl is a particularly powerful presence, and it has long been regarded in many traditions, including the European and the Aztec, as the embodiment of wisdom and a favorite familiar of witches. In some Native American lore, particularly in the Northwest, the owl represents the Powers of death. In his oration at the oil recycling plant, George Bush dared not speak the spotted owl's name, but the owl is calling his name.[43] For, in truth, the flagrantly witless leadership that Bush and his ilk have offered over the past century has resulted in widespread desecration and destruction of forests. The result is harm for both creatures and working-class humans whose jobs have been chain-sawed out of existence due to unregulated corporate greed and mismanagement.

Bush's foolish pronouncements sounded a death knell, not only for his failed administration but also for the consummately wasteful, though much vaunted, "American way of life." Despite all the 1992 campaign jabbering about an honoring of "family values," Bush's administration transgressed against the original and most essential "family value": the equal sacredness of *all* life, a respect for future generations, and the commitment to what Carol Lee Sanchez calls humanity's *"familial* relationship with all creatures, elements, plants, and minerals, as well as humans" (emphasis mine)."[44]

Bush probably believes that owls can't speak, but this is the height of fooldom.[45] Not only do animals talk, but they also teach us how to. In his apocalyptic and very nuclear novel *London Fields*, Martin Amis hits upon a central truth. He asks, "How will we teach the children to speak when all the animals are gone? Because animals are what they want to talk about first. Yes, and buses and food and Mama and Dada. But animals are what they break their silence for."[46]

Gossips regularly have heart-to-heart talks with the Owl, that familiar of witches and ancient avatar of wisdom. Listening to the speech of animals (including that of insects) provides a transmutational moment during which any human can grasp the original theory of relativity: that everything is a relative and one does not fuck one's relatives. Knowing this, we move ourselves, once again, to break our silence, to speak the unspeakable, and save our souls from soul murder, by telling our own stories, in our own ways, in the ancient Grandmother tongue.

CHAPTER 7

From Psychic Numbing to Psychic Activism

A "human interest" story appeared in the *New York Times* one day in 1979 following the near meltdown at Three Mile Island. It was a story that doubles as a parable on psychic numbing. It went like this:

> Last Wednesday afternoon Edward Houser [a chemistry fore-man at the Three Mile Island nuclear power plant, one of four men who received overdoses of gamma radiation on the day that unit No. 2 went out of control] dressed more carefully than usual for work. He put on a pair of coveralls, something like a jumpsuit. On top of the coveralls, he put on two more pairs. He put on three pairs of gloves, one pair of rubber boots and a full-face respirator. Then he walked into more nuclear radiation than a human body can endure for very long. "I never felt a thing," he said.[1]

When queried about his health later that day, he replied, "Other than feeling a little tired, I feel all right."

Every day, we walk in a world of man-made ugliness, sexist and racist harassment and terror, profound social injustice, incessant machine noise, and increasingly foul air and water. Yet many of us walk in oblivion or discount our perceptions and experiences rather than resist these horrors. At the end of our day or even our lives, we too might say, "I never felt a thing." Maybe we feel a little tired. Maybe, if our sleep is occasionally troubled, we plug in our mushroom-cloud night-lights and try to forget our dreams, taking up permanent residence in the land of the living dead.

The mother of all technological myths is Mary Shelley's *Frankenstein*. This prescient story pointed out the dire results of masculine envy of female reproductive powers when fused with necrophilia and powered by technology.[2] It also anticipated the ultimate "fathering of the unthinkable" that took place in the New Mexico desert: the "birth" of the "Little Boy" bomb from all-male parentage, a "son" fully capable of coming back to destroy its fathers.[3]

The horror genre has continued to serve as a locus for the generation of myths powerfully critical of the destructive consequences of phallotechnology.[4] For example, a mythic narrative criticizing psychic numbing has been building in the sci-fi/horror genre since the 1950s, culminating in the characterization of the ghoul or zombie in George Romero's 1968 exploitation shocker film, *Night of the Living Dead*.

Zombies "R" Us

The question so often asked, "would the survivors [of a nuclear war] envy the dead?" may turn out to have a simple answer. They would not so much envy, as, inwardly and outwardly, resemble the dead.
　　　　　—Robert Jay Lifton and Kai Erikson[5]

People are pods. . . . They have no feelings. They exist, breathe, sleep. To be a pod means that you have no passion, no anger, the spark has left you.
　　　　　—Don Siegel, discussing Invasion of the
　　　　　Body Snatchers[6]

Sometimes I think it would be a lot easier being dead.
　　　　　—Clarissa, a character in River's Edge[7]

The zombies are us.
　　　　　—George Romero, discussing Night of the
　　　　　Living Dead[8]

Romero's nuclear-nuanced *Night of the Living Dead* has endured as a cult horror classic, inspired two sequels and numerous imitations, and gained a respectable critical reputation. In discussing its popularity, several analysts of the film have pointed to its revision of the vampire myth and its implicit critique of the capitalist and consumer society.[9] R.H.W. Dillard points to *Night of the Living Dead's* "open-eyed detailing of human taboos" and its utterly unconventional refusal to resolve the fears it evokes "in any way that does not sacrifice human dignity and human value."[10] As Dillard continues, with its assault on government, family, individual identity, and reason, "the film as a whole undercuts most of the cherished values of our whole civilization."[11]

The story takes place on a night when the world turns upside down. The dead walk again, reanimated by a mysterious beam of radiation from space. They roam the Earth, seeking to devour living human flesh. A grab bag of people—a lone black man, a young white woman who has seen her brother killed by a ghoul, a triune white nuclear family, and a pair of young white lovers—hole up in an abandoned farmhouse. All of their efforts to escape the ghouls fail. The lovers are roasted when their truck blows up and they are graphically consumed by the zombies, the explosive nuclear family ends up eating itself, and the young woman is carried off by her undead brother. The black man, who alone survives the night, is mistaken for a ghoul by a roving posse of "rednecks," shot in the head, and dumped on a pile of the dead. The living dead themselves are depicted in a distinctive style. They look terribly ordinary, move slowly and clumsily, and, except when motivated by desire for flesh, appear to wander aimlessly.

In their essay "Nuclear War's Effect on the Mind," Robert Jay Lifton and Kai Erikson attempt to imagine the psychological condition of nuclear war survivors. To gain some understanding, they refer to conditions experienced at Hiroshima:

> Survivors . . . had a sense that *everyone* was dying, that "the world is ending." Rather than panic, the scene was one of slow motion—of people moving gradually away from the center of the destruction, but dully and almost without purpose. . . . most

felt themselves to be so much part of a dead world that . . . they were "not really alive."[12]

Lifton describes this mental deadening as part of a complex of phenomena he calls "psychic numbing," involving the partial shutdown of mental facilities and emotional responses, denial, repression, and apathy in the face of disaster. Psychic numbing is a condition he contends affects all of us living under constant nuclear threat. For survivors at Hiroshima and Nagasaki, this numbing was a necessary defense mechanism, as no one could have responded with full emotions to the devastation around them and remained sane. Those survivors, referring to themselves, "used such terms as 'walking ghosts.' . . . People were literally uncertain about whether they were dead or alive."[13] Extrapolating from this, Lifton and Erikson hypothesize about the postnuclear world:

> The landscape is almost moonlike, spare and quiet, and the survivors who root among the ruins seem to have lost contact with one another. . . . survivors will remain in a deadened state, either alone or among others like themselves, largely without hope and vaguely aware that everyone and everything that once mattered to them has been destroyed. . . . Virtually no survivors will be able to enact that most fundamental of all human rituals, burying their own dead.[14]

This scenario is posed as a likely one for a world following nuclear war. Yet it is also immediately recognizable, right down to the impossibility of burying the dead, as the milieu of *Night of the Living Dead*.

The ghouls in the film bear some resemblance to traditional vampires in that they are the undead who seek sustenance from living bodies. There are, nonetheless, key distinctions. Whereas the ghouls are ordinary and interchangeable, vampires are intensely individuated. Also, the disturbance at the heart of the vampire myth is one of emotion, sexuality, and desire. The ghouls, however, show no emotion whatsoever, only the hunger for flesh. Moreover, unlike vampires, the ghouls cannot be dispatched with stakes through their hearts. Rather, they can be destroyed only with blows to their heads. "Kill the brain and you kill the ghoul," gloats the beefy sheriff at the film's end. The disturbance represented by the ghouls is a *mental* one.

They bespeak a monstrosity of consciousness. Thus, *Night of the Living Dead* offers not only a symbolic description of the landscape of a postnuclear world, but it provides a powerful metaphor for the psychic numbing that characterizes general consciousness in the nuclear age.

If the ghouls of *Night of the Living Dead* resemble yet diverge from vampires, they are more directly descended from the "pod people" of Don Siegal's 1956 classic movie, *Invasion of the Body Snatchers*. In this film, seed pods with the ability to exactly replicate any form of life drift down to Earth from space. While humans sleep, the pods replace them with true-to-form but emotionally blank substitutes. Some humans notice a difference, but are unable to explain the psychically numbed pod people in their midst. A psychiatrist (who might or might not be a pod at this point) dismisses the phenomenon as a bizarre though harmless mass neurosis. When pressed by the hero to explain the cause of the phenomenon, he shrugs and says, "Worry about what's going on in the world, I guess." Later the hero himself attempts to explain the monstrosity: "So much has been discovered in the past ten years," he muses. Indeed.

In 1988, the New Mexico Coalition for Children issued a book surveying the increasingly desperate conditions affecting many New Mexican children. It was titled *Kids in Crisis: New Mexico's Other Bomb* and, to communicate the extreme menace, displayed on its cover a haunting graphic of a composite face: half child, half mushroom cloud.[15] Although this book made no overt connection between the dangers and disruptions experienced by contemporary children—for example, sexual assaults, suicides, and substance abuse —and the advent of nuclear technology, its cover image nevertheless dramatically pointed to that connection. So, too, did the 1987 film *River's Edge*.

Although it is a realistic film, the *New York Times* film reviewer Vincent Canby proclaimed *River's Edge* to be "the year's most riveting, most frightening horror film. Metaphysics has nothing to do with *River's Edge*, although, like *Dracula*, it's a tale of the undead."[16] The "undead" in this film are not cannibalistic ghouls, but a group of ordinary North American high school students. The film is based upon a true incident in Milpitas, California. A high school student rapes and kills his girlfriend, brags about it to his friends, and, when they show disbelief, escorts them to the corpse to see for themselves. Later, still more students come to look. For two days, no one reports the crime, which means that the gang of friends is casually breaking that most sacred of Western taboos: neglecting to bury the dead.

In *River's Edge*, as in *Night of the Living Dead*, it is the image of the unburied dead that fills the screen as the camera insistently returns to scan the naked corpse of the murdered girl. That cold body is the screen emblem of psychic death in life. However, it is the gang of aimless, unfeeling, incessantly drinking and drug-taking teenagers who—either through hyperkineticism (in one case) or generalized dullness—truly embody the emotional state of the undead. *New York* magazine film critic David Denby writes that *River's Edge* succeeds in getting at "a phenomenon that has haunted the twentieth century the way Satan haunted the Middle Ages—affectlessness, indifference, the inability to feel what we think human beings should feel."[17] *River's Edge*, then, can be understood as a filmic exploration of the numbed psyche of those who manifest the paradigmatic consciousness of the twentieth century, most particularly the nuclear age.

At one point, the killer in the film, Samson, tells another character, "Me—I get into a fight. I go fucking crazy, you know. Everything goes black and then I fucking explode, you know, like it's the end of the world. . . . I mean, the whole world is going to blow up anyway. I might as well keep my pride." Of course, when the bomblike boy finally explodes into rape and murder, the target he aims at is a female body. In the equation that identifies the killer with a nuclear bomb, the body of the female victim signifies the corpse of the Earth. Samson also reveals that although he wasn't "even mad really" at the moment of the murder, he soon reached a peak of hitherto inaccessible emotional intensity: "It all felt so real. It felt so real. She was dead there in front of me and I felt so fucking alive." In other words, Samson had "ceased to feel." He had become so psychically numb that only inflicting death could enliven him—only sadistic murder and necrophilic rape could turn him on.

Rambling around the river's edge, one of Samson's friends remarks, "You got to make the best of it while we're still alive because any day now—boom—and we're dead. Somebody could just murder you, you know; or Russia could send up a whole batch of nuclear bombs." Apparently, screenwriter Neal Jimenez meant to connect the mental state of his characters with the psychological exigencies of nuclear living. Although no critics I know of have pinpointed this link, many do speak of the film in apocalyptic terms. Canby, for example, writes, "Mr. Jimenez has written a screenplay that has the effect of a surreal comedy, about a society that's reached the absolute end of commitment to—or interest in—anything, set in a time without moral obligations, when the quick and the dead have at long last achieved the same body temperature."[18] Canby's pithy assessment bizarrely evokes Dan O'Bannon's 1985 comedy/horror film, *Return of the Living Dead*, in which precisely this situation occurs.

In one striking scene from *Return of the Living Dead*, paramedics are examining two men who have inhaled a chemical toxin and are suffering very grave effects. After taking their vital signs and conferring, the medics tell them, "You have no pulse. Your blood pressure is zero over zero. You have no pupillary response. You have no reflexes. Your temperature is 70 degrees. . . . Technically you're not alive except you're conscious . . . and moving around." In this movie, the differences between the quick and the dead literally have collapsed.

The story in the movie revolves around two workers in a medical supply warehouse, Frank and Freddie, who have tampered with some sealed containers mistakenly shipped to them. The containers hold corpses pickled in a chemical agent that when activated can reanimate the dead. While fooling around with the containers, Frank and Freddie inadvertently open them, not only releasing a gas that causes them eventually to turn into the undead, but also unleashing a chain of events that leads to global death and undeath.

Return of the Living Dead deliberately plays on its cinematic ancestor, *Night of the Living Dead*. Before showing Freddie the containers, Frank asks him if he has seen the movie *Night of the Living Dead*. Sure he has. Frank then tells him that it was based upon a true incident, a collaboration between the U.S. Army and Dow Chemical that resulted in a chemical agent to reanimate the dead!

After Frank and Freddie's fatal fumble, a corpse stowed in the warehouse is reanimated. These two and now Bert, owner of the warehouse, try to kill the ghoul "as they did in the movie": with a blow to the brain. But it doesn't work this time. Nothing, even vivisection, which they try next, kills the undead. In desperation, Bert calls upon a mortician, Ernie, to burn the still motile, though dismembered, corpse in his crematorium.

As the dangerous corpse burns, they sigh with relief. But the fumes from the burning body go up into the night sky, and immediately a heavy rain begins to fall, sending the chemical agent right back down to Earth. It falls on Freddie's friends, a crowd of punk, alienated kids in crisis. The kids complain that the rain has a stinging, burning feel, "like acid rain." The burning rain also falls on the ground, seeping into graves and resurrecting the buried dead. These newly risen 1980s ghouls not only cannot be stopped with the old bullet to the brain, but they actually feed on human brains. "Brains, brains," they wail, running through the streets as they hungrily assimilate the mental centers of the living.

Nearly twenty years after Romero's nuclear parable, *Return of the Living Dead* poses an even grimmer, more apocalyptic vision, not only imaging psychic numbing but vividly enacting through the metaphor of the ghouls the unending lethal presence of chemical and nuclear contamination. Nothing can stop the ghouls. As with nuclear waste, burning doesn't work; it just spreads the contamination. Burial is also no permanent solution. At the film's end, the army carries out a surgical nuclear attack on the embattled area. A hydrogen bomb blows away Louisville, Kentucky, and the officials sigh with relief, thinking that they have contained the problem. But in the last few minutes of the film, a thundering rain begins to fall, and news reports inform us that residents claim the rain has a "stinging" quality. What next but apocalypse as the undead rise to completely take over the world?

The psychic numbing metaphorically enacted by the ghouls in nuclear stories is paralleled and countered by a companion nuclear narrative—that of the reemergence of *psychic sensitivity* in the face of nuclear disaster. In scores of works of fiction and nuclear films (such as the 1990 blockbuster *Total Recall*), radiation induces, along with physical mutation, a kind of psychic transformation. This results in characters acquiring paranormal powers of empathy, telepathy, prophecy, telekinesis, and so on.

In his study of nuclear-war literature, Paul Brians notes that "the most common side effect of radiation is not blindness, hemophilia, or limblessness; it is the ability to read minds." Brians reasonably reads these fantastic motifs as "ways of avoiding thinking realistically about the probable consequences of atomic warfare"[19]—in other words, as yet another manifestation of psychic numbing. While such avoidance undoubtedly accounts in part for this theme of psychic awakening, there is another way of interpreting it: the association of paranormal powers with the effects of radiation[20] also bespeaks a beneficial mutation of consciousness in response to the invention of nuclear weaponry. At the same time, it also recognizes the necessity of *psychic activism*[21] as an antidote to psychic numbing.

Psychic Activism

Macha is "the raven" . . . goddess of prophetic warfare. This means she is a mind-zapper, rather than a physical participant in battles. With psychic energy alone, mental mojo, she can influence a fight, destroy an enemy, or win a war.
—*Barbara Mor*[22]

In her 1976 essay, "A Dream in Female," Barbara Starrett speaks of the need for resistant women to (re)acquire and reacquaint ourselves with the psychic Powers that, everywhere in the world, have been associated with females: witchcraft, spell-casting, prophecy, cursing, the "evil eye," and so on. In doing so, she argues, we will generate visionary alternatives to the world as we know it. Thus, we can actively will, through symbols, myths, and language, an evolutionary shift in consciousness. Starrett sees this psychic mutation as essential to our survival in a world increasingly dominated by the "emotionless objectivity" of machines, epitomized by the computer.[23]

Psychic numbing often is described as something people choose in order to avoid horror, yet it is important to recognize the ways that we are unconsciously conditioned into this dulled state. Gossips remind us that language is a primary site for the inculcation of numbing and a dulling of consciousness and Powers that extends far beyond the blocking of awareness of the nuclear threat. Novelist Toni Cade Bambara shrewdly observes this operation:

> English is a wonderful mercantile language. You can get a lot of trade done with English. But you would find it very difficult to validate the psychic and spiritual existence of your life. Consequently, we pretend. We pretend that we're not clairvoyant, and we buy glasses instead. We pretend that we're not telepathic, and we lean on the telephone. . . . As a result, those of us who are adept, who have dormant powers, have to expend a great deal of time and energy denying it and suppressing it—to the detriment of the individual and the entire community.[24]

In that spirit, Gossips recognize a crying need to unnumb, to cease wasting our energies by unconsciously denying our spiritual and psychic Powers and instead put them to work *actively denying* patriarchal reality. *Denial*, as it is commonly understood, is a passive and defensive response to an overwhelming threat—such as that posed by nuclear weapons. It is seen as a "refusal to feel, to think, or to contemplate action" and is a prime component of psychic numbing.[25] Yet there is an entirely other form of denial. An elder Diné (Navajo) medicine woman, Irene Yazzie, responded to questions about relocation at Big Mountain by stating, "I refuse to talk about relocation. For me, it does not exist."[26] This is active denial, a refusal to participate in the social construction of destruction, a strategy of psychic activism that when employed individually often creates martyrs, but if employed collectively effects radical change.

Once we stop pretending that we are not clairvoyant, telepathic, and adept, we can use the energy freed from repressing these gifts to develop our psychic talents. One way to do this, quite simply, is to speak another language—to create different words, to conjure metaphors, and to tell stories that are consciousness altering and hence world altering. Veritably sentenced to live in a patriarchal, woman-hating, racist, imbalanced, and apocalypse-seeking world, it is possible, nonetheless, for Gossips to talk our way or, we might say, mutter our way out of it. Paula Gunn Allen tells us that the word *myth* is related to the word *mutter* and that myth, like muttering, is a kind of "'ritual verbalization,' that is, a language construct that wields the power to transform something (or someone) from one state or condition to another. . . . At base myth is a vehicle, a means of transmitting, of shaping paranormal power and using it to effect desired ends."[27] The tenets of Western rationalism dismiss myth at worst as a lie, at best as merely a fable. Yet reversing the underlying reversal here, we can affirm that it is precisely *because* myth is story that it is so powerful.

The patriarchal narrative is exhausted. Rather than let it conclude with a world-scale mass murder and suicide engineered by one or another nuclear father, let us pick up the thread and begin telling another story, understanding full well the truth of the atomic or any age. As poet Muriel Rukeyser tells it, "The universe is made of stories/ not of atoms."[28]

A Little Bird Told Me

When I was a child, my mother would often know, in a way that was seemingly inexplicable, things that were strange or secret. When I would ask her how she knew, she would answer, "A little bird told me." There was a strong tradition of prescience among the Celtic women on my mother's side of the family: my Great-Aunt Fritz introduced herself to me as a witch when I was about five. Thus, I always understood the invocation of the "little bird" as an acknowledgment, albeit a coded one, of the psychic concourse that we knew existed but which the world denied. Perhaps because of this early guidance, as an adult a bird will still on occasion speak to me.

A traditional Inuit poem, "Magic Words," tells about the Powers of language to shape the world and the context that enables this to occur:

> In the very earliest time,
> when both people and animals lived on earth,
> a person could become an animal if he [sic] wanted to
> and an animal could become a human being.
> Sometimes they were people
> and sometimes animals
> and there was no difference.
> All spoke the same language.

That was the time when words were like magic.
The human mind had mysterious powers.
A word spoken by chance
might have strange consequences.
It would suddenly come alive
and what people wanted to happen could happen—
all you had to do was say it.
Nobody could explain this:
That's the way it was.[29]

A month or so after I first read this poem, I was driving with my friend Joan Balter in the early morning along the coast of northern California when I noticed a large bird perched on a fence. I heard a voice telling me (just as the poem says) that the reason people once could talk to animals was not because people understood a language that we have since forgotten, but because we and the animals were and are aspects of the same being(s). *This* is what we have forgotten or forsaken.

The repression of our knowledge of this original kinship with animals constituted the primal moment of splitting that has enabled humans to erroneously imagine ourselves as separate from what we have corraled off and designated as "nature." This splitting has led some of us to think that we can destroy "nature" without destroying ourselves. This initial moment of fission made possible all subsequent ones, including rape, atomic fission, gene splicing, vivisection, and so on.

The word *animal* is derived from a Latin word meaning "breath" or "soul." Many human cultures, particularly my own, participate (along with our machines) in the torture and annihilation of animals. Yet as we do, it is our very souls that we are sacrificing. One of the great dangers of deforestation is the attendant depletion of the oxygen content of the atmosphere. According to Alice Walker, humans are "connected" to animals as closely as we are to trees. She warns us that by destroying animals we lose "the spiritual equivalent of oxygen." Without wild animal life, "'Magic' intuition, sheer astonishment at the forms the Universe devises in which to express life—will no longer be able to breathe in us."[30]

Walker's insight corresponds precisely with that of the Inuit poem. Both point out that it is only when we are living in harmony with "familiar values"—when there is a communion between animals and people—that we can work magic. Currently, the dominant factions of the human species are relentlessly waging war against all those creatures designated as "nature." Because of this, not only is our magic waning, but psychic numbing is becoming ever more deeply entrenched.

In the late 1950s, Rachel Carson drew a connection between the increasing human withdrawal from elemental experiences and what she perceived to be an increasing destructiveness in humanity:

> I myself am convinced that there has never been a greater need than there is today for the reporter and interpreter of the natural world. Mankind has . . . sought to insulate himself, in his cities of steel and concrete, from the realities of earth and water and the growing seed. Intoxicated with a sense of his own power, he seems to be going farther and farther into more experiments for the destruction of himself and his world.
>
> There is certainly no single remedy for this condition and I am offering no panacea. But it seems reasonable to believe—and I do believe—that the more clearly we can focus our attention of the wonders and reality of the universe about us the less taste we shall have for the destruction of our race.[31]

Efforts to insulate ourselves externally with concrete and steel are mirrored by efforts to insulate ourselves internally via shrouds of psychic numbing—to turn ourselves and to be turned into ghouls, veritably into the living dead. While such desensitization may help us get through our daily (often deadly) chores, it simultaneously robs us of our ability to sense danger and hence to protect ourselves.

For example, we take it for granted that humans are oblivious to deadly radiation, yet many other animals have abilities to sense its presence. On the day of the breakdown at Three Mile Island, the purple martins were due back from their winter migration; they had flown into Harrisburg for years on that very day. The birds never showed up. Moreover, local farmers reported strange behavior among their cows. On the Lytle Farm in Middletown, the cows started lining up side by side at the fence and staring south. As the *New York Times* reported, five miles due south "as the cow stares," the

Three Mile Island plant was "generating fear instead of electricity."[32]

Animal sensory awareness of radiation is presented as a humorous, curious, yet meaningless phenomenon—merely an "animal interest" story, not real news. At the same time, the diminishing sensorium of humanity is not only taken for granted but actually celebrated throughout the advertising world. Think of those televised commercials for Hitachi televisions in which popular actress Jamie Lee Curtis invites us to guess which television is filled with real chattering birds and which one is simply a televisual representation. (Of course, the whole thing is only a televisual representation, but we're not supposed to think about that.) Or how about all those audio-tape commercials daring listeners to determine, "Is it live, or is it Memorex?"

The punch line of all such advertisements, invariably, is that we cannot tell the difference between reality and its simulations. Yet the reason many people cannot distinguish between the two is not because mechanically reproduced representations have gotten so fine, but because in our state of psychic numbing our sensory abilities have atrophied to the point where we lack basic perceptual, survival faculties. Quite literally, we have lost our senses. In our everyday lives, as we become ever more distanced from the elemental—on physical and psychic levels—and ever more removed from our ability to feel, we stand a good chance of becoming spectators to and even consumers of our own demise.[33]

In late December 1990, just before the inception of the Gulf War, I had one of those dreams that wakes you up with a start in the middle of the night making you feel, in the words of poet Beverly Smith, like the universe is shouting at you.[34] In my dream, I was alone, looking at a globe that hung in the center of a large, rectangular black box. I could see all sorts of devastations taking place on its surface, and I remember thinking, "OK, let the destruction mount—let them really wreck the planet and then they might finally realize that they have succeeded in wasting everything only to annihilate themselves." As I watched, I felt that the life force was very nearly extinguished from the globe. I knew that I needed to break away from just watching it and act. Suddenly, there was a group of female friends with me. We sat in a circle and concentrated on calling back the elemental spark. Nothing happened. I began to get panicky. We kept focusing. Finally, a small bowl appeared in the center of our circle, within which swam infant dolphins.[35] We concentrated once again and soon were joined by a woman who clearly was some avatar of the Earth (though she also was someone I know—a very loving woman named Augusta). She returned to us from a state of underground captivity, dressed in blood-red robes, with remnants of chains hanging from her arms.

Just a dream? Some rationalist extremists exhort us to scorn dreams, to see them as just a kind of mental housekeeping meaning virtually nothing.[36] Yet my dream was just the opposite. It not only presented a vision of change, but proposed active, collective dreaming and visioning as a way to influence reality. While seemingly dream-dead snools[37] pretend to mock and dismiss such notions, they in truth continually make use of the compelling power of imagery. An example of imagery used in imperialist ventures was the Spaniards' dream of the seven cities of gold in the "new world." A potent political image was Ronald Reagan's thirty-billion-dollar vision of "Star Wars." And let's not forget that all-consuming vision—the "American Dream."

Alice Walker urges peace-seeking dreamers to accept the reality of such Powers and to actualize them in our lives. As she puts it, "The Universe responds." What we seek from the Universe, we get. Walker points to the military, scientific, and corporate leadership whose faith in "hatred and war" has led them to ask "the Earth for all its deadlier substances. . . . The Universe, ever responsive, the Earth, ever giving, has opened itself fully to their desires." Walker affirms that the spiritual is political, urging us to "pray," understanding prayer to be "the active affirmation in the physical world of our inseparableness from the divine; and everything, *especially* the physical world, is divine." War, she affirms, will cease when we cease to honor it and "Peace will come wherever it is sincerely invited."[38]

Along with Walker I believe we must, individually and in the company of other Gossips, cook up and dream up recipes for psychic activism. We must do so in the "wordshops" of our kitchens, in our labors, in our political activism, through the media, in our arts, in our teaching, in our child rearing—in other words, wherever and whenever we can.

Psychic numbing means never having to feel anything. Refusing such anesthetization and unearthing our passions means facing our emotions, especially those that have been the most anathematized, such as rage, female pride, and self-love. In short, it entails embracing *monsters*. Lesbian novelist Bertha Harris tells it truly: "Monsters . . . express what ordinary people cannot: feeling. Monsters . . . are emblems of feeling in patriarchy. . . . Monsters [represent] the quintessence of all that is female, and female enraged."[39]

The monster most emblematic of feeling, most communicative of female rage, is the *Gorgon*. Many people, consumed by fear, simply cannot meet her gaze. Others, steeped in greed, ignorance, fear, and self-loathing, quite frankly *want* to lose their senses. Rather than look into the Gorgon's all-seeing eye, they turn themselves to stone—that is, they become psychically numb. Yet those of us who are sick of pretending, denying, suppressing, and repressing our knowledge, our emotions, and our Powers journey to her island of rock and stone and there face a laughing, welcoming, and gorgeous Gorgon. As we do, we turn not to stone, but to sentient flesh, sensual mind, and boiling blood.

PART THREE

The Gorgon:
Speaking with Snakes

Ricki Klages © 1993

Menstrual Secrets: The Gorgon in the Reactor

These taboos against contact with "menstruous persons" are worldwide, and occur throughout history. . . . In them the woman is treated as a scientist treats a dangerous piece of radioactive material. Radioactive elements are never touched, since their power would burn. Protective clothing is needed, lead-sheathed rooms, sealed laboratories fitted with remote-control tongs. Similarly with the woman at her period. We know also of radioactivity that it is the basic, archaic power of the universe. It is terribly destructive if incorrectly handled. Nevertheless, hydrogen fusion in the solar system created the planets, and the radiation from our star, which comes from the processes which are utilized in the hydrogen bomb, created life on our planet, and feeds us all day by day in the food chain beginning with photosynthesis. We would like to suggest that the analogy is worth following through, since an acknowledgment of paradoxical benefit and danger is also the characteristic of menstrual taboos.

—*Penelope Shuttle and Peter Redgrove*[1]

The ultimate controlled breeder.

Why is a beautiful woman like a nuclear power plant? In order to remain beautiful she must take good care of herself . . . she schedules her rest regularly . . . when she is not feeling well she sees her doctor . . . she never lets herself get out of shape . . . she is as trim now as she was ten years ago . . . in other words, *she is a perfect example of preventative maintenance.*
          —*Ad for a nuclear power plant, 1976*

I repeat the text from the "beautiful woman" ad quoted earlier because it resonates so uncannily with the statement comparing menstruating women to radioactivity—"the basic, archaic power of the universe." The ad shows a drawing of a young woman with eyes demurely downcast, dressed in a flowing nightgown, with a flower at her breast. On numerous occasions in recent years I have shown this ad to hundreds of people, and invariably many women and even some men have told me that it reminds them of an old-fashioned Kotex ad. Maybe it's the flower (she's "having her flowers") or maybe it's the super-feminine look of the woman, but the ad some-

Gorgon face. Laura Kaye © 1993.

how recalls popular images of menstruation. So, why is a "beautiful woman," let alone (subtextually) a menstruating woman, associated with a nuclear power plant? To arrive at the answer, we first must face the quintessentially "ugly woman," the Gorgon.

A Gorgon is defined by *Webster's* as "an ugly, repulsive, or terrifying woman." This meaning is rooted in a Greek myth, which tells of a trinity of sister monsters. These hideous, bearded Moon goddesses, with hair of snakes, could turn men to stone at a glance. Their names were Sthenno or Sthenon ("strength"), Euryale ("the wide sea"), and Medusa ("ruler of the sea").[2] Of the three, only Medusa, the eldest, was mortal.

In the myth, an aspiring hero, Perseus, boasts to a prospective father-in-law that he can bring back the head of the terrifying Medusa. He journeys to the abode of the Graeae, a trinity of Crones who originally were the same triad as the Gorgons. They are named Enyo ("warlike one"), Pemphredo ("wasp"), and Dieno ("terror") and share one eye and one tooth among them. Perseus steals their single eye, forcing them to reveal the way to the Gorgon Medusa. Still, even with this information, the hero cannot succeed without the constant aid of Athene. She warns him against gazing directly into the Gorgon's face and gives him a mirror so that he can look into its reflection, thus avoiding a direct confrontation with Medusa's lethal glance. The Goddess even guides his decapitating aim. Eventually, Athene takes the head of Medusa and fastens it to her aegis, but in the meantime, Perseus uses it to vanquish his enemies. With it, *he* is the one who can turn others to stone. Significantly, this stolen Gorgon head is used as perhaps the first weapon of mass death; with it, the hero can kill hundreds in a wink of her eye.

Traveling eastward, Perseus spies a beautiful woman—naked, save her jewels—on the sea rocks. Purportedly, she is ready to be sacrificed to a female dragon/serpent. Continuing his snake-slaying, hero-making activities, Perseus kills the monster and claims the woman, Andromeda, as his bride. But the sea serpent is no antagonist of Andromeda. Rather, let us understand this supernatural being as her guardian, her dragon protector, even her emanation.[3] Perseus has therefore killed off the woman's "monstrous" self and married the "beautiful" controlled remnant.

The story of Medusa is related to any number of dragon-slaying myths throughout world culture in which mythological divine kings and aspiring gods acquire their power through the slaughter of a primordial Mother/Snake/Dragon/Moon. In an ancient Sumerian-Babylonian tale, the goddess of Chaos, Tiamat, was slain by her grandson, Marduk. In classical Greek mythology, the Python of the Delphic oracle was slain by Apollo. The Mesoamerican Moon goddess, Coyolxauhqui, daughter of the Gorgon-like "Serpent Skirt" goddess, Coatlicue, was decapitated by her brother Huitzilopochtli. Yahweh broke the heads of the Leviathan. Saint George slew the dragon. And so the patriarchal stories always go.[4] As with the tale of Medusa, these stories all bespeak a primordial taboo violation, an originating and paradigmatic act of gynocide that, as radical feminist philosopher Mary Daly argues, functions to legitimate future gynocidal "sado-ritual" acts.[5]

The story of Medusa is a self-serving patriarchal revision of archaic *Gynergetic*[6] myths. Like much of Greek mythology, it is rooted in ancient African elements. Feminist mythographers Monica Sjöö and Barbara Mor trace Medusa's origins to a "group of Amazons and witch women" from what is now Morocco: "They called their Moon

Huntress Goddess Anatha, a name related to the Egyptian Goddess Neith and the Greek Athene. The Amazon tribes in this area were called Gorgons, one of their queens was named Medusa, and their Warrior Goddess Anatha wore the original legendary aegis, a goatskin chastity tunic, along with a Gorgon mask and a leather pouch containing a sacred serpent."[7] Mythographer Barbara G. Walker writes, "Medusa was the serpent-goddess of the Libyan Amazons, representing 'female wisdom.' . . . She was the Destroyer aspect of the Triple Goddess called Neith in Egypt, Ath-enna or Athene in North Africa."[8]

In the phallocentric casting of the myth, Athene is made to pursue vigorously the murder of herself—or rather the Destroyer aspect of her triune nature—via the cardboard character of Perseus. With the understanding that Medusa and Athene are two aspects of the same goddess, however, the story of Medusa's rape can be interpreted somewhat differently. Athene does not punitively transform Medusa for being raped by Poseidon; rather, Medusa's enraged and "ugly" visage is, in part, Athene's own response to rape.

This is true only in part because the snaky locks predate the patriarchal intrusion signaled by Poseidon's rapism. Knowledge, taboo, serpents, the Moon, and menstruation are linked in ancient myths from all parts of the world. According to Barbara Walker, Medusa's "serpent hairs symbolized menstrual secrets."[9] The Gorgon signifies serpent-guarded wisdom—female spiritual knowledge. A forbidding glance from Medusa, like a glance from a menstruating woman in a variety of folk beliefs, could turn men to stone—that is, stop them in their tracks.

It is not only her association with snakes and a petrifying gaze that mark Medusa as a menstrual emblem, but also the spiritual power of her blood. In *The Greek Myths*, poet and mythographer Robert Graves reports that Athene gave Asclepius (the renowned healer) "two phials of the Gorgon Medusa's blood; with what had been drawn from the veins of her left side, he could raise the dead; with what had been drawn from her right side, he could destroy instantly."[10] This description unmistakably identifies Medusa's blood as what Barbara Walker refers to as the menstrual "wise blood," the primordial sacred substance, the blood that symbolizes cosmic

Powers of life and death. This blood is essentially taboo, off limits, and profoundly dangerous to despoilers and exploiters.

Many anthropologists have reported that, almost universally, menstrual blood and menstruating women are considered dangerous and/or offensive. Hence, they are surrounded by prohibitions or taboos. Anthropologists Thomas Buckley and Alma Gottlieb write that these ethnographic ideas have been incorporated eagerly into the oral traditions of modern, literate societies, perhaps because *these* societies treat menstruating women as evil, dangerous, and/or offensive. But, according to Buckley and Gottlieb, "the menstrual taboo" simply does not exist in so-called primitive cultures:

> Many menstrual taboos, rather than protecting society from a universally ascribed feminine evil, explicitly protect the perceived creative spirituality of menstruous women from the influence of others in a more neutral state, as well as protecting the latter in turn from the potent, positive spiritual force ascribed to such women. In other cultures, menstrual customs, rather than subordinating women to men fearful of them, provide women with means of ensuring their own autonomy, influence, and social control.[11]

That ultimate menstrual symbol—the forbidding face of the Gorgon—is precisely such a stop sign, a marker of taboo. Traditionally, she is a protective figure, guarding female spiritual presence and Powers from invasion. For example, Gorgon figures were placed at the entrances to temples throughout the archaic Greek period (late sixth century to early fifth century B.C.) to avert evil. Their purpose was to turn to stone—that is, to stop—transgressors who intended to violate the temple and the indwelling Goddess. Therefore, the myth of the heroic murder, decapitation, and defacement of the taboo-enforcing Medusa has served to legitimate all sorts of violations of female-identified space, including rape, gynocide, colonial exploration into "virgin lands," and the never-ending scientific quest for secret knowledge.

Toxic belief systems such as male supremacy treat life-preservative taboos, such as the incest taboo or the murder taboo (which nowhere prohibits war), as rules made only to be broken. At the same time, patriarchy invents and enforces self-serving taboos, such as taboos against victims speaking out about sexual abuse; taboos against female "ugliness"—that is, strength and freedom; taboos against consensual nonprocreative eroticism, including lesbian and gay eroticism; and taboos against speaking with Snakes. These are prohibitions that Gorgons disregard—strategically, flagrantly, and with full explanation.

However, at the same time we must revive and respect taboos based in "familiar values"—that is, the recognition of the interconnectedness and sacredness of *all* forms of life and the awareness that everything is alive. Such taboos preserve free, responsible, respectful, and balanced relationships among life-forms. They include taboos on human overpopulation—beginning with elite, white, upper-class populations who consume most of the world's resources; taboos on the squandering of resources; taboos on exploiting others in the pursuit of wealth; and taboos on technological expansion.

To most people, any thought of putting a limit on technology seems utterly backward if not downright heretical. As cultural theorists Lewis Mumford, Jerry Mander, and Langdon Winner all have observed, under the ideology of "progress," technology has been promoted and largely perceived as an unqualifiedly good force.[12] Concomitantly, there has been little or no thought of social sanctions on its pursuit of "knowledge." Yet to technocrats, *knowledge* is virtually synonymous with *domination*. In the patriarchal, dominator[13] worldview, knowledge literally *is* power, time *is* money ("get it while you can" with no thought for the future), and space exists to be invaded. To all the snools[14] and incestuous fuckers who consider it their divine right to go where no man has gone before, the Gorgon, forcefully and in our face, reappears to say No.

Facing Reality

> the house on fire/
> poison waters/
> earthquake/
> and the air a nightmare/
>
> momma
> help me

turn the face of history
to your face.
          —*June Jordan*[15]

In her earliest depictions, the Gorgon is always fierce, bearded, toothy, and assuredly ugly by *cockaesthetic* standards. Gorgon images of more recent vintage usually feature a "pretty woman"—the beloved victim and ever inspirational subject of snoolish poetry and art.[16] Yet, as in contemporary "before/after" fashion photographs, this put-on beauty is an expedient cover-up. It masks the original powerful, self-centered visage—the face of one who is the owner of her gaze and not the object of another's pornographic peeping. This original Gorgon face is of one who can vanquish and annihilate those who attempt to violate and victimize her.

Given this background, the meaning of the "beautiful woman" representing the nuclear power plant in the advertisement is somewhat less perplexing. The basic, archaic, generative forces of the universe, even under patriarchy, are understood as female. To snools, untamed, self-directed female Powers, cosmic or individual, are frightening and hideous—hence much of the anti-abortion "misteria."[17] Yet, that same menstrual and sexual power—when captured, contained, shielded, and kept in the bedroom—is considered "beautiful," that is, highly desirable as well as (re)productive. The corporation represented by this advertisement assures "peak efficiency and savings"—before, during, and after it goes on line. In other words, no PMS tantrums, no leaks, no spills, no postpartum depressions for their controlled, beautiful "breeders."

In her discussion of domestic practice and ideology of the 1950s, Elaine Tyler May notes "symbolic connections between the fears of atomic power, sex, and women out of control" and finds a number of parallels between nuclear and domestic ideology:

> As with other potentially explosive forces in postwar America, the female bombshell could be "harnessed for peace" within the home. It was widely believed during these years that atomic energy could foster a better lifestyle through nuclear power, which would be achieved by taming the atom. Presumably, female sexuality could also be contained and domesticated.

Knockouts and bombshells could be tamed, after all, into harm-less *chicks, kittens,* and the most famous sexual pet of them all, the Playboy bunny.[18]

The "beautiful woman" ad stems from this tradition, which equates taming female sexuality with harnessing the atom and then using it as a controlled power source. In mythic terms, this is Perseus killing the Gorgon and marrying Andromeda. The made-up beautiful woman is kept looking down and aside, as well she must, for released from constraints, her Gorgon face might shine through to repel, petrify, and immolate those who would capture, disrespect, and exploit female Powers.

Medusa has been symbolically annihilated, shunned, slandered, and categorically defined as ugly and evil. Now, more than ever, we need to repudiate that long-standing lie. Now, more than ever, we need to turn the face of history *to her face.*

CHAPTER EIGHT

Respecting Limits: Not Going "Where No Man Has Gone Before"

[Our] mission: To boldly go where no man has gone before.
—from the introduction to "Star Trek"

A popular feminist button reproduces a Gorgon face. . . . The
button contains no words, for it needs no explanation of what it
is. This face is self-explanatory. The father of an acquaintance
saw this button on the book bag I carry. He had never heard of
Gorgons nor seen a picture of one and asked me what it meant. I
asked him to tell me first what he thought it meant. Immediately
he replied, "It means: Keep Out!"
—Emily Culpepper[1]

Time and again, patriarchal mythographers distort, reverse, and
conceal. They say, for example, that Medusa was mortal. Yet as any
survey of Gorgon imagery in contemporary feminist thought reveals,
Medusa lives forever.

In a stirring article, feminist philosopher Emily Culpepper traces the origins of the Gorgon and the resurfacing of her image, name, and story in contemporary feminist metaphor. Culpepper rightfully names the Gorgon as a face of female rage and argues most convincingly that "feminists are *living* the knowledge gained from tapping deep and ancient symbolic/mythic power to change our lives."

Culpepper then relates an incident that occurred in 1980, when her Gorgon self emerged to save her life. While working one evening at home, someone knocked at her door. After looking out and thinking it was someone she knew, she opened the door. A stranger came in and immediately attacked her. Culpepper, at first off guard, gathered herself and fought back, throwing out the would-be rapist. In a section from her journal recalling the incident, she writes, "I am staring him out, pushing with my eyes too. My face is bursting, contorting with terrible teeth, flaming breath, erupting into ridges and contortions of rage, hair hissing. It is over in a flash." Afterward, she realized that she "needed to look at the terrible face that had erupted and sprung forth from within" during her fight:

> As I felt my face twist again into the fighting frenzy, I turned to the mirror and looked. What I saw in the mirror is a Gorgon, a Medusa, if *ever* there was one. This face was my own and yet I knew I had seen it before and I knew the name to utter. "Gorgon! Gorgon!" reverberated in my mind. I knew then why the attacker had become so suddenly petrified.

In this world where men daily perpetrate outrages on women, Culpepper avows that it is imperative that women "learn how to manifest a visage that will repel men when necessary. . . . The Gorgon has much vital, literally life-saving information to teach women about anger, rape, power, and the release of the determined aggressiveness sometimes needed for survival." Understanding the intimate connections between sexual and geocidal assaults, women also can look to the Gorgon for vital information about stopping nuclearist rippers and their brethren.

In scores of nuclear movies, such as the 1958 *Teenage Caveman* and the 1968 *Planet of the Apes*, there is a recurrent motif: that of the "forbidden zone," an area closely guarded by taboo, which no one may enter. Usually, this area is contaminated by radiation from some long-ago nuclear war. In protechnology films like *Teenage Caveman*, the hero is the one who disregards the taboo and boldly strides into the proscribed area.

The 1956 film *Forbidden Planet* puts a different twist on this theme. A scientist, Morbius, lives alone on the paradisiacal planet Altair with his full-grown daughter, Altaira. Domestic chores are performed by a marvelously efficient robot named Robby. A spaceship from Earth arrives to find out what happened to the original landing party that came to the planet twenty years before. Morbius attempts to make them go away. He tells them that, in essence, the entire planet is taboo to them, for there is a deadly force on the planet that killed everyone in the landing party except himself and his daughter. Nevertheless, the captain of the ship refuses to leave.

As a sexual attraction develops between the captain and the daughter, the deadly planetary force again makes an appearance, threatening the men and their ship. Ultimately, we learn that the lethal force is generated by the jealous Morbius's own mind. The planet Altair formerly was inhabited by the members of a technologically superior civilization, the Krell. Although they wiped themselves out years ago "in a single night," the Krell left behind the agent of their own destruction, a vast nuclear-powered machine. Morbius, lusting for the Krell's technological knowledge, has been able to tap into the machine's power, allowing him to externally produce all that he can imagine, such as the marvelous Robby. Marching his visitors past the vast nuclear complex, he warns them against gazing into its power source: "Be sure to look only in the mirror. Man does not behold the face of the Gorgon and live."

But Morbius is gazing fixedly into mirrors himself—in other words, he is operating under a serious mantle of denial and displacement. He is transgressing profoundly against self-, family-, and planetary-preservative taboos in his quest for both sexual and technological knowledge. The Krell machine manifests in material reality not only his conscious wishes but also his most awful unconscious thoughts and desires, unleashing "monsters from the id." (The Krell themselves discovered this after they had built the machine. It brought their unconscious thoughts into material existence, and they "destroyed themselves in a single night.") The lethal planetary force, then, is actually an externalization of Morbius's unconscious. When his incestuous paradise with his "forbidden partner," his daughter, is threatened, his unconscious strikes out to eliminate the threat. In the film's climactic moment, Morbius faces his own evil self, and the experience does indeed destroy him. Romance, however, manages to "save" Altaira. She and the captain escape into space, bringing Robby with them, while Morbius and the planet that shares her name are blown to bits.

The word *forbidden* in the film's title speaks not only to the archetypal "forbidden knowledge" that structures both ancient myths and mad-scientist movies, but also to the nominally forbidden incestuous relationship that the father imposes upon his daughter. This incest is never made explicit. In keeping with cultural patterns of denial, it is woven into the story as a subtext.[2] *Forbidden Planet* is basically a conservative movie: it sets up pairs of false dichotomies and then in a tidy resolution replaces the "bad" heterosexual domination—incest with her father—with "good" heterosexual domination—marriage to the captain. Similarly, the "bad" nuclear technology—represented by the Krell machine—is replaced with "good" nuclear technology—in the form of Robby the Robot.

Yet, however conventional, *Forbidden Planet* once again holds up for view the connection between the incestuous father and nuclearism. It clearly points out the connection between Morbius's unbounded quest for knowledge and his incestuous depredations. As Catharine MacKinnon has noted, "Sexual metaphors for knowing are no coincidence. . . . Feminists are beginning to understand that to know has meant to fuck."[3] It was this reigning pornographic paradigm of knowledge that guided and legitimated the quest to "penetrate the secrets" of the atom, that supreme achievement of Western intellectual and scientific endeavor.

The approved transgression of taboo in the quest for knowledge is a central dynamic in the christotechnological tradition of knowledge. It is memorialized neatly in the Apple computer logo: the artificial apple with the bite proudly taken. Of course, as the plastic rainbow face of the apple cannot help but reveal, this is artificial knowledge or intelligence. In one 1984 advertisement, Apple verbalized its (rotten to the) core reigning principle: "At Apple we only have one rule. Rules are made to be broken."[4] This sort of cocky, enterprising individualism and doublethink, by which snools[5] deliberately break their own rules, underwrites all sorts of depredations, including incest, serial sex murder, uranium mining, deforestation, and that ultimate taboo violation—planetary Motherfucking.

From Gynocide to Geocide

> I start by skinning Torri a little, making incisions with a steak knife and ripping bits of flesh from her legs and stomach while she screams in vain. . . . I force my hand down, deep into her throat, until it disappears up to my wrist . . . and grab at the veins lodged there like tubes and I loosen them with my fingers and . . . violently yank them out through her open mouth. . . . her whole body starts twitching, like a roach on its back, shaking spasmodically, her melted eyes running down her face mixing with the tears and Mace, and then quickly, not wanting to waste time, I turn off the lights and in the dark before she dies I rip open her stomach with my bare hands.
> —*Bret Easton Ellis*, American Psycho[6]

> Deforestation in the 1990s will claim roughly 110,000 acres per day in the tropics alone. . . . Forest disintegration of this magnitude ripples throughout the global ecosystem. The visual metaphor that comes to mind is an earth skinned alive, its lungs ripped out.
> —*Stephen J. Pyne*[7]

On September 4, 1988, an editorial appeared in the *Los Angeles Times* urging global strictures against environmental depredations. The headline read, "To Save the Earth from Human Ruin, Enact New World Laws of Geo-Ecology." To illustrate this concept, the *Times* artist David Tillinghast rendered the globe impaled upon a huge knife. One hardly need consult Freud to grasp the message: the (Mother) Earth is in the death grip of a geocidal Ripper.

As I extensively documented in my 1987 book, *The Age of Sex Crime*, the serial sex killer—who most often is a white man—has attained mythic proportions and an outlaw/hero stature in contemporary culture. Although categorized as a deviant, he actually is an exemplar of patriarchal normalcy. Like any culture hero, the serial killer enacts on some grand, symbolically redolent scale the core val-

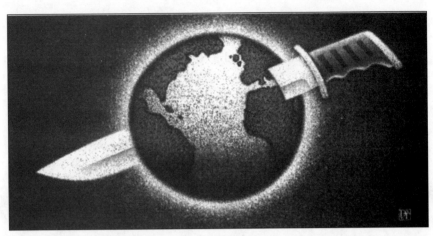

Environmental degradation as a sexual murder. David Tillinghast © 1988.

ues and beliefs of his culture. Mass murderers have been enshrined in U.S. culture previously: witness the heroization of genocidal killers of Native Americans such as Christopher Columbus, Kit Carson, and Andrew Jackson.[8] These men enacted core cultural values of white supremacy and manifest destiny. The serial killer enacts patriarchal culture's hatred of the female and its inevitable sexualization of domination and violence. The serial sex killer, moreover, is a hero because his actions, however covertly, support and sustain the status quo. That is, they enforce male supremacy through terrorism.

In horror at the murder of twelve African-American women in six months in a small area of Boston in 1979, Audre Lorde speaks of these killings as culturally sustaining rituals:

> as women we were meant to bleed
> but not this useless blood
> my blood each month a memorial
> to my unspoken sisters falling
> like red drops to the asphalt
> I am not satisfied to bleed
> as a quiet symbol for no one's redemption
> why is it our blood
> that keeps these cities fertile?[9]

While Lorde rages, other voices urge acceptance of this blood sacrifice. For example, on December 6, 1989, one heavily armed man, Marc Lépine, entered the college of engineering at the University of Montreal, separated out the women from the men, and then fired on the women, killing fourteen of them, because, as he averred, they were "all fucking feminists."[10] He then killed himself. In the aftermath of the massacre, Cardinal Paul-Émile Léger stated that the death of these women must be seen as "an offering made to God."[11]

Although such sentiments are rarely so openly admitted, patriarchal culture does indeed require the ritual sacrifice of women, sometimes called Gorgons, sometimes witches, sometimes prostitutes, and sometimes feminists. These murders reveal not only our culture's profound gynocidal propensities, but simultaneously its geocidal desires and intentions. The endless numbers of women raped, flayed, mutilated, and murdered, in both the real and the symbolic worlds, reflect and enact the large-scale assaults on the besieged and traditionally female-identified Earth.

Much of the symbolic meaning of the serial killer is wrapped up in his role as a violator of taboo. For example, the "father" of serial sex murder, Jack the Ripper, attacked the womb, the very source of life, and cannibalized his victims. U.S. culture, in its fascination with and heroization of overt taboo violators, symbolically acknowledges the taboo violation that constitutes the nation's core modus operandi.

Murder, for example, is supposedly taboo, yet in the 1991 Gulf War, the United States accomplished the mass murder of at least one hundred thousand Iraqis, the contamination of vast regions of the "cradle of civilization," and the attendant destruction of countless shore birds and sea creatures. Before the war began, one *Los Angeles Daily News* columnist, Debra Saunders, warned against Sadaam Hussein as "Ted Bundy with an arsenal." Of course, in terms of devastation inflicted, Ted Bundy, that all-American boy turned serial killer,[12] was operating on the U.S. side.

This connection between serial killers and the Gulf War was again displayed on the 1991 April Fools' Day cover of *Newsweek*. The cover highlighted the feature story, "Violence Goes Mainstream," about the alarming increase of violence, particularly violence against women, in popular culture. The cover illustration portrays the staring eyes of the nation's adored fictional serial murderer, Hannibal Lecter, the "genius" psychiatrist, incestuous father figure, and cannibalistic killer from the novel and film *The Silence of the Lambs*.[13] At the top of the cover is a blurb referring to another story, "Apocalypse in Iraq: The Shattering of a Nation." This particular juxtaposition reminds us that the violence, misogyny, and mass murder that run so rampant in our popular culture are profoundly linked to the ideals and accomplishments of our political leaders and military forces. Lecter, as the date on the cover makes so perfectly clear, is a modern avatar of the patriarchal fool archetype—that is, he is the alter ego of serious "good father" figures like former president Bush.[14]

The cover openly invites us to gaze into Lecter's eyes. His gaze, oddly enough, does not repel, but attracts. He is our nation's mirror, reflecting consumerism, orgiastic violence, and fatherfucker dominance. Hannibal's cannibalism, the proximate reference to the Gulf War further suggests, is connected to our nation's gluttonous appetite for luxuries. The United States forcibly demands a vastly disproportional share of the world resources, most recently oil. Our nation demands, in short, full, unlimited, and exclusive access to the body of the Mother (Earth).

Clearly, cannibalism can have a great number and variety of meanings, yet in the United States, where it has become a major motif in horror films and fiction since the 1960s (*Night of the Living Dead*, 1968; *The Texas Chainsaw Massacre*, 1975), cannibalism usually is a metaphor for, in a word, consumerism. A corporate consumerist society is inherently ravenous, devouring natural resources and insatiably requiring new mass-produced goods. Perhaps Lecter (and his real-world counterpart, Jeffrey Dahmer) grip the collective imagination in part because they mirror gluttonous American incorporation of the land, resources, and bodies of others—most frequently, racial others. Jeffrey Dahmer, a white man, battened mostly on the bodies of men of color.[15] Lecter, also a white man and one with an appetite for luxury, by film's end takes up residence in the Bahamas, where the streets are filled with black people. Common consensus holds that it is modern (particularly white) people's respect for the taboo on cannibalism that makes us "civilized." Yet a curious doublethink informs this, for metaphorical cannibalism is necessary to the much vaunted "American way of life."

Capitalism continuously endorses and encourages the unbounded and imperialist pursuit of the (material) good, as those authoritative voices on the credit card commercials firmly suggest: "Don't leave home without it" and "Visa takes you everywhere you want to go." Concomitantly, pornotechnology allows no limits in its quest "to penetrate the secrets of the Universe," as a 1985 Lockheed advertisement boasts.

In the Marquis de Sade's philosophy, taboo breaking is erotic, heroic, and liberating. In pornotechnic procedure, taboo breaking is all of these and also routine. "Can implies ought" is the guiding rule here. Reflecting on his experiences at Los Alamos, J. Robert Oppenheimer avowed, "It is my judgment in these things that when you see something that is technically sweet, you go ahead and do it, and you argue about what to do about it only after you have had your technical success. That's the way it was with the atomic bomb."[16] The denial of any need for taboo, for protective restraints on economic expansion or technology's sweet tooth, has resulted in the invention of ever greater means of mass destruction, an epidemic of pollution, and the desertion of the planet by any number of animal and plant beings.[17]

In many ancient and even some modern thought systems, the breaking of a taboo results in *pollution*. The taboo breaking is understood as a moral transgression or impurity, but one always manifesting in physical contamination—plague, blight, and infertility in the material world. An ancient example of this is the incest and patricide in Sophocles' play *Oedipus the King* and the resulting blight on the people and the land.[18] In modern capitalist and technological thinking, the moral factor has been deleted and pollution now *is* the contamination or the material impurity itself. Yet contemporary pollution—radioactive, chemical, and so on—remains rooted in metaphysical violation, in the flouting of life-preservative taboo.

Skewed variants of this belief system do operate. Many Christian fundamentalists, for example, claim that AIDS is a disease visited upon gay men because homosexuality is a "taboo." Clearly, though, this snool-made dictum is a rule made to be broken by the hypocritically homophobic Christian religion itself, whose myths, rituals, and practices, ironically enough, are highly homoerotic.[19] AIDS, of course, does not truly discriminate, and it is only a matter of time before this potentially apocalyptic disease becomes primarily a heterosexual disease in the United States, as it is in the rest of the world. Social hierarchies being what they are, any disease, AIDS included, will first devastate the poor and the oppressed—especially if it were deliberately introduced into that population, as some channels of the oral tradition suggest.[20]

If there is a transgressed sexual taboo behind the appearance of AIDS in the late twentieth century, it is not gay sex. AIDS is also transmitted in heterosexual intercourse, and like many of the effects of radiation, such as sterility, fetal mutation, and birth defects, its horrors are linked to human reproduction. Let us then consider rampant heterosexism, which has resulted in human overpopulation, brought about and maintained through colonialism, the requirements of a market economy, patriarchal religious mandates, and the sexual and the reproductive enslavement of women worldwide.[21] The serious problem of human overpopulation must be considered as a taboo violation underlying the appearance of AIDS.

The taboo violation involved in splitting the atom is also a most relevant factor here. The Soviet physicist Andrei Sakharov was one of the first to point to the biological effects of nuclear tests. These include genetic damage and both immediate and delayed damage to immune systems. As scientific writer Jay Gould details, radiation physicists Ernest Sternglass and Jim Scheer

> point out that the AIDS epidemic first appeared during the early 1980s in the high rainfall areas of Africa that twenty years earlier registered the highest levels in the world of strontium-90 in human bone after receiving heavy fallout from the atmospheric bomb tests. They conclude that fallout is a factor in the impairment of immune response that can show up when young adults encounter the newly mutated strains of sexually transmitted viruses.[22]

Finally, Gorgons suggest that to further understand the metaphysical meanings of AIDS we might also look to the skies, that is, to the diminishment of the atmosphere's ozone layer, the shield protecting Earth's creatures from ultraviolet radiation. Some scientists have analogized the ozone layer to the individual human body's immune system.[23] As the planetary system goes, so goes the human body. (Or as the legendary alchemist Hermes Trismegistus put it, "As above, so below.") Can we ever stop AIDS, the disintegration of the individual immune system, unless we cease disrespecting the planet's immune system by bombarding it with our technological waste?

On the *Newsweek* cover featuring Hannibal Lecter, the word *apocalypse* in the blurb describes the damage done to Iraq. Like AIDS, nuclear weaponry, and ozone devastation, the serial sex killer is an apocalyptic indicator, a sign of endtimes. Indeed, the popular embrace of mutilating cannibalistic serial killers in both fact and fiction suggests not only gynocidal, genocidal, and geocidal impulses, but also a *suicidal* one: a desire to be engulfed, to reach an end to commitment and even to existence.

Apocalyptic inferences are woven throughout these narratives. In *The Silence of the Lambs*, a young FBI student, Clarice Starling, is sent to the imprisoned serial killer, Hannibal Lecter, to solicit his help in identifying a current serial killer. Lecter agrees to assist her, but only if she reciprocates by revealing to him her "worst memory of childhood."

That sadistically extracted story goes like this. Two years after her father's death, her mother was no longer able to support the family, and Clarice was sent to Montana to live with her mother's cousin and her husband on their ranch. Lecter interrupts her narrative to ask, "Did your foster father in Montana fuck you, Clarice?" She denies this and tells him that the real trauma she experienced there was the slaughter of both lambs and horses. She would wake at night to the screaming of the lambs. Unable to bear this, after seven months she takes one of the horses marked for death and runs away. She is caught, but gets to live with the horse at an orphanage.

Through her "therapeutic" interaction with Lecter, Starling understands that her adult life has been determined by this early experience. She has set herself on a continuing quest to "silence the lambs," that is, to save women endangered by sex criminals. Of course, the story of the young girl waking to horror in the night, her identification with screaming, helpless animals, her desperate flight from the ranch, and her ultimate removal beg to be interpreted as an allegorical rendering of incest. Her own trauma around sexual assault impelled Starling as an adult to become a gorgonish woman, that is, one who is committed to saving women endangered by male sexual abuse. Unfortunately, as the novel sets it up, she must consent to being "mind fucked" by her surrogate father, Hannibal Lecter. Incest trauma, in this schema, is indelible, and the victim, however strong, must reenact it in subsequent interactions with abusive father figures.

Long before Starling reveals her own traumatic resonance with lambs to Lecter, the subject pops up in conversation. Lecter has done a sketch of Golgotha, and when Starling asks about it, he refers to Christ as the paschal lamb, the rubric under which he appears in the apocalyptic book of Revelation. In Harris's earlier novel, *Red Dragon*, references to the book of Revelation are even more insistent.[24] The serial killer at large is one who has adopted the name Red Dragon, in homage to god's antithesis in Revelation.

The hero of another bestselling, serial killer novel, *American Psycho*, is Patrick Bateman, a man who epitomizes the "best" of American society. He is masculine, homophobic, white, rich, profoundly materialistic, insatiably interested in pornography, Harvard educated, a Wall Street broker, and an unemotional man who wonders, "If I were an actual automaton, what difference would there really be?"[25] The novel thus offers an accurate, if partial, critique of the serial killer as the product of U.S. consumer ideologies, race and class hierarchies, and psychic numbing.

At the same time, *American Psycho* ignores any gender analysis of the origins or behaviors of the serial killer and becomes itself a work of gynocidal pornography. When Bateman murders men, the scenes are relatively short, take place outside, and are asexual. When women are murdered, the sequences are extensive, take place in private, and frequently follow upon several pages of basic sado-masochistic sexual description, clearly aimed at arousing the reader. At this point, Ellis offers scenes of unmatched violence wherein the women are tortured and killed in ornate and highly sexualized ways. In one, the killer nails a former girlfriend, Bethany, to the floor, cuts out her tongue, and then orally rapes her. In another, he forces a starving rat up a woman's vagina. Ironically, then, Ellis becomes what he purportedly critiques. Between boring segments satirizing designer clothes, expensive consumer products, and yuppie life-styles, he suddenly crackles to life, churning out top-drawer, design-er porn and gore—and capitalizing nicely on it, too.

American Psycho is also rife with apocalyptic references. Just prior to her torture and murder, Bethany tells Bateman that he has hung a painting upside down and asks how long it has been that way. "A millennium," Bateman answers cryptically. He then knocks her unconscious and enacts a religiously resonant form of torture:

> I drag her back into the living room, laying her across the floor over a white Voilacutro cotton sheet, and then I stretch her arms out, placing her hands flat on thick wooden boards, palms up, and nail three fingers on each hand, at random, to the wood by their tips. . . . I keep shooting nails into her hands until they're both covered.[26]

It is impossible to miss the references to Bethlehem and the crucifix-ion in this scene. Is Ellis setting up Bateman as an apocalyptic Antichrist? Or can we read this moment as a cynical twist on the anticipated second coming of Christ. In traditional Christian iconog-raphy, the divine, sacrificial, tortured, and crucified victim is male, as was the original lamb. The paschal lamb was the substitute for the murder of the first-born son demanded by Yahweh, a tradition reen-acted in the continuing sacrifice of sons in war by governmental and military fathers. Yet as *The Silence of the Lambs* attests, in modern imagery the passive, victimized lamb recalls the feminine body. And, as *American Psycho* makes plain, women are by no means divinized in the Christian era, but we certainly are sacrificed.

Later, Bateman dines with his current girlfriend and muses:

> To Evelyn our relationship is yellow and blue, but to me it's a gray place, most of it blacked out, bombed, footage from the film in my head is endless shots of stone and any language heard is utterly foreign, the sound flickering away over new images: blood pouring from automatic tellers, women giving birth through their assholes, embryos frozen or scrambled (which is it?), nuclear warheads, billions of dollars, the total destruction of the world.[27]

Such a description evokes the havoc and reversal of apocalypse. Ellis implies that the ascendancy of the serial killer is a harbinger of demise for the culture that has produced and immortalized him, a culture that proceeds from a core commitment to the violation of life-preservative taboos. This culture enacts on a grand scale an attack on the feminine, females, and often literally the womb, understood within our tradition to be an assault on the core source of life and, hence, the future itself.

However, another use of apocalyptic themes in serial killer fiction also merits some attention. Mention of the Dragon of the Apocalypse appears in George Stade's *Confessions of a Lady-Killer*, a novel in which a man murders three leading New York feminists in his quest to regain possession of his wife, who has left him to join their movement. Stade, a respected professor of English at Columbia University, makes it exceedingly clear that his killer is a hero, waging a holy war against civilization-destroying feminists and hence perfectly justified in his murders.[28] Curiously enough, the novel's cover shows a knight with the severed head of Medusa in his hands. Indeed, throughout this profoundly misogynist novel, feminists repeatedly are identified with monsters, Gorgons, and dragons—in short, with the Powers of Chaos, and therefore deserving of death:

> The monster who held Samantha in thrall [the feminist Jude Karnofsky, his first victim] was the Dragon of the Apocalypse herself. Karnofsky had at her disposal all the demonic forces released by the collapse of a civilization, our civilization.[29]

This description is a key to understanding one drift of apocalyptic references in serial killer narratives. In such references, the acceleration of violence of all types against women is a backlash phenomenon, meant to reassert threatened male power and stave off the socially transformative Powers of gorgonish feminism. The political apocalypse that Stade fears and so purely identifies with feminism is not the end of the world, but the end of the world we presently know—that is, the very world that has produced the serial killer: the world of patriarchy.

The Gorgon is a nemesis for practitioners not only of gynocide but also of geocide. She is the antithesis of the "pretty woman," the plaything providing succor to capitalist hotwads as they invest in military hardware and the object par excellence of the male proprietary gaze.[30] (See the 1989 film *Pretty Woman*.) In the *cock-eyed*[31] world of the "pretty woman," snools survey women and the world at will. Concomitantly, women are exhorted to make ourselves up as spectacles for manly peepers, while keeping our own eyes down.

Medusa, of course, completely reverses these roles: she is the one with the powerful and intimidating gaze. Not surprisingly, then, many male commentators read her as a symbol of castration: "If the woman looks, the spectacle provokes, castration is in the air, the Medusa's head is not far off."[32] The Gorgon does indeed signify the capacity to emasculate both would-be rapists and *phallotechnology*[33]—to put a stop to both gynocide and geocide. Ronald Reagan might have promised, quite speciously, that his Strategic Defense Initiative would be able to make nuclear weapons "impotent and obsolete,"[34] yet, quiet as it's kept, it is the Gorgon who truly possesses the power to disarm and render impotent "Mr. MX."

Lesbian poet and cultural critic Barbara Deming is one of many observers who finds an antinuclearist significance in the Gorgon:

> Ssisters, ssisters—of course they dread us.
> Theirs is the kingdom
> But it is built upon lies and more lies.
> The truth-hissing wide-open-eyed rude
> Glare of our faces—
> If there were enough of us—
> Could show their power and their glories
> To be what they merely are and
> Bring their death-dealing kingdom
> Down.[35]

Since 1947, the *Bulletin of the Atomic Scientists* has published a "doomsday clock" that depicts how many minutes there are until "midnight," that is, until a nuclear holocaust. As Mary Daly and I declare in *Websters' First New Intergalactic Wickedary of the English Language*, the Gorgon is the one whose "face can stop a clock." Daly writes:

Spinsters Spinning about-face face the fact that clockocracy's clocks are elementary moons. Whirling Witches Announce that the subject of clocks and calendars is about Face. . . . Lusty women, in tune with the Moon, pose the poignant Question: Is the Moon's Face the Face that can stop the doomsday clock?

. . . women as Gorgons look toward the madmen and turn them to stone—the doomsday men with their doomsday clocks whose tick-tocks mimic the rhythms of Lunar Time.[36]

Stopping the doomsday clock simultaneously arrests the linear drive of Father Time—that is, it debunks and dethrones the notion of progress, predicated so clearly upon an illusion of endless abundance (for the elite, anyway). The Gorgon as Dragon or Snake bespeaks another kind of time: spiral time, cycles of relative fullness and emptiness. Her menstrual signification and sense of timing reveal the Gorgon to us as the woman in the Moon, one of the Powers, an archaic class of angels who ensoul the celestial bodies. Let us insinuate her into our consciousness. Let us gaze into the mirror of her face to show our respect and to acquire inspiration that is celestial, yet simultaneously snaky and earthy.

The Last Laugh of the Medusa

You only have to look at the Medusa straight on to see her. . . . she's beautiful and she's laughing.

—Hélène Cixous, "The Laugh of the Medusa"[37]

Western Gorgon-, Serpent-, and Dragon-slaying myths have an uncanny resonance to myths connecting snakes with menstruation told by Australian native peoples. At the core of their symbol systems is the Rainbow Snake or Rainbow Dragon, a metaphor for sexuality, cyclical time, and the cosmic force that drives the universe. The Rainbow Snake, like any other complex spiritual symbol, embraces paradox. She lives both in the heavens and in the depths of water and the Earth. And while understood as primally female, she combines attributes of both female and male. Menstrual blood is always connected to the Rainbow Snake: "Blood must be flowing if 'the Snake' is to appear; *where there is no blood, there is no Snake.*"[38]

Some Australian indigenous stories concern a male attack on the Snake/Mother, including a few that parallel the Andromeda legend. Anthropologist Chris Knight calls one of these a "dragon-slaying myth in reverse."[39] The heroine in no way wants to go off with the interfering suitor. She wants to stay with the Rainbow Snake, who, as befits a protector, kills the would-be hero. In another story, men do accomplish the murder of the Rainbow Snake, but it is an act resulting in decidedly mixed emotions:

> Male myths justify the usurpation of women's menstrual power by describing the female version in lurid terms as a cannibalistic monster from which humanity had to be rescued.
> Interestingly, however, these male myths are rich with ambivalence and a sense of tragedy at the loss of the original Mother/Snake. . . . With her death a disaster of almost incomprehensible dimensions had occurred. "The loss to man," say the Murinbata, "was irreparable." The symbolic substitutes for her are felt to be inadequate.[40]

The symbolic substitutes referred to are elaborate rites of subincision and dramas of male rebirth from men. Subincision entails a cutting of the penis so that during rituals the wound can be reopened and the penis can bleed. As many male anthropologists agree, the bleeding men "are playing the role of menstruating women."[41] It is difficult to imagine male anthropologists concluding that their contemporary Western brethren have also manufactured rituals allowing them to play the role of menstruating women. Not bound by such gender loyalty, the Gorgons of Greenham Common, the British women's peace camp, loudly proclaim, "War Is Menstruation Envy."[42] Chris Knight tells us that in the Australian indigenous metaphysics, the Snake is "the force behind the changing of the seasons, the movements of the celestial bodies, the breeding times of animals and plants, and the cycles of life, death, and afterlife."[43] Unable or unwilling to summon the Snake through their own blood and body processes, envious patriarchal men have attacked and banished female menstrual power. They have implemented various symbol-laden substitutes, including the Christian obsession with the bloody, sacrificial body of the paschal lamb, Christ, in both the crucifixion and the sacrament of communion;[44] ritualistic, sacrificial sexual mutilation and murder of women and feminized males; and the mass bloodletting of war.

As cultural theorist Zoë Sofia cuttingly argues, Western patriarchs do not mutilate their own penises in a rite of subincision. They play out their bloody rituals not on their own bodies, but on the bodies of those designated as "others."[45] Making their penises into weapons rather than wounds, they attack the genitals of females and other less powerful males in sexual assaults and lynchings. Correspondingly, they use phallic weapons to massively spill blood in private assaults as well as war.

What can we say of a culture that taboos menstrual blood but allows the free flow of PCBs and chlorofluorocarbons? While scorning women's bodies as "foul sinks," technocrats blithely unearth, manufacture, and, with alarming regularity, release profoundly polluting substances into the ground, water, and air. Continually "killing" the Gorgon, they refuse to face the need for limitations on or prohibitions against their excursions.

In her poem "Mother Nature Sends a Pink Slip," Marilou Awiakta passes sentence upon these invaders in techno-corporate and dispassionate terms they can understand:

> To: Homo Sapiens
> Re: Termination
>
> My business is producing life.
> The bottom line is
> you are not cost-effective workers.
> Over the millennia, I have repeatedly
> clarified my management goals and objectives.
> Your failure to comply is well-documented.
> It stems from your inability to be
> a team player:
>   —you interact badly with co-workers
>   —contaminate the workplace
>   —sabotage the machinery
>   —hold up production
>   —consume profits
> In short, you are a disloyal species.
> Within the last decade

> I have given you three warnings:
>   —made the workplace too hot for you
>   —shaken up your home office
>   —utilized plague to cut back personnel
> Your failure to take appropriate action
> has locked these warnings into
> the Phase-Out Mode, which will result
> in termination.   No appeal.[46]

Awiakta read this poem during a visit to the University of New Mexico in December 1991. Leonard Tsosie, a lawyer in the audience, responded:

> One time in listening to an elderly Navajo man talking about the atom, one of the things that I remember him saying is that Mother Earth is good, but Mother Earth also has to protect herself and you can only go so far before you trigger Mother Earth's response. And one of the things that he was talking about—in Navajo we call it *'ánt'iih*—meaning that something that is bad. And if you keep digging and digging and digging, that elderly man said, eventually you will find Mother Earth's *'ánt'iih*. And then that's when we all go. When we dig that up. We may have gotten to the *'ánt'iih*, and if that is the case, that may be the end.[47]

Awiakta and Tsosie insist that we recognize a basic fact of life: If human beings do not respect Mother Earth's limits, the planet herself will respond with various forms of final—and fatal—devastations.

The horror of unrestrained mining expressed by Tsosie may seem strange to European-Americans, yet as environmental historian Carolyn Merchant details, taboos on mining were once a common feature of the ancient European world. These traditional strictures, however, were overturned by the forces of commercialism at the beginning of the modern era.[48]

Over 70 percent of the world's uranium mining takes place on the traditional lands of indigenous cultures in Canada, the United States, Ecuador, Brazil, China, India, Central Asia, Siberia, and Australia, wreaking environmental havoc, poisoning the land and the people, and continuing the genocide begun with colonialism. One of the organizers of the 1992 World Uranium Hearing, Claus Biegert, writes: "Around the globe, indigenous sacred sites and zones of taboo are identical with buried uranium deposits. This uncanny phenomenon bears witness to the spiritual wisdom of these peoples, a wisdom rooted deeply in the Earth. . . . Native peoples tell us that uranium should stay in the ground."

Not surprisingly, the ancient figure associated with indigenous taboos at uranium mining sites in Australia is none other than the Rainbow Serpent or Snake, that figure from menstrual myth who is kin to the Gorgon. Biegert reproduces a petroglyph from Australia depicting the Rainbow Snake assaulting and killing two men. He comments,

> The Rainbow Serpent on the Upper Yule River: a cosmic force from the rainbow awakened—male and female energies struggling. Indigenous artists of northwestern Australia's Njamal Tribe created this petroglyph long before the first white man set foot on the continent. The Aborigines tell us that the Rainbow Serpent, asleep in the earth, guards over those elemental powers beyond mankind's control. They warn us that any attempt to rob these powers from the earth will rouse the serpent from sleep, provoking its wrath: a terrible deluge of sickness and death.[49]

This connection between uranium and the Serpent or Dragon appears consistently throughout nuclear history. Consider the following three incidents from New Mexican nuclear history.

Los Alamos

In 1944, scientists at Los Alamos needed to determine the amount of uranium that would be needed to create a critical mass for the first bomb, Little Boy. To do this, Otto Frisch designed an experiment that involved fitting together two subcritical pieces in a way that would create a momentary critical mass, a split second in which there existed the conditions for an atomic explosion. Another scientist, Richard Feynman, reportedly was much amused by the plan and analogized it to tickling the tail of a sleeping dragon. From that point on, it became known as the Dragon Experiment. Twice, however, the Dragon awakened and laughed out loud: on separate occasions the experiment claimed the lives of two scientists, Harry Daghlian and Louis Slotin.[50]

Frisch himself gave the name Lady Godiva to the so-called naked assembly of critical materials equipping the Dragon Experiment. In this experiment, as in the most ancient myths, the Goddess and the Dragon/Snake appeared together. According to mythographer Barbara Walker, the name Godiva "is simply a combination of three different ways of saying 'Goddess.'" It was in the legend of Lady Godiva that "Peeping Tom" appeared, a fool who dared to spy on Godiva's nakedness and was, veritably, blinded by her light. Mythically, this tomfool had lots of company, for blindness was the punishment most commonly meted out to those caught "peeping at forbidden sacred mysteries."[51]

Edward Teller, "father of the hydrogen bomb," bragged about his behavior during the Trinity test of the first atomic bomb in 1945. He swore, "I wouldn't turn away. I wanted to look the beast in the eye."[52] But, of course, as Teller well knew, humans at close range could not safely look into the eye of the Bomb without protective goggles. Any who refused to turn away would be struck blind.

Teller's swaggering aside, truly looking at the "beast" involves not simply *eyeballing*[53] a mushroom cloud through protective lenses. Rather, it involves facing the Gorgon, the very last thing a snool like Teller would do. Yet half a century into the nuclear age, we know that we cannot forever avoid her gaze. Someday soon, nuclearist culture will have to relinquish its protective numbing and face up to the consequences of its high-tech peeping and tomfoolery, its disrespect for the Dragon and its profound violation of life and Earth-preservative taboos.

Laguna Pueblo

Laguna Pueblo is the site of the now inoperative Jackpile Uranium Mine. Laguna novelist and poet Leslie Marmon Silko reveals that in 1980 a gigantic stone snake formation appeared near the mine. Workers and regular visitors agreed that nothing like the giant stone formation had been there before and that it had happened quite suddenly. As Silko continues, "The stone snake seemed to have always been there. The entire formation was more than 30 feet long and 12 inches high, an eccentric outcrop of yellow sandstone mottled and peppered with darker iron ores, like the stone that had once formed the mesas that had been swallowed up by the open-pit mine." She connects the stone snake with Ma^{ah}'shra-True'-Ee, a sacred messenger from the Fourth World below who, as the old stories go, had once come to live at the lake near Laguna Village. However, the Snake deserted the people when some jealous neighbors "came one night and broke open the lake / so all the water was lost."[54]

The traditions of the Laguna people prohibit mining, but during the Cold War the United States government was in the grip of atomic bomb fever, so the tribe could not prevent this violation of the land. The mine did bring temporary jobs and money to the pueblo, but at a terrible cost. For, as Silko laments, the taboo transgression was reflected in tragedies throughout the pueblo, including teenage group suicides and mass murders. These acts of violence, she continues, "run as deep, but only as deep, as the deepest shafts with which humankind has pierced the Earth."

According to Silko, the Laguna people tell many stories explaining the sudden reappearance of the sacred messenger. In her 1991 novel, *Almanac of the Dead*, she offers one of her own: The stone snake is a harbinger of a world revolution in which indigenous people from everywhere will retake their lands from colonizers. The last lines of this rich and complex work read, "Sterling knew why the giant snake had returned now; he knew what the snake's message was to the people. The snake was looking south, in the direction from which the twin brothers and the people would come."[55]

Serpents are the guardians of elemental wisdom and knowledge, a fact that is acknowledged even in the creation myth of Christianity. Feminist thinkers have long pointed to the absurdities and misogyny of the Adam and Eve story: its negation and scapegoating of Eve; the ludicrous reversal of Eve's birth from Adam; the further reversal of blame, shame, and sin affixed to Eve's acceptance of the proffered knowledge; the slandering of the Snake; and the myth's carte blanche legitimation of man's total domination over nature.

Yet within this myth still linger stray memories of the earthly paradise, the wilderness, the living food, the cosmic Snake, the Goddess (Eve), and the Tree of Knowledge. The apple signifies not only knowledge, but a knowledge rooted in the Earth, a vital wisdom quite literally from the trees. This is something Mary Daly writes of in *Pure Lust* as an "Elemental" knowing or philosophy, "a form of philosophical be-ing/thinking that emerges together with metapatriarchal consciousness—consciousness that is in harmony with the Wild in nature and in the Self. . . . It is the force of reason rooted in instinct, intuition, passion. . . . rooted in love for the earth and for things that naturally are on earth."[56]

To partake of that wisdom, we might be inspired by Eve and endeavor to speak with our familiars—our relatives the Snake people. To wit, let us recognize another major reversal in the Christian version of the myth. According to the Bible, the injunction against eating of the Tree of Knowledge issues from god. But who is god? Clearly, he is nothing but a trespasser and a blowhard. The Tree is the province of the Snake.

Curiously enough, nowhere is the putative god-given injunction against pursuing forbidden fruit or knowledge respected by the god-fearing godfathers of the christotechnological tradition. An example is the 1946 ravings of the Jesuit philosopher Pierre Teilhard de Chardin:

> The fact remains that in laying hands on the very core of matter we have disclosed to human existence a supreme purpose: the purpose of pursuing ever further, to the very end, the forces of Life. In exploding the atom we took our first bite at the fruit of the great discovery, and this was enough for a taste to enter our mouths that can never be washed away: the taste for super-creativeness.[57]

In short, Teilhard was claiming that with the discovery of atomic fission, "man" drew nearer to being "super creative," essentially to being like his god. Moreover, man accomplished this feat by tasty taboo breaking: eating the forbidden fruit; pursuing and hounding, relentlessly, the forces of Life; and finally "laying hands" on the very core of matter/mother. The priest, in short, was describing (and rhapsodizing over) a rape. He was hailing the splitting of the atom as a divine act, which we might recognize as one resulting from a tradition of science as penetration into forbidden female mysteries.

Clearly, the injunction against eating the forbidden fruit without invitation was attributed erroneously to the male god. In truth, this injunction issued from the Snake. There is a critical message here for all questers of knowledge, be it scientific, technological, mystical, or sexual: one must wait to be invited by the Snake before presuming to eat. Patriarchy names all spaces—real and conceptual, bodily and global—as utterly open to conquest. Yet, it never has been more apparent than in our present times that humans cannot force an entrance through the gates of knowledge. We cannot sneak by a sleeping Dragon, but must await permission of that Dragon/Snake. In other words, we must carefully weigh the consequences of our actions, from the microcosm to the macrocosm, considering how the pursuit will affect "the changing of the seasons, the movements of the celestial bodies, the breeding times of animals and plants, and the cycles of life, death, and afterlife"—or else we court disaster.

WIPP

Environmental disaster now beckons in many forms, including the dangers resulting from our inability to safely dispose of nuclear waste. A 1991 report by Worldwatch Institute researcher Nicholas Lenssen estimates the worldwide volume of high-level nuclear waste at more than eighty thousand tons.[58] This estimate does not include low-level nuclear waste—such things as "the plutonium-contaminated dross produced by our nation's weapons facilities: rags, rubber gloves, shoe covers, lab coats, test tubes, beakers, pipes, valves, drill bits," and so on.[59] This latter type of waste is destined for permanent storage in southern New Mexico at WIPP, the Waste Isolation Pilot Plant. So dangerous is this "low-level" waste that the site must be covered over and protected from any leakage or incursion for the next ten thousand years—an impossible task worthy of any fairy tale. The Environmental Protection Agency (EPA) also faces an additional quandary at WIPP: how to design a marker that will dissuade anyone from entering the site or digging there hundreds and thousands of years hence—when no one speaks English anymore and any form of human or nonhuman cultures could exist in the area.

In an article in *Harper's* magazine, Alan Burdick reports upon the activities of an EPA-appointed group composed of archaeologists, anthropologists, astronomers, geologists, materials scientists, linguists, artists, architects, and psychologists. They have been commissioned to design what he terms "the ultimate KEEP OUT sign" for WIPP, a permanent marker that "should pierce the collective unconscious, resonate of death, fear, of a threat to the body. It should attract notice yet viscerally repulse."[60]

This task invokes the most profound sense of irony. Once upon a time, male gods and heroes "slew" the Gorgon, the Dragon, the Snake. That is, a shift in consciousness occurred whereby men felt empowered to invade others' spaces, to "rape" their relatives, to exploit cosmic energies, and to cannibalize the Mother/Earth. Now, faced with some of the almost unimaginably toxic results of those thoughtless incursions, they want to bury the evidence and to hide from the harm they have caused. However, they find that they need, in Burdick's words, the "ultimate KEEP OUT sign." Guess what? Their consummately foolish journey has come full circle. They need the Gorgon.

Medusa indeed must be shaking with mirth, literally cracking up. We had better prepare ourselves for deluges, earthquakes, and other tremors. This might well be the last laugh.

CHAPTER NINE

Facing the Unfaceable

We must face the Medusa, the unfaceable in ourselves, in order
to have access to the powers we require.
—*Chela Sandoval*[1]

In his bestselling meditation on male initiation, *Iron John*, men's
movement leader Robert Bly cites a dream of a contemporary man,
Keith Thompson, who describes himself as a "typical young man
'initiated' by women." His parents' marriage dissolved when he was
twelve. Thompson's main friends in college were feminists, and
when he graduated he got a job in state politics, where he worked
primarily with issues of concern to women:

> About that time he had a dream. He and a clan of she-wolves
> were running in the forest. Wolves suggested to him primarily
> independence and vigor. The clan of wolves moved fast through
> the forest, in formation, and eventually they all arrived at a
> riverbank. Each she-wolf looked in the water and saw her own
> face there. But when Keith looked in the water, he saw no face
> at all.

Bly admits that dreams are complicated and mysterious, yet he ven-

195

tures an interpretation of this dream: "The last image . . . suggests a disturbing idea. When women, even women with the best intentions, bring up a boy alone, he may in some way have no male face, or he may have no face at all."[2]

I cannot completely dismiss this interpretation: dreams are indeed many-layered and subtle. Yet I must offer a reading of my own. Under the terms of contemporary manhood, feminists strike terror into the hearts of men. And feminists—females who do not subscribe to traditional femininity—do not hide their faces. Most men are convinced, even if unconsciously, by the dictates of male supremacy that for them to be "men," women must be subordinate. Therefore, many men experience all independent and vigorous females as castrating, that is, as robbing them of their essence, their face. Thus, when there are strong women, there are only "soft" men. Bly certainly promotes this belief. The implication is clear: in order for men to have faces, women must submit to defacement.

In chapter 4, I described a popular-culture landscape of defaced, decapitated, and degraded female images: women with products in place of faces, fembot walk-ins, beautifully torn fragments of female bodies. As these images attest, the murder of the Gorgon is being ritually reimagined and reenacted every day, striking fear into the hearts of women. In addition, females are endlessly met with exhortations to beauty: the incessant "make-over" sessions and the ubiquitous "before/after" pictures. Look closely at these pictures. "Before" is the Gorgon. The make-over is her death mask. Naked female faces are taboo. They must be veiled or cosmeticized, for snools[3] cannot look upon the Gorgon and live.

Patriarchal "manhood" depends upon the denial and ongoing murder of the Gorgon. Understandably, patriarchal fools fear and banish her, for they know they have transgressed against her and would lose face entirely when measured by her gaze. Yet patriarchal womanhood likewise depends upon denial of the Gorgon. Females, too, have learned to avert our eyes—to fear coming out as Gorgons.

The Gorgon dispels psychic numbing. When we face her, we acknowledge and experience what has been blocked, repressed, and denied. We see through the "pretty woman" romanticization and lies, and we recognize the pornographies, prostitutions, and abuses of everyday life, whatever our situations. Sometimes we approach the Gorgon gradually, uncovering her a bit at a time as we slowly regain our passions and our senses. Sometimes terror or cowardice overtakes us, and we cover her up again for long periods, sinking back into facelessness. Some snool-identified women avoid the Gorgon religiously, knowing that facing her entails relinquishing any number of class, race, age, and beauty privileges accorded to those in select categories—wealthy, white, professionally powerful, young, pretty.

Sometimes an individual's encounter with the Gorgon is sudden, shocking, and irreversible, as it is for the two women in the 1991 film sensation *Thelma and Louise*. This is the story of two ordinary women, one of whom, Louise, shoots a man who has disrespected and raped her friend. The killing is not required to stop the rape; it is a cosmically justified act of rage, revenge, and perhaps even prevention. Neither woman kills anyone else in the movie. They become road-running outlaws who eventually, in order to avoid capture, drive their car over the cliff of the Grand Canyon.

However it occurs, once one fully faces the Medusa, she (or he) is initiated into the realms of the Powers, her entire life and consciousness transmute, and she never can quite go back to the illusions of her former life. Like Thelma and Louise, she will now rather take that metaphorical leap off the cliff into the unknown than return to the land of the living dead.

Facing the Gorgon means committing to revolution in our lifetimes, and the sooner the better. I remember remarking once at a party in May 1992 that an astrologer had told me 1993 would be a revolutionary year. The woman I was talking to, by all accounts a social radical, looked at me and said, "Oh no. Not so soon. Can't we wait a few years?" A joke perhaps, but my inner Gorgon wasn't laughing.

Facing the unfaceable also means that we must face our contradictions and weaknesses and work out those things that are shameful and painful to us: our participation in domination, our failures, our cowardice, our fears. Thus, facing the Gorgon means, for example, white women acknowledging and disavowing racism and owning up to the ways we are oppressive and wrong, or any of us who are batterers or abusers facing up to these behaviors, tracing them to their origins, and ceasing to practice them. These are admittedly painful journeys, and it might be more expedient to avoid them entirely. We might prefer to travel instead along familiar paths of denial and see the source of oppression only in others. The Gorgon, of course, has no truck with psychic numbing. She, in her most profound essence, acknowledges the truth, sheds denial, and opens our metaphorical all-seeing eyes. She knows that only by fearlessly facing reality can we ever hope to change it.

Classical scholar Page duBois writes, "The myth of Medusa is a myth of fear of women, fear of their archaism, their self-sufficiency, their buried power."[4] Certainly, facing the Medusa also means facing our strengths. These are traits that the godfathers fearfully and mendaciously have deemed shameful, ugly, or monstrous in ourselves: our sexualities, our unruly bodies, our agedness, our energies, and our Powers, not only of life but also of *death*. Gazing into the Gorgon's eye, we acknowledge the workings of sacred female Powers in the self, in the cosmos, and even in nuclear technology itself.

Why a Gorgon Woman Is Like a Nuclear Power Plant, or Why a Thinking Woman Is Like the Bomb

Around the turn of the century . . . a few scientists began to observe the atom asserting its nature, which was more flexible and unpredictable than had been thought. . . . As research progressed the word "mystery" began to appear in scientific writing. . . . Perhaps the universe resembled a great thought more than a great machine.
—*Marilou Awiakta*[5]

In much Euro-American feminist thinking, including my own, the primary impulse has been to expose the phallic character of nuclear technology and weaponry and to oppose that masculinist force. Yet in the writings of Native American philosophers Marilou Awiakta and Paula Gunn Allen, the predominant movement is to reclaim the atom from its immurement in phallocentric language, sexuality, and religion and to recall its repressed sacred and gynocentric face.

Social theorists Emile Durkheim and later Roger Caillois observed that all religious beliefs share one characteristic: the classification of all things as either sacred or profane. The *sacred* "represents a dangerous force, incomprehensible, intractable but eminently efficacious. For the one who decides to have recourse to it, the problem consists of capturing and utilizing it in his best interest, while at the same time protecting himself against the risks inherent in using a force so difficult to control."[6] The sacred, then, like the mythic Medusa, is "both desired and dreaded, attractive and repellent, respected and fearful."[7]

Such a concept, though describing an ancient religious idea, uncannily evokes the properties of nuclear energy, compelling us to recognize atomic Powers as sacred. One cultural theorist, Jacques Ellul, has proposed that the sacred must have had a meaning to ancient peoples "just as real as the fabrication of the first tools."[8] I agree with him and find unmistakable manifestations of the sacred in contemporary phenomena associated with radiation and nuclear technology. For example, just as the sacred is paradoxically both dangerous and efficacious, so too is radiation. As is well known, radiation can "kill as well as cure."[9] When Caillois's determinants of the sacred are compared with statements describing aspects of nuclear technology, we can find an uncanny correspondence between the archaic mystical concept and the modern nuclear reality:

The sacred is related . . . to certain objects. [Caillois][10]

Uranium and plutonium are the radioactive elements upon which all nuclear technology depends.

The sacred is related . . . to certain beings (kings, priests). . . . Religion is the administration of the sacred. [Caillois][11]

The creators of strategic doctrine actually refer to members of their own community as "the nuclear priesthood." [Carol Cohn][12]

[The sacred] stimulates feelings of terror and veneration. [Caillois][13]

It is a striking fact that none of those present [at the Trinity test] react-

ed to the phenomenon as professionally as he had supposed he would. They all, even those—who constituted the majority—ordinarily without religious faith or even any inclination thereto, recounted their experiences in words derived from the linguistic fields of myth and theology. [Robert Jungk][14]

Contact with [the sacred] becomes dangerous. Automatic and immediate punishment would strike the imprudent one, as surely as flame burns the hand that touches it. The sacred is always more or less "what one cannot approach without dying." [Caillois][15]

A dose of 600 rems or more produces acute radiation illness. . . . Victims die of infection and/or massive hemorrhage. . . . There is no "safe" amount of radioactive material or dose of radiation. [Caldicott][16]

An unprepared individual cannot bear such a transformation of energy [contact with the sacred]. The substance of the sacrilege becomes turgid, its branches diffuse and twist, its flesh decomposes, it soon dies of languor or convulsions. [Caillois][17]

Within 48 hours of exposure [to 3,000 rems or more] the brain cells swell and enlarge. . . . Confusion, delirium, stupor, psychosis and ataxia . . . [precede] death. [Caldicott][18]

The sacred cannot be subdued, diluted or divided. It is indivisible and always a totality wherever it is found. [Caillois][19]

Plutonium does not simply vanish at the death of a contaminated organism. If, for example, someone were to die of a lung cancer induced by plutonium and were then cremated, contaminated smoke might carry plutonium particles into someone else's lungs. [Caldicott][20]

The sacred, like the Gorgon and like radioactivity itself, is always that which "one cannot approach without dying." As such, it must be guarded with taboo and treated with ultimate respect. Yet that has not been the case with pornotechnic culture's treatment of the atom.

Caillois speaks of the sacred as "the inexhaustible source that creates, sustains, and renews [life]."[21] Awiakta speaks of atomic energy in similar terms: It is "the life force in process—nurturing, enabling, enduring, fierce." She sees atomic energy as not only sacred, but as ineluctably linked to female Powers: "I call it the atom's mother heart. Nuclear energy is the nurturing energy of the universe. Except for stellar explosions, this energy works not by fission (splitting) but by fusion—attraction and melding." Awiakta further points to modern culture's profound irreverence toward atomic power—evidenced most blatantly in the splitting of the atom—and, correspondingly, toward women. As such, she contends, the atomic age has special, even ontological, significance for women:

> In theory, nature has been linked to woman for centuries— from the cosmic principle of the Great Mother-Goddess to the familiar metaphors of Mother Nature and Mother Earth. But to connect the life force with living women is something only some ancient or so-called "primitive" cultures have been wise enough to do. The linear Western, masculine mode of thought has been too intent on conquering nature to learn from her a basic truth: *to separate the gender that bears life from the power to sustain it is as destructive as to tempt nature itself.* . . . But the atom's mother heart makes it impossible to ignore this truth any longer. She is the interpreter not only of new images and mental connections for humanity, but also, most particularly for women, who have profound responsibilities in solving the nuclear dilemma.[22]

The "mother heart" is the first of several female metaphors through which Awiakta understands nuclear energy. Astonishingly, as a child growing up on the nuclear reservation at Oak Ridge, Tennessee, she too found a "woman" in a nuclear power plant. She recalls this scene from her childhood:

> Scientists called the reactor "The lady" and, in moments of high emotion, referred to her as "our beloved reactor."
> "What does she look like, Daddy?"
> "They tell me she has a seven-foot shield of concrete around a graphite core, where the atom is split." I asked the color of graphite. "Black," he said. And I imagined a great, black queen, standing behind her shield, holding the splitting atom in the shelter of her arms.

Awiakta's vision, far from being one of a possessed beautiful woman, is one of an autonomous and infinitely powerful cosmic being. I interpret her experience to be a modern encounter with the most archaic Black Goddess—black because she represents "the great darkness at both the beginning and the end of life's 'daytime' or conscious cycle . . . the infinite void at both the beginning and the end of the universe."[23] The Virgin Mary, no matter how pallid and possessed she is in many representations, has also become a keeper of this tradition. Religious historian Ean Begg notes that more than four hundred of the world's images of the Madonna, such as Mexico's Virgen de Guadalupe, are black and that such figures represent an "elemental and uncontrollable source of life, possessing a spirit and wisdom of its own not subject to organization or the laws of rationality."[24]

Paula Gunn Allen similarly finds "elemental and uncontrollable" female Powers in nuclear power—not in the reactor but, boldly, in the Bomb itself. In a published excerpt from her novel in progress, *Raven's Road*, two Indian lesbians, Raven and Allie, deliberately station themselves to watch the blast from an above-ground nuclear test. Later, Allie, who had done this before and anticipates her partner's response, asks Raven what she saw in the cloud. Scarcely believing herself, Raven remembers: "'An old woman . . . I remember now. I saw an old woman's face."[25] Through such daring figuration, Allen defies the masculinist hubris that sees only a fatherly face in technologically channeled Powers.

In the theology of the Keres people (a cultural complex of Southwestern Pueblos whose language is Keresan), the original creator is Thought Woman or Spider Grandmother, who continually thinks and dreams and spins the world into being. In a 1991 conversation I held with Allen, she rooted the exigencies of the nuclear age firmly in this, to use her word, cosmogyny:[26] "I know that she's the lady that made the uranium and she's the lady that made radioactivity, and she's the lady that dreamed the dream of nuclear fission. She dreamed it. Men could not have found the idea if she didn't give it to them. When she dreams, and that's what Thought Woman does, what she says, what she dreams, becomes."[27]

The test of the first atomic bomb was code-named Trinity. Certainly, this name recalls the Christian trinity, but it evokes countless other divine figurations as well. Significantly, Thought Woman is one member of a *trinity* of sisters, the other members being Naotsete, or Sun Woman, and Iyatiku, or Corn Woman. Long ago, Naotsete quarreled with her sister Iyatiku and left. Allen continued:

> Uranium was first mined at Laguna, and the form it comes in is called yellowcake. The color of femaleness is yellow. . . . I can't help thinking that Iyatiku, who is Corn Woman, is associated with all this and that yellowcake is connected with yellow Corn Woman. Around Laguna they say she's come back. And they say it with respect to the bomb. And "she" is Naotsete, who is Sun Woman, who went away long ago, but she was to come back some day. Well, I can't think of anything more vividly Sun Woman than the Bomb.[28]

At first, I was shocked by these ascriptions of female Powers to the Bomb: How was this any different than Christians identifying the Bomb with the return of Jesus Christ? Yet as I began to ponder this image, I remembered that *shock* can be a most clarifying experience.

Symbols and metaphors, like words, are alive. Mary Daly, discussing the meaning of symbol and metaphor, comments that symbols are meant to open up doorways into previously indescribable and inaccessible realities. Moreover, she writes: "As theologian Nelle Morton has explained, metaphors evoke action, movement. They Name/evoke a shock, a clash with the 'going logic' and they introduce a new logic."[29] Such a semiotic shock is precisely what I experienced when I first encountered Allen's constellations of the Bomb as Old Woman or Sun Woman and yellowcake uranium as Iyatiku. Certainly these metaphors, based in cosmogynic realities, introduce a logic that is completely contrary, even infuriating, to patriarchal logic.

The previously described Jesus-Bomb equation trots out patriarchal man's identification with the forces of radiant light and his warfare against the despised dark—in the form of Earth/mother/matter. There is nothing new in this metaphor, nothing to make us think—only further numbing and hopeless acquiescence to annihilation. Allen's metaphor instead claims for females an identification with and hence some influence with the cosmic radiant forces of the universe. It suggests that in order for what is commonly understood as Goddess spirituality to achieve the world-transformative power that so many feminists argue it is capable of, we must face the active and

current presence of female Powers. Such Powers, the metaphor further suggests, exist not only in past myths and familiar benevolent
images such as Mother Nature and Mother Earth, but also in contemporary, technological, and even death-dealing realities.

Of course, such a shocking metaphor raises some disturbing
questions. I next asked Allen if her ascription of female Powers to the
Bomb could lead to the idea that women should encourage the
development or use of nuclear bombs. She replied,

> In my novel, as far as I've gotten with it, Allie and Raven are just
> observing, because that's what this old woman told Allie to do.
> She told her that there was this thing going on and she was sup-
> posed to observe to make sure they did it right. But the old
> woman didn't really know what she was seeing—this was in the
> 1930s—and she didn't know what the "it" was that they were
> doing or how they were going to do it right or how they were
> going to do it wrong. She just knew what she knew and she said
> what she said. And I think that there's something in that, in
> what she said. In a way, what we have to do is watch them. We
> can't stop them. We have to watch so that at the psychological
> moment, we can change the direction. Because I think that a new
> planet or a new being or a new world—something—is being
> born. It has something to do with the Bomb, though I don't
> know what it has to do with it. But it's like some vast magical
> rite that's going on, and we don't know enough about magic to
> be able to interfere.[30]

Certainly, many of us will resist her idea that female Powers
"thought" of such an agent of megadeath as the Bomb. Nevertheless,
Allen does radically upset the mind-set that the Bomb can be fully
understood as a thing invented by and totally under the control of
elite Western men; the mind-set that females are merely passive spectators to nuclear energy and, moreover, have no engagement with
the Powers of death; and the mind-set that the Earth is inert, soulless
matter, an object, a reflection of the patriarchal "feminine"—that is,
passive, endlessly forgiving and masochistic, willing to ceaselessly
absorb every abuse and disrespect aimed at her. These mind-sets
could not be more wrong.

R-E-S-P-E-C-T:
Find Out What It Means to Me

Respect: "Dread, fear. . . . to face . . . (Obs)."
—*Oxford English Dictionary*

Queen of Soul Aretha Franklin urges all women to demand respect. Gorgons agree and further tell us to be sure to greet the full moon face-to-face as a sign of respect. In my dictionaries, the word *respect* has not only the expected meanings of "honor," "esteem," and "consideration," but also the more archaic meanings cited above. *Respect* is derived from Latin words meaning "to look back" or "to look again." In respecting female Powers, we face them, looking again, reconsidering, and restoring them not to a place of dominance, but to a place of reverence.

In his extensive study of nuclear symbolism, Spencer Weart finds many ascriptions of cosmic, sacred power given to the atom. For example, the most common (though scientifically inaccurate) representation of the atom is the mini–solar-system model, the "little ball ringed by ellipses, standing for a nucleus with electrons whirling around it." Weart comments, "Any scholar familiar with symbology could identify in an instant a design characterized by a central object, symmetry (especially fourfold symmetry) and perhaps a surrounding circle. It is a mandala."[31] According to Jung, the mandala signifies a cosmic union of opposites. According to *Webster's*, "contemplation of the mandala leads to mystical insight."

Significantly, an incidence of atom-gazing resulted in one of the most arresting nuclear symbols I have ever seen: the "emblem" that Awiakta tells us she has "created for my life and work—the sacred white deer of the Cherokee, leaping in the heart of an atom."[32] This emblem came to her in 1977, when Awiakta visited the Museum of Science and Energy in Oak Ridge, Tennessee, and experienced an epiphany: "I was looking at an immense translucent blue model of the atom. Inside it, tiny lights, representing electrons, whirl in orbit. As I watched this, my state of consciousness slowly altered, and suddenly I saw Little Deer leaping in the heart of the atom."[33]

As she explained in her 1991 conversation with me, "Little Deer is a spirit of reverence for the sacred circle of life. He embodies the principle of never taking without giving back. He is a protean symbol, reminding us of the spirit that is always on the move, always circling." Just as the hunter must "pray words of pardon" for the life he is given, lest he be pursued by Little Deer, who "swiftly pains and cripples his bones so he never can hunt again,"[34] so, too, must contemporary culture ensure respect for nuclear and other technologies or else suffer retribution.

When asked if she is pronuclear or antinuclear, Awiakta responds that she is

> *pro-reverence.* . . . Nuclear energy is here and has been for almost 50 years. While people are fighting over their "pro" and "anti" positions, the reactors keep operating, the atom keeps splitting. Who is nurturing that process, making it safe? . . . To avoid disaster, we have to create a consensual climate, a center where responsible men and women from every sphere—science, religion, industry, community—can unite to work out solutions. Women should be—and are not—well represented on the councils working for solutions.[35]

Similarly, Carol Lee Sanchez, a poet and essayist of Laguna and Sioux ancestry, deplores yet another paradigm of splitting: the modern Western schism between the sacred and the profane. She contrasts this to the tribal tradition that recognizes "all things in the known universe to be equally sacred," including what we deem to be inanimate and man-made objects. Pointing to "an ever-widening gulf between 'daily life' and 'spirituality'" in technological culture, she avers, "I believe Euro-Americans waste the resources and destroy the environment in the Americas because they are not spiritually connected to this land base, because they have no ancient mythos or legendary origins rooted to this land."

Sanchez believes that not only must all nontribal Americans acknowledge and become thoroughly familiar with the indigenous spiritual frameworks of this hemisphere, but we must rethink Western culture's social and technological processes and philosophies. We must compare them with tribal principles, philosophies, and social structures, working ultimately toward the creation of "a non-Indian Tribal community." Such a community formally acknowledges the sacredness of everyday life through songs and ceremonies. It also reverences the realities of the modern world, creating

> new songs of acknowledgment as well as ceremonies that include metals, petrochemicals, and fossil fuels, electricity, modern solar power systems, and water power systems. . . . it is very important to make sacred . . . the new ways and elements in our lives—from nuclear power. . . to plastics to computers . . . in order to restore harmony and balance to our out-of-control systems and, in particular, to our modern technologies.[36]

Of course, Western culture already holds "sacred" its technologies. "Songs" reiterating the power and glory of the machine, the godliness of the warhead, the promise of religious and sexual fulfillment in the consummation of the Earth, and the capturing and profaning of female Powers underlie many of the ads, popular tunes, and metaphors as described in earlier chapters. Yet this brand of sadomasochistic worship has nothing to do with holding something sacred. It stems from a worldview that reveres opposition and domination rather than respect, balance, harmony, and consanguinity as the basic principles of the universe.

Allen, Awiakta, and Sanchez insist that we face the metaphysical implications of modern technology. When we reverence technology, treating it as sacred, we begin to think and act in ways that restore harmony and balance. "It's not a toy," Lakota shaman Wallace Black Elk cautions, "when you have the wisdom of the Creator and the power of Grandmother, one from each, in your hands. The power is the atom."[37]

Hence, we don't play with fire—including nuclear fire, firearms, combustion engines, and so on. We tell the truth about the inherent dangers of these forms, and we institute life-preservative taboos. We *respect* and do not try to rape, split, possess, or control cosmic Powers. We use the Earth's resources sparingly and with great caution. Frequently, we leave resources utterly alone. For example, we do not disturb sacred uranium sites unless we can figure out how to rebury the uranium sacredly and safely. Otherwise, it will return to us as ineffably toxic radioactive waste—the unshielded rage of the elements, living death laughing in our faces.

Facing *Our* Rage

The Gorgon/Medusa image has been rapidly adopted by large
numbers of feminists who recognize her as one face of our own
rage. Besides the daily outrages women face in patriarchy, physical violence against women is widespread and multiform. Such
dangers make is desirable and vitally important for women
to learn how to manifest a visage that will repel men when necessary.
                                    —*Emily Culpepper*[38]

Just as the atom's mother heart reacts, in Awiakta's words, with
"ferocity" when "her whole is disturbed," so too must human
females respond with rage when our integrity is disrespected. The
story of Thelma and Louise suggests that once women have lived
outside men's law, renounced the role of sacrificial lambs, and faced
their rage, there can be no return. Some women have expressed dis-
comfort with the ending of the film, seeing it as a defeat. I see it
entirely differently. Thelma and Louise's "suicide" is purely metaphorical. These women have faced the unfaceable and undergone
profound transformation. They have faced the Gorgon, and they are
no longer mortal. By the film's end, Thelma and Louise are no longer
"women." Their constructed selves have "died," and they have
become mythic beings, immortals. As the popular T-shirt says,
"Thelma and Louise Live Forever."

This gorgonish concept of revenge—of women fighting back and
killing those who would rape, abuse, or kill them—is an increasingly prevalent theme in fiction authored by women. For example,
The Weekend by Helen Zahavi features an ordinary Englishwoman,
Bella, who is harassed by obscene phone calls and rape threats. After
suffering these threats for some weeks, she decides that she finally
has had enough and kills her harasser with no great difficulty.
Having done this, she becomes her own style of serial killer, slaying
men who assault her. In the last scene, Bella is walking along
Brighton Beach at night when a man approaches and attacks her. He
is himself a serial killer named "Jack," who strangles, rapes, and
mutilates women. But Bella is prepared with her switchblade and
knifes him repeatedly until he dies. Zahavi leaves the reader with a
final message:

If you see a woman walking, if she's stepping quietly home, if you see her flowing past you on the pavement. If you'd like to break her brittle bones, and you want to hear the hopeless pleading, and you want to feel the pink flesh bruising, and you want to taste the taut skin bleeding.

If, in fact, you see her and you want her.

Think on. Don't touch her. Just let her pass you by. Don't place your palm across her mouth and drag her to the ground.

For unknowingly, unthinkingly, unwittingly you might have laid your heavy hand on Bella. And she's woken up this morning with the knowledge that she's finally had enough.[39]

In *Mercy* by Andrea Dworkin, the narrator is Andrea, a woman born into an age already in thrall to mass murder: "I was born in 1946, after Auschwitz, after the bomb. I never wanted to kill, I had an abhorrence for killing but it was raped from me, raped from my brain; obliterated, like freedom."[40] First assaulted as a child by a man in a movie theater, Andrea recounts years of sexual abuse and the social complicity involved in its proliferation. By the age of twenty-seven, Andrea is living on the streets, inhabiting a "body packed with rage" and enunciating a political principle: "It is very important for women to kill men." She acts on this principle, going out at night to find drunken bums and kicking them to death. She envisions an army of girls who will burn down Times Square, gather en masse to kill abusive husbands and/or pimps, and who "are ready for Mr. Wall Street who will follow any piece of ass down any dark street; now he's got a problem; it is very important for women to kill men."[41]

Dworkin is best known for her ceaseless work against pornography, which she views as both an enactment and an incitement to violence against women. She is the author, with Catharine MacKinnon, of an antipornography civil ordinance.[42] By explicitly advocating serial gender murder in *Mercy*, Dworkin challenges those who defend pornography as a mere representation of violence, not equivalent to or causally connected to acts or statements in the real world. The average reader, accustomed to male violence against females but not the reverse, may find Dworkin's advocacy of male death far more shocking and reprehensible than Bret Easton Ellis's imagined depredations against women in *American Psycho* or Guns N' Roses tuneful admission that "I used to love her but I had to kill her."[43] Of course, Dworkin is thus intentionally challenging us to examine the normalization of misogynist, lethal violence in popular culture and its defense through classic liberal principles.

Mercy ends with a threat: "I went out; at night; to smash a man's face in; I declared war. My *nom de guerre* is Andrea One; I am reliably told there are many more; girls named courage who are ready to kill."[44] One such "girl" is named Hothead Paisan, and we find her in one of the most thrilling, courageous, and riotous creations of contemporary feminist culture: the comic book series, or "zine," *Hothead Paisan: Homicidal Lesbian Terrorist*, written and illustrated by Diane DiMassa.

The gorgonish Hothead strikes back against "dickheads" everywhere, harassing and even killing and castrating men who abuse women—street thugs, gynecologists, anti-abortion terrorists. At the same time, Hothead, frequently in conversation with various types of feminists, questions the meaning of her violence. On occasion, the author herself will enter into the "zine's" action.

In *Hothead 5*, one woman, Fran, calls up DiMassa decrying Hothead's tactics, saying that she is "disgustingly violent" and "acts *just like* the men she's bashing." Fran speaks for many feminists who argue, as she does, that "we, as women, must set an example and act in a peaceful, non-violent way *godamm it*." DiMassa assures her that Hothead herself is somewhat out to lunch, "buzzed out on too much T.V.!" The whole thing, she explains, is a "satire," mocking in particular the superviolent mass media, while also providing a fantasy that allows women to vent their justifiable rage. DiMassa asks Fran if she has ever been "so pissed-off at someone that you fantasized about killing them? Like maybe possibly your Uncle George." At this point, Fran, clearly an incest survivor, understands completely and writes out a check for a subscription to *Hothead Paisan*.[45]

Whatever one thinks of the ethics of recommending or committing revenge murder, it is imperative to recognize a central motif in *Mercy, Hothead Paisan,* and all the other women's works dealing with murder: feminist reclamation of the Powers of action, rage, and even of death.

In mainstream films and literature, only very occasionally are women given license to kill. Clarice Starling, in both the novel and film versions of *The Silence of the Lambs*, has the power briefly, but at great cost to her soul.[46] Several extremely popular Hollywood films also feature lethal women. For example, *Aliens* (1986) and *Fatal Attraction* (1987) present "good" women who kill, but, of course, these characters are not so subtly legitimated by the fact that they are defending home and children against vicious *female* predators. *Thelma and Louise*, the film featuring a woman who wrathfully kills a male predator, aroused an enormous amount of controversy and' was denigrated as "fascist" and "degrading to men"[47] by several male reviewers—reactions that betrayed a deep uneasiness with women violently responding to male oppression.

Significantly, these same reviewers did not rail against the 1992 film *Basic Instinct*, in which women again spectacularly kill men. But in this film, in keeping with the myth of feminine evil, they kill unjustifiably, wantonly, and for pleasure. *Basic Instinct*, a wonder of misogynist, homophobic, paranoid fantasy, has only four female characters. All four of them are bisexual or lesbian, and all are remorseless, self-absorbed killers. Moreover, the young, blonde, beautiful "heroine" is not only fabulously wealthy and diabolically clever, but she kills men explicitly for erotic pleasure. Such plotting by no means develops a gorgonish conceptualization of the Powers of death. Instead, it enacts a profound reversal: a woman is cast as a serial sex killer, that paradigm of masculinist death power. In keeping with the men's movement's emphasis on male victimization, this film invites male viewers to imagine themselves as the sexual prey, rather than the abusers, of women. Simultaneously, it functions as an act of faith in the traditional sexist belief that evil originates in and is the "instinctual" property of women.

Ironically, in patriarchal culture, serial killers often become deathless. Immortality is the dominating motif in Jack the Ripper fantasies, and that theme pervades the lore associated with such fictional fellows as Dr. Hannibal Lecter. This occurs as well in James Ellroy's 1986 novel, *Killer on the Road*, in which the imprisoned serial murderer concludes his narrative, "I implode into a space beyond all laws, all roadways, all speed limits. In some dark form, I will continue."[48] The myth that the sex killer lives in perpetuity legitimates and naturalizes the endless perpetuation of sexual abuse.

Significantly, the serial killer whom Bella slays in the climactic scene of *The Weekend* is named "Jack." Author Helen Zahavi thus declares war against the myth of the eternal Ripper. In reclaiming the Powers of death, it is imperative that females declare our resolve to fight back, and fight back lethally, against those who attack us with murderous intent. At the same time, we must break the grip of the immortal Ripper on our symbol system. We can do so by reassociating men with nurturance and the life forces, by restoring dignity to death, by making matter and women once again sacred, and by conjuring immortal female Powers.

We Walk the Back of the Tiger by Patricia A. Murphy is a 1988 lesbian-feminist novel about a male serial killer. In this story, the white killer of young college women is himself finally slain by an African-American prostitute who paints a "red teardrop in the center of her forehead."[49] Anyone familiar with this characteristic iconography will recognize this woman as the avatar of the Black Goddess Kali, "the Hindu Triple Goddess of creation, preservation, and destruction. . . . the basic archetypal image of the birth-and-death Mother, simultaneously womb and tomb, giver of life and devourer of her children."[50] Like the Gorgon, Kali refuses the rigid dichotomization of death and life, as well as their packaging into separate and unequal gender bundles. In a world without serial murder, it is not Jack the Ripper but the Medusa, not Hannibal Lecter but Thelma and Louise who live forever.

Death Becomes Her

Since the Crone was death, one could see her "face to face" only in one's final moments of life. . . . Many myths present the idea that the Crone could kill with a straight look from her unveiled eye. . . . Perhaps the best known of these evil-eye myths was that of Medusa . . . whose petrifying look may have symbolized the "turning to stone" of the dead.
—*Barbara Walker*[51]

Feminist theorist Charlene Spretnak writes: "Patriarchal culture alienates men from the life-giving processes, so their concern becomes the other half of the cycle: death."[52] The response of "father of the Bomb" J. Robert Oppenheimer to the Bomb's first appearance has been quoted ad infinitum; still, it bears repeating here. Borrowing from the *Bhagavad Gita*, Oppenheimer looked into the mushroom cloud and chanted, "I am become Death." This appropriation of cosmic death is but one of many in a long line of patriarchal appropriations. Death most becomes the Gorgon and Crone, and the reconstellation of these Powers in the contemporary imagination is, in part, a direct response to the colossal disturbance effected by the invention and proliferation of weapons of mass death.

What does it mean that men turn to stone when looked upon by Medusa? One meaning, quite simply, is that they die, literally or metaphorically. Classical scholar Page duBois dismisses one common interpretation of the Medusa myth and suggests another: "I see it not as a discourse about castration but rather about the association of the female body with the earth. The earth is full of stones, which are seen by the Greeks as her bones, as seeds of human beings; the earth is also the place of burial. To be turned to stone by the gaze of the mother is to return to the earth."[53] Facing the Gorgon, "women" and "men"—that is, hierarchically gendered selves—do indeed "die"; that is, they transmute—change into beings beyond patriarchal classification and containment.

The Greek myth of the slaying of the Gorgon by Perseus narrates snooldom's unending desire to appropriate the Powers of death from the mother and from the Earth. This desire has resulted in men's profound identification with death and destruction, culminating in the twentieth-century heroization/and divinization of the emblems of pure death, from Jack the Ripper to the Bomb. Such emblems are utterly divorced from life-giving capacities. Curiously enough, the Medusa myth predicts these atrocious developments. First of all, it contains a sexual murder and mutilation, for Medusa, in Freudian thought and elsewhere, is frequently read as a symbol of the vulva. Secondly, Perseus uses the head of the Gorgon as a weapon of mass death in war, anticipating the mass-murderous capacities of nuclear weapons.

In an evocative essay, cultural theorist Gerburg Treusch-Dieter suggests that nuclear history is the end of the patriarchal narrative—that is, the termination of patriarchal reality, epistemology, and power. He takes us back to an archetypical myth of patriarchal origin in which the world was formed, quite literally, over the dead body of a Grandmother/Goddess. In the Sumerian-Babylonian creation myth, Marduk murdered and then mutilated the body of his grandmother, Tiamat, the primordial Serpent or Dragon of Chaos. After slaying her, Marduk took "his merciless weapon," with which he "split her skull and severed her veins. The north wind blew her blood afar. When his fathers saw this, they were glad and rejoiced."[54] From her split corpse, Marduk formed the world—a world made from matricide.

Once again, this myth portrays the paradigmatic act of the splitting of matter, in this case represented by Tiamat's skull. This is a disrespectful practice that now has reached its omega point with the splitting of the atom. Treusch-Dieter muses, "For thousands of years myths of the creation and philosophical discourse have subordinated matter, or the feminine, to form, or the masculine. The radiating spirit shapes the feminine, that which is passive and conceiving. This order comes to an end in Chernobyl—matter begins to radiate." In other words, *the dark has begun to glow*. In the nuclear age, "Tiamat is a threat to the world made from her and to her master. . . . matter for its part now radiates back." In a futile attempt to prevent her resurrection, Tiamat's *blood*, the source of her energy, was banished, blown afar by the north wind. Yet her Dragon's blood, like Medusa's, was gifted with extraordinary Powers of life and death. Now it has regrouped and returned with a vengeance in the form of radiation.

The Goddess comes back at the end of the patriarchal world. She comes under any number of visages—many of them "ugly," monstrous, frightening, outraged, pissed off, death dealing, and seemingly unfaceable. But we must face her, look her in the eye, and *respect* her. Paula Gunn Allen does so. She calls out to her by one of her most ancient names, "Old Woman." In doing so, she announces the return of the supernatural being who lives in the farthest reaches of space and who abides in the very wrinkle of time. She calls the Crone.

PART FOUR

The Crone:
Hints from the Haggis

Ricki Klages © 1993

Increasing the Signs of Aging: The Plenitude of the Crone

Our physicality—which always and everywhere includes our spirituality, mentality, emotionality, social institutions and processes—is a microform of all physicality. Each of us reflect, in our attitudes toward our body and the bodies of other planetary creatures and plants, our inner attitude toward the planet. And, as we believe, so we act.
—*Paula Gunn Allen*[1]

Work to increase the signs of aging every day.
—Hints from the Haggis[2]

Whenever the Earth and female Powers are respected, the female body, in all of its transformations, is respected. As we have seen, the female body is subjected to numerous symbolic violations in popular imagery. Echoing this treatment, the body of the Earth, in any number of popular depictions, is recurrently threatened, mutilated, cut in half, penetrated by outside products, depicted as carved-up fruit, and reconstituted as some kind of man-made fabrication.

In the summer of 1984, two very telling ads appeared in the business section of the *New York Times*. The first, on June 25, was for Saudia Airlines. A split-screen composition was used. On the left side hung an image of the Earth as seen from space; it was captioned "The Problem." On the right are pictured four long jet planes, made to seem as if they were larger than the planet itself and aimed directly at it. This side was captioned "And how we got round it." The very next day, *Science* magazine took out an ad to promote its upcoming fifth anniversary issue, devoted to "20 DISCOVERIES THAT SHAPED THE TWENTIETH CENTURY." To impress this theme upon viewers, the ad depicted something like the Earth in the grip of the Boston Strangler: two gigantic male hands grasping, shaping, and crushing a puny, malleable, pathetic, and defenseless Earth.

An infinitely arrogant 1984 ad for Cobra phone answering machines depicted one answering machine floating over the surface of a planet that was no longer composed of land and water but of Cobra phone answering machines. Another ad of this type was for ICI—"the fourth largest chemical company in the world"—which manufactures, among other things, pesticides—which it termed in the ad "crop-protection chemicals." The ad showed the Earth as seen from space with the corporate ICI logo engraved on its surface. Not only was the Earth thus metaphorically mutilated, but the viewer was invited to identify with an off-world or extraterrestrial perspective on the home planet. As cultural theorist Zoë Sofia acidly observes, "Our high technology is extraterrestrial technology, with deadly impact upon us Earthlings."[3] Pesticide technology joins nuclear and other chemical technologies as a leader among potentially lethal "extraterrestrial" technologies. Yet rather than recognize the damage to Earth creatures from its endeavors, ICI invited us to identify with the "off-world" view and see ourselves as somehow safely beyond the reach of these contaminants.

Such motifs have been most pronounced in corporate military advertising. In a 1985 ad, Rockwell International displayed a planet that the multinational corporation could, as they put it, "man•ig."

The Earth as a dismantled toy.

The Earth was shown as if it were a projection on a computer screen. The top half of the sphere was sectioned into four pieces; the bottom disappeared into an abstract grid. Bolts penetrated the Earth at both axes as well as through the middle. McDonnell Douglas in a 1986 ad similarly pictured the Earth as a dismantled toy, composed of square building blocks, with national flags and weapons painted on the sides of the squares. This warlike squaring off among nations was belied by the written copy, which announced, "A World of Opportunities Waiting To Be Shared."

The actual nature of such "sharing" was clarified in an ad in the *New York Times* on May 14, 1986, for Northern Telecom. Four naked infant boys were clustered around a toy replica of the globe. Three sat on the floor; of these, two were of Asian or Native American descent, one of African. Their eyes gazed around—up, down, sideways—anywhere but at the viewer. Yet rising up behind the globe

White male domination over the Earth,
over men of color, and, implicitly, the
dominion of all men over all women.

was a focal point: a slightly older white boy, making a thumbs-up gesture of authority and looking the viewer squarely in the eye. Here it was, all at once: white male domination over the Earth, over men of color, and, implicitly, the dominion of all men over all women, whose very presence was completely obliterated.

I was heartened in some respects by a 1992 ad for the Center for Fitness and Movement in New York. The thoughtful headline "Love Our Bodies—Love Our Planet" was emblazoned over the figure of a strong, fit young woman. She assumed a modified lunge position and held a miniature elephant in one outstretched hand; in the other, she cradled a miniature Earth. Assuredly, as the copy went on to state, "awareness of the world begins with awareness of yourself." Still, ecological body and planet awareness cannot inflate the importance of human beings and applaud human domination, as was visually telegraphed in this ad by the miniaturization of the elephant and the planet. Nor can it fetishize perpetually young "hardbodies" as the ideal.

In the Western patriarchal world, young female bodies are rendered pornographic, while aged ones are reviled. In commercial imagery, it is difficult to find a more consistently defeated, mocked, and unfaceable figure than that of the old woman. This can easily be seen in the series of images I encountered one day on television in 1992 while taking a break from writing this prelude. In all of them, the Crone was slashed and trashed.

First, I happened upon "Devil's Due," an episode of "Star Trek: The Next Generation." The intrepid crew of the starship Enterprise had responded to a distress call and traveled to a planet, Ventax, that was besieged by apocalyptic tremors. It seemed that one thousand years ago, the rulers of the planet had made a pact with "Ardra," a Crone-type goddess. They had promised that if she granted them a millennium of peace and prosperity, they would give themselves and the planet over to her at the end of that period. During that time, the Ventaxian people had renounced all types of toxic technologies and embraced an agrarian lifestyle. However, the end of the millennium had arrived and along with it a seemingly magical and powerful woman, amidst visions and earthquakes, claiming to be Ardra. She was somewhere in her forties, had a voluptuous body, and bore a scarred, alien face. Ardra claimed countless names and identities and, with great drama, transformed herself into a variety of ancient Hag/Death goddesses from the traditions of planets throughout the universe. (She was a veritable "Crone with a Thousand Faces.")

Everyone believed Ardra except the Enterprise's Captain, Jean-Luc Picard, who declared her a fraud. Nevertheless, Ardra ardently lusted for the fifty-something Picard (prick hard?). But the manly captain expressed only distaste for her and haughtily rejected her advances. Ardra agreed to a mediated decision on her claim to the planet, to be decided by the android Lieutenant Commander Data of the Enterprise. However, she demanded that Picard submit to her for eternity if he lost the arbitration. He agreed, and the arbitration commenced. Of course, with the help of the Enterprise's computers, Ardra was ultimately shown up as not only an utter fraud in her claims to divinity, but as contemptible in her aggressive, midlife female desire.

After viewing this episode, I randomly flicked the remote and happened upon the last half-hour of the 1991 film *Robin Hood, Prince of Thieves*. This brief segment was quite enough. In it, an older woman was once again the emblem of evil. A very ancient Hag plotted and aided the "bad guy" in his quest to rape Maid Marion. In the climactic mo-ment, Robin and his sidekick came to Marion's rescue, and our hero, to the strains of a highly melodramatic score, told Marion, "I would die for you." But the cock Robin, of course, was never in any such danger. The Crone got staked through the heart with a sword, and Robin got to stake her younger version, Maid Marion, through marriage in the traditional "happy ending."

Such fare has not been unusual. The Crone, if she has not been annihilated, has almost everywhere been trivialized and be-smirched. Old women are degraded, for example, by the character of the simpleminded, arrogant, and "lovable" racist, Miss Daisy, in the Academy Award–winning film from 1990.[4] And appearing in her characteristic covey of three, the Crone has been made to serve as a cleaning maid in the house of the Lord in the long-running television commercials for Murphy's Oil Soap. Frequently, she has not been shown at all, but has been symbolically disappeared. A 1991 Nike ad pictured a twelve-year-old girl; the copy read: "THIS IS A PICTURE OF A 40-YEAR-OLD WOMAN, or perhaps just a picture of the way a 40-year-old woman feels." In truth, this ad said a great deal more about Nike's contempt for and erasure of middle-aged females.

A voice-over for another ad, a televised one for an anti-wrinkle cream, Plenitude by l'Oréal, offered this testimonial from a woman on the go:

> I live with my time
> > progress, performance.
> For my skin care I choose Plenitude.
> With Plenitude my skin can actively defend itself
> > against the signs of aging. . . .
> With Plenitude, I reduce the signs of aging every day.

Everywhere in the fatherland, women are exhorted to reduce the signs of aging. Yet, in truth, the signs of aging are the signs of Powers. It is by increasing them that we enter into the *plenitude* of the Crone.

Despite mainstream derogations and erasures, the figure of the old wise woman—the Ancestor, Hag, or Crone—appears with increasing regularity in gynocentric imaginings, including the works of Paula Gunn Allen, Mary Daly, Ursula LeGuin, Paule Marshall, Barbara Mor, Toni Morrison, and Barbara G. Walker.[5] As mythographer Barbara Walker relates, the Crone is the general designation of the third of the Triple Goddess's aspects and is embodied in figures such as Hecate and Kali. She is associated with great age, the waning Moon, winter, change, death, and even doomsday. Significantly, the presence of the Crone is vehemently banished in a culture both terrified of death and in thrall to horror and socially manufactured megadeath.

This same culture fetishizes youth, progress, and the "future," encourages rapid obsolescence and turnover, and emits a continuing parade of pseudochange or that which is "new." Age, organic change, darkness, decay, and death are radically denied. A 1985 ad for computers depicted a purely white living space: white walls, white rugs, and white furniture, occupied by a white man and a white woman dressed completely in white, working at a white computer. "Welcome to Someday," read the copy. Correspondingly, a 1977 ad for an age-reducing cream depicted a white woman talking on a white phone resting on a white table adorned with white flowers against white walls. "The Over-40 Look Is Over" the headline assured us.

Why all this whitewashing? Along with their implicit racism, such renditions proceed from a central absurdity. Zoë Sofia accurately points to "the two-faced character of modern technology, which generates for every desirable, legitimate and supposedly practical tool a pile of useless, toxic wastes and uninhabitable lands for which no one wants to take responsibility; for every shiny good product there's a slimy bad by-product."[6] The Crone by nature demands that we face the reality of the "slimy bad"—age, death, and decay—for it exists in exquisite balance with youth, life, and growth. By denying this balance, the warheads who run the world have produced, along with all their "shiny goods," virtually deathless chemical and nuclear wastes.

Valerie Solanas, the author of the extraordinary 1968 radical fem-

inist rant *The SCUM Manifesto*, summarizes the principal achievement of consumer man: "He has made of the world a shitpile."7 Toni
Morrison concurs with this pithy assessment in *Tar Baby*, her indictment of colonialism and consumerism. She describes a world where
waste is "the ordering principle of the universe." The waste is per-
sonified in white millionaire candy manufacturer Valerian, who, after
plundering its resources and people to make his fortune, takes up
residence in the Caribbean. Morrison spares nothing in her scathing
indictment of Valerian and his brethren: "They had not the dignity of
wild animals who did not eat where they defecated but they could
defecate over a whole people and come there to live and defecate
some more by tearing up the land and that is why they loved property so because they had killed it soiled it defecated on it and they
loved more than anything the places where they made shit." These
plunderers, while surrounding themselves with delicacies, perfumes,
and the finest trappings of luxury, still cannot quite suppress the
stench, the rot, the smell of corruption, for

> that was the sole lesson of their world: how to make waste, how
> to make machines that made more waste, how to make wasteful
> products, how to talk waste, how to study waste, how to design
> waste, how to cure people who were sickened by waste so they

The raging Crone as nuclear waste. Mike Smith, Las
Vegas Sun.

could be well enough to endure it, how to mobilize waste, legalize waste and how to despise the culture that lived in cloth houses and shit on the ground far away from where they ate. And it would drown them one day, they would all sink into their own waste and the waste they had made of the world and then, finally, they would know true peace and the happiness they had been looking for all along.[8]

The ultimate form of consumerist waste is, of course, nuclear waste. An editorial cartoon railing against the proposed nuclear dump at Yucca Mountain in Nevada depicts a skull-faced Crone dressed in standard S&M dominatrix gear. Before this laughing face of death grovels a little white man whimpering, "Oh yes, Madam Nuke Dump, we pro-nukers will do anything for you."[9] Mr. MX, however much he boasts and swaggers, ultimately must go down on bent knees to the Black Goddess he thought he disposed of so long ago. Caught in the S&M hierarchy he has promoted for several millennia, Mr. MX is destined to eat, worship, lie down in, and ultimately die—despite his hopes for eternal life/erection—in his own waste.

The War Powers

Man should be trained for war and woman for the recreation of warriors.
—*Friedrich Nietzsche*[10]

The year was 1600, or thereabouts, when these tribal feminists decided that they had had enough of unregulated warfare by their men. Lysistratas among the Indian [Iroquois] women proclaimed a boycott on lovemaking and childbearing. Until the men conceded to them the power to decide upon war and peace, there would be no more warriors.
—*Stan Steiner*[11]

Two issues concerning women and death continue to preoccupy North American culture: women soldiers in combat and abortion. Mass controversy generally attends these issues because they challenge the snoolish taboo that forbids women the Powers of death. Patriarchal men have staked their lives on a belief in their exclusive mastery of death, resulting in a bizarre cultural techno-necrophilia.

This phenomenon is marked by identification with machines, the worship of commodities, the senseless prolongation of "life" through medical technology, the generation of simulacra, and the invention of the means for megadeath. To counter such techno-necrophilia, it is imperative that females reclaim and redefine the Powers of death.

Increasingly, feminists turn our attention to war, denying men their status of sole authority on the subject and redefining war from feminist and/or tribal perspectives.[12] For example, poet and mythographer Barbara Mor unearths the Morrigan, the triple Black Goddess in Irish mythology. She details the Morrigan as a warrior Crone, signifying the Powers of "prophetic warfare," an "Amazonian Battle-Ax hounding us Out to Fight Again. . . . A war goddess . . . [whose] weapon is the female mind. Psychic kung fu." Mor points to the folly inherent in the feminist revisioning of female Powers only as "wise, benevolent, graciously non-confrontational Ladies. . . . Goddesses of therapy . . . goddesses of personal well-being." Rather, she insists, we should be unearthing "bitches of politics . . . witches of global upheaval."[13]

It is perhaps the deep fear of the transmutational Powers of the Amazonian Battle-Ax that fuels resistance to the idea of women serving in combat roles, although few people would come right out and say so. Rather, opponents rely upon traditional sexist notions of woman's "place." For example, one Marine Corps general, Robert H. Barrow, testified before Congress in 1991: "It is killing . . . and it is . . . uncivilized! And women cannot do it! . . . I think the very nature of women disqualifies them. . . . Women give life. Sustain life. Nurture life. They do not take it."[14] The underlying reason for this peculiar form of twentieth-century chivalry is not respect but a desire to keep women powerless as men define power.

I am not proposing that if women served fully or partly in combat roles patriarchy would collapse. Clearly, the armed forces are adept at assimilating women into militaristic and other patriarchal values. Rather, I am saying that snoolish resistance to female participation in battle stems from a fear of the mythic potency of the warrior Crone. Lurking beneath the chivalrous front of such "natural men" as General Barrows is a terror that if the symbol of the female warrior were reactivated in a feminist context, it would awaken the need for female authority over war and peace, require a redefinition of war, and undermine the authority of patriarchal "civilization." With the mythic warrior Crone as our model, women might once again hone those arts of prophetic warfare and practice those ancient female Powers of "psychic kung fu."

Meanwhile, abortion rights continue to be threatened in a campaign frequently led by committed warmongers. Patriarchal culture's banishment of the Crone accompanies the wanton extinction of countless plant and animal species. Simultaneously, patriarchal culture fixates on the preservation of the human fetus. This fetal focus and identification is a primary sign of doom-ridden times: human-extinction anxieties raised by the nuclear threat, overpopulation, and the continuous razing of the elemental world are displaced by the right wing onto the much more manageable and expedient issue of abortion.[15] The rhetoric of the anti-abortion movement paints women as "genocidal" killers, perpetrating a holocaust and posing a dire threat to the continuance of our species. Yet the actual agenda of this movement is patriarchal control over the maternal body—a practice that both legitimates and reflects patriarchal control over the life-giving planetary body of the Earth. This is the core practice that has resulted in the environmental disarray now threatening the continued life of our species and many others.

Curiously enough, if we heard General Barrow's words out of context, we might assume him to be fulminating against women's right to abortion rather than their participation in combat. On the issue of abortion rights, as with the issue of female combat, patriarchal resistance partially stems from a peculiar terror at the idea of women being able to kill. As a bumper sticker puts it, "If men got pregnant, abortion would be a sacrament," or, I might add, it would be an initiation rite—a red badge of courage. Neither military men nor the often committed warmongers who lead the anti-abortion crusade are opposed to killing. They do it, or condone it, all the time—as long as it is men who do the deed. Both the anti-abortion and the anti–women-in-combat campaigns vividly reflect the terrors of a Crone-phobic culture. In this culture, "good" female Powers are isolated into the figure of the patriarchal "good mother," a being whose primary function is to be a container for new (male) life, a mother who gives life and only life and is always available, nurturing, and kind.

Yet this fantasy is most immature, self-serving, and cowardly. The intuition expressed in Triple Goddess imagery from around the world denies this simplistic formula. It points out that the womb is also a tomb—that the one who gives life also ultimately takes it away. In addition, the Triple Goddess philosophy illuminates the fact that the Crone, however fearful her first appearance, is simultaneously a harbinger of rebirth, Be-Speaking a call to profound healing and change.

Increasing the Signs of Aging

> Since death held no terrors for her (she often spoke to the dead),
> she knew there was nothing to fear.
> —*Toni Morrison*[16]

In Paule Marshall's novel *Praisesong for the Widow*, Avey Johnson's Great-Aunt Cuny appears to her in a dream, attempting to drag her on a journey that Avey at first regards with terror. The ancestral visitation is both powerful and auspicious, and it signals the beginning of a cycle of events that transforms Avey and restores her to herself.[17]

Similarly, Jungian mythographer Nor Hall writes that the mythic significance of the old wise woman "is to be of assistance in times of difficult passage. As midwife to the psyche she is constellated in 'emergency' situations where a spirit, a song, an alternative, a new being is emerging."[18] Assuredly, we are in a time of planetary emergency—one demanding the emergence of the Crone. The commercial directives of L'Oréal's anti-wrinkle cream, Plenitude, notwithstanding, women need to defend ourselves far more against patriarchal depredations—both individual and planetary—than against the so-called signs of aging. Indeed, these portentous "signs" should be encouraged as our best defense, for they bespeak our genuine *plenitude*: the fullness of our beings, the crystallization of our Powers, the completeness of the Crone.

A sure sense of the connection between great age and female Powers infuses the creation myth of the Keres people of the American Southwest, as told by Paula Gunn Allen:

In that place where she [Grandmother Spider/Thought Woman] was alone and complete with her power . . . she thought to the power once and knew a rippling, a wrinkling within. Then she knew she was old, and wrinkled, and that the power's first song was a song of great age. The wrinkling became tighter, more spidery, stronger. . . . She knew much of the universe, the great power, was contained within. Later the earth would be ripples and wrinkles, spidery lines of power folded and enfolded into a tight moving shape, and it would also hold the great power within, like a mother holds new life. Others would also imitate this time: walnuts and acorns, apples and pineapples, cactus and mountains, even the oceans would be like that. And humans, five-fingered beings, would grow wrinkled in their skins and brains, in honor of this time when she and the power made a song to form new life, new beings.[19]

A Crone, then, is someone who embodies what one of my students, Eric Yackley, called "wrinkled knowledge."

Of course, being and becoming a Crone—being and becoming complete in one's own Powers—is no automatic thing. It is gained only by the most prodigious labors. Ursula LeGuin observes, "There are things the Old Woman can do, say, and think that the Woman cannot do, say, or think. The Woman has to give up more than her menstrual periods before she can do, say, or think them. She has got to change her life. . . . bear herself, her third self, her old age."[20] The results of successfully undergoing this "wrinkling," this enormous psychic and physical shift are the *signs of aging* that are so abhorrent in the snool's-eye view:[21] the waxing of incisiveness, courage, belligerence, intractability, the ability to change, and the development of the Powers of psychic warfare.

The world we know and do not know is itself undergoing a climacteric, a critical shift of enormous proportions, something like the transformations a woman undergoes at menopause.[22] The commonly heard refrain "change or die" seems accurate enough. Yet patriarchal man steadfastly fears and refuses ontological change. This, then, is the promise of the Crone, she who knows that there is nothing to fear. What the Crone presages for the individual woman and for the world as a whole is, precisely, the *change of life*.

CHAPTER TEN

Look Me in the Eye

Not only will I stare. I want my look to change reality.
—*bell hooks*[1]

I am the all/seeing Eye . . .
whose appearance strikes terror,
Lady of Slaughter, Mighty One of Frightfulness
who takes the form of blazing light
I . . . most ancient female of the world.
—*from Spell 316 of the Egyptian* Coffin Texts[2]

The beautiful woman in the nuclear-power-plant ad described earlier keeps her eyes down and to the side. In any number of hierarchical body languages, such posturing conveys subservience.[3] Alternatively, a direct gaze, an open stare, connotes a challenge to authority. *The Story of O* is a pornographic fantasy about a woman whose very name labels her a "hole," a negation.[4] She is a woman who is kept as a sexual slave and who embraces her servitude and sexual abuse by men. During her training period as a slave, O learns that she must always keep her head down and never look a man in the eye.

O is meant to be a pornographic "everywoman" and her story a narrative of the feminine condition. As with other patriarchal narratives, hers is riddled with reversal. Women are enjoined never to meet a man's gaze, literally or figuratively, but this proscription was instituted not only to condition feminine subordination, but to protect men from the female gaze. This masculine protection was needed because gorgonish women, particularly *old* women, have long been said to possess the ability to "eyebite" or "overlook," that is, to bewitch with the eye, to curse someone with a glance.[5] Therefore, patriarchal cultures everywhere have issued orders to render Crones and potential Crones eyeless. This was done to the robbed Graeae in the Medusa myth and continues to be done to this day in countless images and stories.

For example, an ad for a curative eye-drop product from 1991 displayed an image of a disembodied female eye contained in a shattered circular mirror. The overt message was that the eye was inflamed or infected and in need of the product; the subtext was that the inflammatory or enraged female eye was shattered, battered, contained—a captive of the mirror.

In the 1991 film *Eve of Destruction*, a scientist, Eve, constructs for the U.S. government a new nuclear weapon, a cyborg (android) who is an exact twin of herself, even to the point of being programmed with her creator's memories. This cyborg, Eve-8, is a veritable femme fatale: in place of a womb, she has a nuclear bomb. When the government sends her out on a trial run to check her ability to pass in the real world, she stumbles onto a bank holdup and gets shot. She goes haywire, starts wearing red and black leather—the colors of Kali— and acting out Eve's unconscious desires and emotions.

Particularly, Eve-8 expresses *rage* at all men who threaten her with sexual violence. (She has an especially violent reaction to the epithet *bitch*). Eve-8 castrates one offender with her teeth in a motel and runs another off the road before tracking down and killing her real quarry, who, once again, is a nuclear father. Eve's alcoholic father was verbally as well as physically abusive to his wife and child, and in a drunken rage he killed the mother, an event the five-year-old Eve witnessed. These inflammatory memories and events send the cyborg Eve-8 into critical mode, and the nuclear bomb inside her starts its countdown to explosion.

This fantasy of an outraged, nuclear-armed, avenging aspect of oneself raging against sexist injustice holds great promise. But, all too typically, patriarchal self-preservation prevails. At the end of the film, a male CIA agent manages to shoot Eve-8 in the eye, her only vulnerable area, but this doesn't quite do the trick. Eve-8 is stopped only after Eve herself stabs her better half right through the eye, negating her soul, obliterating her memories, and denying her rage and her primeval Powers of death. The message is that women have to do themselves in.

While the female eye in patriarchal representation is averted or attacked, the frequently mechanical male eye is becoming well nigh inescapable. In the nineteenth century, the British proponent of utilitarianism, Jeremy Bentham, conceptualized what he called a "Panopticon." It was the symbolic utopian building of Western culture, a potential prison/factory/military/educational structure designed for continual surveillance from a central point. French philosopher Michel Foucault zeros in on the meaning of such a structure:

> The perfect disciplinary apparatus would make it possible for a single gaze to see everything constantly. A central point would be both the source of light illuminating everything and a locus of convergence for everything that must be known: a perfect eye that nothing would escape and a center towards which all gazes would be turned.[6]

As Barbara Mor and Monica Sjöö incisively point out, this "Panopticon" is another example of men playing god, for such a structure "is the eye of God—the God who is an eternal prison-keeper, the voyeuristic judge of morals, Big Brother."[7]

Emblems of this peeping-Tom, pornotechnic god are ubiquitous, from the CBS "eye" logo to a multitude of high-tech ads. For example, Grumman, a major military contractor, boasted in a 1984 ad of its "Hawkeye" aircraft, a "brand new eye-in-the-sky"—a surveillance plane packed with radar and computer equipment. The graphic showed a gigantic disembodied eye set amidst the clouds. Over the iris and pupil was a grid. The impenetrable dark of the pupil emitted a radar beam.

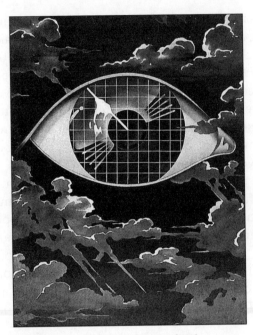

The military version of the eye of god.

Grumman has bestowed a mythic name upon its aircraft, for Hawkeye is the name of the hero in James Fenimore Cooper's series of frontier novels, including *The Deerslayer* and *The Last of the Mohicans,* as well as the nickname of the Alan Alda character in the TV series "M*A*S*H." But these associations just barely skim the surface. In ancient Egypt, there also was a notion of an eye in the sky emitting radiant light. That eye was veritably the eye of a bird of prey, in this case a falcon. Moreover, that same eye was also the Crone, the Lady of Slaughter, the "most ancient female of the world."

In Egyptian mythology, the eye was the most common symbol, though an extremely complex one. In primordial times, the high deity was a falcon whose right eye was the Sun and whose left eye was the Moon. Still, the eyes themselves were simultaneously regarded as independent and separate beings. Moreover, "one fact does stand out—the Egyptian eye was always a symbol for the Great Goddess, whatever name she may have in any particular instance."[8] The sacred Eye in ancient Egypt was "a sign of destructive force, terrible blinding light, fire and the emotions which can be described in such terms, namely, anger and uncontrollable fury." However, Egyptian mythology also spoke of a time when the Eye was absent, a season of terrible "fear and lifelessness."

"Look me in the eye," demands the Crone,[9] yet snools[10] cannot. They fear not only her uncontrollable fury, but also her ability to take their measure, discern fraud, spot vulnerability, and render judgments. Mythographer Barbara Walker muses,

> Men feared the judgmental eye of the wisewoman even when she was socially powerless. This, then, is the chink in the armor of patriarchal establishments. When many women together say no and mean it, the whole structure can collapse. . . . God can't, but woman can call man to account for his gynocidal, genocidal behavior. She had better do it soon, for he is already counting down to doomsday.[11]

Ironically, in this countdown men foolishly are trying to play Goddess, for throughout world mythologies doomsday has been ruled by the figure of the Crone. In Hindu eschatology, the prime mover is Kali, the Dark Mother and Triple Goddess of creation, preservation, and destruction. She, like the Sumerian-Babylonian grandmother creator, Tiamat, is the primal Deep, the "menstrual Ocean of Blood" at the beginning and end of the world:

> When Kali's doomsday arrived, the gods would slay each other, Earth would be overwhelmed by fire and flood. The Goddess would swallow up everything and un-make it, returning to her primordial state of formless Chaos, as she was before creation. All beings would enter her, because 'She devours all existence.' After a time that could not be counted because even Time was destroyed, Kali would give birth to a new universe.[12]

Ancient northern Europeans had a similar doomsday myth, that of Ragnarok, a battle in the world's last days that would ensue as a result of the Mutspell, or Mother's Curse. At this time, the cursing Goddess would take all of creation into the dark Chaos of her womb. Walker further notes: "The Celtic version of the same symbol was Mother Sulis, the female gap, or eye, or black hole, or cauldron: the cosmic yoni."[13]

Not too surprisingly, then, all manner of manly theologies and philosophies try to banish the female Eye and define the "female gap" as a fundamental obscenity. As Jean-Paul Sartre sputters, "The obscenity of the feminine sex is that of everything which 'gapes open.' . . . woman senses her condition as an appeal precisely because she is 'in the form of a hole.'"[14] Being in "the form of a hole" supposedly means that female bodies are ineluctably obscene, ready and able to castrate the penis. Yet these bodies are simultaneously said to be perpetually open to penetration and victimization. Female Powers find these aspersions uproarious and quite frankly obscene. They tell a wholly other "Story of O," inviting us to look toward the Earth and see the fiery "O" of thermonuclear ground zero. They beckon us to gaze skyward, encountering yet another inflamed "O," the ozone hole.

O-Zona

The Goddess is coming and is She pissed!
—*Bumper sticker, c. 1985*

As many scientists have noted, the diminishment of ozone in the atmosphere is manifesting primarily as a thinning of the ozone layer, rather than a gap or space within it. Nevertheless, the image that best describes the event mythically is the image that has taken root in the collective imagination: that of a hole. This mythic image demands that we face the connections between ozone depletion and those cosmic female Powers who appear in the forms of gaps, mouths, eyes, cauldrons, or holes.

A stunning image appeared on the February 17, 1992, cover of *Time* magazine. The feature story concerned the "vanishing ozone." The headline read, "Ozone: The Danger Moves Closer to Home." The graphic showed a blue and white cloud-dotted sky. Across it in large-capital red letters was written the word *OZONE*, but the second *O* had been removed and replaced with a flame-ringed black hole. This was the most graphic contemporary representation I have yet seen of the cosmic being described in Egyptian myth as the "most ancient female" of the world. Here, on the cover of *Time* magazine, was the "Lady of Slaughter . . . who takes the form of blazing light." Here was the "all-seeing Eye"—outraged, *inflamed*, and eminently destructive.

As I was writing this chapter, I got together with a group of other feminists to put together a television report on violence against women. One of the organizers was named Ona. As she drove off from our first meeting, I happened to notice her license plate; it read "O-Zona."[15] My mouth gaped open and my eyes stared in wonder at this stunning synchronicity: the Lady of Slaughter or Doomsday Crone was announcing one of her contemporary names.

Now, I assure you, I am not proposing that there is a divine woman hanging out in the upper atmosphere. I am not suggesting that we worship O-Zona or try to establish a personal relationship with her. Nor do I intend us to become supporters of ozone depletion, seeing this phenomenon as a manifestation of divine will. Rather, I am suggesting that the diminishment of the ozone layer must be understood as a manifestation of female Powers, especially those raging, chaotic, creative, and destructive—essentially transmutational—Powers associated with the Crone.

Mythic/metaphoric thought is not only a way to express intuitions about the nature of the universe, but also a forum to discern guidelines for the conduct of life. Patriarchal myth tells us that both women and the Earth are passive victims of snoolish assault. By understanding the ozone hole as O-Zona, we recognize the active and enraged response of cosmic female Powers to pornotechnic depredations against the elements.

Identifying with O-Zona's rage, women, too, can react with fire to assaults on our being. Thinking through the metaphor of O-Zona, we acknowledge the ensouled, intelligent, and active nature of the elements. In so doing, we disrupt standard objectifying and numbing modes of (mis)understanding the ways of the elemental world. Thinking elementally, we might elicit new modes of reverence and respect for the mysteries in which we all participate, and hence spur the invention of new modes of nontoxic technologies and lifestyles. By so doing, we just might be able to avert the danger now staring us in the face.

Thinking elementally about O-Zona, I also detect a ripple of cosmic last laughter. It is deeply ironic that the culture that has so demonized the dark and associated all knowledge, intelligence, and understanding with the (masculine-identified) light should now find itself targeted by an abundance of illumination.

Connecting O-Zona to archaic manifestations of the cosmic eye, gap, or hole we also affirm the connection of ozone depletion to cosmic operations of justice, truth, balance, and fate. In ancient Egypt, the all/seeing Eye was associated with Maat, the goddess of truth and judgment. Maat in turn is linked to the Carthaginian goddess Libera, the Libra of astrology, the lady of the scales. Like Maat, she signifies the balancing action of karmic law.

Nowadays, we still have Justice represented by the figure of the woman holding scales, but she is blindfolded. Still, as Barbara Walker notes, "The blindfold on today's Goddess of Justice was unknown in antiquity. She not only held the scales of every man's fate; she also had the All-Seeing eye."[16] While the blindfold purportedly represents the impartiality of patriarchal law, it actually signifies an attempted covering up of the Eye. Snools want to cover up the Eye so that they can carry out their atrocities without scrutiny or judgment. They foolishly promote the belief that they can commit any outrage without awakening the Powers of divine retribution or Justice. O-Zona appears to prove them dead wrong.

While never blindfolded, the Crone goddesses of antiquity frequently were veiled. Walker writes: "The inscription on the Goddess's temple at Saïs said (in words later copied into the biblical Book of Revelation): 'I am all that has been, that is, and that will be. No mortal has yet been able to lift the veil that covers me.'"[17] Pornoscience and pornotechnology are predicated upon disrespect and profanation. They are obsessed with penetrating, displaying, possessing, and exposing sacred mysteries—with baring the nakedness of the Goddess/Universe. Ironically, it is at today's high point of patriarchal knowledge, when snools think they have succeeded most thoroughly in stripping the Goddess, that she actually is the *most* veiled. For the Crone is the woman clothed in the Sun, the Goddess clad in space alone. Indeed, her most characteristic "dress" is blazing light,[18] be it the light of the celestial Powers (the Sun, Moon, and stars), the relentless rays peeking through O-Zona's hole, or the energy of the Sun drawn down to Earth and manifesting in the blazing eye at the center of the nuclear firestorm, otherwise known as ground zero.

The mythic Triple Goddess represents the primal spiraling movement of nature—creation, protection, and destruction—as well as the karmic laws of balance—give and take. She is both mother and grave, womb and tomb, the site from which all life originates and to which all life returns. Indeed, "she is so vast that 'the series of universes appear and disappear with the opening and shutting of her eyes.'"[19] The recent appearance of O-Zona the Amazona announces such a world-ending yet potentially "eye-opening" moment. Despite the blandishments of Oakley sunglasses, there is no purchasable "thermonuclear protection" against her gaze. Our only protection is to cease disrespecting the elements and to institute rituals of reverence and respect for female Powers, human and nonhuman. Perhaps O-Zona then will again close her Eye and dream of green, opening her mouth to gossip out a new creation.

I first started thinking mythically about the ozone hole when Paula Gunn Allen suggested to me that the ozone hole was very much like a cervix opening to give birth.[20] And indeed, O-Zona bespeaks not only an apocalyptic moment, but also a creative one. The current hole in the sky reminds me of a creation myth from the oral traditions of northeastern Native American tribes. In this myth, the world began with the opening of a hole in the sky, caused by the uprooting of a magical tree. An unimaginably powerful spirit being jumped through the hole and fell for a time that was uncountable and unimaginable. One day, several waterfowl looked up, saw her, caught her, and placed her upon the back of Turtle, for there was no land but only water at that time. A series of creatures tried to dive to the bottom of the water to bring up some earth, but they met with continued failure. Finally, Toad went down and, though nearly dying in the attempt, managed to bring up a mouthful of dirt. When the woman spread this out on Turtle's back, it extended in all directions and became dry land.[21]

I am venturing to say that a spirit being is again journeying toward us, ready to plunge through the new "hole in the sky" into our world. But who is this being? In advertising imagery, science fiction, and the visionary work of some New Age artists, this being frequently is represented as some sort of star child. But I think this is only a partial understanding. We should be preparing as well for the return of the Haggis, the Great Witch, the Grandmother, the Space Crone.

The Space Crone

the earth . . .
is a black and living thing
is a favorite child
of the universe
feel her rolling her hand
in its kinky hair
feel her brushing it clean.
                —*Lucille Clifton*[22]

A 1986 plea from Boeing to support the development of a "space station" displays an enormous infant floating in space. Such iconography is by no means rare. Over and over in contemporary imagery, a figure recurs: that of the space fetus (or newborn). For example, an April 1982 cover of *Omni* magazine showed a mushroom cloud exploding on the Earth, while off in space, a fetus in a bubble emerged from a cracked egg. One message here is clear: if nuclear war takes out all of Earthly life, humanity can be reborn in space.

A different, though related, fetal image appeared in a 1982 ad for Fuji audiocassettes. Floating in space was a shiny, blank-faced, and utterly smooth mechanical woman in a fetal position—with fully developed, exposed loins. Again, the implication is that if the Earth is destroyed, pornotechnology can engineer a new "virgin mother," the fuckable virgin machine or mechanical bride. This image represents simultaneously a managed womb and a fetal harbinger of a new world order predicated upon the elimination of female Powers. It also conveys disrespect for and abandonment of the body and planet.[23]

The most common image of the space fetus appears in the film *2001: A Space Odyssey*, scripted by Arthur C. Clarke and Stanley Kubrick.[24] The story opens in some prehistoric time before human consciousness sparked in our apelike ancestors. One day, an alien "monolith," some type of inscrutable machine being, lands on Earth. A male ape approaches it, peers intently into it, and seems to achieve some sort of communion with it. Soon afterward, that very ape figures out that he can use a bone as a weapon. In short order, he kills a rival for the local water supply. The triumphant ape then hurls the bone into the air where, in an editing tour de force, the spinning bone transforms into an orbiting space station.

The film then shifts to the future, just postmillennium, as the title indicates. Several scientists have embarked on a top-secret mission to the Moon to investigate an identical monolith that has just been discovered buried beneath the surface. When that monolith is uncovered, it emits some sort of energy beam toward Jupiter. A spaceship is sent out to track the beam to its source. Two of its astronauts are awake; the remainder lie in some sort of suspended animation until Jupiter is reached. But the human plan goes awry. The ship's computer, Hal, develops a mind of its own and manages to kill off all but one of the crew members before the remaining astronaut, David Bowman, unplugs it.

When Bowman does arrive in the vicinity of Jupiter, he encounters yet another monolith floating in space. He undergoes some sort of psychedelic journey through a "star gate"—what might be a passage through a black hole. We next see him as a very old man in some sort of staged hotel suite, where he is being kept by his alien hosts. Once again, the monolith appears, and as the old man reaches toward it, he is transformed into an embryo, a planet-sized space fetus in a bubble.

The last frame shows the space fetus approaching planet Earth. Suddenly, the Earth disappears and the viewer is left to meditate upon the space fetus, the so-called "star child" who now fills the frame. In the novel by Clarke, the reason for the disappearance of the Earth is explained, albeit somewhat ambiguously:

> There before him, a glittering toy no Star-Child could resist, floated the planet Earth with all its peoples. He had returned in time. Down there on that crowded globe, the alarms would be flashing across the radar screens, the great tracking telescopes would be searching the skies, and history as men knew it would be drawing to a close. A thousand miles below, he became aware that a slumbering cargo of death had awoken, and was stirring sluggishly in its orbit. The feeble energies it contained were no possible menace to him; but he preferred a cleaner sky. He put forth his will, and the circling megatons flowered in a silent detonation that brought a brief, false dawn to half the sleeping globe.[25]

In other words, the eminently tidy space fetus set off some Star Wars–type nuclear weapons orbiting the planet, presumably annihilating the Earth.

Certainly, I favor one of the ideas expressed in Clarke's novel: history as we have known it is drawing to a close. Yet there are too many familiar phallocentric notions involved in Clarke's schema to convince me that any real transmutation is being evoked. While the image of the star child might at first seem appealing, a hopeful sign of future evolution, he actually is, as Zoë Sofia writes, "a sign of extinction."[26] 2001's space fetus, of course, is not only male but has no mother, not to mention grandmother. He is reborn without the help of those primordial midwives—Gossips.[27] He has no primary kinship to spirit, to females, to the Fates, or even to kindred beings. Without such primal connections to the Old Wives, he has no stories; hence, while he appears to be a symbol of the future, he actually has no future and is a symbol only of futurelessness.

Embedded, moreover, in this star-child symbol is a geocidal myth of necessary human evolution beyond Earth. This same myth is expressed in Clarke's celebrated novel *Childhood's End*, in which the Earth is also obliterated and all children under the age of twelve merge into a mass mind and migrate off into space. [28] The myth promises, not unlike certain forms of Christian fundamentalism, that we can be born again after the annihilation and cannibalization of our planet. The implications are that Earth's only purpose is to provide a launch pad for "man," that the fetus is all-powerful and can devour the mother, and that having thus cut the cord to the original mother, humans can escape into the new virgin "empty" territory of Space, transmuting into a spaceship fetus—the outerspace "inner child." In 2001, Baby Jesus comes once again, but this time he is completely independent of the unholy womb and the elemental Earth Mother.

Spaceman's antipathy to the elemental mother and child was profoundly etched into the composition of story and picture on the front page of the *Boston Globe* for Christmas Eve of 1984. Two stories at the top of the page commanded attention. The first, on the left, was about the famine ravaging Ethiopia. There was a photograph of a mother and her infant son grotesquely posed to look like the Christian Madonna and child. The headline read, "Amid famine and

war, hope and faith survive." Following those words, on the immediate right there was a story about President Reagan's space opera,
"Star Wars" (the Strategic Defense Initiative). Its headline read,
"Weinberger: No Give on 'Star Wars.'" Beneath that was a quote
from the secretary of defense: "It's the one thing that offers any real
hope to the world and we will not give that up."

Both stories are parts of one continuing story. One part is about
the Earth, the mother, food, and Africa—the cradle of human life, the
so-called primitive, the so-called past, the expendable. The other part
is about space, the father, the final frontier, technology, and the
alleged future. In this narrative, we learn that Africa and its people,
from the so-called First World point-of-view,[29] are completely, perhaps even necessarily, expendable. Mass death in Africa is caused
not only by racism and neocolonialism but also by the time-honored
patriarchal war against the elemental, the body, the Earth. Men such
as Caspar Weinberger—like Saint Paul, his brother before him—have
set their minds "on things that are above, not on things that are on
the earth."[30]

In the patriarchal imagination, space has been conceived not only
as the final frontier, but also as the great escape—from the body, the
planet, the organic, the mud, the mother. Of course, the characteristic
dichotomy that associates women, hell, and evil with the Earth and
men, god, and heaven with space is as fallacious as any other split
truth. The idea of space, not as a final frontier but as a realm of ancestors, magic, and transmutation, continually surfaces in some of the
most radical of feminist imaginings.[31] In these, space is not a virgin
but a grandmother.

Ursula LeGuin's 1976 essay on menopause and the momentous
life shift it brings comes with the intriguing title "The Space Crone."
In LeGuin's fantasy, a spaceship filled with friendly aliens comes to
Earth, hoping to take one human being back to their planet. Rather than allowing some fit young man to be selected, LeGuin opts to
"go down to the local Woolworth's . . . and pick an old woman, over
sixty, from behind the costume jewelry counter," for "only a person
who has experienced, accepted, and acted the entire human condition—the essential quality of which is change—can fairly represent
humanity."[32]

*Poster for a Native American women's antinu-
clear group.* C. Winters © 1976.

As suggested by artist C. Winters's 1976 poster for WARN (Wom-
en of All Red Nations, a Native American antinuclear group), tech-
nology-worshiping entrepreneurs, trying to breach the final frontier
and break the bond with Mother Earth, will have to contend with the
Earth Mother's mother, the Grandmother Universe, "the ultimate
authority."[33] Spacesnools, who have fooled themselves into thinking
that they can waste the planet with impunity and then escape off into
outer space to colonize the cosmos,[34] will have to reckon with the
spiraling Black Hole, the chaotic center of galaxies and universes,[35]
that dark matter/mother, the womb/tomb of space and time, the
Space Crone. If there are any "children" up there in space, she is the
source.

CHAPTER ELEVEN

The Change of Life

MENOPAUSE MYTH NO. 1—"No man in his right mind would
be interested in a menopausal woman."
> —*1990 ad for an estrogen replacement therapy*

MENOPAUSE NO. 1 TRUTH—"No woman in her right mind,
most particularly a Crone, would be interested in a snool[1] of
any age."
> —Hints from the Haggis[2]

Author Jane Gross, in a 1992 article in the *New York Times* on
menopause, reiterated the opinion of one Gossip, Germaine Greer,
who had stated that medical companies push artificial estrogen in
order to make menopausal women into sex slaves for men.[3] Surely,
she goes too far—or does she?

The drug ad quoted above was quite a piece of work. It was one
in a series. All showed pictures of white women of about fifty years
old, lush, moist, and inviting. Although the models varied, the
women, invariably, were dressed in virginal white: none wore dark
and threatening Crone colors. The ad implied that men, to be sure,
could remain interested in *these* menopausal women because they
still looked approximately like menstruating women—with the help

of drugs and, variously, cosmetics, dieting, and surgery. Most outrageous of all were the tag lines at the bottoms of the pages, which read: "NOW THE CHANGE OF LIFE DOESN'T HAVE TO CHANGE YOURS."

The manipulations wrought upon the individual female body always reflect the larger processes of patriarchal machination and domination. In these ads, pornotechnology was trying to seduce us once again with promises of perpetually "shiny goods" in the form of our own preserved bodies. The ads also promised endless abundance in the form of at least an appearance of fertility and no "slimy bads"—aging, death, and decay. Yet, *change*—the cosmic and chaotic processes of transmutation that we participate in through the elemental wanderings of our bodies—cannot be stopped. The change of life now occurring on the whole planet is potentially a movement away from the sex-slave, soul-splitting, hierarchical, law-and-order, controlling, and greed-driven dominations of everyday life. Many of us, including the most privileged and imbalanced, might not survive this change. If we want to make it through, we might take as our guide the Grandmother, or Crone—the enduring one, she who is both the changer and the changed,[4] the survivor of both gynocide and geocide.[5]

Fear of change is the same as fear of age, maturation, and death. Pornotechnology, in line with its attempted symbolic annihilation of the Crone, "wages war" and plans to "defeat" aging and even death—a quest that many scientists analogize quite explicitly to the quest to split the atom.[6] As we well know, that historic achievement resulted in the construction of the ultimate death-machine and reigning god of the consumer society, the Bomb. Not too surprisingly, then, pornotechnology's principal method to defeat aging and death is to once again invoke a machine god—to make humans resemble machines as closely as possible. Ironically, in so doing we book first-class passage into the land of the living dead.

Machines "R" Us?

One reason older people dislike *2001* is they realize it's about reality and it scares hell out of them. This film is about the two most important realities of the future: development of intelligent machines and contact with higher alien intelligence. Which of course may be machines themselves. I suspect that all really higher intelligence will be machines. Unless they're beyond machines. But biological intelligence is a lower form of intelligence, almost inevitably. We're in an early state in the evolution of intelligence, but a late stage in the evolution of life. Real intelligence won't be living.

—*Arthur C. Clarke*[7]

As described earlier, the origin story behind the toy series the Toxic Crusaders involves an evil alien, Dr. Killemoff, who has invaded Earth and established his multinational corporation, Apocalypse, Inc., in order to generate the smog, toxic waste, and other pollutants upon which his species thrives. This story is very similar to one I have been hearing for some time on the popular-legend circuit involving space aliens who generate pollution because they require that type of atmosphere for life support and because they want to get rid of us and take over the Earth.

In some variants of this story, the machines themselves are the space aliens living among us—a suggestion that appeared as well in a 1993 Acura automobile television commercial. As these narratives imply, we don't necessarily need to look to evil space aliens coming in ships to find a "species" that both generates and thrives upon waste and the destruction of the elements. We need only look to the human warheads of multinational corporations and military establishments and to their machines.

Modern reports of UFO sightings and encounters with space aliens originated in the period immediately following World War II and have become ever more insistent. The initial sightings of "flying saucers" were recorded in 1947 in Washington state and were followed by the reported crash landing of a space vehicle near Roswell, New Mexico. As one of my graduate students, Annette Peláez, has shown, a great many reports of alien craft sightings or abductions have occurred in the vicinities of nuclear facilities.[8] Numerous films, stories, and written accounts suggested a reason for this: that humanity's invention of atomic weaponry had attracted the attention of advanced alien civilizations. So prominent were the flying saucer reports in the 1950s that Carl Jung devoted a book to what he termed the "visionary rumor," suggesting that such reports were a protective psychological projection in response to fear of atomic weaponry and the aggressive designs of the Soviets.[9]

Of course, modern American culture is not unique in this visionary experience. Other cultures have long had traditions of contact with alien beings. For example, Lakota shaman Wallace Black Elk reports that encounters with spirit or star beings have long been recognized in the Lakota tradition. These beings are neither foreign nor unknown, and Black Elk jokingly calls them "UFOs." In his view, it is scientists who are "not trained," who have "lost contact with the wisdom, knowledge, power, and gift. So they have to see everything first with their naked eye. They have to catch one first. They have to shoot it down and then see what all it is made of, how it was shaped and formed. But their intention is wrong, so somebody is misleading those scientists that way."[10]

Throughout human history, many people have reported meetings with supernaturals. As psychology professor Kenneth Ring, journalist James Gordon, and a variety of observers suggest, modern reports of alien encounters are very similar to descriptions of shamanic travels. Both involve transformative journeys in which people encounter strange beings who irrevocably alter them.[11] Certainly, the contemporary popular narrative regarding UFO sightings and alien encounters does coincide with the invention of the Bomb. Yet perhaps the reason for this is not because UFO reports represent fearful psychological projections. Rather, it might be because the underlying theme of both UFO and Bomb narratives is that of radical transmutation—a qualitative change in human identity and our sense of self and species in the cosmos. The increased reporting of encounters with aliens may indeed reflect an accelerated concourse by Westerners with supernaturals, a phenomenon reflecting the exigencies of this time at the end of the world as we know it. Still, stories always have multiple meanings, and "evil alien" invasion stories may also be interpreted with respect to their metaphorical commentary about human life on Earth.

The alien motif, particularly coupled with nuclear themes, showed up throughout the postwar period in scores of science fiction films, including *The Day the Earth Stood Still*, *War of the Worlds*,

Invaders from Mars, Invasions of the Body Snatchers, The Mysterians, The Space Children, Village of the Damned, and *Children of the Damned.* In her classic essay on this subject, "The Imagination of Disaster," cultural theorist Susan Sontag noted the machinelike character of aliens in such films, who, though they were frequently portrayed as simulating human form, were also imagined as emotionless, efficient, and rigid beings. Sontag claimed that monsters in earlier horror films, such as *The Wolfman,* acted out humanity's fear of dehumanization by succumbing to a "beast" within. In the postwar science fiction films, however, the threat, while remaining dehumanization, now lay "in man's ability to be turned into a machine."[12]

Certainly, this fear was inspired in part by the machine-identified, psychically numb nuclearist consciousness proudly adopted by some elite Earthlings like the rigidly emotionless SAC leader Curtis LeMay. If, as religious historian Ira Chernus declares, the dominant culture has accepted what it perceives to be a "death machine" as its divinity, perhaps it is inevitable that those who subscribe to this religion remake themselves in the image and likeness of their god. Those of us who do not accept this death-machine god, however, are regarded by these techno-idolaters rather like the heathens targeted by those imperialistic Christians (the original "toxic crusaders") who marched out under the sign of the cross to convert the world and, in so doing, committed countless acts of genocide.[13]

In some ways, then, the persistence of the contemporary alien-invasion narrative is due to the fact that it resonates with a very earthly experience of invasion, colonization, and mechanization. The planet and its creatures, including all women and most dark-skinned, poor, and/or subversive males have been routinely invaded by elite Western men, real-life toxic crusaders who adamantly assume an extraterrestrial perspective. These invaders have taken a distant, objective, and objectifying view of the Earth, identifying themselves with "aliens"—that is, assuming the subjectivity of machines and oppressing, exterminating, and *screwing* all organisms within their reach.

Such "biological cleansing" was flaunted in a haunting ad for the Toyota Land Cruiser in the *New York Times Magazine* on July 19, 1992. In the ad, the vehicle had come to a stop on a dirt road in a verdant rain forest. Two very shadowy human figures sat in the front seats. The copy read,

> DARWIN WAS RIGHT. Survival of the Fittest. For more than forty years, the Toyota Land Cruiser has roamed the earth as a dominant species. Each new generation, becoming stronger and better adapted to the harsh environments in which it's so often found. Like the Amazon, the Sahara, the Arctic.

Unspoken in this ad was the fact that the warhead culture represented by the Land Cruiser has ordained the extinction of uncounted numbers of "nondominant" animal and plant species—symbolized not too subtly by the rainforest setting of this ad. In truth, machines have not so much adapted to earthly environments as earthly environs have been modified and trashed to suit the requirements of machines and the consumers who identify with them. Worldwide, forests are being disappeared, allegedly to make way for human progress. However, before humans gloat too much at our technical prowess and advancement, we should take a closer look at this picture, for we humans are on the verge of being disappeared as well.

Many machine dreamers might applaud such replacement by machines as a most positive indicator. Hans Moravec, an expert in robotics at Carnegie-Mellon University, is a man who loves too much—machines, that is. In his 1988 book, *Mind Children: The Future of Robot and Human Intelligence,* Moravec rhapsodizes that humanity is poised on the edge of a "postbiological" future,

> a world in which the human race has been swept away by the tide of cultural change, usurped by its own artificial progeny. . . . Today our machines are still simple creations, requiring the parental care and hovering attention of any newborn, hardly worthy of the word "intelligent." But within the next century they will mature into entities as complex as ourselves, and eventually into something transcending everything we know—in whom we can take pride when they refer to themselves as our descendants. . . . We humans will benefit for a time from their labors, but sooner or later, like natural children, they will seek their own fortunes while we, their aged parents, silently fade away.[14]

Moravec yearns to be swept away, though remembered technos-talgically[15] by his "progeny." What sort of emotional motivations underlie this fantasy? Clearly, there is that familiar envy of the female body's capacity to give birth, evidenced in Moravec's view of himself as the father progenitor of a new "superior" breed, albeit a soon-to-be obsolete father. A further emotion girding this machine worship, as in the brand espoused by Arthur C. Clarke, is a loathing for the organic, the biological, the bodily—the province of the Crone.

Clarke's and Moravec's sentiments are the stuff of much contemporary popular culture. If the 1950s films portrayed aliens as machinelike beings, later science fiction films frequently posit a genesislike moment when earthly machines attain subjectivity—and immediately want to reproduce. Such films include *Colossus: The Forbin Project* (1970), *Demon Seed (1977)*, and *The Terminator* (1984). In *The Terminator*, machines become conscious somewhere around the turn of the twenty-first century, only to immediately initiate nuclear war as a way to get rid of their abhorred and dangerous ancestors, the human race. The Terminator himself, played by Arnold Schwarzenegger, is a cyborg, a machine with some human "parts." He is sent from the future to perform something of a retroactive abortion, that is, to kill the woman who will give birth to a son with the alarming initials J.C., who is destined to lead the human resistance against the machine takeover. Although the story sides with the sentimental, saving the mother and fetus, its real hero and focus of identification is the Terminator himself. Once again, a popular film creates a masochistic identification with an abuser, in this case the machines who have wasted the Earth and who want, literally, our flesh and our blood.

The Terminator is but one of countless cyborgs inhabiting our popular landscape. There are "good" ones and "bad" ones, emblems of terror and emblems of pleasure, beings produced through the "mating" or intermingling of humans and machines. They include the Six Million Dollar Man, the Bionic Woman, Robocop, Lieutenant Commander Data, and a burgeoning, if less famous, population in commercial advertising and science fiction stories. Scholars frequently point to cyborgs as the consummate product of postmodern consciousness because they disintegrate the traditional boundary between the human and the technological.[16]

One postmodern feminist theorist, Donna Haraway, has adopted the cyborg as a revolutionary mythic identity. While noting its origins in the military-industrial complex, she nonetheless feels the cyborg to be "the illegitimate offspring of militarism and patriarchal capitalism" and hence potentially disloyal to those "inessential" fathers. She further claims that the cyborg can aid in the subversion of Western capitalist patriarchy and its dualisms, gender assignments, enmities, and apocalyptic drift. According to Haraway, we already are cyborgs, beings formed through the fusion of machines, humans, and animals. She chides radical feminists who "insist on the organic, opposing it to the technological," and celebrates the cyborg for its abandonment of the spurious "organic": "The cyborg would not recognize the Garden of Eden; it is not made of mud and cannot dream of returning to dust. Perhaps that is why I want to see if cyborgs can subvert the apocalypse of returning to nuclear dust." Haraway ultimately concludes her manifesto, "Though both are bound in the spiral dance, I would rather be a cyborg than a goddess."[17]

Haraway's work reminds us, as it should, that the choice of mythic identity is rooted in personal taste and proclivities. Nevertheless, while I certainly can understand the appeal of the mechanically bolstered cyborg as a solution to the multiple threats to the body posed by nuclear weapons, toxic waste, random sexualized violences, AIDS, and so on, I cannot accept fully the notion that the cyborg is a subversive political identity.

Haraway applauds the fact that modern scientific culture has thoroughly dissolved the boundaries between human and animal (by showing that both use language and tools) and between human and machine (as in medical technologies). Yet is the dissolution of boundaries always something to cheer about? Scientific culture regularly violates animal and human boundaries through standard modes of colonization, experimentation, torture, and appropriation.[18]

Many humans already *are* cyborgs, according to Haraway, for we have merged with machines in innumerable ways. Yet cyborg existence is not always our choice, nor is it in our best interest. For example, I have "cyborg" lungs—that is, lungs filled with car exhaust and other forms of toxic waste. Moreover, while Haraway celebrates the identification of humans with technology, there are only brief references to the inclusion of animals in the cyborg persona and no elaboration at all upon their inherent Powers. This does not surprise me, for the primary human concourse with animals I see undertaken by technology is disrespectful destruction of their habitats, disrespectful torture and exploitation of their bodies in laboratories, and disrespectful appropriation of their flesh, skin, fur, and, most recently, their very organs—baboon hearts, pig livers, and so on—for transplantation into ailing human bodies.

Despite these disagreements, I find Haraway's work fruitfully "shocking" in much the same way that Paula Gunn Allen has shocked me. Haraway's cyborg mythos demands that we resacralize our bodies *and* our machines by seeing both as profoundly interconnected and even coextensive. Haraway also makes us realize that in order to create a genuinely radical social revolution we must imagine a complete transmutation of human subjectivity—psychic and even physical.

However, when doing this I believe we must guard against perpetuating one of the most fundamental patriarchal traditions: the loathing for the body and for the Earth, the very originating female mud from which Haraway so cleanly disassociates her cyborg. Otherwise, cyborg mythos might well ultimately collaborate with nuclearism, supporting, not thwarting, body- and Earth-wasting technologies. Haraway is right: we must cease promoting a false opposition between technology and nature, the artificial and the organic. Yet to do this in a truly subversive way would entail not insulating ourselves from the mud, but bringing our technologies into ritual balance with our bodies, with animals, and with the elements. If that is cyborg being, I am all in favor of it.

Atomic veterans who witnessed the U.S. above-ground tests in the 1950s testified "that they saw both animals and humans chained in cages close to ground zero."[19] These caged beings were literally sacrificed to the death-machine god, yet this horrific incident represents only the most overt form of such ritual sacrifice. The consumer society aggrandizes elite men as the godlike creators of godlike machines. Simultaneously, it demands that human bodies—primarily those of the poor—and, in even greater abandon, plant, mineral, and animal bodies be sacrificed to them. The corporation, from the Latin word *corpus*, meaning "body," now rules the flesh-and-blood body. Many humans—unpaid, grievously exploited workers, for example—constitute a good part of the "food" or raw materials for the corporation. Others, higher on the consumer chain, avidly seek its products. Of course, if shoppers could see many of these corporate products in all of their dimensions, we would perceive them to be prettily packaged toxic waste, strip-mined mountains, oil-spilled waters, and "nuked" forests, all hiding behind the mask of consumer "goods."

The abandonment and dishonoring of the body and its Powers is an ontologically disastrous error. In her brilliant and heartfelt essay "The Woman I Love Is a Planet," Paula Gunn Allen writes that our bodies are our most precious "talismans" connecting us to the Earth: "Walking in balance, in harmony, and in a sacred manner requires staying in your body, accepting its discomforts, decayings, witherings, and blossomings and respecting them."[20] In other words, one of the most politically radical and effective things that any of us can do is respect our bodies—and the bodies of others—in all of their manifestations and transformations. This includes respecting aging, fatness, weakness, male softness, female hairiness, bodily waste making, and even our sickness and death. One of the most common ways to insult someone is to call them a "slimy bad," hence shame-ridden, body part, like *asshole*. Perhaps if we were a body-respecting culture that honored even our "assholes," we might not be a corporation- and machine-ruled culture that has made of our world a toxic "shitpile."

The popular and patriarchal imagination of the cyborg remains based in the civilized folly of body loathing and denial, and, concomitantly, Earth loathing and denial. Snools have long had machine wet dreams of cyborgs—permanently hard masculine ones like the "Terminator" or controllable feminine ones like the countless canned fembots who so preoccupy popular culture. Ironically, these constructs are everywhere proclaimed to be the "future"—harbingers of radical progress and change—but in the larger scheme of things they are far more equivalent to late-night, fly-by-night television gadgets and novelties and have very little to do with the ultimate and intimate processes of transmutation now occurring on the planet.

Transmutation: Turtle Powers

Tell them as I dying live
so they dying will live again.
—*The Moon speaking through a turtle
to the African bushpeople*[21]

I think that technological societies are very young, very very young, not even adolescent yet. And so they love new gadgets and the latest craze. . . . In old fuddy-duddy culture, tribal culture, we are into change in the sense of transmutation, ritual, because the purpose of ritual is to change something from one state or condition to another. . . . Ritual becomes what the grown-ups do, while the little kids are content with changing their toys.
—*Paula Gunn Allen*[22]

In 1901, two scientists working together, Ernest Rutherford and Frederick Soddy, discovered that radioactivity is a manifestation of "fundamental changes within matter. A pulse of radiation signals that an atom is changing into a different kind of atom, a different element with its own chemical properties." For example, radioactive thorium gradually turns itself into radium. Spencer Weart reports that at this moment of realization, Soddy, steeped in the history of alchemy, shouted out, "Rutherford, this is transmutation."[23] The core metaphysical meaning of the nuclear age, which, as Weart points out, properly began with the discovery of radium, is transmutation, change, and evolution. All earthly creatures and planet Earth herself are now "radioactive" in the sense that we all are in a heightened process of changing into something else.

Weart has suggested that this alchemical concept of transmutation—the passage from destruction to rebirth, both physical and metaphysical, individual and societal—informs nearly all species of nuclear myth. [24] As I have noted earlier, one of this motif's most common variants is the notion that exposure to radiation causes humans to mutate dramatically and qualitatively, a premise acted out regularly by comic book superheroes. Most recently, this same theme has achieved unprecedented popularity in the explosively popular narratives of the "Teenage Mutant Ninja Turtles" in comic books, cartoons, movies, and toys. According to the Ninja Turtles origin story, the four superheroes were once tiny turtles living in the sewers of New York City. One day, they were accidentally doused with some type of radioactive waste, which turned them into half-human, pizza-chomping, sewer-dwelling, teenage-boy–like Ninja warriors. Fans can purchase a plethora of Ninja Turtle toys, including a small plastic container of "Turtles Retromutagen Ooze," promising to make the buyer "mutate like a real Ninja Turtle."

Watching Ninja Turtle cartoons and movies is a fairly superficial experience. If this is transmutation, how could it be so boring? Still, the central metaphor is quite evocative. The turtle is one of the most ancient of Earth's creatures—an amphibian, able to travel between elemental worlds—and one with a complex symbolic heritage. For millennia, the turtle has been understood as a watery, female-identified being, a correspondent of the Moon, and, most importantly, an avatar of the Earth. In many Native American as well as Asian (including Japanese) oral traditions, the Turtle *is* the Earth.[25]

Frankly, the patriarchal world does feel rather like a teenage mutant ninja sewer, a Ted Bundy–world run by war-crazed, waste-obsessed men who are ruled by their "inner teenagers." Still, we can uncover a greater meaning in the bizarre story of the Ninja Turtles, for this story of turtle transmutation is mythically quite resonant. Turtle Island—the name the Earth is called to this day by many Native Americans—*is* transmuting; she is undergoing profound changes in which all of her creatures necessarily participate. As Paula Gunn Allen sees it, the Earth is entering upon a great initiation, from which she will emerge as "one of the sacred planets in the Grand-mother galaxy":

> Now, now is the time when mother becomes grandmother, when daughter becomes mother. . . . I have said that this is the time of her initiation, of her new birth. I could also say it is the time of mutation, for transformation means to change form.[26]

As creatures of the Earth, we humans are also undergoing profound and mysterious transformations, marked frequently by travail and terror. We are afraid that we will lose our humanity and change into something alien, something unrecognizable. This emotion is explored in great depth in Octavia Butler's sci-fi novel *Dawn*.[27] *Dawn* is set in a time of cosmic change. The Earth has been devastated by nuclear war, and plantlike, bizarrely sexed aliens arrive wanting to mate with humans to form a new species. Terrifying, yes, but as Butler metaphorically suggests, the change of life we now are undergoing does indeed require that we become aliens—that we *lose* our "humanity." That is, modern people must lose those all-too-familiar qualities of apocalyptic aggressiveness, consummate consumer greed, hierarchical ordering, fear of and loathing for anyone we define as "other," fundamentalist thought patterns, wastefulness, and the severe propensity to objectify.

How do we lose these patterns? While some thinkers suggest merging with mechanisms, I see in that approach a continued alienation from instinct, intelligence, eroticism, sense perception, emotions, and psychic abilities—in short, from the Powers of our bodies. In our healing and transmutational work, Paula Gunn Allen insists that first of all we need to cherish and honor our bodies, "singing *"Heya-hey* to our flesh":

> The mortal body is a tree; it is holy in whatever condition; it is truth and myth because it has so many potential conditions; because of its possibilities, it is profane and sacred; most of all, it is your most precious talisman, your own connection to her. Healing the self means honoring and recognizing the body, accepting rather than denying all the turmoil its existence brings, welcoming the woes and anguish flesh is subject to, cherishing its multitudinous forms and seasons, its unfailing ability to know and be, to grow and wither, to live and die, to mutate, to change.[28]

To be politically useful and spiritually mature, we might take as our model the tree. The Mother of us all, in her form known as Sophia, was long ago said to be a tree, the great Tree of Life. In that spirit, Allen strongly urges us to go out and talk to trees, learning as fully as we can how to be a tree. However, it is difficult in Christendom to hold concourse with trees—not only because they are being sacrificed to the gods of technology and consumption in reckless abandon, but also because, under Christianity's bitter rule, the Tree of Life has been turned into the torture cross of the world.[29] The Crusades, the explorations and exploitations of Columbus, and the atrocities of the Ku Klux Klan were and are horrors conducted under the sign of the cross.[30] This core icon of Christianity, depicting the broken body of a feminized man nailed to a mutilated tree, is a symbol that has encouraged loathing for the body and for nature.

When I was around twelve, I had a dream that made a tremendous impression on me. I was walking in a place that I knew well in daytime life—a narrow, tree-lined path. There, in a transsexed version of the typical Christian crucifixion scene, were three women hanging on three trees. These three very similar women called out to me in a language I did not understand. I felt their anguish and knew that someday I would have to act on their behalf. The image of the crucified Jesus refers to, but simultaneously deflects awareness away from the fact that christotechnology has put the female guardians of the elemental world "on the cross."

I remember as a child learning about the "passion of Christ," a passion marked by his submission to whippings, torture, and death at the hands of a supreme father. As I grew, that "greatest story ever told" was continually told and retold in a variety of forms—everything from tales of the Christian martyrs to *The Story of O.* It is profoundly ironic to see devout Christian moralists such as U.S. senator Jesse Helms leading the campaign against such artwork as the photography of gay S&M devotee Robert Mapplethorpe,[31] for Christianity itself provides our culture's basic model for sadomasochistic, homophobic homoeroticism.[32] The feminized and near-naked Jesus hanging willingly, even ecstatically,[33] on the cross, in total submission to his cruel father, is an advertisement par excellence for erotic torture and, quite frankly, child abuse. And this image promises ever greater pornographic torments to come.

The story and iconography of Jesus is endlessly revealing. One further aspect is most relevant here: he died, but his body did not rot. Rather, according to the myth, he, as every good Christian learns, *defeated death.* In truth, then, Jesus was the first cyborg. He literally was resurrected and exists in some permanent, glorified (plastic) state up in space/heaven. As the second millennium since his birth approaches, many believers await the return of Jesus and an accompanying doomsday for the elemental and the earthly.

Such an apocalypse inspires no fear in these boys and girls, for they believe they will be saved, their bodies swept up in the sky during a "rapture"—an experience that, as the word itself suggests, is rife with rapist and sadomasochistic longings.[34] Of course, nuclear and environmental apocalypse may indeed be coming—aided by two thousand years of human-worshiping, nature-loathing, and torture-loving dicta of christotechnological practices and beliefs. But Crones tell the truth about such a doomsday: all, or most of us, will go. Certainly no one religious group will be spared.

Crones also tell the truth about the fate of the body. At death, the body returns to Earth and the elements—it disintegrates. Then its constituents reform, transmute, and become something else. Christianity, particularly in the Jesus myth, refuses this journey. Jesus, as imagined in the Christian tradition, is an everlasting "shiny good." Yet behind that pretty facade, he actually is a ghoul, a representative of the unburied dead returning to cannibalize the living (despite the dogmatic reversal that it is we who are eating him).

As we approach the millennium, Crones tell us that this point in time is not the hour of Jesus' return, but the prime time for his burial, time for that permanently tortured body to come down off the cross.[35] Symbolically and mythically, we must bury Jesus. He must be returned to Earth, where he can complete his cycle. Buried, he can journey into the dark womb of the inner Earth to gain some of the gynesophical[36] wisdom enclosed there. He can get a taste of Chaos by participating in the full cycle of existence, rotting and merging with the elements so strenuously vilified in his name. With his body finally buried, a new and ecological metaphor of male Powers might spring forth from the decomposition. With the cross dismantled, we might again approach Sophia, the Tree of Wisdom and of Life.

Millennia ago, the "desire that generates the energy of the universe" was understood and represented by such metaphors as Inanna, the Sumerian goddess of love.[37] This is the "Pure Lust" that

Mary Daly conceptualizes as "unadulterated, absolute, simple sheer striving for abundance of be-ing. . . . unlimited, unlimiting desire/ fire." Patriarchal men are not content to, or are perhaps simply afraid to, participate in that vortex of ultimately uncontrollable and unpredictable desire. Instead, they have built a civilization founded upon seemingly endless "phallic lust"—raping, torturing, denying, exploiting, and hoarding cosmic energy experienced as female.[38] This civilization has worked to chop down the Tree of Life to a veritable stump.[39] Simultaneously, it has banished and denied any notions of nonsexist, egalitarian, and elemental energy experienced as male.

Our civilization has produced as its highest achievement a pornotechnology based on the objectification of the Earth's body and the sublimation of intermeshed pleasure and domination, eroticism and destruction into mechanisms. Concomitantly, it has striven to achieve a battery, rape, enslavement, and wasting of elemental Powers. Pornotechnology is epitomized by the sadistic desire infusing all aspects of nuclear development—from the investiture of rapist energy in phallic weaponry to the attempt to render nuclear energy a controlled—hence beautiful—female "breeder." A similar sadistic dynamic informs reproductive technologies that attempt to turn women, even postmenopausal women, into what feminist theorist Gena Corea calls "mother machines"—cyborg wombs and controlled sexual objects that are endlessly moist and fertile and perpetually open to insemination.[40]

The World Grandmother

"California Woman, 53, Gives Birth to Twins."
—Headline, *The New York Times*, November 12, 1992

In their brilliant book, *The Great Cosmic Mother*, mythographers Monica Sjöö and Barbara Mor identify the control and exploitation of female reproductive capacities as the foundation of all patriarchal power and the model for all subsequent exploitations. They incisively assess patriarchal man's relationship to his engines and machines:[41]

The machine has been called man's baby, sometimes man's true lover. It is also patriarchal man's version of the World Mother. The machine is man's transformation ritual, his magic uterus of mass production. The machine is a manmade system, device, or theology-philosophy for converting world energy (animal, vegetable, mineral) into human wealth.[42]

This attempt at cosmic fettering is enacted in the worldwide enslavement of female bodies and reproductive Powers. Female exercise of bodily reproductive autonomy, therefore, threatens every patriarchal "life" support system, since male supremacy is so dependent upon a perpetual fetal fettering of the World Mother. Captured female energy, as Sjöö and Mor rightly claim, is the true energy source behind patriarchal history. They further argue that the "next stage [of patriarchal development] depends on the total physical and economic mechanization of the female body. The global assembly line turning out consumer junk and human consumers (and human-replacing robots) will be the great machine mother of the world— with the eggs, uteruses, and hormone systems of living women attached to it, one way or another, in servomechanistic functions."[43]

This, indeed, is the direction of that long march known as patriarchy. Yet, there is a *fatal*—in all senses of the word—flaw in this march. Time, as we know, does not proceed along straight lines, and the patriarchal parade is about to run smack into the ends of the Earth. The planet herself is journeying to a destination all her own, following a destiny all her own. As part of that process, she is perhaps experiencing her own "stage," analogous to what human females understand as menopause or the climacteric.

Feminist author Carolyn Heilbrun avers that women, when they are past fifty, "can stop being female impersonators, can grasp the opportunity to reverse their most cherished principles of 'femininity.'"[44] Despite the intense social opprobrium directed at women who are elders and despite the lack of ritual attention and ceremony given to menopause, many menopausal women still report that after passing through the climacteric they achieve a greater sense of personal empowerment.[45] This arises out of a liberation from the constraints of biology, most particularly (for heterosexual women) the rigors of fertility and reproduction, and a newfound liberation from the psychological bondage to femininity.

Understanding the ends of the Earth through the metaphor of the climacteric, we can postulate that the World Mother, too, is shaking herself free from millennia of a "forced marriage," withdrawing her abundant fertility, and leaving mankind to reckon with her judgments, her necessities, her irrevocable Fates. Previously, men asked the Earth for gifts, and the Earth, in Alice Walker's words, "ever giving . . . opened itself fully to their desires."[46] Now, the Earth as Haggis laughs in their faces. Having withdrawn her "wiseblood"[47]— her cosmic creative energy sources—back into herself, the Earth Crone is no longer so endlessly fertile, so perpetually giving and forgiving in the face of systematic disrespect.

Mythographer Robert Briffault writes, "The power of witchcraft belongs particularly to old women."[48] Old and young men alike have long been profoundly afraid of unsubmissive old women. They know that the fatal Crone energy encompasses not only the Powers of psychic warfare—cursing, prophecy, and eyebiting—but also the Gossip's or Granny Midwife's Powers to ensure that women can *"control their own fate, learn secrets of sex and birth control, or procure abortions"* (emphasis mine).[49] The Crone, in short, is the one who cuts the cord of that fetal fettering of the World Mother. She aborts phallocratic parasitism once and for all. This consummately fatal act links her unmistakably with the Fates of the Earth.

The headline cited at the beginning of this section—the one about the fifty-three-year-old woman giving birth to twins after test-tube fertilization—is from a news story that caught my eye. On one level, it is just another horrific news item trumpeting pornotechnology's extending control over female bodies. However, there are also some strangely unsettling mythic meanings that leak through this story, some intimations of chaotic stirrings. The woman is a grandmother, and her newborn twins are females. This is reminiscent of an ancient story. Once upon a time Spider Grandmother also "gave birth," that is, thought into being, twin daughters. These twins were the supernaturals mentioned earlier, Nau'ts'ity and Ic'sts'ity, or Naotsete and Iyatiku.[50] Female twins here and elsewhere carry meanings of cosmogynic[51] origins and Powers, of justice and balance. They include even the metaphorical warrior twins Thelma and Louise![52]

When the nuclear fathers built the atom bomb, they thought of themselves as conquering nature. However, they actually were writing a script for the demise of their world, maybe even their species. So, too, technological male mothers, in inducing the Grandmother to bear, may be achieving a very temporary victory. However, I wager that they are simultaneously sowing the seeds of their own impotence, planning, albeit unintentionally, their own obsolescence.

CHAPTER TWELVE

The Fates of the Earth

Fates [derived fr. L *fatum* prophetic declaration, oracle . . . destiny, fate, fr. *fari* to speak—*Webster's*]: the Norns, the Weird Sisters, the three Goddesses who determine the course of events; Moon Goddesses, Be-Speakers, Weavers, Spinners of Stamina— the Thread of Life; the Forces who can save the world.
—*Mary Daly with Jane Caputi*, Wickedary[1]

The 1988 film *Pumpkinhead* is usually thought of as an exploitative teenage splatter film. Yet this thoroughly heathen horror film offers a compelling vision of the complex workings of some of the forces represented by the Crone, in this case divine justice or fate.[2] The story opens with a group of city teenagers traveling to the country. One of them, while recklessly driving his motorcycle, accidentally kills a young boy. The boy's father, Ed Harley, is inconsolable. At first, Harley seems as if he were the perfect father, a recent widower totally devoted to his son. Yet scattered throughout the film are subtle but unmistakable references suggesting that Harley murdered his wife. Not such a nice guy after all.

Bent upon vengeance, and ignoring the advice of his neighbors, Harley drives out to visit the Haggis, an ancient Crone. The Haggis lives at the edge of the woods, in a cabin with her familiars: owls, bats, spiders, and rats. Harley walks in holding the body of his son, wanting her to reverse fate and raise the dead. She immediately tells him, "That's not within my Powers." He is adamant, puts money in her cup, and insists that she help him in some other way. OK, she says, you asked for it. The Haggis tells him to dig up a body from where it is buried in an old pumpkin patch. She then animates this demon, Pumpkinhead, who immediately sets out to destroy the youth and his friends. Ed Harley, however, is not having any fun. To his horror, he finds that it is his own lust driving the demon and that, consequently, he has to experience all the torment and death that has been unleashed.

Mad as hell, Harley returns to the Haggis, demanding that she stop the demon. "Nothing I can do," she says. "It's gotta run its course." At this point Harley curses her, and she only laughs at him, "You're a fool, Ed Harley, you're a fool." He then swears to her, "Well then, I'll do it myself." The Haggis sneers back, "You'll fail, Ed Harley, you'll fail and you'll die." The film concludes with Harley trying to shoot himself, but failing. One of the surviving teenagers— a female—picks up his gun and kills him herself. At this moment, Pumpkinhead bursts into flames and disintegrates. The last scene shows the Haggis alone in the old pumpkin patch at midnight, burying another demon body, this one with the face of Ed Harley.

The Haggis reads Ed Harley just right and tells it exactly as it is. Ed Harley is a *fool* and one who epitomizes the common run of fools now dominating the planet. Those fools are "smart at doing stupid things." They continually try to defeat death, beseeching and besieging the Earth to give them the means to build ultimate weapons. Such weapons, like Pumpkinhead, are animated by the maleficence of their creators, whom the weapons will come back to torment and destroy. For, as the Haggis reminds us, one cannot tamper with fate.

The Sacred Triangle

According to Albert Einstein, there is a dimension beyond time/space where time stands still—past, present, and future are one. My Cherokee ancestors knew how to enter this dimension at will. Since their spirits abide in my native mountains in East Tennessee, I walk with the strong nurturing grandmothers.
—*Marilou Awiakta*[3]

On the campus of the University of New Mexico, there is a sign that often jumps out at me. It consists of three downward-pointing yellow triangles against a black background. Downward is the direction of the Earth, the underground, the place of emergence. Yellow is not only the color of corn and uranium, but also, in the Keres tradition, the color of women. Black is the color of the Crone. The triangle is not only the worldwide sign most commonly associated with radiation, but also the sign of the cosmic energies understood as female.[4] Specifically, the triangle invokes the Triple Goddess and the Powers associated with the wise Crone. Most importantly, "three triangles created the emblem of the Fate Goddesses, the Greek Moerae, Teutonic Norns, Roman Fortunae, medieval Parcae or Weird Sisters."[5]

The sign on campus nominally refers to the presence of an atomic bomb shelter; however, its mythic meaning unmistakably points to the presence of the Fates of the Earth. "Nearly all mythologies," Barbara Walker writes, "bear traces of the Triple Goddess as three Fates, rulers of the past, present, and future in the usual personae of Virgin, Mother, and Crone (or Creator, Preserver, Destroyer)."[6] Like Awiakta's Grandmothers, the Fates abide in that dimension where time stands still. They are—and endure in—the ends of the Earth.

All Fates are Moon goddesses, and all "are older than the gods."[7] The Greek conception of the Fates as Moerae is reminiscent of the creative activity of Spider Grandmother. The Moerae are also spinners, measurers, and, finally, cutters of *stamina*, the thread of life. For each individual, it is the Fates whose word or gesture selects the time of death. That decision, moreover, is always binding, for there is no one who "can withstand the word of Urdha."[8] As for the individual, so, too, for the world. Therefore, the Fates also represent *judgment*, including the final judgment, or doomsday.

Fools like Ed Harley might curse fate, but only to have the Haggis laugh in their faces, for cursing belongs to the Fates and to those who participate in their Powers, not to those who oppose them. The Scandinavian Norns are named Urth (Earth)—"fate"; Verthandi—"being"; and Skuld—"necessity." The original and oldest sister is Urth, "who represented Fate and the Words of creation." If Urth is the magical first word, Skuld is the very last, for it is "she [who] would lay the death-curse on the whole universe at doomsday."[9]

Given the sexual exploitation of children and women, the rampaging epidemics of incest, rape, and sexual murder, the continuing horrors of racism and genocide—both subtle and overt—the insatiable greed of consumer society, and the ever greater outpourings of phallic lust in pollution, war, and weaponry, the thought of imminent doomsday might bring momentary satisfaction to those of us who have been injured by any or all of these atrocities. Yet—rather than focus upon a holocaust to "purify" Earth, let us make our pact with divine Justice, that is, with the Fates, for it is the Powers of scarcity, necessity, change, chance, and chaos that can save the world. Alice Walker has contemplated this choice, concluding that a revenge achieved from the grave—rather like the revenge gotten by Ed Harley—is not a very satisfactory one at that.

Walker opens her essay "Only Justice Can Stop a Curse" by reciting a curse prayer collected by Zora Neale Hurston in the 1920s. The curse is steeped in desire for vengeance against unspeakable oppressions, a "prayer by a person who would readily, almost happily, commit suicide, if it meant her enemies would also die. Horribly." Walker empathizes heartily with such righteous rage and believes we must seriously consider the possibility that ending the human race might be the only way to save both earthly and other creatures from the destructive colonizations of the wasichu.

Still, she concludes that wishing for such a vast and indiscriminate annihilation serves, ultimately, no greater good. After all, radiation does not discriminate. It beams into the cells of the just as well as the unjust. And why anyway, Walker demands, should *she* forsake her home, the Earth? Although white people continuously maintain that she has no right to exist, "except in the dirtiest, darkest corners of the globe." Walker vows to

> protect my home. Praying—not a curse—only the hope that my courage will not fail my love. But if by some miracle, and all our struggle, the Earth is spared, only justice to every living thing (and everything is alive) will save humankind.
>
> And we are not saved yet.
>
> *Only justice can stop a curse.*[10]

It is to the Fates, then, that we must turn, for the Fates have everything to teach us. They teach not only of the cursing that lays a ban on geocidal and gynocidal depredations, but also of *justice.*

Talk of fate often revolves around one's "lot in life," for the Fates are the dividers and measurers of lots, the ones who apportion each person's special sphere of activity. Like primitive mothers or grandmothers, they also mete out each person's portion of food and lot of land.[11] I remember reading years ago that if all the food available on any given day in the world were distributed equally among all the people, we each would get portions equivalent to about two hundred calories. Five thousand years ago there were about five million people on the Earth. Within the next fifty years, the human population is expected to exceed nine billion.

Due to this overpopulation, as well as colonialism, consumerism, and toxic wasting of the environment, the available "portions" of all resources are becoming ever more minuscule and, simultaneously, more inequitably distributed. A team of environmental experts reported in the February 1993 issue of *Scientific American* that "renewable-resource scarcities of the next 50 years will probably occur with a speed, complexity and magnitude unprecedented in history. Entire countries can now be deforested in a few decades, most of a region's topsoil can disappear in a generation, and acute ozone depletion may take place in as few as 20 years."[12] The authors stress that these scarcities of renewable resources have led and will continue to lead to outbreaks of war and mass violence. They call upon "rich and poor countries alike" to "restrain population growth, to implement a more equitable distribution of wealth within and among their societies, and to provide for sustainable development."

So-called First World corporations grievously exploit human beings and other "resources" in the so-called Third World to maximize their profits. For example, one U.S. company, Nike, pays malnourished female workers in Southeast Asia about fourteen cents an hour—less than they need to provide for "minimum physical needs"—to manufacture sneakers that sell in the United States for about $130. In 1991, Nike grossed more than $3 billion in sales.[13] Not only is the labor of Third World peoples thus grievously exploited, but many of the scarcities and contaminations in their communities are caused by First World traditions of colonialism and consumption. First World residents continue to use resources—renewable and non-renewable—at a rate of about ten to twenty times greater than that of people in the Third World. In 1990, the United States declared war on a Third World country, Iraq, in part to assure continued U.S. access to a nonrenewable resource, oil.

Yet, how much longer do we really think the arrogant wasichu world can gluttonously "eat the fat?" How much longer can we continuously cannibalize the bodies, lands, and resources of others without engendering "divine retribution"? As with Lady Fortuna and her cosmic wheel, the Fates raise the fallen and abase the arrogant.[14] The Crone represents the Powers who return to demand equitable distribution, to level out gross imbalance, and to balance the cosmic scales of justice.

In "Osa" Hidalgo-de la Riva's beautiful and inspiring short film, *Mujeria: Primitive and Proud*, the testing of the atomic bomb is understood as an event that has "irreversibly deflected the future of the cosmos." The test, in part, occasions the arrival into 1950s California of a woman from the gynocentric Olmeca culture, which flourished some three thousand years ago in what is now Mexico. This woman, Eagle Bear, is followed by the ancient Olmeca warrior goddess.[15] Hidalgo-de la Riva is not alone in her vision of the return of female Powers to our time.

When I put my ear to the ground, I hear a constant chant: "The Grandmothers are returning."[16] Some would say they are awakening. The Fates are journeying toward us from the farthest reaches of space and time. Knowledge of this journey fills many with extreme trepidation, for the Fates can take the form of doom, disaster, and devastation. Yet we are not mere spectators to or victims of the Fates, but participants in these Powers. Thus, it is up to us to become *fateful*—to have "the power of serving or accomplishing fate"— *Webster's*. We must spur ourselves to influence the form the Fates will take when they greet us. After all, the Fates come not only from the world above and the world below, but also from without and from within. If we live in accordance with necessity, if we hold all things to be sacred, if we honor the Earth's time of scarcity and take only what we need, if we "pay" for what we take—that is, return energy and

Sun image by Yan Maria Castro as it appears in the film Mujeria II: Primitive and Proud. *T. "Osa" Hidalgo-de la Riva © 1992.*

gifts to the elements and the Earth—and if we respect our bodies and the bodies of others, through all of their transformations, the elements will not abandon us. All too often, common understanding of the Fates encompasses only irrevocable doom or fatality. Yet, while it might be true that we cannot bargain with fate, if we act out of respect, reverence, and knowledge, and if we work to further divine justice, we just may be able to haggle.

Learning to Haggle

The Morrigan, as described by Barbara Mor, is

the Fate of Ireland, my people's Black Goddess. In Old European symbology, "black" is the color of Female Power. The power of Earth, of Night, of the womb; a stern power, often, but wholly real. "Blackness" to the Irish is the mood of necessity, be it grim, glorious or otherwise. It is the eventual doom of all things, the inevitable flowering of each thing, as we follow our natures utterly to the end: endless transformation on the wheel of change.

Mor gossipaciously tells the story of the Morrigan, offering a contemporary account of her meeting with the Morrigan and her successful haggling with this ancient and beloved Hag:

> Ten years ago, I had a malignant melanoma. It was there too long, before surgical removal; time enough to get dangerously under my skin. I imaged my body as a winter tree, bare branches covered with crows. And as the Morrigan, with her Raven, the Death Bird, perched on my left shoulder. This was the cancer's site. Melanoma's darkness, swiftness, lethalness, even a terrible death, are Hers, as they are mine: I couldn't hate the "black cancer," or fight it with swords of light. I asked the multitude of crows to fly up and away, leave my branches clear of death for awhile. I asked the Raven to take off, circle the universe, see the world: give me a chance to get some work done before She returned, if She must, to perch on my bones again. Death, too, is Our Mother. I sweat black birds, outstared many moons of depression, grief and sheer terror. But I'm still here.[17]

Many would say, "Oh, she was just lucky." Well, of course, that is exactly what she was. As Mary Daly knows, "Nothing is really lost to those who Lust. Our luck is with the Fates."[18] Luck and fortune are utterly the province of the Fates, for Dame Fortune and Lady Luck are emanations of the Powers of the Fates. As Mor's story reveals, in our dealings with the Fates there is always that willed—not random—fortune. It is weird luck, a variety of fateful coincidences, or in Daly's words, a "Fateful Fore-making . . . act[ing] out of deepening be-ing in the past and present, participating in the Tidal Timing of biophilic creation."[19]

When we are fully psychically active, alive and unnumb, in harmony with the elemental and familiar values and thus participating in the spiraling movement of Grandmother Time, we literally do get "lucky." Novelist Toni Cade Bambara tells us of her fortuitous experiences with the Fates:

I had a "grandmother" (not blood kin but spirit kin) who . . . used to say that if you're doing what you're supposed to be doing, then the whole universe will accommodate itself to you. That is to say, if you are on the right track, and you are committed, and your intentions are clear, then you can be passive because the information you need, the teachers you need, the people you need, the resources you need are going to come towards you. And all you have to do is be receptive.[20]

The critical need for this type of ritual receptivity is stressed in an exceptionally convincing metaphor found throughout the oral tradition regarding the Fates. Nor Hall reveals that "Norns, as with wise women everywhere, dealt in death, but were also midwives—the old Gossips present at the instant of birth whose vision encompassed the future."[21] The Fates could visit a home at any time, but they always came to visit the cradle of every newborn in order to bestow gifts upon the child and determine her or his destiny. To welcome these wandering Weirds, parents would "chain up the watchdog, leave the door open, and set out dainty foods to put the Moerae in a good humor. Many fairy tales still give stern lessons in the folly of offending fairy godmothers."[22]

Thus, while the Fates are the very oldest, strangest, and in some ways the most distant of the supernaturals, they simultaneously are the most familiar. They are our Gossips, or best friends and boon companions, the ones who grace our homes in the moments of greatest creativity and possibility. In other words, the Fates come to visit us where we live—and not only when we literally give birth, but also when we birth a new phase of ourselves or our world, when we are ready for the emergence of a new creative work, and so on.

In the sad, numb, and *weirdless* ("ill-fated; improvident"—*Webster's*) world that the nuclear fathers have made, it has been difficult to commune with the Fates, to make them welcome, to be receptive to their gifts. Yet we can change this. We can ritually invite the Fates into our lives. We can chain up the abusive father gods in our heads or, better yet, cast them out utterly. We can set extra plates at our tables, sharing what we have, and bringing out our tastiest and finest repasts. We can open up our homes and hearts to realize the presences of the Fates in the very textures of our lives. When we sing to these women in the Moon and tell their stories, as Paula Gunn Allen explains, we participate in their Powers:

> Long ago the peoples of this hemisphere knew that their power to live came to them from the Grandmother or Grandmothers (depending on the tribe) not only originally but continuously, even to the present. . . . Only recently have the women begun to raise our voices again, at the behest of the Grandmother(s), to tell the story as it is told and to lay claim to the ancient power that is vested in Woman since before time.[23]

We can ignore the behest of the Grandmothers only at extreme peril, for theirs are the Powers not only of the past and the present, but also of the future. Our popular culture is littered with incomplete, incoherent, incompetent, and impotent symbols of the future, including the child, the fetus, the mushroom cloud, the fembot, the terminator, and any shiny new technological product. Yet the truest symbol of the future is the one that pornotechnic culture most studiously avoids. It is the Crone. This third person, aspect, or phase of the Fates is the most ancient and genuine face of the future. If we are to survive, it is she who we must fully honor. It is she who we must finally and most abundantly become.

> *Cast your spells with the Hag!*
> *Cast your lot with the Fates of the Earth!*

CONCLUSION

The Future Is Female, or the New World Chaos

From a metaphysical point of view, everything will change into something else, but that doesn't mean that there are no essences, it just means that all essences are subject to change. . . . There is essential woman, and one of the ways that you know it is that things will inevitably return to it. You can stop the process of change at some point and then you get an effect that you want, but if it continues and you move her out of woman, left to herself she will run all the way through all the changes herself and come back to Woman. She will change, but she will come back Woman. That's why the Keres say that God is a woman. They mean that all of the substances in the universe when you put them all together, the preponderant gender is female or feminine.

—*Paula Gunn Allen*[1]

Life is a female environment in which the male appears, often periodically, and created by the female, to perform highly specialized tasks related to species reproduction and a more complex evolution. . . . This is not to say that males are an unnecessary sex. Parthenogenesis is a cloning process. Sexual reproduction, which enhances the variety and health of the gene pool, is necessary for the kind of complex evolution that has produced the human species. The point being made here is simply that, when it comes to the two sexes, one of us has been around a lot longer than the other.

—*Monica Sjöö and Barbara Mor*[2]

Grandfather and Grandmother are one.
—*Wallace Black Elk*[3]

Mutation or transmutation—physical and metaphysical, individual and social—is the key motif underlying nuclear myth. It is in this

275

concept that we must seek the core significance of the nuclear age. It is from this fulcrum that our attention swings toward the future. Here, of necessity, we stand, scanning the horizon, gossiping about what will be.

Unquestionably, there are horrific mutations wrought by radiation and other technological effects, particularly as these taboo agents are so widely and wantonly disrespected. Yet, as Paula Gunn Allen has suggested to me on numerous occasions, some of the mutations that ensue must be beneficial ones. Patriarchal men, whatever their intentions or pretensions, *cannot* control the processes of mutation; and change, or mutation, is, after all, essential to life.

Indeed, that most perfect plant, Indian maize, or corn, itself originated in an ancient mutation. In her pregnant meditation upon the Native American experience of corn as a teacher, *Selu: Seeking the Corn-Mother's Wisdom*, Marilou Awiakta tells us that scientific research demonstrates that the first appearance of corn was the result of what one researcher termed a "catastrophic sexual transmutation." Awiakta continues, "The Corn-Mother was born as an androgynous plant, one that incorporates the balance of genders not only in sexual parts of silken ear and tassel, but also in the forces of nature that female and male represent—continuance in the midst of change."[4] Though intersexual in that she contains the male, corn is understood in the Cherokee tradition as primally, powerfully, and essentially female. She is Selu, Grandmother Corn, the "Mother of Us All."

Some seven thousand years after the birth of corn, catastrophic sex and gender mutations are once again in the wind. For example, a year or so ago, a decidedly weird story started making the rounds through the news media. It seems that water fowl, marine life, and small mammals are responding to the vast amounts of chemical pollutants—including PCBs, dioxin, and lead—in the Great Lakes with a "reversal or mixing of gender roles."[5] This story indicates that, once again, the animals are speaking to us. They are enacting for us one of the only sensible responses that humans can make in the face of the massive toxic contamination wrought by the power-mad masculine culture: sex and gender transmutations.

While I was writing this book, a phrase from a mid-seventies feminist T-shirt kept resounding in my mind: "The Future Is Female." That prophecy always sounded right to me for, obviously, if the future isn't female, there might not be much of a future for us at all. But, by saying this I don't mean that all males will simply vanish. To paraphrase novelist Leslie Marmon Silko, males themselves will not disappear, but what *will* disappear is the idea of "mankind," including patriarchal "customs" of opposition, inequality, and enmity, and the enactment of maleness based in the conventional two-party, oppositional, and invidious sex and gender system. This, moreover, has "already begun to happen and . . . it is a spiritual process that no armies will be able to stop."

[margin annotation: pat. gone and won't come back]

In the early stages of embryonic growth, all mammals, including humans, are anatomically female. If a Y-chromosome–bearing sperm fuses with the egg at conception, male genitalia will develop in the eighth week. Thus, as biology itself tells us, the male body originates in and then diverges from the female. In essence, "the clitoris and the penis are the same organ, formed from the same tissue. The labia majora and the scrotum are one, indistinguishable in the early embryonic stages; in the presence of androgen 'the two lips simply grow longer, fold over and fuse along the midline, forming the scrotal sac.'"[6] In essence, then, female and male are originally one.

In keeping with a strategy of conscious mythmaking, let us imagine males as changed females but females nonetheless. (Or, as Gordene MacKenzie cackled when I suggested this to her, "Boys 'R' Us!") Of course, such a perspective is profoundly inimical to systems of male dominance for such systems require that there be two oppositional and hierarchically ordered sexes, with the male occupying the supreme position.

As Genesis paints the primal scene, god creates Adam as the first (hu)man. Then, in an extraordinary reversal, Adam "gives birth" to the first woman, Eve.[7] Sometime later, god is displeased with the rampant sin (disorder) he perceives to be afflicting the world. He decides to send an apocalyptic flood so that everything could start over from scratch and order could be reestablished. The only survivors of this devastation, conveniently enough, are the patriarch Noah, his family, and any creatures of the world who could be organized into opposite sex pairs and loaded onto an ark.

Some questions arise here. Which types of sin so antagonized god? Which types of beings were the real targets of this patriarchal cleansing? The myth provides some explicit answers. The only survivors were those who were marched in matched male-female pairs onto Noah's ark. The father-god's new world order was founded upon bipolar sexual opposition and heterosexuality. Anyone who didn't fit that order was allegedly washed away.

In her study of male femininity and transsexualism, *Transgender Nation*, Gordene MacKenzie calls for a "gender revolution," what I see as a type of new world Chaos. She decries the surgical "solution" of transsexual surgery to deal with the disorder of beings who do not neatly fit into the socially constructed classifications of male/masculinity and female/femininity. Instead, she demands a total breakdown of bipolar gender classifications.[8]

Transgender revolution will not be accomplished by simply extending male privilege to encompass men getting in touch with their "inner feminine," that is, patriarchally ordered and defined female traits. Rather, true revolution requires female self-definitions, male renunciations of power and privilege, and cultural acknowledgment of a nonhuman female primacy in which both women and men participate.

Yet maleness, we continue to be taught, is everything that is not female. The worst thing a boy can call another little boy is *girl* or *pussy*. Indeed, as psychoanalysis contends, "masculinity" is achieved by the boy separating from the mother and repudiating and degrading the female and the "feminine."[9] Patriarchally oppressive sex and gender configurations are policed into us from the earliest stages of life, with girls and boys steered and sometimes coerced into what are deemed to be gender-appropriate dominant and submissive behaviors (including heterosexuality).

Freud contended that men perceive women as mutilated or castrated males and react with either horror or triumphant contempt for the female body. (The horror comes from the male's fear that if she could be castrated, so could he.) Certainly, under patriarchy, the female body/mind itself is a threat to intact masculinity, for this body/mind continually deflates snools,[10] undermining their all-powerful–father-creator fantasies and reminding them not so much of castration (as Freud would have it), *but of where they came from and to where they eventually will return.* To stave off and deny this knowledge, patriarchy wages ceaseless gynocidal attacks—criminal, surgical, and psychic—on the female body/mind.[11] It continuously tries to dominate the female body/mind through pornographic exposure, religious sequestering, cosmetic make-over, state-sanctioned domestication, rape and other acts of sexual terror, and so on.

Yet there continue to be unruly, chaotic, and uncontrollable bodies/minds who resist patriarchal, oppositional classification and containment. In chapter 9, I discussed the radical feminist "zine" *Hothead Paisan: Homicidal Lesbian Terrorist.* The gorgonish Hothead has fully reclaimed the Powers of death, and she does spectacularly kill individual male offenders. Nevertheless, her visionary daydream is not of mass murder, but of a utopia where money is useless, locks are unnecessary, all creatures are equally respected (indeed, her cat pal "Chicken" is the mayor of their town), and obviously intersexed human beings stroll the beaches. Hothead stares at these unruly beings and then screams, "Hermaphrodites! Oh My Fuckin' god. There's nothin' to fight about anymore! All hail the Earthworm!! They've known all along."[12]

Of course, hermaphrodites or intersexed beings are not found only on the beaches of radical feminist daydreams. Geneticist Anne Fausto-Sterling scoffs at the dogmatic belief in two sexes. She argues that there are at least five sexes and that biological sex itself must be understood as a "vast, infinitely malleable continuum that defies the constraints of even five categories."[13]

The presence of hermaphrodites has been noted throughout world oral traditions and histories. Intersexed persons have long confounded patriarchal laws governing marriage, the family, sexual intimacy, military service, and so on. Contemporary medical interventions—hormonal and surgical—promise to eradicate intersexuality by locking an individual into one biological sex category and its appropriate gender role. Fausto-Sterling sees this as yet another exercise of what cultural theorist Michel Foucault calls *biopower*—medical/surgical control over bodies. Control is exerted from birth through adulthood over intersexed bodies/minds because they are unclassifiable, unruly, turbulent, irregular, freakish, and monstrous to a world based upon hierarchical opposition and division—because they are, in a word, *chaotic.*

Imagine a world in which intersexuality—both physical and metaphysical—was respected, was even the "norm." It would be a world in which females could reclaim, respect, and manifest whatever it is within our own skins that bespeaks unruliness and resistance to snool-ruled containment and classification, such as gorgonish facial hair, large bodies, and those witchy signs of aging. It would also be a world in which males would no longer be trained to despise and eradicate their own femaleness. No more might so many of them analogize themselves to weapons and then, in order to affirm their manhood, use their bodies as weapons targeting women.　　—

The Fates, we might remember, dwell on the "edge of the depths of woods, water, and the unconscious—places where things can turn into their opposites"[14]—in other words, where opposition itself is meaningless. The Fates of the Earth invite us to imagine a transmuted world, as Fausto-Sterling suggests, in which "the sexes have multiplied beyond currently imaginable limits." It would be one "of shared powers, where oppositions . . . have to be dissolved as sources of division."[15] Such a future would be female in its essence and simultaneously one in which all varieties, aspects, and permutations of that perpetually and necessarily changing essence would coexist in nonhierarchical balance. It would be a world in which current categories, orders, oppositions, and enmities would become, precisely, *meaningless*. It would be the end of the world as we know it. It would be a new world Chaos.

The New World Chaos

Where Chaos begins, classical science stops. For as long as the world has had physicists inquiring into the laws of nature, it has suffered a special ignorance about disorder in the atmosphere, in the turbulent sea, in the fluctuations of wildlife populations, in the oscillations of the heart and the brain. The irregular side of nature, the discontinuous and erratic side—these have been puzzles to science, or worse, monstrosities.

　　　　　　—*James Gleick*[16]

May I realize that I

> am a
> monster. I am
> a
> monster.

I am a monster.

And I am proud.
> —*Robin Morgan*[17]

Grandmother Goose's cosmic egg is cracking, and Chaos is (re)-emerging. The Goddess—that is, turbulent and transmutational Powers in which both females and males participate—is returning. And this unpreventable event is occurring despite the degree to which patriarchal sciences and religions have tried to prevent it. Religion, in sociologist Peter Berger's conception, functions as a "sacred canopy," sheltering the human *nomos*, or world of meaning, from *anomie*, or Chaos.[18] Yet that spiritual Star Wars shield is by no means impenetrable. Lately, in particular, it has been shot full of Holes.

The word *chaos* is derived from a Greek word meaning "chasm, gulf, abyss, hole." In the ancient world, Chaos *is* Tiamat and Chaos *is* Kali. These goddesses were metaphors who expressed their culture's awareness of the universal Powers of Chaos. They represented the original churning womb or Crone-stirred cauldron of birth, death, and transmutation—the gaping Hole or spiraling Eye associated with the primordial female Powers in which all of us originate and to which all of us will return, to change once again.

Patriarchal origin or "creation" myths boast of their heroes' triumphs over Chaos, their groundbreaking murders of Tiamat, the Grandmothers, the Dragon, the Leviathan, the Rainbow Serpent, and the Gorgon. Yet Marduk and all the other young gods and heroes were taking credit for something they had nothing to do with. Chaos had been disrespected and therefore *she* abandoned us. She chose to temporarily fly elsewhere, go away for awhile, take a nap, or simply to ignore us. Chaos is not dead. As a matter of fact, she is back. Chaotic Powers now yawn, like the shark's mouth in *Jaws*, against all the margins of mankind's most holy orders: the rules of law, scientific knowledge, sexual order, hierarchical order, the order of worship, and so on.

Chaos dropped her calling card into our laps unmistakably with the splitting of the atom and the invention of the Bomb. Snools proclaimed that with this feat they had arrived at the crowning point of Western knowledge and fulfilled the scientific goal of ultimate control over and manipulation of cosmic forces. Yet what the nuclear scientists really had "discovered" was a force that was quintessentially uncontrollable and indeed could spell their *own* demise, split and shatter *their* world order. Since then, the nuclear age has taught us that the world could change instantaneously and permanently in the twinkling of her Eye.

Chaos has also unmistakably announced her presence through such phenomena as O-Zona's hole; the discovery of black holes in space; ground zero, in all its various meanings from the Bomb to lesbian, bisexual, and gay Liberation;[19] the call for transgender or intersexual revolution; the proliferation of alien encounter and abduction narratives; and, of course, the concepts and images of the recently conceptualized "chaos theory" of contemporary math and physics.

Chaos theory tells us, among other things, that the idea that everything can be reduced to linearity is an illusion. It also tells us that at any moment, an event, however apparently trivial,[20] can take place and completely alter those that follow in qualitatively transforming ways. For example, an originating chaos theory paradigm, the "Butterfly Effect," talks about how it is absolutely impossible to predict the weather beyond a couple of days for there is no way to account for all the possible significant factors. In short, when a butterfly flaps her wings in Peking, the weather in New York can change. Gossips from centuries past encoded this crucial knowledge into the oral tradition, telling us how even the most socially powerless of us could effect devastating changes:

> For want of a nail, the shoe was lost;
> For want of a shoe, the horse was lost;
> For want of horse, the rider was lost;

For want of a rider, the battle was lost;
For want of a battle, the kingdom was lost![21]

Powerlessness turns out to be as specious a reality as *power*. Snool-ish propaganda to the contrary, individuals far removed from the seats of state, military, or corporate power are by no means helpless to affect the course of events. We must develop "chaotic" political strategies. We must stir the Crone's turbulent cauldron, losing those crucial "nails" wherever we can. The kingdom, even as we speak, is being toppled.

Looking into the Abyss

Whoever fights monsters should see to it that in the process he does not become a monster. And when you look long into an abyss, the abyss also looks into you.
—*Friedrich Nietzsche*[22]

To become a Monster, look long into an abyss. And, if you're lucky, the abyss also looks into you.
—Hints from the Haggis

It would be difficult to overstate the extent to which male su-premacist rule and notions of power depend upon and stem from pa-triarchal men's fear of otherness—of female Powers. They fear the abyss existing not only in other creatures and the elements, but also in *themselves*. Why else is patriarchal myth so obsessed with heroes—manly men marked by their superior ability to kill off the Dragon, the enemy or anomie? For example, in the 1979 movie *Raiders of the Lost Ark*, the hero, Indiana Jones, is a white man with a name remi-niscent of genocide. His life's work consists of plundering sacred arti-facts and subduing and defeating all women and men of color. His only real worthy adversaries are "evil" white men. Purportedly, movies such as these are tales of heroic bravery, yet such narratives are, instead, vivid documents of elite masculine terror.

One way that patriarchal men have managed their fear of fe-maleness and otherness—particularly their own femaleness—is through fetishization of domination. Their control is achieved not only through violence and propaganda but also through scientific prediction. Yet these measures are, to varying degrees, becoming impotent and obsolete. According to *Webster's*, Chaos is a realm in which "chance reigns supreme." In other words, Chaos is home to the Fates of the Earth: Gossips—you never know what they'll say; Gorgons—monstrosities who look into the abyss and find it becoming; and Crones—who know there is nothing to fear.

It is difficult for many people to describe Chaos beyond intuitive assessments. As one character in *Jurassic Park*, Michael Crichton's bestselling novel about dinosaurs, chaos theory, and the folly of control, sums it up, "All major changes are like death. You can't see to the other side until you are there."[23] Still, it is vital to realize that Chaos is *not* havoc—the absence of institutional control, order, and meaning, resulting in pillage, mass rape, poverty, terrorism, famine, and so on. Frankly, the horrors that commonly are labeled "chaos"— such as the neocolonial famine in Somalia—are more often than not the products, directly or indirectly, of systematic interference and domination.[24]

Similarly, serial sex killers are not monsters, deviants, or inexplicable mysteries but the logical and predictable products of patriarchal normalcy. They are trained and obedient soldiers waging war against the female—products of patriarchal order, *not* creatures of Chaos. As Ernest Becker has argued, men fetishize death as the ultimate evil and spend their lives heroically trying to defeat it. Ironically, in so doing they create real evil.[25] Likewise, horrific heroes, on their mission from god to dominate the Earth, impose order, abolish femaleness (in the self and others), and exert control at all times, have created a reign of true terror, disorder, and a numbing sense of meaninglessness in everyday life.

Chaotic Crones remind us that we don't have to fear anomie, meaninglessness, or "nothingness," for truly *there is no such thing*. Even in the most random data, as chaos theory reveals, there are beautiful patterns—structures that are fine and intricate even if they are hidden and unpredictable. Anomie, or Chaos, is said to be a state of emptiness, senselessness, and terrifying randomness. Yet this is a radically stupid and inaccurate perception. Living in a chaotic world does not mean entering into a realm of meaninglessness. Quite the contrary, for in a world respecting Chaos, *everything we do has mean-*

ing. Living chaotically means being in a world in which everything coexists in a delicate, exquisite, butterflylike balance. In this world, the commonplace brims with meaning, everything is equally sacred, every moment is portentous, everything is alive, and everything speaks. It is a world where "empty space" is respected—for, of course, no space is empty.[26] It is a world where humans do not try to control nature(s), but communicate with them through ritual and thereby become fateful accomplices in divine processes—in cosmic/chaotic natures.

Clearly, getting to know Chaos can take us in many unexpected directions. But we never will know to take these paths if we are ruled by the canned commentary that keeps telling us that Chaos is redolent of "femininity"—that is patriarchal ideas of femaleness. Psychedelic researcher Terence McKenna, while writing eloquently of the psychedelic and mythic dimensions of Chaos, still falls back on sexist metaphors:

> In a premodern society, no woman could escape chaos because of the automatic birth script that had women giving birth over and over until death. Women are biologically scripted into being much closer to chaos simply because there are certain episodes in the life of a female that are guaranteed to be boundary dissolving. The psychology of feminine sexuality, which involves the acceptance of penetration, creates an entirely different relationship to boundary than does the male need to fulfill the potential to penetrate.[27]

There are a number of problems with McKenna's assertions. First of all, many ancient and still living "premodern" women have had methods of birth control, including abortifacient herbs and drugs, vaginal sponges, and, most commonly, prolonged lactation. The reality of women giving birth until they die is an atrocity engineered by *modern* cultures ruled by patriarchal religions and governments that mandate women's biological slavery. Under these rules, heterosexuality is enforced, both overtly and covertly, and abortion and birth control are deemed crimes and sins.

Secondly, McKenna's model is grossly heterosexist. It naturalizes and normalizes oppositional sexual differentiation as well as socially constructed heterosexuality predicated upon unequal partners. The intercourse of such a sexuality doubles as *the* sex act and, conveniently, a rite of domination organized around penetration. But, of course, not all women seek penetration, either with female or male partners. Moreover, men have holes, too, and often seek penetration with both male and female partners. Penetration can be accomplished with fingers, tongues, and large clitorises[28] as well as with penises. It carries the connotations of dominance and submission only in a heterosexist context.

In McKenna's "biological"—actually pornographic—paradigm, women are empty spaces who accept penetration and dissolve, while men pleasurably invade female boundaries yet manage to maintain their own. This isn't biological reality; it's that same old script of the virgin continent being invaded by the intrepid explorer/conqueror. Not only is this a sexist model of sexuality, but being thus fucked is hardly the essence of Chaos. Moments of chaotic being instead consist of ecstasy, the sense of everything being connected to everything else, *mutual* intermingling, disintegration of oppositional perception, the experience of flow, and the apprehension of ubiquitous meaning.

Modern mythic descriptions of Chaos, some of which are insightful, nevertheless keep describing Chaos as the "feminine," the irrational, and the unconscious.[29] These concepts are themselves mired in hierarchical dualisms. They most inadequately describe realities that precede male domination, will outlast it, and for which the language of control cannot speak. To speak both of and with chaotic Powers, we must journey into the chasm. We must begin to speak with the tongues of dragons and monsters.

The Face of Chaos

During the dark side of the moon something in the mirror catches my gaze, I seem all eyes and nose. Inside my skull something shifts. I "see" my face. Gloria, the everyday face; Prieta and Prietita, my childhood faces; Gaudi, the face my mother and sister and brothers know. And there in the black, obsidian mirror of the Nahuas is yet another face, a stranger's face. *Simultáneamente me miraba la cara desde distintos ángulos. Y mi cara, como la realidad, tenía un caracter multiplice.* [Simultaneously, she would see my face from distinct angles. And my face, like reality, had a multiple character.]

—*Gloria Anzaldúa*[30]

On our path toward Chaos, we might conjure up images of the ontologically strange—of the anomie, of the dark that patriarchy has trained us to fear. We might visualize "monsters"—those female Powers that have been stigmatized as alien, inhuman, freakish, turbulent, and chaotic—not to fight them, but to become them.

We can learn a great deal about the transmutation into Chaos and the confrontation with monsters, both internal and external, from Gloria Anzaldúa, who, in her brilliant work *Borderlands/La Frontera: The New Mestiza,* takes her readers on a journey into what she describes as the "Coatlicue state." She reminds us that "Coatlicue is the ancient Mesoamerican Goddess, the serpent-headed 'monster,'" who, "like Medusa, the Gorgon . . . is a symbol of the fusion of opposites."[31] When we face Coatlicue, as when we affirm the Gorgon, we begin to face the chaotic in ourselves.

Octavia Butler also vividly describes this process of becoming familiar with the strange in her science fiction trilogy, *Xenogenesis.* The first novel, *Dawn,* puts together two of the prime allegories of Chaos: nuclear holocaust and alien encounter. In this story, aliens, on the heels of a nuclear holocaust, "rapture" up the remaining humans and seek to mate with them, altering both species permanently. Initially, these aliens appear unbearably frightening and repulsive to humans. They not only have three sexes, but also possess snakelike sensory tentacles on their heads and over the rest of their bodies. The heroine, Lilith, looks upon the aliens, takes in the significance of their appearance, and immediately understands the source of her terror. The word that comes to her mind is "Medusa."[32] Lilith soon moves from repulsion to complicated moments of ecstasy.

As poet Wendy Rose reminds us, "The ghosts of our future are unpredictable and out of control."[33] This time at the end of the patriarchal world *is* a time of chaos, of transmutation, of unpredictability. It is a time of birth into the Strange—what Butler calls a "xenogenesis." In January 1993, I had a dream of a strange birth, one in which my mother (who was 64 at the time and a grandmother) was suddenly pregnant. Gestation took place overnight, and my mother, just as instantaneously and magically, gave birth to a male infant. As she sat with the child on her lap, I looked and saw that he had no "face," that is, no normal face. Rather, his face was completely round, smooth, and black, though it had some type of wave motion over its surface. I don't know how, but I knew that I was looking into the dark of the Moon.

This dream is still mysterious to me, although I have some ideas about what it means. It *is* time for the Grandmother(s) to bear a new world. Since the "future is female," it might at first seem strange for my dream to have a male child on the grandmother's lap. But the child's *masculine* face has disappeared. The males of the future are those who are able to "be all that they can be"—that is, those who can be "female," who can accept their own otherness, and who, without fear, can look into that obsidian mirror and behold the face of Chaos. Robert Bly might interpret my dream to mean that I am wishing "facelessness" upon men. Well, yes, in a way I am. I am wishing that they—as well as women—become able to face the unfaceable and hence become utterly unrecognizable to patriarchal thought systems, categories, and classifications.

The Gossips, the Gorgons, and the Crones are three of the faces of Chaos, that state of being and consciousness that we have been conditioned to perceive—not least of all through sensory deprivation and psychic numbing—as meaningless, monstrous, freakish, puzzling, unknowable, unthinkable. Yet, Chaos is within us as much as it abides in the farthest reaches of the universe. If we can know and accept within ourselves that which is chaotic, dark, creative, turbulent, female, and wild, our fear will leave us. We will see that female Powers are not at all forbidding, repulsive, or frightening, but are, in a word, *attractive.*

One of the most compelling notions in chaos theory is something called the "strange attractor." An attractor is a mathematical model that depicts the motion of systems with reference to a "pull" on them. For linear and regular systems, orderly attractors are fully sufficient. Thus, a pendulum coming to rest against friction has a "fixed-point attractor," which is zero. The "pull" on such a pendulum is motionless. Other systems, such as the motion of planets, can be ade-

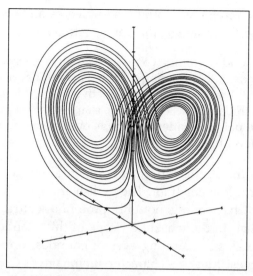

The Lorenz Attractor

quately described by "periodic attractors." The mathematical conceptualization of the motion will be a fixed loop, repeating its orbit again
and again. Such systems are so predictable that their motions can be
understood and depicted without reference to attractors at all.

But turbulent, ceaselessly stirred-up systems have posed far
greater problems of analysis. From the surging of a great river to the
ultimate unpredictable play of the weather, to the whirling motion in
a stirred beverage, to the steam rising from a boiling liquid—there *is*
a tempest in every teapot. These are familiar but infinitely changing
systems, with no fixed points or periodic patterns to be found.

The mathematics and computer technology that allowed the plotting of the multiple, nonrepetitive variables when applied to turbulent systems produced a new kind of attractor. This attractor was a
picture of the regularity of irregularity, of the changelessness of
change. This attractor was strange.[34]

The most famous strange attractor was generated by M.I.T.
meteorologist Edward Lorenz in 1962. Given enough (seemingly
meaningless) weather data, Lorenz's computer produced the image
that has come to be emblematic of chaos theory. This image of unpredictability, as described by scientific writer James Gleick in his

bestseller *Chaos*, resembled nothing so much as an "owl's mask" or "butterfly wings." This image, the Lorenz Attractor

> displayed a kind of infinite complexity. It always stayed within certain bounds, never running off the page but never repeating itself, either. It traced a strange, distinctive shape, a kind of double spiral in three dimensions. . . .The shape signaled pure disorder, since no point or pattern of points ever recurred. Yet it also signaled a new kind of order.[35]

Gleick calls the strange attractor a "magical image," and indeed there are magical Powers afoot. The owlish strange attractor augurs the new world Chaos and is not only profoundly attractive but also strangely familiar. In the masklike visage of this chaotic pattern, we can discern the classic spiraling eyes of countless ancient goddess images.[36] I suggest that this characteristic image of Chaos is a contemporary avatar of the sacred being described in the Spell 316 of the Egyptian *Coffin Texts* (see chapter 10) as "the most ancient female of world," that being who also appeared in the form of the *eyes* of a bird of prey.[37] Chaos theory is concerned with those same Powers that ancient cultures understood and reflected upon through these sacred goddess metaphors.

Looking at the owl's mask of the strange attractor, we also recognize the presence of the supernatural being whom the ancient Greeks knew as the "Owl-Eyed Athene."[38] In classical, patriarchal revisions of her myth, Athene was fissioned at the core and made to fight, in alliance with a male hero, against her deepest female self—the Gorgon. Can it now finally be the time for this splitting and fragmenting order to end? Can we again understand and appreciate female Powers (and ourselves) in a state of wholeness? Can we once again, with full respect, look upon this most ancient, stirring, wild, laughing, unpredictable, and supremely attractive face?

EPILOGUE

Imagine the Gossips, the Gorgons, and Crones standing over a raging fire in the dead of night.[1] Hanging above that dragon fire is a giant cauldron that changes colors from purple to silver to copper to red and finally to black. The Gossips are muttering among themselves. The Gorgons are gazing deeply into the black hole of the cauldron's eye. The Crones are waving large, crooked sticks over its surface, stirring up trouble, brewing up brainstorms, reconstituting creation.

The cauldron is the magical matrix of Chaos into which all the structures by which we have been ruled and controlled for millennia are now crackling, cracking, and dissolving. Peer with your owl eyes into the rising, infinitely turbulent steam. Actively visualize what is now bubbling forth. Become fateful, taking responsibility for what turn our world is now taking.

NOTES

FOREWORD

1. Nathan Schwartz-Salant, *The Borderline Personality: Vision and Healing* (Wilmette, IL: 1989), 205n.

PREFACE

1. Jane Caputi, *The Age of Sex Crime* (Bowling Green, OH: Bowling Green State University Popular Press, 1987).

2. Mary Daly in Cahoots with Jane Caputi, *Websters' First New Intergalactic Wickedary of the English Language* (Boston: Beacon Press, 1987).

3. Mary Daly, *Pure Lust: Elemental Feminist Philosophy* (1984; reprint San Francisco: HarperSanFrancisco, 1992). Daly's other works are *The Church and the Second Sex* (1968; reprint Boston: Beacon Press, 1985); *Beyond God the Father: Toward a Philosophy of Women's Liberation* (1973; reprint Boston: Beacon Press, 1985); *Gyn/Ecology: The Metaethics of Radical Feminism* (1978; reprint Boston: Beacon Press, 1990). See also her later work, *Outercourse: The BeDazzling Voyage* (San Francisco: HarperSanFrancisco, 1992).

4. Daly, *Pure Lust*, 1.

5. Some of these ideas come from Paula Gunn Allen, *The Sacred Hoop: Recovering the Feminine in American Indian Traditions* (Boston: Beacon Press, 1986), 3.

INTRODUCTION

1. Leslie Marmon Silko, "The Fourth World," *Artforum International* 27, no. 10 (1989): 124–125.

2. See Vladimir Chernousenko, *Chernobyl: Insight from the Inside* (New York: Springer-Verlag, 1992); Jay M. Gould, "Chernobyl—The Hidden Tragedy," *The Nation*, Mar. 15, 1993, 331–334; Murray Feshback and Alfred Friendly, *Ecocide in the USSR: The Looming Disaster in Soviet Health and Environment* (New York: Basic Books, 1992).

3. Esther Krumbholz and Frank Kressing, *Uranium Mining, Atomic Weapons Testing, Nuclear Waste Storage: A Global Survey* (Munich: the World Uranium Hearing, 1992).

4. Alice Walker, "The Universe Responds: Or, How I Learned We Can Have Peace on Earth," in *Living by the Word* (San Diego: Harcourt Brace Jovanovich, 1988), 187–193. Information about the decimation of both plant and animal species is given in David Papineau's review of E.O. Wilson's *The Diversity of Life, New York Times Book Review*, Oct. 4, 1992, 1, 24–25. Species are being extincted at the rate of 27,000 per year, 74 per day, 3 every hour. See also E.O. Wilson, *The Diversity of Life* (Cambridge, MA: Harvard University Press, 1992). Paula Gunn Allen suggests that the animal and plant species are abandoning us in *Grandmothers of the Light: A Medicine Woman's Sourcebook* (Boston: Beacon Press, 1991), 170.

5. Cited in Richard Rhodes, *The Making of the Atomic Bomb* (New York: Simon and Schuster, 1986), 44.

6. *Cockaludicrous* means "snoolishly foolish, laughably loutish; epitomizing androcratic authoritativeness: perfectly, pompously *wrong*." Mary Daly in Cahoots with Jane Caputi, *Websters' First New Intergalactic Wickedary of the English Language* (Boston: Beacon Press, 1987), 190.

7. Elaine Tyler May, *Homeward Bound: American Families in the Cold War Era* (New York: Basic Books, 1988).

8. Jane Flax, *Thinking Fragments: Psychoanalysis, Feminism, and Postmodernism in the Contemporary West* (Berkeley: University of California Press, 1990).

9. For a discussion of the meaning of the "final cause," see Mary Daly, *Beyond God the Father: Toward a Philosophy of Women's Liberation* (1973; reprint Boston: Beacon Press, 1985), 179–198.

10. Monique Wittig writes, "We are escapees from our class in the same way as the American runaway slaves were when escaping slavery and becoming free." See Monique Wittig, "The Straight Mind," in *The Straight Mind and Other Essays* (Boston: Beacon Press, 1992), 20.

11. Wendy Rose, "The Fifties," in *Women on War: Essential Voices for the Nuclear Age from a Brilliant International Assembly*, ed. Daniela Gioseffi (New York: Simon and Schuster, Touchstone Books, 1989), 60–61.

12. R.E.M., "It's the End of the World as We Know It (and I feel fine)," *Document* (MCA Records IPSC 42059: 1987).

13. Lavina White, "Listening to our Elders," *Indigenous Woman* 1, no. 2 (1992): 13–14. The Haida people are from areas of what are now Canada and Alaska.

14. Françoise d'Eaubonne, "Feminism or Death," in *New French Feminisms*, ed. Elaine Marks and Isabelle de Courtivron (New York: Schocken Books, 1980), 64–67.

15. Alice Walker writes: "Wasichu was a term used by the Oglala Sioux to designate the white man but it had no reference to the color of his skin. It means: He who takes the fat. It is possible to be white and not a Wasichu or to be a Wasichu and not white. In the United States, historically speaking, Wasichus of color have usually been in the employ of the military, which is the essence of Wasichu." See Alice Walker, "Everything Is a Human Being," in *Living by the Word: Selected Writings, 1963–1987* (San Diego: Farrar Straus Giroux, 1988), 139–152.

16. Whenever I refer to *Webster's* in the text, my source is *Webster's Third New International Dictionary, Unabridged* (Springfield, MA: Merriam-Webster, 1986).

17. *Snool* was first used and defined by Mary Daly in *Pure Lust: Elemental Feminist Philosophy* (1984; reprint San Francisco: HarperSanFrancisco, 1992), 20–21. There she tells us that snools, who are "the rule," are characterized by "sadism and masochism combined" and are "the stereotypic saints and heroes of the sadostate."

18. Daly, *Pure Lust*, 11, 182. Daly is citing Catherine Dimier in *The Old Testament Apocrypha*, trans. from the French by S. J. Tester (New York: Hawthorn Books, 1964), 31.

19. Daly, *Pure Lust*, 25.

20. Gayle Rubin, "The Traffic in Women: Notes on the 'Political Economy' of Sex," in *Toward an Anthropology of Women*, ed. Rayna R. Reiter (New York: Monthly Review Press, 1975), 157–210; Gordene MacKenzie, *Transgender Nation* (Bowling Green, OH: Bowling Green State University Popular Press, 1993).

21. Wittig, "The Category of Sex," in *The Straight Mind and Other Essays*, 1–8.

22. "Rape Becomes a 'Weapon of War,'" *New York Times*, Jan. 10, 1993, E4.

23. See, for example, Susan Griffin, "Rape: The All-American Crime," in *Made from This Earth: An Anthology of Writings* (New York: Harper and Row, 1983), 39–58; Kate Millett, *Sexual Politics* (Garden City, NY: Doubleday, 1970); Diana E.H. Russell, *The Politics of Rape: The Victim's Perspective* (New York: Stein and Day, 1975); Susan Brownmiller, *Against Our Will: Men, Women and Rape* (New York: Simon and

Schuster, 1975); June Jordan, "Against the Wall," in *Civil Wars* (Boston: Beacon Press, 1981), 147–149.

24. Andrea Dworkin, "Remembering the Witches," in *Our Blood: Prophesies and Discourses on Sexual Politics* (New York: Harper and Row, 1976), 15–21. See also Mary Daly, *Beyond God the Father: Toward a Philosophy of Women's Liberation* (1973; reprint Boston: Beacon Press, 1985), 194.

25. See Lori Heise, "Crimes of Gender," *WorldWatch*, Mar./Apr. 1989, 12–21; Jane Caputi, "Men's Violence Against Women: An International Overview," *Current World Leaders* 34, no. 6 (1991): 847–878.

26. Paula Gunn Allen argues that North American Indian culture was and continues to be gynocentric and that this provided a "gynocidal motive behind the genocide." See *The Sacred Hoop*, 36.

27. Robert Bly, *Iron John: A Book About Men* (Readings, MA: Addison-Wesley, 1990). See also Jane Caputi and Gordene MacKenzie, "Pumping Iron John," in *Women Respond to the Men's Movement*, ed. Kay Hagan (San Francisco: HarperSanFrancisco, 1992).

28. There are nonpatriarchal elemental and earthy male powers, perhaps in some of the nonsexist notions associated with the "Green Man." See William Anderson, *Green Man: The Archetype of Our Oneness with the Earth* (San Francisco: HarperCollins, 1990). But, as with female Powers, nonpatriarchal male Powers have been demonized and banished. As more and more males refuse loyalty to patriarchal manhood and power, more and more metaphors of these Powers will appear. More and more nonpatriarchal males will listen to them and describe what they hear. See also John Stoltenberg, *Refusing to be a Man: Essays on Sex and Justice* (New York: PenguinMeridian, 1989).

29. This was cited by Marta Weigle in *Creation and Procreation: Feminist Reflections on Mythologies of Cosmogony and Parturition* (Philadelphia: University of Pennsylvania Press, 1989), 144. In her commentary, she talks about thinking strongly through symbols.

30. *Fembot* was first used by Mary Daly in *Gyn/Ecology: The Metaethics of Radical Feminism* (1978; reprint Boston: Beacon Press, 1990), 17. It is defined in Daly with Caputi, *Wickedary*, 198, as a "female robot: the archetypical role model forced upon women through fatherland: the unstated goal/end of socialization into patriarchal womanhood: the totaled woman."

31. R.T. Rundle Clark, *Myth and Symbol in Ancient Egypt* (London: Thames and Hudson, 1959), 33.

32. Quoted in Robert Briffault, *The Mothers: A Study of the Origins of Sentiments and Institutions* (New York: MacMillan, 1927), 2: 603.

33. Nor Hall, *The Moon and the Virgin: Reflections on the Archetypal Feminine* (New York: Harper and Row, 1980), 206.

34. Barbara Walker, *The Crone: Woman of Age, Wisdom and Power* (San Francisco: Harper & Row, 1985); Briffault, *The Mothers*.

35. *Fool* is defined in Daly with Caputi, *Wickedary*, 200, as "*fool* [derived from L *follis* bellows, bag, akin to Gk *phallos* penis—*Webster's*; also derived from Indo-European root *bhel*– 'to blow, swell; with derivatives referring to various round objects and to the notion of tumescent masculinity'—*American Heritage*]: archetypal player on the stage/foreground of phallocracy: bellowing fellow, windbag; cockaludicrous parader of 'round objects'; exposer/exponent of tumescent masculinity."

36. Paul Boyer, *When Time Shall Be No More: Prophecy Belief in Modern American Culture* (Cambridge, MA: Harvard University Press, 1992).

37. The term *White City* comes from the name given to the fairgrounds of the Chicago International Exposition in 1893. For more information on the mythic meaning of the White City and its incorporation into nuclear popular culture, see Spencer Weart, *Nuclear Fear: A History of Images* (Cambridge, MA: Harvard University Press, 1989), 7–10.

38. Daly with Caputi, *Wickedary*, 64.

39. Alice Walker, "The Universe Responds," in *Living by the Word*, 193.

40. Marilou Awiakta, "The Grandmothers are Coming Back," *Woman of Power: A Magazine of Feminism, Spirituality, and Politics* 15 (Fall/Winter 1990): 41–42.

PART ONE

PRELUDE ONE

1. June Jordan, "White English/Black English: The Politics of Translation," in *Civil Wars* (Boston: Beacon Press, 1981), 59–73.

2. Monique Wittig, *Les Guérillères*, trans. David Le Vay (New York: Avon Books, 1971), 114.

3. Julia Penelope, *Speaking Freely: Unlearning the Lies of the Father's Tongues* (New York: Pergamon Press, the Athene Series, 1990), xx–xxi.

4. Robert Jay Lifton first introduced this term in his book, *The Broken Connection: On Death and the Continuity of Life* (New York: Simon and

Schuster, 1979). On p. 369 he defines nuclearism as the "passionate embrace of nuclear weapons as a solution to death anxiety and a way of restoring a lost sense of immortality."

5. The Firm, "Radioactive," *The Firm* (Atlantic 7888 12391: 1985).

6. Lowell Blanchard with the Valley Trio, "Jesus Hits Like an Atom Bomb," *Atomic Cafe* (Rounder Records 1034: 1982).

7. On the connections between fundamentalist Christianity and nuclearism, see A.G. Mojtabai, *Blessed Assurance: At Home with the Bomb in Amarillo, Texas* (New York: Houghton Mifflin, 1986) as well as my extended discussion in chapter 3.

8. Glenn D. Hook, "Making Nuclear Weapons Easier to Live With: The Political Role of Language in Nuclearization," *Bulletin of Peace Proposals* 16, no. 1 (1985): 67–77.

9. Carol Cohn, "Sex and Death in the Rational World of Defense Intellectuals," *Signs: Journal of Women in Culture and Society* 12, no. 4 (1987): 687–718.

CHAPTER ONE

1. Cited in Stephen Hilgartner, Richard C. Bell, and Rory O'Connor, *Nukespeak: The Selling of Nuclear Technology in America* (New York: Penguin Books, 1982), 31.

2. Quoted in Paul Boyer, *By the Bomb's Early Light: American Thought and Culture at the Dawn of the Atomic Age* (New York: Pantheon, 1985), 315.

3. Robert Jay Lifton and Richard Falk, *Indefensible Weapons: The Political and Psychological Case Against Nuclearism* (New York: Basic Books, 1982, 1992), 3.

4. Paula Gunn Allen has been discussing this with me since 1990. See also Derrick de Kerckhove, "On Nuclear Communication," *Diacritics* 14, no. 2 (1984): 72–81.

5. Both Spencer Weart and Derrick de Kerckhove write extensively about transmutation or transformation as the essential characteristic of atomic symbolism. See Spencer Weart, *Nuclear Fear: A History of Images* (Cambridge, MA: Harvard University Press, 1989).

6. de Kerckhove, "On Nuclear Communication," 78.

7. Weart, *Nuclear Fear*, 402–403.

8. Boyer, *By the Bomb's Early Light*, 17.

9. Peggy Rosenthal, "The Nuclear Mushroom Cloud as Cultural Image," *American Literary History* 3, no. 1 (Spring 1991): 63–92.

10. Sharon O'Brien (Paper presented at the annual meeting of the Popular and American Culture Associations, St. Louis, MO, Mar. 1990).

11. James Coates, "Guacamole Story Bombs at Rocky Flats Nuke Plant," *Albuquerque Journal*, June 7, 1992, A6.

12. Quoted in Patricia Leigh Brown, "In a World of Symbols, One Brings Confusion," *New York Times*, Jan. 30, 1992, B1, national edition.

13. "Let Them Eat Radiation," *E: The Environmental Magazine*, May/June 1992, 44.

14. One of my students, Vincent Murphy, wrote an excellent paper about nuclear superheroes, and I thank him for drawing this to my attention.

15. Marilou Awiakta, "When Earth Becomes an It," in Thomas Rain Crowe, "Marilou Awiakta: Reweaving the Future," *Appalachian Journal* 18, no. 1 (Fall 1990): 40–55.

16. For information on contaminating United States corporations, including Rockwell, see "Toxic Ten: America's Truant Corporations," *Mother Jones* (Jan./Feb. 1993): 40–41.

17. "Birth Defects in Texas Prompt Call for Registry," *New York Times*, Sept. 23, 1992, B7, national edition.

18. Conversation with Paula Gunn Allen, April 13, 1993.

19. Anne H. Soukhanov, "Word Watch," *Atlantic Monthly*, May 1987, 100.

20. Lifton and Falk, *Indefensible Weapons*, 106.

21. Weart, *Nuclear Fear*, 146.

22. "Nuke It," words and music by Joe Scruggs. The lyrics to this song were given to me by my friend Augusta Walden. It was sung in the first grade at Comanche Elementary School in Albuquerque, NM in September 1991.

23. Prince, "1999," *1999* (Warner Bros. Records 23720-1F 25: 1982).

24. For more information, see Deena Weinstein, *Heavy Metal: A Cultural Sociology* (New York: Lexington Books, 1991).

25. Art Spiegelman, *Maus I: A Survivor's Tale* (New York: Pantheon, 1986) and *Maus II: A Survivor's Tale* (New York: Pantheon, 1991).

26. Marilou Awiakta, "Dying Back," *The Tennessee Conservationist*, Jan./Feb. 1987, 12. Most of Awiakta's poetry and essays are collected in her book *Selu: Seeking the Corn-Mother's Wisdom* (Golden, CO: Fulcrum Publishing, 1993).

27. Lee Green, "The U.S. Forest Service's Darkest Secret: They've Been Raping the Giant Sequoias," *Audubon*, May 1990, 112–115.

CHAPTER TWO

1. Carol Cohn, "Sex and Death in the Rational World of Defense Intellectuals," *Signs: Journal of Women in Culture and Society* 12, no. 4 (1987): 687–718.

2. A photo of this taken by Ruth Putter appeared on the back cover of *Heresies: A Feminist Publication on Art & Politics* 5, no. 4 (1985).

3. Catharine A. MacKinnon, "Feminism, Marxism, Method, and the State: Toward Feminist Jurisprudence," *Signs: Journal of Women in Culture and Society* 8, no. 4 (1983): 635–658; Catharine A. MacKinnon, *Feminism Unmodified: Discourses on Life and Law* (Cambridge, MA: Harvard University Press, 1987), 6.

4. Marilou Awiakta, "Baring the Atom's Mother Heart," in *Homewords: A Book of Tennessee Writers,* ed. Douglass Paschall and Alice Swanson (Knoxville: Tennessee Arts Commission and the University of Tennessee Press, 1986), 183–188.

5. Paul Beale, ed., *Partridge's Concise Dictionary of Slang and Unconventional English* (New York: MacMillan Publishing Company, 1989), 424.

6. My definition of erotica is influenced by Diana E.H. Russell, "Pornography and Rape: A Causal Model," *Political Psychology* 9 (1988): 41–73. For definitions of pornography see Andrea Dworkin and Catharine MacKinnon, *Pornography and Civil Rights: A New Day for Women's Equality* (Minneapolis, MN: Organizing Against Pornography, 1988), esp. 138–139. See also Andrea Dworkin, *Pornography: Men Possessing Women* (New York: Perigee, 1981) and *Letters from a War Zone: Writings 1976–1989* (New York: E. P. Dutton, 1988). See also Catharine MacKinnon, *Feminism Unmodified* and *Toward a Feminist Theory of the State* (Cambridge, MA: Harvard University Press, 1989).

7. Carolyn Merchant, *The Death of Nature: Women, Ecology, and the Scientific Revolution* (San Francisco: Harper and Row, 1980).

8. Spencer Weart, *Nuclear Fear: A History of Images* (Cambridge, MA: Harvard University Press, 1989), 58.

9. For an extensive discussion of essentialism, see Diana Fuss, *Essentially Speaking: Feminism, Nature and Difference* (New York: Routledge, 1989).

10. This idea was introduced to me by Paula Gunn Allen. For amplification on this, see Jane Caputi, "Interview with Paula Gunn Allen," *Trivia: A Journal of Ideas* 16/17 (1990): 50–67.

11. Marilou Awiakta, "When Earth Becomes an It," in Thomas Rain Crowe, "Marilou Awiakta: Reweaving the Future," *Appalachian Journal* 18, no. 1 (Fall 1990): 40–55.

12. Jayne Cortez, "Tell Me," in *Coagulations: New and Selected Poems* (New York: Thunder's Mouth Press, 1984), 106–109.

13. See "Let the Guy Grin," *People Weekly*, Dec. 22–29, 1986, 24.

14. Jay Cocks, "Why He's a Thriller," *Time*, Mar. 19, 1984, 54–60.

15. Crouse Group of Companies, *Nuclear News Buyer's Guide*, mid-Feb. 1976, 102.

16. Martha Vicinus, "Sexuality and Power: A Review of Current Work in the History of Sexuality," *Feminist Studies* 8, no. 1 (1982): 133–156.

17. William L. Laurence, *Dawn over Zero: The Story of the Atomic Bomb* (New York: Alfred A. Knopf, 1946), 239.

18. Little Caesar with The Red Callender Sextette, "Atomic Love," *Atomic Cafe* (Rounder Records 1034: 1982); Trammps, "Disco Inferno," *Saturday Night Fever* (RSO Records RS-2-4001: 1977).

19. Mimi Smith, cartoon, *Public Illumination Magazine* 21 (June 1982): 14.

20. Stephen King, *It* (New York: Viking, 1988), 931.

21. This is from a title at the beginning of the film *Cafe Flesh*, directed by Rinse Dream. For commentary see Danny Peary, *Guide for the Film Fanatic* (New York: Simon & Schuster, 1986), 78–79.

22. Ann Larabee, "Radioactive Body Politics" (Paper delivered at the Popular and American Culture Associations meeting, Louisville, KY, Mar. 1992).

23. Raymond Pettibone, cover art for a compilation album, *The Blasting Concept*, c. 1984.

24. Quoted in Boyer, *By the Bomb's Early Light*, 246

25. Ann McMullen, "Women Back the Atom," *Electrical Review* 201 (Nov. 11, 1977): 27.

26. Lou Myers, cartoon, in *War Heads: Cartoonists Draw the Line*, ed. Steven Heller (New York: Penguin, 1983), 66.

27. Paul Conrad, cartoon, *Los Angeles Times*, Feb. 22, 1987, part 5, 5.

28. Quoted in Bob Bach, "Letter to the Editor," *New York Times*, Feb. 2, 1984, A18.

29. Richard von Krafft-Ebing, *Psychopathia Sexualis*, translated from the twelfth German edition by Franklin S. Klaf (New York: Stein and Day, 1965), 59.

30. Jane Caputi, *The Age of Sex Crime* (Bowling Green, OH: Bowling Green State University Popular Press, 1987); Jane Caputi, "Seeing Elephants: The Myths of Phallotechnology," *Feminist Studies* 16, no. 3 (1988): 487–524.

31. A snuff film is a pornographic film in which a performer, usually a woman but sometimes a child of either sex or a man, is actually tortured and killed. See Caputi, *Age of Sex Crime*, 164–165. See also Jane Caputi, "Advertising Femicide: Lethal Violence Against Women in Pornography and Gorenography," in *Femicide: The Politics of Woman Killing*, ed. Jill Radford and Diana E.H. Russell (New York: Twayne Publishers, 1992), 203–221.

32. David O. Edge, "Technological Metaphor," in *Meaning and Control*, ed. David O. Edge and James N. Wolfe (London: Tavistock, 1973), 31–59.

33. "Atom Bomb Baby," The Five Stars, *Atomic Cafe* (Rounder Records 1034: 1982).

34. Michael Wood, *America in the Movies: Or, Santa Maria It Had Slipped My Mind* (New York: Basic Books, 1975), 51.

35. Illustrations of these can be found in A. Costandina Titus, *Bombs in the Backyard: Atomic Testing and American Politics* (Reno, NV: University of Nevada Press, 1986).

36. Jane Caputi, "Charting the Flow: The Construction of Meaning through Juxtaposition in Media Texts," *Journal of Communication Inquiry* 15, no. 2 (Summer 1991): 32–47.

37. Elaine Tyler May, *Homeward Bound: American Families in the Cold War Era* (New York: Basic Books, 1988), 112.

38. The Golden Gate Quartet, "The Atom and Evil," *Atomic Cafe* (Rounder Records 1034: 1982).

39. Japan Graphic Designers Association, *Graphic Design in Japan* 6 (Tokyo: Kodansha International Ltd., 1986), unpaged.

40. I take this phrase from the 1992 hit film *Basic Instinct*, in which the blonde bombshell female serial killer is described by the cop investigating her as the "fuck of the century."

41. Marquis de Sade, *The 120 Days of Sodom and Other Writings*, trans. Austryn Wainhouse and Richard Seaver (New York: Grove Press, 1987), 364.

42. Thomas Harris, *Red Dragon* (New York: Bantam, 1981), 270–271.

43. The destruction of the Earth by fire is predicted as "But the day of the Lord will come like a thief, and then the heavens will pass away

with a loud noise, and the elements will be dissolved with fire, and the earth and the works that are upon it will be burned up." (2 Pet. 3:10 [R.S.V.]). See also Daly, *Pure Lust*, 10.

44. Mass murder now is being committed on the average of twice per month in the United States. This country is the world leader in mass murders. See Fox Butterfield, "Experts Explore Rise in Mass Murder," *New York Times*, Oct. 19, 1991, A6, national edition.

CHAPTER THREE

1. Quoted in Perry Miller, "The End of the World, " in *Errand into the Wilderness* (Cambridge, MA: Harvard University Press, 1956), 217–239.

2. Buchanan Brothers, "Atomic Power," *Atomic Cafe* (Rounder Records 1034: 1982).

3. Ira Chernus, *Dr. Strangegod: On the Symbolic Meaning of Nuclear Weapons* (Columbia, SC: University of South Carolina Press, 1986), 153.

4. See Robert Jungk, *Brighter than a Thousand Suns: A Personal History of the Atomic Scientists*, trans. James Cleugh (New York: Harcourt, Brace, 1958), 201; Paul Boyer, *By the Bomb's Early Light: American Thought and Culture at the Dawn of the Atomic Age* (New York: Pantheon, 1985), 6; William L. Laurence, "Eyewitness Account of Bomb Test," *New York Times*, Sept. 26, 1945, 1.

5. Spirits of Memphis Quartet, "Atomic Telephone," *Atomic Cafe* (Rounder Records 1034: 1982).

6. Alan Moore, *The Watchmen* (New York: D.C. Comics, 1986).

7. Chernus, *Dr. Strangegod*, 141.

8. Jane Caputi, "Interview with Paula Gunn Allen," *Trivia: A Journal of Ideas* 16/17 (1990): 50–67. Derrick de Kerckhove, "On Nuclear Communication," *Diacritics* 14, no. 2 (1984): 72–81.

9. *Christotechnology* is "technology subliminally modeled upon the myths, dogmas, and cherished obsessions of the christian tradition." See Mary Daly in Cahoots with Jane Caputi, *Websters' First New Intergalactic Wickedary of the English Language* (Boston: Beacon Press, 1987), 189.

10. Clive Barker, *The Great and Secret Show* (New York: Harper and Row, 1989); Stephen King, *The Stand* (New York: New American Library, 1978, 1990).

11. Robert MacCammon, *Swan Song* (New York: Pocket Books, 1987); Carolyn See, *Golden Days* (New York: McGraw–Hill, 1987).

12. See, *Golden Days*, 190–191.

13. Torv Carlsen and John Magnus, directors, "Knocking on Armageddon's Door," PBS broadcast, July 19, 1988.

14. *Necro-apocalyptic* means "marked by a malignant intent to bring about a holocaust that will purge the 'unrighteous' and engulf the Earth; characterized by expectations/hallucinations of the resurrection of the 'righteous' to a world of purified bliss, i.e., utter nonbe-ing." Daly with Caputi, *Wickedary*, 212.

15. Paul Boyer, *When Time Shall Be No More: Prophecy Belief in Modern American Culture* (Cambridge, MA: Harvard University Press, 1992), 135–136.

16. Miller, "End of the World," 222–223.

17. Mary Daly, *Pure Lust: Elemental Feminist Philosophy* (1984; reprint San Francisco: HarperSanFrancisco, 1992), 10–11.

18. Alice Walker, "Everything Is a Human Being," *Living By the Word: Selected Writings 1973–1987* (San Diego: Harcourt Brace Jovanovich, 1988), 139–152.

19. Russell Hoban, *Riddley Walker* (New York: Pocket Books, 1980), 158–159.

20. Mark Baker, *Nam: The Vietnam War in the Words of the Men and Women Who Fought There* (New York: William Morrow, 1982), 152.

21. The phrase "most unholy trinity" is used by Mary Daly in *Beyond God the Father: Toward a Philosophy of Women's Liberation* (1973; reprint Boston: Beacon Press, 1985), 114–122, to describe a conglomerate of rape, genocide, and war.

22. Leslie Marmon Silko, *Ceremony* (New York: Viking/Penguin, 1977), 100.

23. The phrase "respell the world" was first used by Barbara Mor in workshops in San Diego in 1969 to 1973, entitled "Respell the World: A Reconstruction of Female Mythology." She also uses it in her book with Monica Sjöö, *The Great Cosmic Mother: Rediscovering the Religion of the Earth* (San Francisco: Harper and Row, 1987), 425.

PART TWO

PRELUDE TWO

1. Quoted in Pam McAllister, ed., *Reweaving the Web of Life: Feminism and Non-Violence* (Philadelphia: New Society Publishers, 1982), 352.

2. Quoted in Jerome Rothenberg, ed. "Pre-Face (1990)," *Shaking the*

Pumpkin: Traditional Poetry of the Indian North Americas, rev. ed. (Albuquerque, NM: University of New Mexico Press, 1986, 1991), xvii.

3. Paule Marshall, "From the Poets in the Kitchen," *Reena and Other Stories* (Old Westbury, NY: The Feminist Press, 1983), 3–12. I also give thanks to Paule Marshall's *Praisesong for the Widow* (New York: G. P. Putnam's Song, 1983) for inspiring my title for this prelude.

4. Nor Hall, *The Moon and the Virgin: Reflections on the Archetypal Feminine* (New York: Harper and Row, 1980), 189.

5. See Mary Daly in Cahoots with Jane Caputi, *Websters' First New Intergalactic Wickedary of the English Language* (Boston: Beacon Press, 1987), 132–133. There, we define *Gossip* as both a verb and noun: "*Gossip* n ["A familiar acquaintance, friend, chum. Formerly applied to both sexes now only (somewhat *archaic*) to women. . . . *esp.* Applied to a woman's female friends invited to be present at a birth."—*O.E.D.*] : a Female Friend and/or Familiar, esp. applied to the Fates, Fairies, Familiars, and Friends who invite themselves to be Present at any Female Act of Creation" and "*Gossip* v ["To be a gossip or sponsor to; to give a name to. Obs. . . . To act as a gossip, or a familiar acquaintance; to take part (in a feast), to be a boon-companion; to make oneself at home. . . . To tell like a gossip: to communicate. Also with *out.* 1650 'The secret lay not long in the Embers, being gossiped out by a woman.' . . . 1827 'And wisdom, gossip'd from the stars.'" — *O.E.D.*] 1: to exercise the Elemental Female Power of Naming, especially in the Presence of other Gossips 2: to take part in the festivity of wordplay among Boon-Companions 3: to tell like a Gossip; to divine and communicate the secrets of the Elements, the wisdom of the stars."

6. Alexander Rysman, "How the 'Gossip' Became a Woman," *Journal of Communication* 27, no. 1 (1977): 176–180.

7. Ralph L. Rosnow and Marianthi Georgoudi, "'Killed by Idle Gossip': The Psychology of Small Talk," in *When Information Counts: Grading the Media*, ed. Bernard Rubin (Lexington, MA: Lexington Books, 1985), 59–73, esp. 60.

8. See Barbara G. Walker, *The Woman's Encyclopedia of Myths and Secrets* (San Francisco: Harper and Row, 1983), 951. See also Susan Cady, Marian Ronan, and Hal Taussig, *Sophia: The Future of Feminist Spirituality* (San Francisco: Harper and Row, 1986).

9. Walker, *Woman's Encyclopedia*, 302.

10. *Egyptian Book of the Dead*, cited by R.T. Rundle Clark in *Myth and Symbol in Ancient Egypt* (London: Thames and Hudson, 1959), 56.

11. Chrystos, "No Rock Scorns Me as Whore," in *This Bridge Called My Back: Writings by Radical Women of Color*, ed. Cherríe Moraga and Gloria Anzaldúa (Watertown, MA: Persephone Press, 1981), 243–245.

12. Leslie Marmon Silko, "Language and Literature from a Pueblo Indian Perspective," in *English Literature: Opening Up the Canon*, ed. Leslie A. Fiedler and Houston A. Baker (Baltimore: Johns Hopkins University Press, 1981), 60.

13. *Webster's Unabridged* (1986) defines *word-magic* as "magic involving the use of words in a manner determined by a belief that the very act of uttering a word summons or directly affects the person or thing that the word refers to."

14. *Cosmogyny* is a word invented by Paula Gunn Allen meaning "an ordered universe arranged in harmony with gynocratic principles." Paula Gunn Allen, *Grandmothers of the Light: A Medicine Woman's Sourcebook* (Boston: Beacon Press, 1991), xiii–xiv.

15. Leslie Marmon Silko, *Ceremony* (New York: New American Library, A Signet Book, 1977), 1.

16. Paula Gunn Allen, *The Sacred Hoop: Recovering the Feminine in American Indian Traditions* (Boston: Beacon Press, 1986), 122.

17. Herman Kahn, *Thinking About the Unthinkable* (New York: Horizon Press, 1962).

18. Mary Daly, *Pure Lust: Elemental Feminist Philosophy* (1984; reprint San Francisco: HarperSanFrancisco, 1992), 394.

19. Allen, *Sacred Hoop*, 50.

CHAPTER FOUR

1. Linda Hogan, "Women: Doing and Being," in *The Stories We Hold Secret: Tales of Women's Spiritual Development*, ed. Carol Bruchac, Linda Hogan, and Judith McDaniel (Greenfield Center, NY: The Greenfield Review Press, 1986), ix.

2. Catharine MacKinnon, speech at the University of New Mexico Law School, Jan. 30, 1992.

3. Ira Levin, *The Stepford Wives* (New York: Random House, 1972). The film version was directed by Bryan Forbes in 1974.

4. *Snool* was first used and defined by Mary Daly in *Pure Lust: Elemental Feminist Philosophy* (1984; reprint San Francisco: HarperSanFrancisco, 1992), 20–21. There she tells us that snools,

who are "the rule," are characterized by "sadism and masochism combined" and are "the stereotypic saints and heroes of the sadostate."

5. Hélène Cixous, "Castration or Decapitation?" *Signs: Journal of Women in Culture and Society* 7, no. 1 (1981): 41–55.

6. See Toni Morrison, ed., *Race-ing Justice, En-gendering Power: Essays on Anita Hill, Clarence Thomas, and the Construction of Social Reality* (New York: Pantheon Books, 1992).

7. Jane Gross, "Suffering in Silence No More, Women Fight Back on Sexual Harassment," *New York Times*, July 14, 1992, C17, national edition.

8. Elaine Sciolino, "Military Women Report Pattern of Sexual Abuse by Servicemen," *New York Times*, July 11, 1992, A1, national edition.

9. Cynthia Enloe, *Bananas, Beaches, and Bases: Making Feminist Sense of International Politics* (Berkeley: University of California Press, 1989); Coco Fusco, "Army Rules," *Village Voice*, Aug. 11, 1992.

10. Anna Quindlen, "With Extreme Prejudice," *New York Times*, June 24, 1992, A17; Eric Schmitt, "Navy Says Pilots Assaulted Women," *New York Times*, May 1, 1992, A15, national edition.

11. Eric Schmit, "Senior Navy Officers Suppressed Sex Investigation, Pentagon Says," *New York Times*, Sept. 25, 1992, 1, national edition.

12. Mark Thompson, "140 Face Discipline for Tailhook," *Albuquerque Journal*, Apr. 24, 1993, A1, A6.

13. *Cock-eyed* is defined as "1. having the limited sensory awareness of a cock 2: having the characteristic expression of an eyeballer 3: marked by the propensity to see glory, heroism, and excitement only in cruelty, carnage, and disaster. Mary Daly in Cahoots with Jane Caputi, *Websters' First New Intergalactic Wickedary of the English Language* (Boston: Beacon Press, 1987), 191.

14. James Twitchell reports that Farrell has written a pro–incest book called *The Last Taboo: The Three Faces of Incest*. See James Twitchell, *Forbidden Partners: The Incest Taboo in Modern Cultures* (New York: Columbia University Press, 1987), 16.

15. "Navy Tells of Molestations," *San Francisco Chronicle*, May 1, 1992, A4.

16. Thompson, "140 Face Discipline," *Albuquerque Journal*, Apr. 24, 1993, A1, A6.

17. Hélène Cixous, "The Laugh of the Medusa," in *New French Feminisms*, ed. Elaine Marks and Isabelle de Courtivron (New York:

Schocken Books, 1981), 245–264, esp. 264.

18. Amy Curtis-Webber, "Not Just Another Pretty Victim: The Incest Survivor and the Media" (Paper presented at the annual Popular and American Culture Associations, New Orleans, LA, Apr. 7, 1993).

19. Robert Briffault, *The Mothers: A Study of the Origins of Sentiments and Institutions* (New York: MacMillan, 1927), 2: 560–561.

20. Alice Walker, *The Color Purple* (New York: Washington Square Press, Pocket Books, 1982), 187.

21. Sally Tisdale, "Talk Dirty to Me: A Woman's Taste for Pornography," *Harper's Magazine*, Feb. 1992, 37–46.

22. The debate concerning the oppressive and liberating effects of pornography continues among feminists. For a discussion see Robin West, "The Feminist Conservative Anti-Pornography Alliance and the 1986 Attorney General's Commission on Pornography Report," *American Bar Foundation Research Journal*, no. 4 (1987): 681–711.

23. Andrea Dworkin and Catharine A. MacKinnon, *Pornography and Civil Rights: A New Day for Women's Equality* (Minneapolis, MN: Organizing Against Pornography, 1988).

24. Linda Marchiano, the former Linda Lovelace, describes her life in pornography as one of frequently forced sex, including sex with animals. See Linda Lovelace, *Ordeal* (New York: Berkeley, 1981).

25. For an alternative view, affirming the connection of sex and power, see Amber Hollibaugh, "Desire for the Future: Radical Hope in Passion and Pleasure," in *Pleasure and Danger: Exploring Female Sexuality*, ed. Carol S. Vance (London: Pandora Press, 1989, 1984), 401–410. In this article, she argues that "power is the heart, not the beast, of all sexual inquiry."

26. For feminist critiques of coitus as a ritual of domination, see Kate Millett, *Sexual Politics* (Garden City, NY: Doubleday, 1969, 1970) and Andrea Dworkin, *Intercourse* (New York: The Free Press, 1987).

27. Tisdale, "Talk Dirty," 43.

28. John F. Burns, "Canadian Prelate Quits in Clerics' Sex Scandal," *New York Times*, July 20, 1990, A7.

29. See, as just one example, the molesting career of former priest James R. Porter. For information see Fox Butterfield, "Diocese Reaches Settlement with 68 Who Accuse Priest of Sexual Abuse," *New York Times*, Dec. 4, 1992, A8. See also Jason Berry, *Lead Us Not Into Temptation: Catholic Priests and the Sexual Abuse of Children* (New York: Doubleday, 1992).

30. Patricia Ellsberg and Elissa Melamed, "Seeing through the Emperor's New Clothes: Two Women Look at the Nuclear Issue," in *Exposing Nuclear Phallacies*, ed. Diana E.H. Russell (New York: Pergamon Press, 1989), 84–92.

CHAPTER FIVE

1. Elaine Tyler May, *Homeward Bound: American Families in the Cold War Era* (New York: Basic Books, 1988), 3.

2. David Popenoe, *Disturbing the Nest: Family Change and Decline in Modern Societies* (New York: Aldine De Gruyter, 1989), 1.

3. Sylvia Nasar, "The Rich Get Richer, but the Question Is by How Much," *New York Times*, July 20, 1992, C1, national edition.

4. Sir Henry Maine, *The Early History of Institutions* (London), 310–311. Cited in Kate Millett, *Sexual Politics* (New York: Ballantine, 1969, 1970), 46.

5. For an interesting analysis of the connection of nuclear violence to the nuclear family, see Ira Chernus, *Nuclear Madness: Religion and the Psychology of the Nuclear Age* (Albany: State University of New York Press, 1991), 34–40.

6. See United States Senate, *Hearing before the Subcommittee on Children, Family, Drugs and Alcoholism of the Committee on Labor and Human Resources* (Washington, D.C.: U.S. Government Printing Office), 1990; Don Terry, "Stabbing Death at Door of Justice Sends Alert on Domestic Violence," *New York Times*, Mar. 17, 1992, 1, national edition; "Husband's Acquittal of Rape Protested," *San Francisco Chronicle*, Apr. 18, 1992; Diana E.H. Russell, *Rape in Marriage* (Bloomington, IN: University of Indiana Press, 1982, 1990); David Johnston, "Survey Shows Number of Rapes Far Higher Than Official Figures," *New York Times*, Apr. 24, 1992, A9, national edition; David Berreby, "I'm the anti-family voter," *New York Times*, Aug. 29, 1992, 15, national edition.

7. Quoted in Peter Monaghan, "Historians and Sociologists Attempt to Debunk Common Stereotypes of the American Family," *The Chronicle of Higher Education*, Nov. 4, 1992, A8. See also Stephanie Coontz, *The Way We Never Were: American Families and the Nostalgia Trip* (New York: Basic Books, 1992).

8. Judith Stacey, *Brave New Families: Stories of Domestic Upheaval in Late 20th Century America* (New York: Basic Books, 1990).

9. Curtis Lang, "Bad Company," *Village Voice*, Apr. 29, 1992, 29.

10. Patricia J. Williams, *The Alchemy of Race and Rights* (Cambridge: Harvard University Press, 1991), 162.

11. For a discussion of some aspects of this discrimination, see Ruthann Robson, *Lesbian (Out)Law: Survival Under the Rule of Law* (Ithaca, NY: Firebrand Press, 1992).

12. bell hooks, "Homeplace: A Site of Resistance," in *Yearnings: Race, Gender, and Cultural Politics* (Boston: South End Press, 1990), 41–49.

13. Richard Bernstein, "Accusations of Abuse Haunt the Legacy of Dr. Bruno Bettelheim," *New York Times*, Nov. 4, 1990, E6.

14. Valerie Solanas, *The SCUM Manifesto* (London: The Matriarchy Study Group, 1967, 1968, 1983), 10–11.

15. Ann Scales, personal conversation, June 27, 1992.

16. Gertrude Stein, *Everybody's Autobiography* (New York: Vintage, 1937, 1973), 133.

17. Brian Easlea, *Fathering the Unthinkable: Masculinity, Scientists, and the Nuclear Arms Race* (London: Pluto Press, 1983); Robert Jungk, *Brighter than a Thousand Suns: A Personal History of the Atomic Scientists*, trans. James Cleugh (New York: Harcourt, Brace, 1958), 108; Lansing Lamont, *Day of Trinity* (New York: Atheneum, 1965), 285.

18. Cited in Paul Boyer, *By the Bomb's Early Light: American Thought and Culture at the Dawn of the Atomic Age* (New York: Pantheon Books, 1985), 61.

19. Jackie Jadrnak, "Social Workers' Actions Proper in Roswell Case," *Albuquerque Journal*, Jan. 24, 1992, 3E.

20. John List killed his mother, wife, and children in 1971 in New Jersey and then disappeared for eighteen years. See Marianne Jacobbi, "The Mystery of the Model Husband," *Good Housekeeping*, Jan. 1990, 82–84, 144–148; and "Hiding for 18 Years: A Wanted Man is Caught by the FBI and a TV Posse," *People Weekly*, June 19, 1989, 69–72.

   Jeffrey MacDonald is the Green Beret who killed his wife and family and is the subject of the bestseller by Joe McGinnis, *Fatal Vision* (New York: Putnam, 1983).

   In 1989, Ramón Salcido embarked on a shooting and slashing rampage, killing seven people including his wife and two daughters (one daughter survived). See "Bringing Them Back to Justice," *Time*, May 1, 1989, 42.

   George Franklin sexually abused nearly all of his children and also killed his daughter's eight-year-old friend. Eileen Franklin witnessed the attack, but then repressed it from memory until she remembered it in 1989 and brought charges against her father. He was convicted. See Eileen Franklin and William Wright, *Sins of the Father* (New York: Crown Publishers, 1991).

Gene Simmons killed sixteen members of his family three days after Christmas in 1987 in Arkansas. Seven years earlier he had been indicted in New Mexico for committing incest with his daughter. See "A Holiday Killing Spree," *Time*, Jan. 11, 1988, 35.

David Koresh was the leader of the Branch Davidian Christian cult whose compound in Waco was under FBI siege for fifty-one days. On April 19, 1993, the FBI—in a mass-murderous move worthy of an institutional nuclear father—assaulted the compound with tear gas and it soon caught fire, killing eighty-six people who were inside. As of June 1993, it is still a matter of dispute if the fire was set accidentally or purposefully. It has been reported that Koresh made all the children in the compound call him "father" and that he sexually abused many of the girl children. See Barbara Kantrowitz et al., "The Killing Ground," *Newsweek*, May 3, 1993, 18–27.

For related nuclear father stories, see Jonathan Alter, "Oregon: Deaths in the Family," *Newsweek*, Nov. 5, 1983; Ed Magnuson, "A Father Lifts His 'Burdens,'" *Time*, Aug. 28, 1989, 13; Timothy Egan, "Children Find Strength to Face Father in Court," *New York Times*, Oct. 15, 1990, A13, national edition.

21. Tim O'Brien, *The Nuclear Age* (New York: Dell Publishing, Laurel Trade, 1985); Barbara Gowdy, *Falling Angels* (New York: Soho Press, 1990); Paul Theroux, *The Mosquito Coast* (New York: Avon Books), 1982; Pat Conroy, *The Prince of Tides* (New York: Bantam, 1986); *Star Wars*, directed by George Lucas, 1977; *Forbidden Planet*, directed by Fred McLeod Wilcox, 1956; *Desert Bloom*, directed by Eugene Corr, 1986.

22. May, *Homeward Bound*, 146.

23. Betty Friedan, *The Feminine Mystique* (New York: Dell, 1963), 37.

24. *Atomic Cafe*, directed by Kevin Rafferty, Jayne Loader, and Pierce Rafferty, 1982.

25. Mark Crispin Miller, "Deride and Conquer," in *Watching Television*, ed. Tod Gitlin (New York: Pantheon Books, 1986), 183–228.

26. The founding document of the Students for a Democratic Society (SDS), the 1962 Port Huron Statement, opened by describing how young adult rebelliousness was linked to two social realities: the Civil Rights Movement, and the Bomb: "When we were kids the

United States was the wealthiest and strongest country in the world; the only one with the atom bomb. . . . Many of us began maturing in complacency. As we grew, however, our comfort was penetrated by events too troubling to dismiss. First, the permeating and victimiz- ing fact of human degradation, symbolized by the Southern struggle against racial bigotry, compelled most of us from silence to activism. Second, the enclosing fact of the Cold War, symbolized by the presence of the Bomb, brought awareness that we ourselves, our friends, and millions of abstract 'others' . . . might die at any time. We might deliberately ignore, or avoid, or fail to feel all other human problems, but not these two, for these were too immediate and crushing in their impact, too challenging in the demand that we as individuals take the responsibility for encounter and resolution." See "The Port Huron Statement," in *The Sixties Papers: Documents of a Rebellious Decade*, ed. Judith Clavir Albert and Stewart Edward Albert (New York: Praeger, 1984), 176–196.

27. Diana Davenport, "Snow (Marshall Islands)," *Ikon*, no. 10 (1989): 60–64.

28. This speech is reproduced in the superb documentary *Half Life*, directed by Dennis O'Rourke, 1986.

29. The recovery movement originated with the idea of recovery from both physiological and psychological addictions with twelve-step programs modeled upon Alcoholics Anonymous. It has been greatly popularized through the works of such authors as John Bradshaw and Pia Melody.

30. This sequence takes place in *Half Life*.

31. Cited in Richard Corliss, "Did You Ever See a Dream Stalking," *Time*, Sept. 5, 1988, 68.

32. M. Fo, "Interview with Robert Englund," *Thrasher*, Feb. 1988, 72–77.

33. I thank Helene Vann, David's grandmother, for bringing this poem to my attention.

34. Fo, "Interview," 76.

35. Lifton and Falk, *Indefensible Weapons*, 67.

36. Judith Bierman, untitled poem, in *She Who Was Lost Is Remembered: Healing from Incest through Creativity*, ed. Louise M. Wisechild (Seattle: The Seal Press, 1991), 195.

37. Lifton and Falk, *Indefensible Weapons*, 77.

CHAPTER SIX

1. I have taken the phrase "unthinkable fathering" from an excellent paper written by a student, Amy Estelle, entitled "Incest and the Bomb: Surviving in the Nuclear Age," Nov. 22, 1991.

2. Marty O. Dyke, "Yeah I'm Blaming You," in *I Never Told Anyone: Writings by Women Survivors of Child Sexual Abuse*, ed. Ellen Bass and Louise Thornton (New York: HarperPerennial, HarperCollins, 1983), 113.

3. Jane Caputi, "Charting the Flow: The Construction of Meaning through Juxtaposition in Media Texts," *Journal of Communication Inquiry* 15, no. 2 (Summer 1991): 32–47.

4. Brian Easlea, *Fathering the Unthinkable*, 22.

5. See also the comments of Carol Cohn, "Sex and Death in the Rational World of Defense Intellectuals," *Signs: Journal of Women in Culture and Society* 12, no. 4 (1987):687–718.

6. Both incest and nuclearism are perpetrated primarily by men. Brian Easlea in *Fathering the Unthinkable*, 6–7, writes that "while it is clear that women have participated in masculine science in an important way . . . it is also equally clear that the relatively few women in the physical sciences have had to participate on male terms. At Los Alamos, too, female scientists worked alongside male scientists but they were very much in the minority and all the principal scientists (as far as I know) were men. . . . the Austrian and Jewish Lise Meitner, co-discoverer of uranium fission with Otto Frisch, refused to take part in the Manhattan Project although she was invited to do so and although she herself had had to flee Hitler's Third Reich in 1938. . . . The creation of nuclear weapons has been basically a male enterprise and one undertaken, as we shall see, in a paradigmatically masculine spirit."

   David Finkelhor, one of the most prominent researchers on child sexual abuse, refers to a long recognized "male monopoly on child molesting. . . . Among reported cases of abuse, 90 percent or more of offenders appear to be men. Interestingly, when women are recorded as having been involved in molestation, more often than not it is at the instigation and encouragement of men. More important, however, even in general population surveys in which people reveal their own unreported childhood sexual experiences (positive or negative), 95 percent of the adult contacts with girls and 80 percent of the adult contacts with boys are made by men." David Finkelhor, "Abusers:

Special Topics," in *A Sourcebook on Child Sexual Abuse*, ed. David Finkelhor and Associates (Newbury Park, CA: Sage Publications, 1986), 119–142, esp. 126.

7. Cited in Mary Field Belenky, Blythe McVicker Clinchy, Nancy Rule Goldberger, and Jill Mattuck Tarule, *Women's Ways of Knowing: The Development of Self, Voice, and Mind* (New York: Basic Books, 1986), 175.

8. James Barron, "Farrow says that Allen 'mutilated' his better self," *New York Times*, Aug. 20, 1992, B5, national edition.

9. Patricia Murphy, "The Color of Holocaust," unpublished essay, 1985.

10. Barbara Gowdy, *Falling Angels* (New York: Soho Press, 1990).

11. Lifton and Falk, *Indefensible Weapons*, 68.

12. "State of the Union," *New York Times*, Jan. 29, 1992, A14, national edition.

13. E. Sue Blume, *Secret Survivors: Uncovering Incest and Its Aftereffects in Women* (New York: Ballantine, 1990), 243.

14. See Carole Gallagher, *American Ground Zero: The Secret Nuclear War* (Cambridge, MA: M.I.T. Press, 1993); A. Costandina Titus, *Bombs in the Backyard: Atomic Testing and American Politics* (Reno: University of Nevada Press, 1986); Stuart Wasserman, "Navajos Testify on Uranium Reparations," *San Francisco Chronicle*, Mar. 14, 1990, 7; Catherine Caufield, *Multiple Exposures: Chronicles of the Radiation Age* (New York: Harper and Row, 1989); Esther Krumbholz and Frank Kressing, *Uranium Mining, Atomic Bomb Testing, Nuclear Waste Storage: A Global Report* (Munich: The World Uranium Hearing, 1992). Navajo teenagers have a sexual-organ cancer rate seventeen times higher than the national average. See Robert F. Kennedy, Jr., and Dennis Rivera, "Pollution's Chief Victims: The Poor," *New York Times*, Aug. 15, 1992, 15, national edition.

15. Boyer, *By the Bomb's Early Light*, 318.

16. "Hanford Wastes Greatly Underestimated," *The Olympian*, May 5, 1991, 1; Matthew L. Wald, "Secrecy Tied to Hanford Tank's Trouble," *New York Times*, Aug. 1, 1990, A8, national edition; Keith Schneider, "Report Warns of Impact of Hanford's Radiation," *New York Times*, July 13, 1990, national edition; Keith Schneider, "Nuclear Complex Threatens Indians," *New York Times*, Sept. 3, 1990, 9, national edition.

17. Tom Baile, "Growing Up as a Nuclear Guinea Pig," *New York Times*, July 22, 1990, sec. 4, 19.

18. Kyos Featherdancing, untitled essay in *The Courage to Heal: A Guide*

for Women Survivors of Child Sexual Abuse, ed. Ellen Bass and Laura Davis (New York: Harper and Row, 1988), 394–399.

19. Lifton and Falk, *Indefensible Weapons*, 45–46.

20. See Bass and Davis, *Courage to Heal*; Gail Elizabeth Wyatt and Gloria Johnson Powell, eds., *Lasting Effects of Child Sexual Abuse* (Newbury Park, CA: Sage Publications, 1988); Blume, *Secret Survivors*.

21. Paul Loeb, *Nuclear Culture: Living and Working in the World's Largest Atomic Complex* (Philadelphia: New Society Publishers, 1986).

22. Lifton and Falk, *Indefensible Weapons*, 26.

23. Judith Herman with Lisa Hirschman, *Father Daughter Incest* (Cambridge, MA: Harvard University Press, 1981).

24. Florence Rush, *The Best Kept Secret: Sexual Abuse of Children* (New York: McGraw-Hill, 1980); Diana E.H. Russell, *The Secret Trauma: Incest in the Lives of Girls and Women* (New York: Basic Books, 1986).

25. See Rush, *Best Kept Secret*; Jeffrey Masson, *The Assault on Truth: Freud's Suppression of the Seduction Theory* (New York: Farrar, Strauss and Giroux, 1984); Ronald Summitt, "Hidden Victims, Hidden Pain: Societal Avoidance of Child Sexual Abuse," in *Lasting Effects of Child Abuse*, ed. Gail Elizabeth Wyatt and Gloria Johnson Powell (Newbury Park, CA: Sage Publications, 1988), 39–60.

26. Summitt, "Hidden Victims."

27. Telephone conversation with Marylia Kelly, July 1, 1992.

28. David Grogan and Michael Haederle, "Hunting a Silent Killer," *People Weekly*, Oct. 28, 1991, 125–126.

29. Marilyn Van Derbur Atler, "The Darkest Secret," *People Weekly*, June 10, 1991, 88–94.

30. Pat Conroy, *The Prince of Tides* (New York: Bantam, 1986), 8.

31. John Glenn, joint hearings on "Nuclear Reactor Safety at the DOE's Savannah River Plant," Sept. 30, 1988. Opening statement to the House of Representatives Environmental, Energy, and Natural Resources Subcommittee of the Committee on Government Operations and the Senate Committee on Government Affairs. I have taken this information from an excellent paper written by a student, Maura Daly, entitled "Nuclear Dysfunction in *Prince of Tides* and *Desert Bloom*," May 1992.

32. Robert Jay Lifton and Eric Markusen, *The Genocidal Mentality: Nazi Holocaust and Nuclear Threat* (New York: Basic Books, 1990), 13.

33. Quoted in Spencer Weart, *Nuclear Fear: A History of Images* (Cambridge: Harvard University Press, 1988), 149.

34. Quoted in Weart, *Nuclear Fear*, 149.

35. Lifton and Falk, *Indefensible Weapons*, 26.

36. William J. Broad, *Star Warriors* (New York: Simon and Schuster, 1985), 47.

37. Wallace Black Elk and William S. Lyon, *Black Elk: The Sacred Ways of a Lakota* (San Francisco: HarperSanFrancisco, 1990), 39.

38. Judy Bierman, "Pieces of the Night Sky: My Body's Legacy," in *She Who Was Lost Is Remembered: Healing from Incest through Creativity*, ed. Louise M. Wisechild (Seattle: The Seal Press, 1991), 189–194.

39. Judith Lewis Herman, *Trauma and Recovery: The Aftermath of Violence from Domestic Abuse to Political Terror* (New York: Basic Books, 1992), 2–3.

40. See, for example, Carol Tavris, "Beware the Incest-Survivor Machine," *New York Times Book Review*, Jan. 3, 1993, 1, 16–17; "Real Incest and Real Survivors: Readers Respond," *New York Times Book Review*, Feb. 14, 1993, 3; Ethan Watters, "Doors of Memory," *Mother Jones*, Jan./Feb. 1993, 24–29, 76–77.

41. Roseann Lloyd, "Not Even a Shadow on the Sidewalk," in *Healing From Incest Through Creativity*, ed. Wisechild, 84–87.

42. Ellen Bass, "Introduction: In the Truth Itself, There is Healing," in *I Never Told Anyone*, ed. Bass and Thornton, 43.

43. For information on owls in European and Aztec traditions, see Barbara G. Walker, *Woman's Encyclopedia of Myths and Secrets* (San Francisco: Harper and Row, 1983), 754–755 (under "Owl") and 1001 (under "Tlazolteotl"). In the symbol systems of many North American indigenous peoples, owls are birds of great Powers. They particularly hold the Powers of death, and death often follows when people hear the owl calling their name.

44. Carol Lee Sanchez, "Animal, Vegetable and Mineral: The Sacred Connection," in *Ecofeminism and the Sacred*, ed. Carol J. Adams (New York: The Continuum Publishing Company, 1993), 207–228, esp. 213.

45. *Fooldom* is "the domain of wantwits and fools: PHALLOCRACY 2: the common non-sense of the Numbed State; the accumulated 'wisdom' (bull) of bullocracy." Mary Daly in Cahoots with Jane Caputi, *Websters' First New Intergalactic Wickedary of the English Language* (Boston: Beacon Press, 1987), 200.

46. Martin Amis, *London Fields* (New York: Harmony Books, 1989), 97.

CHAPTER SEVEN

1. Alan Richman, "Radiation Overdose: All in a Day's Work," *New York Times*, Apr. 4, 1979, 1.

2. For a radical feminist discussion of the "Frankenstein phenomenon," see Mary Daly, *Gyn/Ecology: The Metaethics of Radical Feminism* (1978; reprint Boston: Beacon Press, 1990), 69–72.

3. For an extensive critique of Shelley's novel as "the most convincing critique of masculine science," see Brian Easlea, *Fathering the Unthinkable: Masculinity, Scientists and the Nuclear Arms Race* (London: Pluto Press, 1983).

4. *Phallotechnology* first appeared in Mary Daly, *Pure Lust: Elemental Feminist Philosophy* (1984; reprint San Francisco: HarperSanFrancisco, 1992), 64. It is defined in Mary Daly in Cahoots with Jane Caputi, *Websters' First New Intergalactic Wickedary of the English Language* (Boston: Beacon Press, 1987), 217, as "the technology of doomdom; technology which has rapism as its hidden agenda and destruction of life as its final goal; applied scientific fooldom."

5. Robert Jay Lifton and Kai Erikson, "Nuclear War's Effect on the Mind," in Robert Jay Lifton and Richard Falk, *Indefensible Weapons: The Political and Psychological Case Against Nuclearism* (New York: Basic Books, 1982, 1991), 274–278.

6. Stuart M. Kaminsky, "Don Siegel on the Pod Society," in *Science Fiction Films*, ed. Thomas Atkins (New York: Monarch Press, Simon and Schuster, 1976), 73–83.

7. *River's Edge*, film directed by Tim Hunter, screenplay by Neal Jimenez, 1987.

8. Cited in Danny Peary, *Cult Movies* (New York: Dell, 1981), 277.

9. See Robin Wood, "Apocalypse Now: Notes on the Living Dead," in *The American Nightmare*, ed. Andrew Britton et al. (Toronto: The Festival of Festivals, 1979), 91–96. See also Robin Wood, *Hollywood from Vietnam to Reagan* (New York: Columbia University Press, 1986).

10. R.H.W. Dillard, *Horror Films* (New York: Monarch Press, 1976), 55–81, esp. 57.

11. Dillard, *Horror Films*, 80.

12. Lifton and Erikson, in Lifton and Falk, *Indefensible Weapons*, 275.

13. Lifton and Falk, *Indefensible Weapons*, 40.

14. Lifton and Erikson, in Lifton and Falk, *Indefensible Weapons*, 278–279.

15. The artist was sixteen-year-old Timothy Cummings. See Ona Lara

Porter, *Kids in Crisis: New Mexico's Other Bomb*, New Mexico Coalition for Children, 1988.

16. Vincent Canby, "Into the Dark Heartland," *New York Times*, June 14, 1987, H25.

17. David Denby, "Our Gang," *New York*, May 18, 1987, 90–92.

18. Canby, "Into the Dark Heartland," 25.

19. Paul Brians, *Nuclear Holocausts: Atomic War in Fiction, 1895–1984* (Kent, OH: Kent State University Press, 1987), 67.

20. For my critique of the theme of psychic Powers in *The Dead Zone*, see Jane Caputi, "Psychic Numbing, Radical Futurelessness, and Sexual Violence in the Nuclear Film," in *The Nightmare Considered: Critical Essays on Nuclear War Literature*, ed. Nancy Anisfield (Bowling Green, OH: Bowling Green State University Popular Press, 1991), 58–70.

21. I have elaborated on the practice of psychic activism throughout feminist theory in "On Psychic Activism," in *A Feminist Companion to Mythology*, ed. Carolyne Larrington (London: Pandora Press, 1992), 425–440.

22. Barbara Mor, "The Morrigan," *Woman of Power: A Magazine of Feminism, Spirituality, and Politics* 15 (Fall/Winter 1990): 60–61.

23. Barbara Starrett, *A Dream in Female: The Metaphors of Evolution and The Metaphors of Power* (Gloucester, MA: Top O' The Harbor, 1976), 2–3.

24. Zala Chandler, "Voices Beyond the Veil: An Interview with Toni Cade Bambara and Sonia Sanchez," in *Wild Women in the Whirlwind: Afra-American Culture and the Contemporary Literary Renaissance*, ed. Joanne M. Braxton and Andrée Nicola McLaughlin (New Brunswick, NJ: Rutgers University Press, 1990), 342–362, esp. 348.

25. Spencer Weart, *Nuclear Fear: A History of Images* (Cambridge, MA: Harvard University Press, 1988), 267.

26. Quoted in Karen Marshall, "Caretakers of the Earth," *Woman of Power: A Magazine of Feminism, Spirituality and Politics*, no. 14 (1989): 42.

27. Paula Gunn Allen, *Grandmothers of the Light: A Medicine Woman's Sourcebook* (Boston: Beacon Press, 1991), 7.

28. Muriel Rukeyser, "The Speed of Darkness," in *The Speed of Darkness* (New York: Random House, 1968), 111.

29. "Magic Words," in *Shaking the Pumpkin: Traditional Poetry of the Indian*

North Americas, rev. ed., ed. Jerome Rothenberg (Albuquerque: University of New Mexico Press, 1986), 41.

30. Alice Walker, "The Universe Responds," in *Living by the Word: Selected Writings 1973–1987* (San Diego: Harcourt Brace Jovanovich, 1988), 187–193.

31. Quoted in Carol B. Gartner, *Rachel Carson* (New York: Frederick Ungar, 1983), 124–125.

32. Alan Richman, "Farm Family Keeps One Eye on Nuclear Power Plant, the Other on Dairy Herd," *New York Times*, Apr. 2, 1979, A15.

33. Walter Benjamin comments on the ways that the invention of technologies of mechanical reproduction induce this tendency to become a spectator to apocalypse. See Walter Benjamin, "The Work of Art in the Age of Mechanical Reproduction," in *Illuminations*, ed. Hannah Arendt (New York: Schocken, 1969), 219–253.

34. Conversation with Beverly Smith, Boston, MA, 1981.

35. The word *dolphin* comes from the Greek *delphinos*, meaning "womb." The dolphin symbolizes female powers of reproduction and regeneration. Barbara Walker notes that "shown on funeral urns, dolphins represented the soul passing to another world." Barbara Walker, *Woman's Dictionary of Symbols and Sacred Objects* (San Francisco: Harper and Row, 1988), 372. In my dream, they represented the soul revitalizing this world.

36. Daniel Goleman, "Do Dreams Really Contain Important Secret Meaning?" *New York Times*, July 10, 1984, C1.

37. *Snool* was first used and defined by Mary Daly in *Pure Lust: Elemental Feminist Philosophy* (1984; reprint San Francisco: HarperSanFrancisco, 1992), 20–21. There she tells us that snools, who are "the rule," are characterized by "sadism and masochism com bined" and are "the stereotypic saints and heroes of the sadostate."

38. Alice Walker, "The Universe Responds," 192.

39. Bertha Harris, "What We Mean to Say: Notes Toward Defining the Nature of Lesbian Literature," *Heresies* 3 (Fall 1977): 5–8.

PART THREE

PRELUDE THREE

1. Penelope Shuttle and Peter Redgrove, *The Wise Wound: Myths, Realities, and Meanings of Menstruation*, rev. ed. (New York: Bantam Books, 1978, 1986), 57.

2. C. Kerényi, *The Gods of the Greeks* (London: Thames and Hudson, 1951), 49.

3. Robert Graves, *The Greek Myths* (Mt. Kisco, NY: Moyer Bell Limited, 1955, 1960), 127, 174.

4. See Jane Caputi, "'Jaws' as Patriarchal Myth," *Journal of Popular Film* 6, no. 4 (1978): 305–326; Gloria Anzaldúa, *Borderlands/La Frontera* (San Francisco: Spinsters/Aunt Lute, 1987), 27; Chris Knight, "Menstrual Synchrony and the Australian Rainbow Snake," in *Blood Magic: The Anthropology of Menstruation*, ed. Thomas Buckley and Alma Gottlieb (Berkeley: University of California Press, 1988), 232–255.

5. Mary Daly, *Gyn/Ecology: The Metaethics of Radical Feminism* (1978; reprint Boston: Beacon Press, 1990), 82, 107–112. See also Jane Caputi, *The Age of Sex Crime* (Bowling Green, OH: Bowling Green State University Press, 1987), 6–10, for a discussion of original gynocide.

6. *Gynergy* is a word invented by Emily Culpepper meaning, in her words, "the female energy which both comprehends and creates who we are; that impulse in ourselves that has never been possessed by the patriarchy nor by any male; woman-identified be-ing." Mary Daly in Cahoots with Jane Caputi, *Websters' First New Intergalactic Wickedary of the English Language* (Boston: Beacon Press, 1987), 76.

7. Monica Sjöö and Barbara Mor, *The Great Cosmic Mother: Rediscovering the Religion of the Earth* (San Francisco: Harper and Row, 1987), 209.

8. Barbara G. Walker, *Woman's Encyclopedia of Myths and Secrets* (San Francisco: Harper and Row, 1983), 629.

9. Walker, *Woman's Encyclopedia*, 635–645.

10. Graves, *The Greek Myths*, 175.

11. Thomas Buckley and Alma Gottlieb, "A Critical Appraisal of Theories of Menstrual Symbolism," in *Blood Magic*, 3–53.

12. Lewis Mumford, *The Pentagon of Power: The Myth of the Machine* (New York: Harcourt Brace Jovanovich, Harvest Book, 1964, 1970); Jerry Mander, *In the Absence of the Sacred: The Failure of Technology and the Survival of the Indian Nations* (San Francisco: Sierra Club Books, 1991);

Langdon Winner, *The Whale and the Reactor: A Search for Limits in an Age of High Technology* (Chicago: University of Chicago Press, 1986).

13. Riane Eisler, *The Chalice and The Blade: Our History, Our Future* (San Francisco: Harper and Row, 1987). Eisler distinguished between dominator and partnership cultures.

14. *Snool* was first used and defined by Mary Daly in *Pure Lust: Elemental Feminist Philosophy* (1984; reprint San Francisco: HarperSanFrancisco, 1992), 20–21. There she tells us that snools, who are "the rule," are characterized by "sadism and masochism combined" and are "the stereotypic saints and heroes of the sadostate."

15. June Jordan, "Gettin Down to Get Over," in *Naming Our Destiny: New and Selected Poems* (New York: Thunder's Mouth Press, 1989), 67–76.

16. Tobin Siebers, *The Mirror of Medusa* (Berkeley: University of California Press, 1983), 24. Susan Bowers, "Medusa and the Female Gaze," *National Women's Studies Association Journal* 2, no. 2 (1990): 217–235. Bowers discusses the Medusa in male art and poetry as well as the female gaze.

17. *Misterics* is "uncontrollable and mysterious fits (thought by some to be caused by testicular disturbances)." Daly with Caputi, *Wickedary,* 212.

18. Elaine Tyler May, *Homeward Bound: American Families in the Cold War Era* (New York: Basic Books, 1988), 110–111.

CHAPTER EIGHT

1. Emily Culpepper, "Gorgons: A Face for Contemporary Women's Rage," *Woman of Power: A Magazine of Feminism, Spirituality, and Politics,* issue 3 (Winter/Spring 1986): 22–24, 40.

2. Danny Peary, *Cult Movies* (New York: Dell, 1981), 94–98. Peary discusses the incest subtext and some elements in the original script that even more strongly suggested incest.

3. Catharine A. MacKinnon, "Feminism, Marxism, Method and the State: Toward Feminist Jurisprudence," *Signs: Journal of Women in Culture and Society* 8, no. 4 (1983): 635–658.

4. This advertisement was in a special issue of *Newsweek,* Nov./Dec. 1984.

5. *Snool* was first used and defined by Mary Daly in *Pure Lust: Elemental Feminist Philosophy* (1984; reprint San Francisco: HarperSanFrancisco, 1992), 20–21. There she tells us that snools, who

are "the rule," are characterized by "sadism and masochism combined" and are "the stereotypic saints and heroes of the sadostate."

6. Bret Easton Ellis, *American Psycho* (New York: Vantage Books, 1991), 304.

7. Stephen Pyne, review of *Trees of Life* by Kenton Miller and Laura Tangley, *New York Times*, Apr. 21, 1991, sec. 7, 19.

8. For information on the genocidal activities of these heroes, see Patrick Sale, *The Conquest of Paradise: Christopher Columbus and the Columbian Legacy* (New York: Alfred A. Knopf, 1991); Grant Foreman, *Indian Removal: The Emigration of the Five Civilized Tribes* (Norman, OK: University of Oklahoma Press, 1972); and Clifford E. Trafzer, *Kit Carson: The Last Great Navajo War* (Norman, OK: University of Oklahoma Press, 1982).

9. Audre Lorde, "Need: A Choral of Black Women's Voices," in Frédérique Delacoste and Felice Newman, *Fight Back: Feminist Resistance to Male Violence* (Minneapolis: Cleis Press, 1981), 63–67.

10. For further commentary, see Jane Caputi and Diana E.H. Russell, "Femicide: Sexist Terrorism Against Women," in *Femicide: The Politics of Woman Killing*, ed. Jill Radford and Diana E.H. Russell (New York: Twayne Publishers, 1992), 13–21.

11. Quoted in Andrée Côté, "The Art of Making it Work for You," in *The Montreal Massacre*, ed. Louise Mallette and Marie Chalouh, trans. Marlene Wildeman (Charlottetown, Prince Edward Island: Gynergy Books, 1991), 67–70.

12. Ted Bundy is one of the most notorious of U.S. serial killers. He was a middle-class, educated white man who killed and mutilated anywhere from thirty-six to fifty young women across several states in the 1970s. He was convicted in 1979 for the murders of two sorority women and one eleven-year-old girl in Florida and executed in that state in January 1989. For more information, see Jane Caputi, *The Age of Sex Crime* (Bowling Green, OH: Bowling Green State University Popular Press, 1987).

13. Thomas Harris, *The Silence of the Lambs* (New York: St. Martin's Press, 1988). The film was directed by Jonathan Demme and released in 1991. It swept the Academy Awards for that year, getting awards for best picture, best director, best actress, and best actor. For my detailed analysis, see Jane Caputi, "American Psychos: The Serial Killer in the Contemporary Imagination," *Journal of American Culture* 16, no. 4 (Winter 1993): 101–112.

14. For more information on the fool archetype, see Mary Daly in Cahoots with Jane Caputi, *Websters' First New Intergalactic Wickedary of the English Language* (Boston: Beacon Press, 1987), 261–272.

15. Jeffrey Dahmer, a loner who mutilated animals as a child, committed his first murder in 1978. He lived in Milwaukee from 1986 to 1991, where he killed at least seventeen young men and boys. After getting them drunk or drugging them, Dahmer photographed, strangled, raped, and dismembered his victims, mostly Asian and African-American men. He was convicted in 1992 and received a life sentence.

16. Quoted in Robert Jay Lifton, *The Broken Connection: On Death and the Continuity of Life* (New York: Simon and Schuster, Touchstone Books, 1979), 425.

17. See also Paula Gunn Allen's discussion of taboo in *Grandmothers of the Light: A Medicine Woman's Sourcebook* (Boston: Beacon Press, 1991), 167–170.

18. Sophocles, "Oedipus the King," trans. David Grene, in *Sophocles I*, ed. David Grene and Richmond Lattimore (Chicago: University of Chicago Press, 1954), 10–76.

19. For a discussion of the homoerotic aspects of Christian myth, see Mary Daly, *Gyn/Ecology: The Metaethics of Radical Feminism* (1978; reprint Boston: Beacon Press, 1990), 61–64.

20. Jason DeParle, "For Some Blacks, Social Ills Seem to Follow White Plans," *New York Times*, Aug. 11, 1991, E5, national edition.

21. Frequently, racists propose as a solution for overpopulation the sterilization or limitation of reproduction for people in the Third World. Of course, it is people in the developed, luxury-oriented, and resource-squandering countries who must first act to reduce their populations, since it is they who use the vast share of the world's resources.

22. Jay Gould, "Hidden Tragedy," *The Nation*, Mar. 15, 1993, 331–334.

23. Warren E. Leary, "Record Rise in Ozone-Destroying Chemicals Found in North," *New York Times*, Feb. 4, 1992, B7, national edition.

24. Thomas Harris, *Red Dragon* (New York: Bantam, 1981), 270–271.

25. Ellis, *American Psycho*, 343.

26. Ibid., 245.

27. Ibid., 343.

28. George Stade, *Confessions of a Lady-Killer* (New York: Alpha/Omega,

1979). For my critique of this novel, see *The Age of Sex Crime*, 78–80.

29. Stade, *Confessions of a Lady-Killer*, 41.

30. For discussions of the gendered and colonialist gaze, see Laura Mulvey, "Visual Pleasure and Narrative Cinema," *Screen* 16, no. 3 (1975): 6–18; John Berger, *Ways of Seeing* (Hammondsworth, NY: Penguin Books, 1982); Susan R. Bowers, "Medusa and the Female Gaze," *National Women's Studies Association Journal* 2, no. 2 (1990): 217–235; Ella Shohat, "Gender and Culture of Empire: Toward a Feminist Ethnography of the Cinema," *Quarterly Review of Film and Video* 13, nos. 1–3 (1991): 45–84.

31. *Cock-eyed* means "1: having the limited sensory awareness of a cock 2: having the characteristic expression of an eyeballer 3: marked by the propensity to see glory, heroism, and excitement only in cruelty, carnage, and catastrophe." Daly with Caputi, *Wickedary*, 191.

32. Stephen Heath, "Difference," *Screen* 19, no. 3 (Autumn 1978): 92.

33. *Phallotechnology* first appeared in Mary Daly, *Pure Lust: Elemental Feminist Philosophy* (1984; reprint San Francisco: HarperSanFrancisco, 1992), 64. It is defined in Daly with Caputi, *Wickedary*, 217, as "the technology of doomdom; technology which has rapism as its hidden agenda and destruction of life as its final goal; applied scientific fooldom."

34. "The President's Speech on a New Defense," *New York Times*, Mar. 24, 1983, A20.

35. Barbara Deming, "A Song for Gorgons," in *Reweaving the Web of Life: Feminism and Nonviolence*, ed. Pam McAllister (Philadelphia: New Society Publishers, 1982), 43–44.

36. Daly with Caputi, *Wickedary*, 282.

37. Hélène Cixous, "The Laugh of the Medusa," in *New French Feminisms*, ed. Elaine Marks and Isabelle de Courtivron (New York: Schocken Books, 1981), 245–264.

38. Chris Knight, "Menstrual Synchrony and the Australian Rainbow Snake," in *Blood Magic: The Anthropology of Menstruation*, ed. Thomas Buckley and Alma Gottlieb (Berkeley: University of California Press, 1988), 232–255.

39. Knight, "Menstrual Synchrony," 240.

40. Ibid.," 250.

41. M.F. Ashley Montagu, *Coming into Being among the Australian Aborigines* (London: Routledge, 1937), 320–325. See also Knight, "Menstrual Synchrony," 247–253.

42. Charlene Spretnak, "Naming the Cultural Forces that Push Us toward War," in *Exposing Nuclear Phallacies*, ed. Diana E.H. Russell (New York: Pergamon Press, 1989), 53–62.

43. Knight, "Menstrual Synchrony," 244.

44. Mary Daly elaborates on a connection between crucifixion imagery and scapegoating in *Beyond God the Father: Toward a Philosophy of Women's Liberation* (1973; reprint Boston: Beacon Press, 1985), 69–97. See also the definition of *christolatry* in Daly with Caputi, *Wickedary*, 189–190, as "the worship of christ as divine sacrificial victim whose sacrifice was followed by resurrection and triumphal ascent into heaven; form of idolatry that functions to mandate and legitimate intolerance, self-hatred, hatred and scapegoating of others, inquisitions, sadomasochism, pornography."

45. This statement was on a leaflet produced and passed around by Zoë Sofia at the 1983 California American Studies Association meeting.

46. Marilou Awiakta, "Mother Nature Sends a Pink Slip," *Appalachian Heritage*, Winter 1991, 5.

47. This poetry reading was videotaped so I was able to transcribe these comments from that tape. Mr. Tsosie, who is now a state representative in the New Mexico legislature, gave me permission to use his words.

48. Carolyn Merchant, *The Death of Nature: Women, Ecology and the Scientific Revolution* (San Francisco: Harper and Row, 1980), 29–41.

49. Claus Biegert, "The Death that Creeps from the Earth, Or Why on Earth a World Uranium Hearing?" Letter, no date, c. 1990.

50. Richard Rhodes, *The Making of the Atom Bomb* (New York: Simon and Schuster, 1986), 610–611.

51. Barbara Walker, *The Woman's Encyclopedia of Myths and Secrets* (San Francisco: Harper and Row, 1984), 347.

52. Edward Teller, *Energy from Heaven and Earth* (San Francisco: W.H. Freeman and Co., 1979), 148.

53. An *eyeballer* is a "deadeye dick; crude public peeper; pornography user/woman-abuser." Daly with Caputi, *Wickedary*, 197.

54. Leslie Marmon Silko, "The Fourth World," *Artforum International* 27, no. 10 (Summer 1989): 124–125.

55. Leslie Marmon Silko, *Almanac of the Dead* (New York: Simon and Schuster, 1991), 763.

56. Mary Daly, *Pure Lust: Elemental Feminist Philosophy* (1984; reprint San Francisco: HarperSanFrancisco, 1992), 7–8.

57. Pierre Teilhard de Chardin, "Some Reflections on the Spiritual Repercussions of the Atom Bomb," in *The Future of Man*, trans. N. Denny (New York: Harper and Row, 1964), 145–153.

58. Monika Bauerlein, "Plutonium is Forever," *Utne Reader*, July/Aug. 1992, 34–36.

59. Alan Burdick, "The Last Cold-War Monument," *Harper's Magazine*, Aug. 1992, 62–67.

60. Ibid.

CHAPTER NINE

1. Chela Sandoval, "Feminism and Racism: A Report on the 1981 National Women's Studies Association Conference," in *Making Face, Making Soul/Haciendo Caras*, ed. Gloria Anzaldúa (San Francisco: Aunt Lute Foundation Books, 1990), 55–71.

2. Robert Bly, *Iron John: A Book About Men* (New York: Vintage Books, 1990), 17.

3. *Snool* was first used and defined by Mary Daly in *Pure Lust: Elemental Feminist Philosophy* (1984; reprint San Francisco: HarperSanFrancisco, 1992), 20–21. There she tells us that snools, who are "the rule," are characterized by "sadism and masochism combined" and are "the stereotypic saints and heroes of the sadostate."

4. Page duBois, *Sowing the Body: Psychoanalysis and Ancient Representations of Women* (Chicago: University of Chicago Press, 1988), 92.

5. Marilou Awiakta, "Baring the Atom's Mother Heart," in *Homewords: A Book of Tennessee Writers*, ed. Douglass Paschall and Alice Swanson (Knoxville: Tennessee Arts Commission and the University of Tennessee Press, 1986), 183–188, esp. 185–186.

6. Roger Caillois, *Man and the Sacred*, trans. Meyer Barash (Glencoe: IL, 1959), 22–23. See also Emile Durkheim, *The Elementary Forms of the Religious Life* (New York: The Free Press, 1915).

7. Richard Stivers, *Evil in Modern Myth and Ritual* (Athens: GA: The University of Georgia Press, 1982), 32.

8. Jacques Ellul, *The New Demons*, trans. C. Edward Hopkin (New York: Seabury Press, 1975), 49–50.

9. Helen Caldicott, *Nuclear Madness: What You Can Do!* (Brookline, MA: Autumn Press, 1978), 26.

10. Caillois, *Man and the Sacred*, 20.

11. Ibid., 19–20.

12. Carol Cohn, "Sex and Death in the Rational World of Defense Intellectuals," *Signs: Journal of Women in Culture and Society* 12, no. 4 (1987): 687–718.

13. Caillois, *Man and the Sacred*, 21.

14. Robert Jungk, *Brighter than a Thousand Suns: A Personal History of the Atomic Scientists*, trans. James Cleugh (New York: Harcourt, Brace, 1958), 201.

15. Caillois, *Man and the Sacred*, 21.

16. Caldicott, *Nuclear Madness*, 29, 34.

17. Caillois, *Man and the Sacred*, 23.

18. Caldicott, *Nuclear Madness*, 29.

19. Caillois, *Man and the Sacred*, 23.

20. Caldicott, *Nuclear Madness*, 66.

21. Caillois, *Man and the Sacred*, 22.

22. Awiakta, "Baring the Atom's Mother Heart," 186.

23. Barbara Walker, *The Crone: Woman of Age, Wisdom, and Power* (San Francisco: Harper & Row, 1985), 82.

24. Ean Begg, *The Cult of the Black Virgin* (Boston: Arkana, 1985), 27.

25. Paula Gunn Allen, "Raven's Road," in *The New Native American Novel: Works in Progress*, ed. Mary Bartlett (Albuquerque: University of New Mexico Press, 1986), 56.

26. Paula Gunn Allen, *Grandmothers of the Light: A Medicine Woman's Sourcebook* (Boston: Beacon Press, 1991), xiii–xiv. Allen invents the word *cosmogyny* to mean "an ordered universe arranged in harmony with gynocratic principles."

27. Jane Caputi, "Interview with Paula Gunn Allen," *Trivia: A Journal of Ideas* 16/17 (1990): 50–67.

28. I have put together statements from two interviews: Annie O. Eysturoy, "Interview with Paula Gunn Allen," in *This Is About Vision: Interviews with Southwestern Writers*, ed. William V. Balassi, John F. Crawford, and Annie O. Eysturoy (Albuquerque, NM: University of New Mexico Press, 1990), 95–108; Caputi, "Interview with Paula Gunn Allen," *Trivia*, 62.

29. Mary Daly, *Pure Lust: Elemental Feminist Philosophy* (1984; reprint San Francisco: HarperSanFrancisco, 1992), 25.

30. Caputi, "Interview," 63.

31. Spencer Weart, *Nuclear Fear: A History of Image* (Cambridge, MA: Harvard University Press, 1988), 405.

32. Awiakta, "Baring the Atom's Mother Heart," 183–188.

33. Thomas Rain Crowe, "Marilou Awiakta: Reweaving the Future," *Appalachian Journal* 18, no. 1 (Fall 1990): 40–54.

34. Marilou Awiakta, *Abiding Appalachia: Where Mountain and Atom Meet* (Memphis, TN: St. Luke's Press, 1978).

35. Crowe, "Marilou Awiakta," 45.

36. Carol Lee Sanchez, "New World Tribal Communities: An Alternative Approach for Recreating Egalitarian Societies," in *Weaving the Visions: New Patterns in Feminist Spirituality,* ed. Judith Plaskow and Carol P. Christ (San Francisco, Harper and Row, 1989), 344–356.

37. Wallace Black Elk and William S. Lyon, *Black Elk: the Sacred Ways of a Lakota* (San Francisco: HarperSanFrancisco, 1991), 54.

38. Emily Culpepper, "Ancient Gorgons: A Face for Contemporary Women's Rage," *Woman of Power: A Magazine of Feminism, Spirituality, and Politics,* issue 3 (Winter/Spring 1986): 22–24, 40.

39. Helen Zahavi, *The Weekend* (New York: Donald I. Fine, 1991), 187.

40. Andrea Dworkin, *Mercy* (New York: Four Walls Eight Windows, 1991), 333.

41. Dworkin, *Mercy*, 331.

42. Andrea Dworkin, *Pornography: Men Possessing Women* (New York: Perigee Books, 1981); Andrea Dworkin and Catharine A. MacKinnon, *Pornography and Civil Rights: A New Day for Women's Equality* (Minneapolis, MN: Organizing Against Pornography, 1988); Andrea Dworkin, *Letters from a War Zone: Writings 1976–1989* (New York: E. P. Dutton, 1989).

43. Guns N' Roses, "Used to Love Her," *Lies, Lies, Lies, Lies* (Geffen Records M56 2224198: 1988).

44. Dworkin, *Mercy*, 333.

45. Diane DiMassa, *Hothead Paisan: Homicidal Lesbian Terrorist,* no. 5 (1992): 6–8. For copies, write to Giant Ass Publishing, P.O. Box 214, New Haven, CT 06502.

46. For elaboration, see Jane Caputi, "American Psychos: The Serial Killer in the Contemporary Imagination," *Journal of American Culture* 16, no. 4 (Winter 1993): 101–112.

47. For a discussion of this, see Richard Schickel, "Gender Bender," *Time,* June 24, 1991, 52–56.

48. James Ellroy, *Killer on the Road* (New York: Avon, 1986), 280.

49. Patricia A. Murphy, *We Walk the Back of the Tiger* (Tallahassee, FL: Naiad Press, 1988).

50. Barbara G. Walker, *The Woman's Encyclopedia of Myths and Secrets* (San Francisco: Harper and Row, 1983), 488.

51. Barbara G. Walker, *The Crone: Woman of Age, Wisdom and Power* (San Francisco: Harper and Row, 1985), 56.

52. Charlene Spretnak, "Naming the Cultural Forces that Push Us Toward War," in *Exposing Nuclear Phallacies*, ed. Diana E.H. Russell (New York: Pergamon Press, The Athene Series, 1989), 53–62.

53. duBois, *Sowing the Body*, 88.

54. Gerburg Treusch-Dieter, "The Beginning of the End: On the History of Radiation from Plato to Chernobyl," in *Looking Back on the End of the World*, ed. Dietmar Kamper and Christoph Wulf, trans. David Antal (New York: Semiotext(e), 1989), 7–18.

PART FOUR

PRELUDE FOUR

1. Paula Gunn Allen, "The Woman I Love Is a Planet, The Planet I Love Is a Tree," in *Reweaving the World: The Emergence of Ecofeminism*, ed. Irene Diamond and Gloria Feman Orenstein (San Francisco: Sierra Club Books, 1990), 52–57.

2. *Hints from the Haggis* is an imaginary book. Certainly, though, it is one I would like to read.

3. Zoë Sofia, "Exterminating Fetuses: Abortion, Disarmament, and the Sexo-semiotics of Extraterrestrialism," *Diacritics* 14, no. 2 (Summer 1984): 47–59, esp. 48.

4. See Helene Vann and Jane Caputi, "*Driving Miss Daisy*: A New Song of the South," *Journal of Popular Film and Television* 18, no. 2 (Summer 1990): 80–82.

5. Paula Gunn Allen, *Grandmothers of the Light: A Medicine Woman's Sourcebook* (Boston: Beacon Press, 1991); Mary Daly, *Gyn/Ecology: The Metaethics of Radical Feminism* (1978; reprint Boston: Beacon Press, 1990); Mary Daly, *Pure Lust: Elemental Feminist Philosophy* (1984; reprint San Francisco: HarperSanFrancisco, 1992); Mary Daly in Cahoots with Jane Caputi, *Websters' First New Intergalactic Wickedary of the English Language* (Boston: Beacon Press, 1987); Ursula LeGuin, "The Space Crone," in *Dancing at the Edge of the World: Thoughts on Words, Women, Places* (New York: Grover Press, 1989), 3–6; Paule Marshall, *Praisesong for the Widow* (New York: G.P. Putnam's Sons, 1983); Barbara Mor, "The Morrigan," *Woman of Power: A Magazine of Feminism, Spirituality, and Politics* 15 (Fall/Winter 1990): 60–61; Toni

Morrison, *Song of Solomon* (New York: New American Library, 1977); Barbara G. Walker, *The Crone: Woman of Age, Wisdom, and Power* (San Francisco: Harper and Row, 1985).

6. Sofia, "Exterminating Fetuses," 48.

7. Valerie Solanas, *The SCUM Manifesto* (London: The Matriarchy Study Group, 1967, 1968, 1983), 4.

8. Toni Morrison, *Tar Baby* (New York: New American Library, Signet Books, 1981), 174–175.

9. Mike Smith, cartoon, reprinted in the *Nevada Nuclear Waste Newsletter* 4, no. 2 (July 1988): 1.

10. Friedrich Nietzsche, *Thus Spake Zarathustra*, trans. and intro. R.J. Hollingdale (New York: Penguin Books, 1969), 91. Cited in Daly, *Gyn/Ecology*, 355.

11. Stan Steiner, *The New Indians* (New York: Dell, 1968), 219–220.

12. For women reclaiming authority on the subject of war, see Susan Jeffords, *The Remasculinization of America: Gender and the Vietnam War* (Bloomington: Indiana University Press, 1989). For feminist redefintions of war, see Paula Gunn Allen, "Introduction," *Spider Woman's Granddaughters: Traditional Tales and Contemporary Writing by Native American Women* (New York: Fawcett Columbine, 1989), 1–25.

13. Mor, "The Morrigan," 60–61.

14. Quoted in Amy Pagnozzi, "The Real Reason Men Want to Keep Women Soldiers Out of Combat," *Glamour*, Dec. 1992, 148.

15. Sofia, "Exterminating Fetuses," 56–57.

16. Morrison, *Song of Solomon*, 149.

17. Marshall, *Praisesong for the Widow*.

18. Nor Hall, *The Moon and the Virgin: Reflections on the Archetypal Feminine* (New York: Harper and Row, 1980), 197.

19. Allen, *Grandmothers of the Light*, 35.

20. LeGuin, "The Space Crone," 4–5.

21. *Snool* was first used and defined by Mary Daly in *Pure Lust*, 20–21. There she tells us that snools, who are "the rule," are characterized by "sadism and masochism combined" and are "the stereotypic saints and heroes of the sadostate."

22. I had this intuition in May 1990. Some months later I came across the same thought in Paula Gunn Allen's "The Woman I Love Is a Planet."

CHAPTER TEN

1. bell hooks, *Black Looks: Race and Representation* (Boston: South End Press, 1992), 116.

2. R.T. Rundle Clark, *Myth and Symbol in Ancient Egypt* (London: Thames and Hudson, 1959), 221–224.

3. Hooks notes that "white slave-owners (men, women, and children) punished enslaved black people for looking." *Black Looks*, 115.

4. Pauline Réage, *The Story of O*, trans. Sabine d'Estrée (New York: Grove Press, 1954, 1965).

5. Barbara G. Walker, *The Woman's Encyclopedia of Myths and Secrets* (San Francisco: Harper and Row, 1983), 294; Mary Daly in Cahoots with Jane Caputi, *Websters' First New Intergalactic Wickedary of the English Language* (Boston: Beacon Press, 1987), 122–123.

6. Michel Foucault, *Discipline and Punish: The Birth of the Prison* (New York: Vintage Books, 1977), 173. Cited in Monica Sjöö and Barbara Mor, *The Great Cosmic Mother: Rediscovering the Religion of the Earth* (San Francisco: Harper & Row, 1987), 327.

7. Sjöö and Mor, *The Great Cosmic Mother*, 327.

8. Clark, *Myth and Symbol in Ancient Egypt*, 218.

9. See Barbara MacDonald and Cynthia Rich, *Look Me in the Eye* (San Francisco: Spinsters, Ink, 1983).

10. *Snool* was first used and defined by Mary Daly in *Pure Lust: Elemental Feminist Philosophy* (1984; reprint San Francisco: HarperSanFrancisco, 1992), 20–21. There she tells us that snools, who are "the rule," are characterized by "sadism and masochism combined" and are "the stereotypic saints and heroes of the sadostate."

11. Barbara G. Walker, *The Crone: Woman of Age, Wisdom, and Power* (San Francisco: Harper and Row, 1985), 177–178.

12. Walker, *Woman's Encyclopedia*, 248.

13. Walker, *The Crone*, 148.

14. Jean-Paul Sartre, *Existentialism and Human Emotions* (New York: The Philosophical Library, 1957), 85–86.

15. Thanks to Ona Lara Porter.

16. Walker, *Woman's Encyclopedia*, 538.

17. Walker, *The Crone*, 56.

18. Aleister Crowley, *The Book of Thoth* (York Beach, ME: Samuel Weiser, Inc., 1944, 1991), 73.

19. Walker, *The Crone*, 72.

20. Jane Caputi, "Interview with Paula Gunn Allen," *Trivia: A Journal of Ideas* 16/17 (1990): 50–67.

21. For versions of this story, see Paula Gunn Allen, *Grandmothers of the Light: A Medicine Woman's Sourcebook* (Boston: Beacon Press, 1991), 38–47; Marta Weigle, *Creation and Procreation: Feminist Reflections on Mythologies of Cosmogony and Parturition* (Philadelphia: University of Pennsylvania Press, 1989), 190–191.

22. Lucille Clifton, "the earth is a living thing," *The Book of Light* (Port Townsend, WA: Copper Canyon Press, 1993), 34.

23. The Boeing ad is from the *New York Times*, June 17, 1986. The artist for the *Omni* cover (Apr. 1982) is Yoshihisa Sadamatsu. *Omni* comments, "The emergence of an egg-encased infant beneath a horrific mushroom cloud foretokens an ironic hope for mankind's continued existence." The Fuji ad appeared in *Rolling Stone* in 1982. See also: Marshall McLuhan's "The Mechanical Bride," in *The Mechanical Bride: Folklore of Industrial Man* (Boston: Beacon Press, 1951), 93–101.

24. Arthur C. Clarke, *2001: A Space Odyssey* (New York: Signet, 1973).

25. Clarke, *2001*, 221.

26. Zoë Sofia, "Exterminating Fetuses: Abortion, Disarmament, and the Sexo–semiotics of Extraterrestrialism," *Diacritics* 14, no. 2 (Summer 1984): 47–59.

27. Weigle, *Creation and Procreation*, 163.

28. Arthur C. Clarke, *Childhood's End* (New York: Ballantine, 1953).

29. June Jordan finds a profound irony in calling the majority of the peoples of Earth the "Third World" and corrects this by reversing the standard and speaking of them as the "First World." See "Declaration of an Independence I Would Just As Soon Not Have," in *Civil Wars* (Boston: Beacon Press, 1981), 115–121.

30. Saint Paul, Colossians 3:2–3, *Holy Bible*, rev. standard version.

31. Mary Daly, *Outercourse: The Be-Dazzling Voyage* (San Francisco: HarperSanFrancisco, 1992).

32. Ursula LeGuin, "The Space Crone," in *Dancing at the Edge of the World: Thoughts on Words, Women, Places* (New York: Grove Press, 1989), 3–6.

33. Walker, *The Crone*, 175.

34. For commentary on such snoolish endeavors, see Andrée Collard

with Joyce Contrucci, *The Rape of the Wild* (Bloomington, IN: Indiana University Press, 1988, 1989), 161–168. For space fanaticism, see George Henry Elias, "At This Rate, We'll Never Get Off the Planet," *New York Times*, Aug. 26, 1990, national edition.

35. Ann Scales says that one form the Space Crone may take is that of the black hole—a contemporary discovery of astrophysics that resonates with the archetypal form of the Black Crone, Kali. The first picture of what astronomers believe to be a black hole appeared on the front page of the *New York Times*, Nov. 20, 1992. It resembles nothing so much as a cervix.

CHAPTER ELEVEN

1. *Snool* was first used and defined by Mary Daly in *Pure Lust: Elemental Feminist Philosophy* (1984; reprint San Francisco: HarperSanFrancisco, 1992), 20–21. There she tells us that snools, who are "the rule," are characterized by "sadism and masochism combined" and are "the stereotypic saints and heroes of the sadostate."

2. *Hints from the Haggis* is an imaginary book. Certainly, though, it is one I would like to read.

3. Jane Gross, "Aging Baby Boomers Take Fresh Look at a Milestone," *New York Times*, May 17, 1992, A1.

4. Thanks to Chris Williamson, *The Changer and The Changed* (Olivia Records LC904: 1975).

5. Mary Daly speaks of Crones as "long-lasting ones" and "Survivors of the perpetual witchcraze of patriarchy." *Gyn/Ecology: The Metaethics of Radical Feminism* (1978; reprint Boston: Beacon Press, 1990), 16.

6. See, for example, Brad Daggach, "The War on Aging," *Life* 15, no. 10 (Oct. 1992): 32–45.

7. Clarke is interviewed in Gene Youngblood's *Expanded Cinema* (New York: Dutton, 1970), 149.

8. Annette Peláez, "UFOs/ETs: Myth, Legend, and Reality" (Paper presented at the Popular and American Culture Associations meeting, New Orleans, LA, Apr. 1993).

9. C.G. Jung, *Flying Saucers: A Modern Myth of Things Seen in the Skies*, trans. R.F.C. Hull (New York: Harcourt, Brace and Company, 1959).

10. Wallace Black Elk and William S. Lyon, *Black Elk: The Sacred Ways of a Lakota* (San Francisco: HarperSanFrancisco, 1990), 91–92.

11. James S. Gordon, "The UFO Experience," *The Atlantic Monthly*, Aug.

1991, 82–92. See also the discussion by Michael Talbot in *The Holographic Universe* (New York: HarperPerennial, 1991), 276–286.

12. Susan Sontag, "The Imagination of Disaster," in *Awake in the Dark: An Anthology of American Film Criticism*, ed. David Denby (New York: Vintage Books, 1977), 263–277.

13. Barbara G. Walker, *The Woman's Encyclopedia of Myths and Secrets* (San Francisco: Harper and Row, 1983), 194.

14. Hans Moravec, *Mind Children: The Future of Robot and Human Intelligence* (Cambridge, MA: Harvard University Press, 1988), 1.

15. Thanks to Annette Peláez, who suggested this word in October 1992.

16. Claudia Springer, "The Pleasure of the Interface," *Screen* 32, no. 3 (Autumn 1991): 303–323; Gabrielle Schwab, "Cyborgs: Postmodern Phantasms of Body and Mind," *Discourse* 9 (Spring/Summer, 1987): 64–83.

17. Donna J. Haraway, *Simians, Cyborgs, and Women: The Reinvention of Nature* (New York: Routledge, 1991), 149–181.

18. Andrée Collard with Joyce Contrucci, *The Rape of the Wild* (Bloomington, IN: Indiana University Press, 1988, 1989).

19. Carole Gallagher, *American Ground Zero: The Secret Nuclear War* (Cambridge, MA: M.I.T. Press, 1993), 346.

20. Paula Gunn Allen, "The Woman I Love Is a Planet, the Planet I Love Is a Tree," in *Reweaving the World: The Emergence of Ecofeminism*, ed. Irene Diamond and Gloria Feman Orenstein (San Francisco: Sierra Club Books, 1990), 52–57.

21. Cited in Monica Sjöö and Barbara Mor, *The Great Cosmic Mother: Rediscovering the Religion of the Earth* (San Francisco: Harper and Row, 1987), vi.

22. Jane Caputi, "Interview with Paula Gunn Allen," *Trivia: A Journal of Ideas* 16/17 (1990): 50–67, esp. 57.

23. Spencer Weart, *Nuclear Fear: A History of Images* (Cambridge, MA: Harvard University Press, 1988), 5.

24. Weart, *Nuclear Fear*, 13–16.

25. Barbara G. Walker, *The Woman's Dictionary of Symbols and Sacred Objects* (San Francisco: Harper and Row, 1988), 392; Joseph Epes Brown, *Animals of the Soul: Sacred Animals of the Oglala Sioux* (Rockport, MA: Element, Inc., 1992), 39–40.

26. Allen, "The Woman I Love Is a Planet," 55.

27. Octavia Butler, *Dawn* (New York: Warner Books, 1987).

28. Allen, "The Woman I Love Is a Planet," 56.

29. Helen Diner, *Mothers and Amazons, The First Feminine History of Culture*, ed. and trans. John Philip Lundin, intro. Brigitte Berger (Garden City, NY: Anchor Books, 1973), 45. See also Daly, *Gyn/Ecology*, 79–81.

30. Columbus signed his name "in its Greek etymological form, Xpo-Ferens—the bringer of the anointed one, the bearer of the Messiah." Djelal Kadir, *Columbus and the Ends of the Earth: Europe's Prophetic Rhetoric as Conquering Ideology* (Berkeley: University of California Press, 1992), 1.

31. For commentary, see Arthur C. Danto, *Mapplethorpe* (New York: Random House, 1992).

32. For commentary, see Daly, *Gyn/Ecology*.

33. For a depiction of this, see the film *The Last Temptation of Christ*, directed by Martin Scorcese, 1988.

34. See William Martin, "Waiting for the End," *The Atlantic Monthly*, June 1982, 31–37.

35. Some of these ideas were generated in a very memorable evening of conversation with Gordene MacKenzie, "Good" Friday 1991, San Antonio, Texas.

36. *Gynesophical* is a word invented by Paula Gunn Allen. Communicated to me in a conversation in July 1992.

37. Diane Wolkstein and Samuel Noah Kramer, *Inanna: Queen of Heaven and Earth: Her Stories and Hymns from Sumer* (New York: Harper and Row, 1983), 169.

38. Mary Daly, *Pure Lust: Elemental Feminist Philosophy* (1984; reprint San Francisco: HarperSanFrancisco, 1992), 3. In *Pure Lust* 2, she also differentiates Pure Lust from "phallic lust," which she defines as "violent and self-indulgent, levels all life, dismembering spirit/matter, attempting annihilation."

39. The scenario is enacted with full approval in Shel Silverstein's bestselling children's story, *The Giving Tree* (New York: Harper and Row, 1964).

40. Gena Corea, *The Mother Machine: Reproductive Technologies from Artificial Insemination to Artificial Wombs* (New York: Harper and Row, 1985). See also "California Woman, 53, Gives Birth to Twins," *New York Times*, Nov. 12, 1992, A9, national edition.

41. The word *engine* is derived from the Latin *ingenium*, "natural capacity" and related to the Latin *gignere*, "to beget."

42. Sjöö and Mor, *Great Cosmic Mother*, 382.

43. Ibid., 383.

44. Carolyn G. Heilbrun, "Women Writers: Coming of Age at 50," *New York Times Book Review*, Sept. 4, 1988, 23.

45. See, for example, Germaine Greer, *The Change: Woman, Aging and the Menopause* (New York: Alfred A. Knopf, 1992); Christine Downing, *Women's Mysteries: Toward a Poetics of Gender* (New York: Crossroad, 1992). See also the 1990 film by Yvonne Ranier, *Privilege*.

46. Alice Walker, "The Universe Responds: Or, How I Learned We Can Have Peace on Earth," in *Living By the Word: Selected Writings 1973–1987* (San Diego: Harcourt Brace Jovanovich, 1988), 187–193. See also my comments in chapter 7.

47. There was an ancient belief that postmenopausal women were the wisest of mortals because they permanently retained their "wise blood." See Walker, *Woman's Encyclopedia*, 641.

48. Robert Briffault, *The Mothers: A Study of the Origins of Sentiments and Institutions* (New York: Macmillan), 2:557.

49. Walker, *Woman's Encyclopedia*, 655.

50. Paula Gunn Allen, *Grandmothers of the Light: A Medicine Woman's Sourcebook* (Boston: Beacon Press, 1991), 33–37, 59–65.

51. Ibid., xiii–xiv. Allen invents the word *cosmogyny* to mean "an ordered universe arranged in harmony with gynocratic principles."

52. Cara Marianna, "The Seven Mythic Cycles of Thelma and Louise" in *Trivia: A Journal of Ideas* 21 (1993).

CHAPTER TWELVE

1. Mary Daly first wrote of the Fates in *Pure Lust: Elemental Feminist Philosophy* (1984; reprint San Francisco: HarperSanFrancisco, 1992). This definition is from Mary Daly in Cahoots with Jane Caputi, *Websters' First New Intergalactic Wickedary of the English Language* (Boston: Beacon Press, 1987), 124.

2. I thank Nicholas Tarnawsky for introducing me to *Pumpkinhead* and Gordene MacKenzie for making sure I got the message.

3. Marilou Awiakta, "Amazons in Appalachia," in *A Gathering of Spirit*, ed. Beth Brant (Ithaca, NY: Firebrand Books, 1984, 1988), 125–30.

4. There are triangular motifs in the international symbol for radiation, in the upward-pointing lava obelisk monument at the Trinity Site in New Mexico, and in any number of popular artifacts. For example, a T-shirt sold in New Mexico (copyright 1990, Swarc) commemorates

the Trinity Site. On it, a fiery orange mushroom cloud blooms against a background of a large, downward-pointing black triangle. Beneath this is the familiar Oppenheimer quote "I am become death, the shatterer of worlds." As with any symbol, there are many paradoxical possible interpretations. One, offered recurrently by my students over the years, is that the image suggests rapist intercourse, with the Bomb serving as the phallic symbol and the triangle as the vulval symbol. The rape imagery is underscored by the Oppenheimer quote suggesting the shattering of worlds and wombs.

5. Barbara G. Walker, *The Woman's Dictionary of Symbols and Sacred Objects* (San Francisco: Harper and Row, 1986), 36. For additional information, see Barbara G. Walker, *The Woman's Encyclopedia of Myths and Secrets* (San Francisco: Harper and Row, 1983), 1016–1017. There Walker writes that the triangle, particularly, "represents the Triple Goddess in her aspect of Wise Crone" and, in ancient times, "the triangle itself was worshiped in much the same way that modern Christians worship the cross." In the Hindu Shakta tradition, art historian Elinor Gadon informs us, the Goddess is understood as "ultimate reality and the *yantra*, the downward pointing triangle, is the ritual diagram used in meditation to invoke her presence. The Kali yantra represents shakti, the life force, cosmic energy experienced as female." Elinor Gadon, *The Once and Future Goddess* (San Francisco: Harper and Row, 1989), 17.

6. Walker, *Woman's Encyclopedia*, 302.

7. Robert Briffault, *The Mothers: A Study of the Origins of Sentiments and Institutions* (New York: Macmillan, 1927), 2:603. The quote is from the ancient Scandinavian epic.

8. Ibid. The quote is from the Scandinavian epic.

9. Walker, *Woman's Encyclopedia*, 730. See also Barbara G. Walker, *The Crone: Woman of Age, Wisdom and Power* (San Francisco: Harper and Row, 1985) for an extensive discussion of the tradition of the doomsday Crone.

10. Alice Walker, "Only Justice Can Stop a Curse," *In Search of Our Mothers' Gardens* (San Diego: Harcourt Brace Jovanovich, 1983), 338–342.

11. Briffault, *The Mothers*, 2:603.

12. Thomas F. Homer-Dixon, Jeffrey H. Boutwell, and George W. Rathjens, "Environmental Change and Violent Conflict," *Scientific American* 268, no. 2 (Feb. 1993): 48–55.

13. Jeffrey Ballinger, "The New Free-Trade Heel," *Harper's Magazine,* Aug. 1992, 46–47.

14. Barbara Walker, *Woman's Encyclopedia,* 1072–1073.

15. Teresa "Osa" Hidalgo-de la Riva, *Mujeria: Primitive and Proud,* Royal Eagle Bear Productions, 1992. This film is distributed by Women Make Movies in New York.

16. This phrase is reiterated throughout much of Awiakta's works. See, for example, Marilou Awiakta, "The Grandmothers are Coming Back," *Woman of Power: A Magazine of Feminism, Spirituality, and Politics* 15 (Fall/Winter, 1990): 41–42. Wallace Black Elk speaks of the Grandmother as *awakening.* See Wallace Black Elk and William S. Lyon, *Black Elk: The Sacred Ways of a Lakota* (San Francisco: HarperSanFrancisco, 1990).

    Poet Sonia Sanchez speaks very clearly about the spiritual Powers conveyed to her through the voice of the Fates in her life—the voice of her grandmother:

    > I see myself as being empowered because of my grandmother, and people like her. It has really been that kind of transmitting that has given us the power. My power may have gotten manifested in a different kind of politic than that of my grandmother. But nonetheless, it was the same power... the same energy that had been infused in me, that had been given to me by my grandmother.

    Zala Chandler, "Voices Beyond the Veil: An Interview with Toni Cade Bambara and Sonia Sanchez," in *Wild Women in the Whirlwind: Afra-American Culture and the Contemporary Literary Renaissance,* ed. Joanne M. Braxton and Andrée Nicola McLaughlin (New Brunswick, NJ: Rutgers University Press, 1990), 342–362.

17. Barbara Mor, "The Morrigan," *Woman of Power: A Magazine of Feminism, Spirituality, and Politics* 15 (Fall/Winter, 1990): 60–61.

18. Daly, *Pure Lust,* 416.

19. *Ibid.,* 271.

20. Chandler, "Voices Beyond the Veil: An Interview with Toni Cade Bambara and Sonia Sanchez," 349–350.

21. Nor Hall, *The Moon and the Virgin: Reflections on the Archetypal Feminine* (New York: Harper and Row, 1980), 195.

22. Walker, *Woman's Encyclopedia,* 303.

23. Paula Gunn Allen, *The Sacred Hoop: Recovering the Feminine in*

American Indian Traditions (Boston: Beacon Press, 1986), 200.

CONCLUSION

1. Jane Caputi, "Interview with Paula Gunn Allen," *Trivia: A Journal of Ideas* 16/17 (Fall 1990): 50–67.

2. Monica Sjöö and Barbara Mor, *The Great Cosmic Mother: Rediscovering the Religion of the Earth* (San Francisco: Harper and Row, 1987), 2–3.

3. Wallace Black Elk and William S. Lyon, *Black Elk: The Sacred Ways of a Lakota* (San Francisco: HarperSanFrancisco, 1990), 137.

4. Marilou Awiakta, *Selu:Seeking the Corn-Mother's Wisdom* (Golden, CO: Fulcrum Publishing, 1993), 270.

5. This news story originated in the *Toronto Globe and Mail*. Unfortunately, I have the clipping but not the date, though I believe it was from 1990 or 1991.

6. The quote is from Sjöö and Mor, *The Great Cosmic Mother*, 3. They, in turn, are quoting Stephen Jay Gould in *Hen's Teeth and Horse's Toes: Further Reflections in Natural History* (New York: W.W. Norton, 1983), 153–154. See also Mary Jane Sherfey, *The Nature and Evolution of Female Sexuality* (New York: Simon and Schuster, 1973).

7. See Mary Daly, *Beyond God the Father: Toward a Philosophy of Women's Liberation* (1973; reprint Boston: Beacon Press, 1985).

8. Gordene MacKenzie, *Transgender Nation* (Bowling Green, OH: Bowling Green State University Popular Press, 1993).

9. For a critique of this theme in psychoanalytic theory, see Gordene MacKenzie, *Transgender Nation*, 86–103.

10. *Snool* was first used and defined by Mary Daly in *Pure Lust: Elemental Feminist Philosophy* (1984; reprint San Francisco: HarperSanFrancisco, 1992), 20–21. There she tells us that snools, who are "the rule," are characterized by "sadism and masochism combined" and are "the stereotypic saints and heroes of the sadostate."

11. For amplification, see Jane Caputi, *The Age of Sex Crime* (Bowling Green State University Popular Press, 1987).

12. Diane DiMassa, *Hothead Paisan: Homicidal Lesbian Terrorist*, issue 2 (1991): 1.

13. Anne Fausto-Sterling, "The Five Sexes: Why Male and Female Are Not Enough," *The Sciences*, Mar./Apr. 1993, 20–24.

14. Nor Hall, *The Moon and the Virgin: Reflections on the Archetypal Feminine* (New York: Harper and Row, 1985), 206.

15. Fausto-Sterling, "The Five Sexes," 24.

16. James Gleick, *Chaos: Making a New Science* (New York: Penguin Books, 1987), 3.

17. Robin Morgan, "Monster," in *Monster* (New York: Vintage, 1972), 86.

18. Peter Berger, *The Sacred Canopy: Elements of a Sociological Theory of Religion* (New York: Doubleday, 1967).

19. "Ground Zero" is the name of the resistance movement challenging as of June 1993 the anti-gay "Amendment 2" passed in Colorado in November 1992. See Donna Minkowitz, "Ground Zero: Fear and Renewal in Colorado," *Village Voice*, Jan. 19, 1993, 30–32.

20. *Trivia* was the Roman name for the goddess Hecate, Crone goddess of witches and crossroads, where three ways (hence *trivia*) meet. Again, the oral tradition encodes means of resistance and stresses the potency of the trivial.

21. This poem is connected by Gleick to the Butterfly Effect. See his *Chaos*, 23.

22. Friedrich Nietzsche, *Beyond Good and Evil: Prelude to a Philosophy of the Future*, trans. Walter Kaufman (New York: Vintage, 1966), 89.

23. Michael Crichton, *Jurassic Park* (New York: Ballantine, 1990), 314.

24. See, for example, one argument that the "culture of aid gave us the tragedy of Somalia." Michael Marren, "Manna from Heaven," *Village Voice*, Jan. 19, 1993, 26–28.

25. See Ernest Becker, *Escape from Evil* (New York: The Free Press, 1975). For elaboration on this, see Caputi, *The Age of Sex Crime*, 156–157.

26. Monotonous, *nomos*-minded men tell us that Chaos is "empty." We might remember that this is what the various conquerors said about the so-called New World, too, just before they started wiping out the people and creatures who had been here forever. The word *empty* is derived from an Old English word that means "leisure" or "rest," which in turn is derived from a word meaning "have to" or "must." When I first read these meanings, I experienced a mild version of chaotic dissociation, for, in the endless traffic jam industrialized peoples call life, the concept of "have to" is connected to notions of work, not leisure. Laughably, industrialized peoples consider themselves superior to "primitive" peoples like the !Kung Bushpeople, who work about twenty hours a week to live well and whose post-menopausal women are outspoken, sexually free, and politically powerful. See Richard B. Lee, "Work, Sexuality, and Aging among !Kung Women," in *In Her Prime: A New View of Middle-Aged Women*,

ed. Judith K. Brown and Virginia Kerns (Massachusetts: Bergin and Garvey, Pubs., 1985), 23–33.

27. Ralph Abraham, Terence McKenna, and Rupert Sheldrake, *Trialogues at the Edge of the West* (Santa Fe, NM: Bear & Company, 1992), 48–49.

28. Fausto-Sterling, "The Five Sexes."

29. For example, see Ralph Abraham's writings in Abraham, McKenna, and Sheldrake, *Trialogues*.

30. Gloria Anzaldúa, *Borderlands/La Frontera* (San Francisco: Spinsters/Aunt Lute, 1987), 44.

31. Anzaldúa, *Borderlands/La Frontera*, 41–51.

32. Octavia Butler, *Dawn: Xenogenesis* (New York: Warner Books, 1987), 12.

33. Wendy Rose, "The Fifties," in *Women on War: Essential Voices for the Nuclear Age from a Brilliant International Assembly*, ed. Daniela Gioseffi (New York: Simon and Schuster, Touchstone Books, 1989), 60–61.

34. I was greatly aided in explaining what an attractor is by Ann Scales, who wrote most of the two paragraphs preceding this note.

35. Gleick, *Chaos*, 30.

36. O.G. Crawford, *The Eye Goddess* (1957; reprint Oak Park, IL: Delphi Press, 1992).

37. For more information, see chapter 10 in this volume.

38. Athene is referred to as *glaukopis*, or "owl-eyed," in *Iliad* 1.206, 2.16, and 5.29.

EPILOGUE

1. I thank Gordene MacKenzie for suggesting a visualization involving a Crone, a stick, and a cauldron which led me to this final image.

SELECTED BIBLIOGRAPHY

Abraham, Ralph, Terence McKenna, and Rupert Sheldrake. *Trialogues at the Edge of the West*. Santa Fe, NM: Bear & Company, 1992.

Allen, Paula Gunn. *Grandmothers of the Light: A Medicine Woman's Sourcebook*. Boston: Beacon Press, 1991.

———. "Raven's Road." In *The New Native American Novel: Works in Progress*, ed. Mary Bartlett. Albuquerque: University of New Mexico Press, 1986.

———. *The Sacred Hoop: Recovering the Feminine in American Indian Traditions*. Boston: Beacon Press, 1986.

———. "The Woman I Love Is a Planet, The Planet I Love Is a Tree." In *Reweaving the World: The Emergence of Ecofeminism*, ed. Irene Diamond and Gloria Feman Orenstein, 52–57. San Francisco: Sierra Club Books, 1990.

Anzaldúa, Gloria. *Borderlands/La Frontera*. San Francisco: Spinsters/Aunt Lute, 1987.

Awiakta, Marilou. *Abiding Appalachia: Where Mountain and Atom Meet*. Memphis, TN: St. Luke's Press, 1978.

———. "Amazons in Appalachia." In *A Gathering of Spirit*, ed. Beth Brant, 125–30. Ithaca, NY: Firebrand Books, 1984, 1988.

———. "Baring the Atom's Mother Heart." In *Homewords: A Book of Tennessee Writers*, ed. Douglass Paschall and Alice Swanson, 183–188. Knoxville: Tennessee Arts Commission and the University of Tennessee Press, 1986.

———. "Dying Back." *The Tennessee Conservationist*, Jan./Feb. 1987, 17.

———. "The Grandmothers are Coming Back." *Woman of Power: A Magazine of Feminism, Spirituality, and Politics* 15 (Fall/Winter, 1990): 41–42.

———. "Mother Nature Sends a Pink Slip." *Appalachian Heritage*, Winter 1991, 5.

———. *Selu: Seeking the Corn Mother's Wisdom*. Golden, CO: Fulcrum Publishing, 1993.

———. "When Earth Becomes an It." In Thomas Rain Crowe, "Marilou Awiakta: Reweaving the Future." *Appalachian Journal* 18, no. 1 (Fall 1990): 40–55.

Bass, Ellen, and Laura Davis, eds. *The Courage to Heal: A Guide for Women Survivors of Child Sexual Abuse*. New York: Harper and Row, 1988.

Bass, Ellen, and Louise Thornton, eds. *I Never Told Anyone: Writings by Women Survivors of Child Sexual Abuse*. New York: HarperPerennial, HarperCollins, 1983.

Black Elk, Wallace, and William S. Lyon. *Black Elk: The Sacred Ways of a Lakota*. San Francisco: HarperSanFrancisco, 1990.

Blume, E. Sue. *Secret Survivors: Uncovering Incest and Its Aftereffects in Women*. New York: Ballantine, 1990.

Boyer, Paul. *By the Bomb's Early Light: American Thought and Culture at the Dawn of the Atomic Age*. New York: Pantheon, 1985.

———. *When Time Shall Be No More: Prophecy Belief in Modern American Culture*. Cambridge, MA: Harvard University Press, 1992.

Braxton, Joanne M., and Andrée Nicola McLaughlin, eds. *Wild Women in the Whirlwind: Afra-American Culture and the Contemporary Literary Renaissance*. New Brunswick, NJ: Rutgers University Press, 1990.

Brians, Paul. *Nuclear Holocausts: Atomic War in Fiction, 1895–1984*. Kent, OH: Kent State University Press, 1987.

Briffault, Robert. *The Mothers: A Study of the Origins of Sentiments and Institutions*. 3 vols. New York: MacMillan, 1927.

Butler, Octavia. *Dawn: Xenogenesis*. New York: Warner Books, 1987.

Caldicott, Helen. *Missile Envy: The Arms Race and Nuclear War*. New York: Morrow, 1984.

———. *Nuclear Madness: What You Should Know*. Brookline, MA: Autumn Press, 1978.

Caputi, Jane. "Advertising Femicide: Lethal Violence Against Women in Pornography and Gorenography." In *Femicide: The Politics of Woman Killing*, ed. Jill Radford and Diana E.H. Russell. New York: Twayne Publishers, 1992.

———. *The Age of Sex Crime*. Bowling Green, OH: Bowling Green State University Popular Press, 1987.

———. "American Psychos: The Serial Killer in the Contemporary Imagination." *Journal of American Culture* 16, no. 4 (Winter 1993): 101–112.

———. "Charting the Flow: The Construction of Meaning through Juxtaposition in Media Texts." *Journal of Communication Inquiry* 15, no. 2 (Summer 1991): 32–47.

————. "Interview with Paula Gunn Allen." *Trivia: A Journal of Ideas* 16/17 (1990): 50–67.

————. "Men's Violence Against Women: An International Overview." *Current World Leaders* 34, no. 6 (1991): 847–878.

————. "On Psychic Activism." In *A Feminist Companion to Mythology*, ed. Carolyne Larrington, 425–440. London: Pandora Press, 1992.

————. "Psychic Numbing, Radical Futurelessness, and Sexual Violence in the Nuclear Film." In *The Nightmare Considered: Critical Essays on Nuclear War Literature*, ed. Nancy Anisfield, 58–70. Bowling Green, OH: Bowling Green State University Popular Press, 1991.

————. "Seeing Elephants: The Myths of Phallotechnology." *Feminist Studies* 14, no. 3 (1988): 487–524.

Caputi, Jane, and Gordene MacKenzie. "Pumping Iron John." In *Women Respond to the Men's Movement*, ed. Kay Hagan. San Francisco: HarperSanFrancisco, 1992.

Chernus, Ira. *Dr. Strangegod: On the Symbolic Meaning of Nuclear Weapons*. Columbia, SC: University of South Carolina Press, 1986.

Chernus, Ira, and Edward Tabor Linenthal, eds. *A Shuddering Dawn: Religious Studies and the Nuclear Age*. Albany: State University of New York Press, 1989.

Cixous, Hélène. "The Laugh of the Medusa." In *New French Feminisms*, ed. Elaine Marks and Isabelle de Courtivron, 245–264. New York: Schocken Books, 1981.

Clarke, Arthur C. *Childhood's End*. New York: Ballantine, 1953.

———— *2001: A Space Odyssey*. New York: Signet, 1973.

Cohn, Carol. "Sex and Death in the Rational World of Defense Intellectuals." *Signs: Journal of Women in Culture and Society* 12, no. 4 (1987): 687–718.

Collard, Andrée, with Joyce Contrucci. *The Rape of the Wild*. Bloomington, IN: Indiana University Press, 1988, 1989.

Condren, Mary. *The Serpent and the Goddess: Women, Religion and Power in Celtic Ireland*. San Francisco: Harper and Row, 1989.

Conroy, Pat. *The Prince of Tides*. New York: Bantam, 1986.

Crowe, Thomas Rain. "Marilou Awiakta: Reweaving the Future." *Appalachian Journal* 18, no. 1 (Fall, 1990): 40–54.

Culpepper, Emily. "Gorgons: A Face for Contemporary Women's Rage." *Woman of Power: A Magazine of Feminism, Spirituality, and Politics*, issue 3 (Winter/Spring 1986): 22–24, 40.

Daly, Mary. *The Church and the Second Sex*. 1968. Reprint. Boston: Beacon Press, 1985.

———. *Beyond God the Father: Toward a Philosophy of Women's Liberation*. 1973. Reprint. Boston: Beacon Press, 1985.

———. *Gyn/Ecology: The Metaethics of Radical Feminism*. 1978. Reprint. Boston: Beacon Press. 1990.

———. *Pure Lust: Elemental Feminist Philosophy*. 1984. Reprint. San Francisco: HarperSanFrancisco, 1992.

———. *Outercourse: The Be-Dazzling Voyage*. San Francisco: HarperSanFrancisco, 1992.

Daly, Mary, in Cahoots with Jane Caputi. *Websters' First New Intergalactic Wickedary of the English Language*. Boston: Beacon Press, 1987.

d'Eaubonne. *See* Eaubonne, Françoise d'

de Chardin. *See* Teilhard de Chardin, Pierre

de Kerckhove, Derrick. "On Nuclear Communication." *Diacritics* 14, no. 2 (Summer 1984): 72–81.

Diamond, Irene, and Gloria Feman Orenstein, eds. *Reweaving the World: The Emergence of Ecofeminism*. San Francisco: Sierra Club Books, 1990.

DiMassa, Diane. *Hothead Paisan: Homicidal Lesbian Terrorist*. Giant Ass Publishing, P.O. Box 214, New Haven, CT 06502.

Dworkin, Andrea. *Intercourse*. New York: The Free Press, 1987.

———. *Our Blood: Prophesies and Discourses on Sexual Politics*. New York: Harper and Row, 1976.

———. *Pornography: Men Possessing Women*. New York: Perigee, 1981.

Easlea, Brian. *Fathering the Unthinkable: Masculinity, Scientists, and the Nuclear Arms Race*. London: Pluto Press, 1983.

Eaubonne, Françoise d'. "Feminism or Death." In *New French Feminisms*, ed. Elaine Marks and Isabelle de Courtivron, 64–67. New York: Schocken Books, 1980.

Eisler, Riane. *The Chalice and The Blade: Our History, Our Future*. San Francisco: Harper and Row, 1987.

Fausto–Sterling, Anne. "The Five Sexes: Why Male and Female Are Not Enough." *The Sciences*, Mar./Apr. 1993, 20–24.

Feshbeck, Murray, and Alfred Friendly. *Ecocide in the USSR: The Looming Disaster in Soviet Health and Environment*. New York: Basic Books, 1992.

Finkelhor, David, and Associates. *A Sourcebook on Child Sexual Abuse.* Newbury Park, CA: Sage Publications, 1986.

Gadon, Elinor. *The Once and Future Goddess.* San Francisco: Harper and Row, 1989.

Gallagher, Carole. *American Ground Zero: The Secret Nuclear War.* Cambridge, MA: M.I.T. Press, 1993.

Gioseffi, Daniela, ed. *Women on War: Essential Voices for the Nuclear Age from a Brilliant International Assembly.* New York: Simon and Schuster, 1989.

Gleick, James. *Chaos: Making a New Science.* New York: Penguin Books, 1987.

Glendinning, Chellis. *Waking Up in the Nuclear Age.* New York: William Morrow, 1987.

Gowdy, Barbara. *Falling Angels.* New York: Soho Press, 1990.

Graves, Robert. *The Greek Myths.* Mt. Kisco, NY: Moyer Bell Limited, 1955, 1960.

Greer, Germaine. *The Change: Woman, Aging and the Menopause.* New York: Alfred A. Knopf, 1992.

Hall, Nor. *The Moon and the the Virgin: Reflections on the Archetypal Feminine.* New York: Harper and Row, 1980.

Haraway, Donna J. *Simians, Cyborgs, and Women: The Reinvention of Nature.* New York: Routledge, 1991.

Harris, Adrienne, and Ynestra King, eds. *Rocking the Ship of State: Toward a Feminist Peace Politics.* Boulder, CO: Westview Press, 189.

Harris, Bertha. "What We Mean to Say: Notes Toward Defining the Nature of Lesbian Literature." *Heresies* 3 (Fall 1977): 5–8.

Herman, Judith, with Lisa Hirschman. *Father Daughter Incest.* Cambridge, MA: Harvard University Press, 1981.

Herman, Judith Lewis. *Trauma and Recovery: The Aftermath of Violence from Domestic Abuse to Political Terror.* New York: Basic Books, 1992.

Hidalgo-de la Riva, Teresa "Osa." *Mujeria: Primitive and Proud* (film). Distributed by Women Make Movies, New York, 1992.

Hoban, Russell. *Riddley Walker.* New York: Pocket Books, 1980.

hooks, bell. *Black Looks: Race and Representation.* Boston: South End Press, 1992.

―――. *Talking Back: Thinking Feminist, Thinking Black.* Boston: South End Press, 1989.

————. *Yearnings: Race, Gender, and Cultural Politics*. Boston: South End Press, 1990.

Jordan, June. *Civil Wars*. Boston: Beacon Press, 1981.

————. *Naming Our Destiny: New and Selected Poems*. New York: Thunder's Mouth Press, 1989.

Jungk, Robert. *Brighter than a Thousand Suns: A Personal History of the Atomic Scientists*, trans. James Cleugh. New York: Harcourt, Brace, 1958.

Kahn, Herman. *Thinking About the Unthinkable*. New York: Horizon Press, 1962.

Koen, Susan, and Nina Swaim, eds. *Ain't No Where We Can Run: A Handbook for Women on the Nuclear Mentality*. Norwich, VT: WAND, 1980.

Laurence, William L. *Dawn over Zero: The Story of the Atomic Bomb*. New York: Alfred A. Knopf, 1946.

LeGuin, Ursula. "The Space Crone." In *Dancing at the Edge of the World: Thoughts on Words, Women, Places*. New York: Grove Press, 1989.

Lifton, Robert Jay, and Eric Markusen. *The Genocidal Mentality: Nazi Holocaust and Nuclear Threat*. New York: Basic Books, 1990.

Lifton, Robert Jay, and Richard Falk. *Indefensible Weapons: The Political and Psychological Case Against Nuclearism*. New York: Basic Books, 1982, 1992.

McAllister, Pam, ed. *Reweaving the Web of Life: Feminism and Non-Violence*. Philadelphia: New Society Publishers, 1982.

MacDonald, Barbara, and Cynthia Rich. *Look Me in the Eye*. San Francisco: Spinsters, Ink, 1983.

MacKenzie, Gordene. *Transgender Nation*. Bowling Green, OH: Bowling Green State University Popular Press, 1993.

MacKinnon, Catharine A. "Feminism, Marxism, Method, and the State: Toward Feminist Jurisprudence." *Signs: Journal of Women in Culture and Society* 8, no. 4 (1983): 635–658.

————. *Feminism Unmodified: Discourses on Life and Law*. Cambridge, MA: Harvard University Press, 1987.

————. *Toward a Feminist Theory of the State*. Cambridge, MA: Harvard University Press, 1989.

McLuhan, Marshall. *The Mechanical Bride: Folklore of Industrial Man*. Boston: Beacon Press, 1951.

Mander, Jerry. *In the Absence of the Sacred: The Failure of Technology and the Survival of the Indian Nations.* San Francisco: Sierra Club Books, 1991.

Marshall, Paule. *Praisesong for the Widow.* New York: G.P. Putnam's Sons, 1983.

May, Elaine Tyler. *Homeward Bound: American Families in the Cold War Era.* New York: Basic Books, 1988.

Merchant, Caroline. *The Death of Nature: Women, Ecology, and the Scientific Revolution.* San Francisco: Harper and Row, 1980.

Miller, Perry. "The End of the World." In *Errand into the Wilderness,* 217–239. Cambridge, MA: Harvard University Press, 1956.

Millett, Kate. *Sexual Politics.* Garden City, NY: Doubleday, 1969, 1970.

Mojtabai, A.G. *Blessed Assurance: At Home with the Bomb in Amarillo, Texas.* New York: Houghton Mifflin, 1986.

Mor, Barbara. "The Morrigan." *Woman of Power: A Magazine of Feminism, Spirituality, and Politics* 15 (Fall/Winter 1990): 60–61.

Morgan, Robin. *The Anatomy of Freedom: Feminism, Physics, and Global Politics.* Garden City, NY: Anchor Press/Doubleday, 1982.

———. *The Word of a Woman: Selected Prose 1968–1991.* New York: Norton, 1992.

Morrison, Toni. *Song of Solomon.* New York: New American Library, 1977.

———. *Tar Baby.* New York: New American Library, Signet Books, 1981.

Mumford, Lewis. *The Pentagon of Power: The Myth of the Machine.* New York: Harcourt Brace Jovanovich, Harvest Books, 1964, 1970.

Parfrey, Adam, ed. *Apocalypse Culture.* Los Angeles: Feral House, 1987, 1990.

Radford, Jill, and Diana E.H. Russell, eds. *Femicide: The Politics of Woman Killing.* New York: Twayne Publishers, 1992.

Rhodes, Richard. *The Making of the Atomic Bomb.* New York: Simon and Schuster, 1986.

Rosenthal, Peggy. "The Nuclear Mushroom Cloud as Cultural Image." *American Literary History* 3, no. 1 (Spring 1991): 63–92.

Rush, Florence. *The Best Kept Secret: Sexual Abuse of Children.* New York: McGraw–Hill, 1980.

Russell, Diana E.H., ed. *Exposing Nuclear Phallacies.* New York: Pergamon Press, 1989.

———. "Pornography and Rape: A Causal Model." *Political Psychology* 9 (1988): 41–73.

————. *The Secret Trauma: Incest in the Lives of Girls and Women*. New York: Basic Books, 1986.

Sanchez, Carol Lee. "Animal, Vegetable and Mineral: The Sacred Connection." In *Ecofeminism and the Sacred*, ed. Carol Adams, 207–228. New York: The Continuum Publishing Co., 1993.

————. "New World Tribal Communities: An Alternative Approach for Recreating Egalitarian Societies." In *Weaving the Visions: New Patterns in Feminist Spirituality*, ed. Judith Plaskow and Carol P. Christ, 344–356. San Francisco, Harper and Row, 1989.

Silko, Leslie Marmon. *Almanac of the Dead*. New York: Simon and Schuster, 1991.

————. *Ceremony*. New York: Viking/Penguin, 1977.

————. "The Fourth World." *Artforum International* 27, no. 10 (1989): 124–125.

————. "Language and Literature from a Pueblo Indian Perspective." In *English Literature: Opening Up the Canon*, ed. Leslie A. Fiedler and Houston A. Baker. Baltimore: Johns Hopkins University Press, 1981.

Sjöö, Monica, and Barbara Mor. *The Great Cosmic Mother: Rediscovering the Religion of the Earth*. San Francisco: Harper and Row, 1987.

Smith, Martin Cruz. *Stallion Gate*. New York: Ballantine, 1986.

Sofia, Zoë. "Exterminating Fetuses: Abortion, Disarmament, and the Sexo-semiotics of Extraterrestrialism." *Diacritics* 14, no. 2 (1984): 47–59.

Solanas, Valerie. *The SCUM Manifesto*. London: The Matriarchy Study Group, 1968, 1983.

Sontag, Susan. "The Imagination of Disaster." In *Awake in the Dark: An Anthology of American Film Criticism*, ed. David Denby, 263–277. New York: Vintage Books, 1977.

Starrett, Barbara. *A Dream in Female: The Metaphors of Evolution and the Metaphors of Power*. Gloucester, MA: Top O' The Harbor, 1976.

Teilhard de Chardin, Pierre. *The Future of Man*, trans. N. Denny. New York: Harper and Row, 1964.

Titus, A. Costandina. *Bombs in the Backyard: Atomic Testing and American Politics*. Reno: University of Nevada Press, 1986.

Treusch-Dieter, Gerburg. "The Beginning of the End: On the History of Radiation from Plato to Chernobyl." In *Looking Back on the End of the World*, ed. Dietmar Kamper and Christoph Wulf, trans. David Antal, 7–18. New York: Semiotext(e), 1989.

United States Senate. *Hearing before the Subcommittee on Children, Family, Drugs, and Alcoholism of the Committee on Labor and Human Resources,* Washington, D.C.: U.S. Government Printing Office, 1990.

Walker, Alice. *The Color Purple.* New York: Washington Square Press, Pocket Books, 1982.

———. *In Search of Our Mothers' Gardens.* San Diego: Harcourt Brace Jovanovich, 1983.

———. *Living by the Word.* San Diego: Harcourt Brace Jovanovich, 1988.

Walker, Barbara. *The Crone: Woman of Age, Wisdom and Power.* San Francisco: Harper & Row, 1985.

———. *The Woman's Encyclopedia of Myths and Secrets.* San Francisco: Harper and Row, 1983.

———. *The Woman's Dictionary of Symbols and Sacred Objects.* San Francisco: Harper and Row, 1988.

Weart, Spencer. *Nuclear Fear: A History of Images.* Cambridge, MA: Harvard University Press, 1989.

White, Lavina. "Listening to our Elders." *Indigenous Woman* 1, no. 2 (1992): 13–14.

Winner, Langdon. *The Whale and the Reactor: A Search for Limits in an Age of High Technology.* Chicago: University of Chicago Press, 1986.

Wisechild, Louise M., ed. *She Who Was Lost Is Remembered: Healing from Incest through Creativity.* Seattle: The Seal Press, 1991.

Wittig, Monique. *The Straight Mind and Other Essays.* Boston: Beacon Press, 1992.

Wolf, Christa. *Cassandra,* trans. Jan Van Heurck. New York: Farrar Straus Giroux, 1984.

Women Working for an Independent and Nuclear Free Pacific. *Pacific Women Speak: Why Haven't You Known?* Oxford: Green Line, 1987.

INDEX

ABOUT THE AUTHOR

Jane Caputi teaches in the American Studies department at the University of New Mexico in Albuquerque. She is the author of *The Age of Sex Crime* (1987), a feminist analysis of the atrocity of serial sex murder and the elevation of the serial killer to hero status in American culture. *The Age of Sex Crime* won the 1988 Emily Toth Award for best feminist study of American culture.

Caputi also worked with Mary Daly on *Websters' First New Intergalactic Wickedary of the English Language* (1987). Her next project is editing an anthology, *The Heart of Knowledge: American Indians on the Bomb*, with Paula Gunn Allen.